The Court and Court Society in Ancient Monarchies

Monarchy was widespread as a political system in the ancient world. This volume offers the first substantial discussion of ancient monarchies from the viewpoint of the ruler's court. The monarchies treated are Achaemenid and Sasanian Persia, the empire of Alexander, Rome under both the early and later Caesars, the Han rulers of China and Egypt's Eighteenth Dynasty. A comparative approach is adopted to major aspects of ancient courts, including their organisation and physical setting, their role as a vehicle for display, and their place in monarchical structures of power and control. This approach is broadly inspired by work on courts in later periods of history, especially early modern France. The case studies confirm that ancient monarchies created the conditions for the emergence of a court and court society. The culturally specific conditions in which these monarchies functioned meant variety in the character of the ruler's court from one society to another.

A. J. S. SPAWFORTH is Professor of Ancient History at the University of Newcastle. His publications include *Hellenistic and Roman Sparta: A Tale of Two Cities* (with Paul Cartledge, 2nd edition, 2002), *The Complete Greek Temples* (2006) and co-editing, with Simon Hornblower, *The Oxford Classical Dictionary* (3rd edition revised, 2003).

The Court and Court Society
in Ancient Monarchies

Edited by

A. J. S. SPAWFORTH

CAMBRIDGE UNIVERSITY PRESS

Cambridge, New York, Melbourne, Madrid, Cape Town, Singapore, São Paulo

Cambridge University Press
The Edinburgh Building, Cambridge CB2 8RU, UK

Published in the United States of America by Cambridge University Press, New York

www.cambridge.org
Information on this title: www.cambridge.org/9780521874489

First published 2007

Printed in the United Kingdom at the University Press, Cambridge

A catalogue record for this publication is available from the British Library

Library of Congress Cataloguing in Publication data
The court and court society in ancient monarchies / edited by A. J. S. Spawforth.
      p.   cm.
Includes bibliographical references and index.
ISBN 978-0-521-87448-9 (hardback)
1. Courts and courtiers.   2. Kings and rulers, Ancient.   3. Monarchy.   I. Spawforth, Antony.
GT3510.C67   2007
395.5 – dc22   2007009045

ISBN 978-0-521-87448-9 hardback

Contents

Figures

Table

Notes on contributors

MARIA BROSIUS is Reader in Ancient History at the University of Newcastle upon Tyne. Her publications include *Women in Ancient Persia (559–331 BC)* (1996, repr. 1998, 2002), *The Persian Empire from Cyrus II to Artaxerxes I* (2000), and *The Persians: An Introduction* (2006). She has edited a volume on *Ancient Archives: Concepts of Record-Keeping in the Ancient World* (2003), and (with A. Kuhrt) *Persian Studies: Essays in Memory of D. M. Lewis* (1998).

JEREMY PATERSON is Senior Lecturer in Ancient History at the University of Newcastle upon Tyne. He is primarily a social and economic historian of the Roman world, with a particular interest in the wine trade. He recently edited, with Jonathan Powell, *Cicero the Advocate* (2004) and is currently working on a book about the ancient economy. His interest in the nature of power has already appeared in a study of emperors' jokes and will reappear in the research he is undertaking on the relationship between Christians and Roman emperors.

ROWLAND SMITH is Lecturer in Ancient History in the School of Historical Studies at Newcastle University. In his research he works chiefly on the cultural and social history of the high and late Roman empire, and on pagan responses to Christianisation: he is the author of *Julian's Gods: Religion and Philosophy in the Thought and Action of Julian the Apostate* (1995). His recent publications include a study of patronal imagery in fourth-century Rome and a chapter in the *Blackwell Companion to the Roman Empire* (2006) on the representation of the Roman past in the historiography of the imperial age.

TONY SPAWFORTH is Professor of Ancient History at the University of Newcastle upon Tyne. His publications include (with P. A. Cartledge) *Hellenistic and Roman Sparta: A Tale of Two Cities* (1989; 2nd edition, 2002), the third edition (with S. Hornblower) of *The Oxford Classical Dictionary* (3rd edition revised, 2003), and many contributions on aspects of the Greek world under Roman rule. He is currently preparing a book on the Roman reshaping of Greek cultural identity in the Principate.

KATE SPENCE is an Affiliated Lecturer in the Faculty of Oriental Studies at the University of Cambridge and a Fellow of the McDonald Institute for Archaeological Research, also at the University of Cambridge. Her research focuses on the monumental and domestic architecture of ancient Egypt. She has excavated at several sites in Egypt including Akhenaten's capital at el-Amarna where she was involved in the re-examination of the North Palace.

HANS VAN ESS has held a chair in Chinese Studies at the University of Munich since 1998. His main interests include the history of Chinese thought with a special emphasis on Confucianism, early Chinese historiography, early Chinese poetry and the history of relations between China and central Asia. Among his publications are two books on the introduction of Confucianism as a state orthodoxy under the Han and on the Neo-Confucian movement under the Sung, as well as an introduction to Confucianism for a general readership. Currently he is working on a comparison of the two first Chinese standard histories.

JOSEF WIESEHÖFER is Professor of Ancient History at the University of Kiel (Germany) and director of its Institute for Classical Studies. He is a member of the Centre for Asian and African Studies at Kiel University, editor of *Oriens et Occidens* and co-editor of *Asien und Afrika*, *Achaemenid History* and *Oikumene*. His main interests lie in the history of the ancient Near East and its relations with the Mediterranean world, social history, the history of early modern travelogues and the history of scholarship.

Acknowledgements

The editor and contributors warmly acknowledge their major debt to the British Academy which funded the bulk of the costs of a workshop in 2004, which brought all the contributors together in Newcastle. The idea for an interdisciplinary project of this kind was stimulated by the collaborative atmosphere of the School of Historical Studies at Newcastle; Jeremy Boulton, Head of School, also gave welcome additional funds for the costs of the workshop. For helpful advice in the course of the project Tony Spawforth would like to thank Yuri Pines, Naomi Standen, Roel Sterckx, Rosalind Thomas and Philip van der Eijk. For practical support the project is grateful to Sarah Francis and the staff in the School Office. All contributors owe a debt of gratitude to Michael Sharp at Cambridge University Press for his constructive interest in the project from its inception, and to the Press's two anonymous assessors, whose comments improved an earlier draft of the text. Tony Spawforth, finally, would like to thank his fellow-contributors for their magnificent engagement with the courts project, and for their good-natured responsiveness to editorial nagging.

Tony Spawforth

Abbreviations

AchHist	*Achaemenid History*
AJA	*American Journal of Archaeology*
AJP	*American Journal of Philology*
Akk.	Akkadian
ANET	*Ancient Near Eastern Texts relating to the Old Testament*, ed. J. B. Pritchard, 3rd rev. edn. Princeton (1969)
AnSt	*Anatolian Studies*
AntAfr	*Antiquités Africaines*
Bab.	Babylonian
BEFAR	*Bullétin de l'Ecole française à Rome: Antiquité*
CahDAFI	*Cahiers de la Délégation Archéologique Française en Iran*
CIL	*Corpus Inscriptionum Latinarum* (1863–)
CQ	*Classical Quarterly*
CR	*Classical Review*
DB	Darius (Inscriptions of) Bisitun
DF	E. Gibbon, *Decline and Fall of the Roman Empire*, ed. O. Smeaton, vols. I–VI, London (1910)
DHA	*Dialogues d'Histoire Ancienne*
DN	Darius (Inscriptions of) Naqsh-i Rustam
DOP	*Dumbarton Oaks Papers*
DP	Darius (Inscriptions of) Persepolis
DS	Darius (Inscriptions of) Susa
EA	*Egyptian Archaeology*
Elam.	Elamite
EncIr	*Enciclopedia Iranica*, ed. E. Yar-Shater (1985–)
FGH	C. and T. Müller, *Fragmenta Historicorum Graecorum* (1841–72)
FGrH	F. Jacoby, *Fragmente der griechischer Historiker* (1923–)
Gr.	Greek
GRBS	*Greek, Roman and Byzantine Studies*
grI	Greek version of the royal inscription(s)
HHS	*Hou Han-shu*
HS	*Han-shu*

ILS	H. Dessau, *Inscriptiones Latinae Selectae* (1892–1916)
IrAnt	*Iranica Antiqua*
JÖB	*Jahrbuch des österreichischen Byzantinistik*
JRA	*Journal of Roman Archaeology*
JWCI	*Journal of the Courtauld and Warburg Institutes*
LÄ	*Lexikon der Ägyptologie*
MAAR	*Memoirs of the American Academy in Rome*
MCAAS	Memoirs of the Connecticut Academy of Arts and Sciences
MDAI(R)	*Mitteilungen des deutschen archäologischen Instituts: Römische Abteilung*
mpI	Middle Persian version of the royal inscription(s)
Neh.	Book of Nehemiah
NPi	(Inscription of) N(arseh from) P(aikul)i (ed. H. Humbach and P. O. Skjærvø, 1978–83)
*OCD*³	S. Hornblower and A. Spawforth (eds.), *The Oxford Classical Dictionary*, 3rd edn. Oxford (2003)
paI	Parthian version of the royal inscription(s)
PdP	*Parola di Passato*
PF	R. T. Hallock, *Persepolis Fortification Tablets*. Chicago (1969)
PFs	R. T. Hallock, 'Persepolis Fortification texts', *CahDAFI* 8: 109–36
PFS	Persepolis Fortification Seals
RE	A. Pauly, G. Wissowa and W. Kroll, *Real-Encyclopädie der klassischen Altertumswissenschaft* (1893–)
SAA	State Archives of Assyria
SC	Ssu-ma T'an and Ssu-ma Ch'ien (eds.), *Shih-chi (Records of the Scribe)*. Peking (1959)
ŠH	(Inscription of) Sh(abuhr I from) H(ajjiabad)
SHA	Scriptores Historiae Augustae
*SIG*³	W. Dittenberger, *Sylloge Inscriptionum Graecarum*, 3rd edition (1915–24)
ŠKZ	(Inscription of) Sh(abuhr I on the) K(a'ba-i) Z(ardusht at Naqsh-i Rustam), ed. P. Huyse (1999)
SO	*Symbolae Osloenses*
SSC	*Shi-san ching chu-shü (The Thirteen Classics)*
StIr	*Studia Iranica*
XP	Xerxes (Inscriptions of) Persepolis
YClS	*Yale Classical Studies*
ZAW	*Zeitschrift für alttestamentliche Wissenschaft*
ZPE	*Zeitschrift für Papyrologie und Epigraphik*

Introduction

TONY SPAWFORTH

Taking the field of ancient history as a whole, including the Middle and Far East as well as Europe and the Mediterranean, the monarchical court cannot be said to have occupied centre-stage in a way that might seem justified by the prevalence of monarchy as a system of power in antiquity.[1] The reasons for this relative neglect are complex and cannot all be unpacked here.[2] But one, certainly, is the sense of the court as a 'moribund social formatio[n]'[3] which has permeated western consciousness since the French Revolution. Backstairs influence, intrigue and flattery: these generic phenomena of courts have earned themselves a bad reputation in western democracies which pose as the mirror-opposites of 'old-regime' arrangements of power, and in the study of ancient monarchies they are often sidelined, or their association by ancient writers with 'bad' or 'weak' rulers, or with whole societies classed as degenerate, as the ancient Persians were by the ancient Greeks (Brosius in this volume), taken at face value.[4] In those nineteenth-century European monarchies which survived, especially after 1848, constitutionalism was the order of the day, as it had been (at least notionally) in the United Kingdom since 1688. Perhaps unsurprisingly, then, in the nineteenth and for much of the twentieth century the students of monarchical institutions in the ancient world have often been preoccupied with modernist attempts to define their legal basis – as with the Macedonian kings, say, or the early

---

[1] I am grateful to the two anonymous assessors of this book, and above all to my collaborators in this project, for comments which have helped to define and refine the issues raised in this Introduction.

[2] A further indication – apart from this book – that a change is afoot is the conference on 'Royal Courts and Capitals' (Istanbul, October 2005) which compared ancient, Islamic and European courts and included two Roman historians among the speakers: see the conference report: Mansel 2006.

[3] Elias 1983: 8. Cf. ibid.: 'As far as [courts] still exist in developed countries, they have lost much of their earlier power and prestige. As compared to the time of their apogee, the court societies of our day are mere epigones. The representatives of rising social formations usually regard these remnants of a past era with mixed feelings.' In the UK this last point is probably more true now than in the period after the First World War when Elias wrote.

[4] In the UK media some newsprint journalists activate a depreciatory stereotype of the court to criticise government when it is seen to act in an insufficiently open and democratic way: thus 'the court of King Tony [Blair]', the 'courtiers' including unofficial advisors like Alistair Campbell.

Roman emperors. In the legacy of earlier generations of scholars, there are obvious exceptions to this sidelining of the court, such as the researches of L. Friedländer on early imperial Rome or H. Berve on Alexander the Great, and these have proved mighty bulwarks for at least two of the chapters in this book (Spawforth; Paterson). But even these studies tend to be descriptive rather than analytical. As the contributors to this book have found out, the court as a central entity within the monarchies which they study has often been taken for granted (Brosius; Spawforth), or scarcely conceptualised at all (Wiesehöfer; van Ess; Spence). A related reason for this neglect is the traditional separation in western scholarship of the 'trappings' from the 'substance' of power. The 'trappings' involve aspects of monarchy which scholars trained to focus on the history of events or institutions have traditionally found hard to take seriously as objects of study – ceremonial, say.[5] They also involve the crossing of interdisciplinary boundaries: the study of palaces, gardens, costume and iconography is traditionally the field of art historians and archaeologists; the study of feasts – a subject which often comes up in this book – is arguably more the domain of the social scientist; and so on. Finally, this interdisciplinary complexity is nowadays being reinforced by the gendered approaches which are reappraising the role of women in rulers' courts, both ancient and modern. The prejudice in most if not all ancient societies against women rulers (see Spence in this volume on Eighteenth Dynasty Egypt) has meant that powerful royal women have often been presented as 'unnatural' by ancient (male) writers, from Achaemenid queens and princesses to the younger Agrippina, when in fact this sort of influence is a sociological phenomenon arising more or less naturally from the embedding of a ruler's exercise of power in the domestic setting of the court.

What, then, is a 'court'? All the chapters in this book have sought to answer this question with reference, first, to contemporary perceptions. In some ancient societies a word for 'court' is harder to track down than in others, and here the issue may require more lexicographical research (Spence and Wiesehöfer in this volume). Elsewhere, with Chinese *ch'ao*, say, meaning literally 'morning audience', a modern dictionary may retroject today's sense of 'court', a meaning of which the Han Chinese may not have been fully conscious (van Ess in this volume). It is clear, though, that the ancient Greeks and Romans had conceptualised the court at least to some degree.[6] Thus the Greek word from which the modern neologism 'aulic' derives, *aulē*, along with the Latin equivalent *aula*, is used by ancient writers

---

[5] There are, of course, significant exceptions to this, e.g. Price 1984; Cannadine and Price 1987.

[6] Winterling 1997: 151 n. 1. Quite how much is debated: Herman 1997: 204–5; Gregor 1997: 31.

both of the ruler's dwelling as a physical entity and in a more abstract sense of the people to be found there – 'those *peri tēn aulēn*' (see Spawforth, Paterson and Smith in this volume).

This idea, that 'the court' is both the spatial framework of the ruler's existence and also the social configuration with which he shares that space, is fundamental in modern attempts to define and analyse the court. It might be argued that the word 'household' then starts to look like a perfectly adequate alternative to 'court', in the sense of the members of the ruler's family cohabiting in his dwelling, along with their domestic attendants and bodyguards. There is some cogency in this viewpoint. But a concept is needed which takes account of more than simply household personnel. For a start, the dwellings of ancient rulers were the focus for decision-making and governance in monarchies which were all (in the case of the ones studied in this book) personal and more or less absolutist. Factored into the ruler's entourage in this kind of 'Weberian' patrimonial monarchy, therefore, must be the comings-and-goings of political 'helpers' and, in some cases (the late Roman and Han Chinese empires, say: see Smith and van Ess in this volume), a fledgling state bureaucracy. The apocryphal saying of Louis XIV, 'L'état c'est moi', could not be more misleading about the complex reality of the exercise of royal power in pre-Revolutionary France, where 'ideas, practices and even institutions' did much to limit – albeit not control – the French king's 'theoretically formidable' authority (Antoine 1989: 175–9). Some such formulation, albeit with less emphasis (perhaps) on 'institutions', could be put forward in summary of the powers of most, if not all, the monarchies studied in this book (the *nomoi* or 'customs', say, which restrained the Macedonian king). For this reason, the ruler's space was also the potential site of exchanges between ruler and all manner of subjects who were not necessarily members of his household or even in any sense his officials. This space, finally, was also where envoys of foreign powers were received. The attempts by each side to control or manage these exchanges gave rise to the theatricality often thought of as characteristic of courts: pomp and circumstance on one side; a carefully controlled demeanour, incorporating deference, ingratiation and flattery, on the other. The semantic field 'court' best conceptualises the idea of a social configuration characterised by these distinctive modes of communication.

The chapters which follow highlight the state elites as the key-group of subjects in the workings of ancient courts. The study of monarchical courts, then, is unavoidably a form of elite history, since no ancient monarchies (or at least, none of those studied here) conceived themselves as instruments of 'people power', even if gift-giving to the masses (the 'bread and circuses' of imperial Rome) was one of 'the necessary costs of stable autocratic government' in antiquity.[7] The court in its physical sense was not entirely isolated from the people – the linkage of the late Roman imperial palace to the hippodrome is the most striking example of the quasi-integration of ordinary subjects into the spatial configuration of the courts studied here (Smith in this volume). More often, however, as the following chapters show, the court turns out to be a place where issues of access to the ruler seem mainly to focus on the elites: these were the people whose face-to-face encounters with the ruler Akhenaten's Window of Appearance (Spence in this volume), say, or Alexander's state tent (Spawforth in this volume), not to mention feasts and hunts (Smith in this volume), were – to differing degrees – intended to manage. Ancient monarchs, like those of later periods, relied on trustworthy servants with whom they were obliged to share their power if territories were to be administered, armies commanded, and other functions of ancient-world governance discharged. From the ruler's point of view, management of relations with his elites was critical, since it was this group which provided both his key helpers and, as often as not, the most potent source of attempts to supplant him. The chief spatial and social setting in which both ruler and elites sought to manage their mutual interaction was the court. In the following chapters the manner of this interaction is shown to be culturally specific in different ancient societies in a range of ways; in all chapters, however, it is a recurrent and a major theme. Most chapters distinguish an 'inner' from an 'outer' court, the former comprising the ruler and those whom service or kinship kept more or less permanently in his vicinity, the latter denoting members of the elite who were a more intermittent presence, in part by virtue of the coming-and-going between centre and periphery imposed on them by the delegated power with which the ruler entrusted them.

Ancient courts, then, were complex entities. In negotiating this complexity, contributors to this volume were able to take their bearings in part thanks to the edifice of current scholarship on medieval and early modern courts inspired, as even his critics concede, by the German social historian Norbert Elias.[8] Elias was the first scholar to impart scholarly rigour to the study of monarchical courts. His doctorate was first published in 1933. As *Die höfische Gesellschaft* ('The Court Society') it only became widely known a generation later, however, following the publication of a new (and different) German edition in 1969. This was translated into French in 1974, with English translation by Edmund Jephcott following in 1983.

---

[7] Paterson 2004.   [8] E.g. the comment of Duindam 2003: 7.

Elias centred his work on the court of Louis XIV and his successors at Versailles, for his picture of which he was heavily reliant on the brilliant but partisan memoirs of a courtier, the duc de Saint-Simon (1675–1753). The text of Elias is rich and dense. One of his central propositions, that the court society of pre-Revolutionary France marked a necessary stage in the 'socio-genesis' of the nineteenth-century French state, does not directly concern this book. Another, however, is more relevant. Basing himself on Saint-Simon, Elias posed the question: How do hereditary monarchies of the patrimonial type reproduce themselves from one ruler to the next, often over a period of centuries? He argued that the crucial relationship in this type of monarchy was between the ruler and the elites (see above), and that the court was the means by which each sought to bring influence to bear on the other – its fulcrum. In his case study, Louis XIV was cast as a conserving ruler, third king of the Bourbon line, whose chief aim was to maintain his inherited position of power. Louis achieved this by constructing the 'hyper-palace' of Versailles. Here he ensnared the kingdom's elite – the French high nobility – by means of an elaborate system of etiquette. This kept grandees in their place by conferring or withholding prestige-fetishes, such as the notorious privilege of holding the candlestick at the royal coucher. The Versailles system worked for Louis XIV, according to Elias, because it manipulated the aristocratic outlook of noble courtiers and in particular their obsession with honour and distinction. For the monarchy, Versailles offered the means to replace the real power of the high nobility with honorific functions.

Elias' arguments have not escaped a revisionist assault from historians in recent years. In particular, it is argued that he exaggerated the absolutism of Louis XIV and underplayed the fact that Louis and his courtiers were engaged in a mutual negotiation, in which the latter exchanged their attendance and their deference for royal patronage and the wherewithal to maintain traditional aristocratic status-goals;[9] and, even if Louis XIV can be said to have dominated his court, this was less obviously the case with his two successors, where the reverse could seem more the case.[10] Even so, the work of Elias still remains perhaps the richest source of reflections on the ruler's court as a social configuration. One of its strengths is that it constantly stands back and risks general observations about power, monarchy

[9] Duindam 1995; 2003: esp. 7–10 with earlier refs.
[10] E.g. Louis XVI's 'très-arrière-cabinet', with the comment of Verlet 1983: 525: 'Le superlative dit, à lui seul, le développement du mal dont souffre le souverain, repoussé chez lui plus loin par la pression de ses courtesans, dans ce château [Versailles] où il étouffe.' But see Hours 2002 for an Eliasque reappraisal of Louis XV's 'strategy of control of his Court'.

and social structure. The interest of these for scholars of ancient courts can be
gauged by the number of citations of Elias in the chapters which follow. For
students of ancient courts, Elias is also highly stimulating for his analysis –
less fresh in 2007, of course, than at the time when he wrote it – of the 'substance' of monarchical rule by means of the 'trappings', and for insisting on
the importance of sociological concepts, notably conspicuous consumption
and status, in trying to understand the workings of courts. Less remarkable
now, to be sure, than when he originally wrote, this kind of approach, while
it may seem commonsensical these days in some fields of history-writing,
cannot be said to be taken for granted in the study of antiquity.

In recent years the work of Elias has started to attract historians tending
one particular corner of antiquity, namely Greece and Rome. In the 1970s
the potential of the Eliasque approach was recognised by Keith Hopkins,
well known for using methodology informed by the social sciences to break
new ground in studies of the Roman empire.[11] In the mid-1990s, in his
chapter on the court of the Julio-Claudian emperors for the *Cambridge
Ancient History* Andrew Wallace-Hadrill acknowledged his debt to Elias,[12]
as did Gabriel Herman in an original study of Hellenistic court politics
and court etiquette (see below).[13] More recently there has been a spate of
German studies of ancient (classical) courts within the Elias tradition led
by the wide-ranging historian Aloys Winterling, who worked first on the
court of the early modern electors of Cologne[14] before turning to ancient
(classical) courts, above all the Roman imperial court.[15] This volume is
greatly indebted to the contributions of Winterling and his colleagues. That
said, their work is not well known in Anglophone scholarship.

Turning to the present volume, it was born out of a common conviction
among the contributors that our understanding of ancient monarchies could
be usefully improved by viewing them through the optic of the court. A first
aim is to explore ways of adding conceptual rigour to an aspect of ancient
rulership which, as noted earlier, has tended to be taken for granted, if it has
been considered at all. A second aim is to take the Elias-inspired debate about
the court to a range of ancient societies. To an extent this approach has been
anticipated by Winterling (1997), in a collection which looked comparatively
at the ruler's court across the sweep of classical antiquity. The Newcastle
project, however, sought to take the discussion of ancient courts out of this
classical 'box' and to adopt a cross-cultural perspective. Egypt, Persia and

[11] Hopkins 1978: 181. See Smith in this volume.   [12] Wallace-Hadrill 1996: 285 n. 13.
[13] Herman 1997.   [14] Winterling 1985.
[15] Winterling 1997b; 1998; 1999. In the later stages of the preparation of this volume another
collective work of German scholarship has appeared which explicitly seeks to 'theorise' the
court: Butz, Hirschbiegel and Willoweit 2004.

China were chosen for a number of reasons. Diversity is one. Han China was clearly not influenced by the practices of the classical world; nor was Egypt in the period studied by Spence in this volume. Along with Persia, all three were ancient societies where little or no explicit attempt has so far been made to model the ruler's court, and this chance to experiment was a further attraction. Eighteenth Dynasty Egypt, moreover, was at best a proto-historic society, and Spence's investigation necessarily addresses the methodological challenge of melding historiographic models with archaeological evidence to a far greater extent than other chapters in the book. Within classical antiquity, Alexander the Great was an attractive figure because on the one hand his court ceremonial is relatively well attested, while on the other he tends to be seen chiefly as a military, not an aulic, figure. As already noted, the court of the Roman emperors is far from being virgin territory. But we felt that there was still room for reviewing the imperial court in an explicitly comparative way. The Roman Principate allows the initial stages in the creation of a court society to be followed in some detail by the usual standards of ancient evidence. The two chapters on Rome by Jeremy Paterson and Rowland Smith not only debate with Elias, but also take account of recent German work as yet relatively unknown in the Anglosphere. With all the ancient states under review, in one respect the project sought to compare like with like. States were chosen which combined strong monarchies with empire in the periods of their history examined in this book, because these seem to be the conditions in which, historically, court culture has tended to flourish.

The Newcastle project explicitly adoped an interdisciplinary approach, and all contributors are aware of, and in different ways have been stimulated by, contemporary court studies. Inevitably, the figure of Elias looms large. It is important to stress, however, that the project was not intended to be merely reactive to Elias and modern court studies. Indeed, the collection is not touting a methodology as such, nor does it espouse any one model of the court. In fact, despite the impact of *The Court Society* on modern work on the court, currently there appears to be no authoritative model of a court to which early modern historians all subscribe.[16]

In order to strike a balance between diversity and the coherence of theme required to sustain a multi-authored approach, the editor provided an initial briefing paper for contributors to consult when writing their first drafts. All contributors attended a workshop in Newcastle in May 2004, where each pre-circulated draft was discussed among the group. The workshop concluded by subscribing to a common agenda around which final contributions

---

[16] Note Duindam 2003: 318–20.

could cohere.[17] Various issues were agreed to merit discussion, although it was up to individual contributors to decide where the emphasis should lie.

It was proposed that each paper in its final form should reflect on two broad questions: whether it was legitimate to talk of a 'court' in the specific monarchy being discussed, and how crucial the ruler's court was for understanding the machinery of power in the double sense of actual decision-making and power's 'representation'. To pursue these questions, further issues were identified which should, or could, be considered.

1 Can the concept of a 'court' and of 'courtiers' be identified in contemporary thought and language?
2 Who belongs to the court? How does membership break down into different status groups? Is it helpful to think in terms of an inner and outer court of, respectively, people permanently in the ruler's personal vicinity and others whose presence is temporary?
3 How are the people closest to the ruler recruited? How far is the ruler's freedom to recruit these people tempered by, for instance, established career-structures, where these can be said to exist at all?
4 What structures of communication characterise the court? How is physical access to the ruler articulated? In the interaction between ruler and courtiers, what part is played, and for what 'structural' reasons, by flattery and servile opportunism, or intrigue, or faction?
5 What is the relationship of the ruler's domestic setting or household function to decision-making? How far, and for what particular reasons, do members of the household, including relations and domestic functionaries, influence decision-making?
6 Does the ruler's residence function as a site of representation? 'Representation' embraces the whole range of forms of symbolic communication, such as art and architecture, ceremony and costume, which legitimate the ruler's authority.
7 Does the court display 'stateliness', in the sense of clearly amounting to an institution in its own right, acquiring organisational complexity, or coming to function of its own volition, or influencing social attitudes, or generating an autonomous 'court society'?
8 How important is the court as a symbol of social order, a place where social ranking is put on display and different elite groups are integrated by means of ceremony?

---

[17] Particular thanks are owed to Josef Wiesehöfer, who kindly offered the workshop a preview of Butz et al. 2004, a volume which, at the time, was still in press.

In considering this wide range of issues, contributors were of course left free to place the emphasis where they thought fit. But the working definition of the court and court society was intended to ensure a measure of rigour when contributors sought to assess – as they were encouraged to – whether a genuine court phenomenon could be diagnosed for a given society, that is, an entity which clearly went beyond the inevitable 'group dynamics around leaders' (Duindam 2003: 318; but see Spence in this volume).

From the outset, it was clear that the ancient sources would be a critical constraint in the investigation of these issues. All contributors were therefore asked to make explicit the strengths and drawbacks of the source material at their disposal. It cannot be emphasised enough how limited these sources are when compared to those, for example, available to the modern historian studying the court of Louis XIV. In this last case, the material includes works of literature and reports by observers (Saint-Simon's memoirs; the missives of foreign ambassadors), courtiers' journals (the marquess de Dangeau's notably[18]), official records of court departments and court ceremonies, royal artefacts, and of course the royal residences themselves, which, even if destroyed or (as in the case of Versailles) severely altered since the Revolution, are still copiously documented by the surviving archives.

The ancient societies viewed here exemplify enormous diversity in the different sorts of limitations imposed by the evidence. For classical antiquity we are heavily reliant on the artful works of a literary elite predisposed – by cultural tradition as much as by political feeling – to sing the praises of personal autonomy and view monarchy with ambivalence. In Alexander's case this literary bias is further skewed by the fact that the extant Alexander-historians wrote, at the earliest, some three centuries after Alexander's death; inevitably, they import the cultural colouring of their (Roman) time. Ancient Chinese historiography provides the basis for the study of the Han Chinese court and displays similar difficulties for the modern historian (van Ess in this volume): the great Ssu-ma Ch'ien was critical of imperial policy; the *Book of the Later Han* was composed some four centuries after the start of the Later Han period; and so on. The most striking feature of the sources for the Achaemenid Persian period is the authority of a body of contemporary writing from a largely hostile, neighbouring culture (Greece), which used (and arguably distorted) representations of the Achaemenid empire

---

[18] Along with the memoirs of Dangeau's grandson, the duc de Luynes, this journal suggests the enormous interest which a court society takes in what might seem to modern historians to be the trivia of the king's day, including details of the king's drinking, sleeping and hunting habits, recalling Alexander's journal (*ephēmerides*), a work held by some modern scholars to be an ancient fiction (Hammond 1983: 5–10).

as a means of constructing the cultural 'other'; this can be offset to a limited degree by contemporary documents and archaeology, given full weight by Brosius in this volume. Sasanian Persia, likewise, has left behind no contemporary literature of its own about the court, although there is relevant material in the literary culture of a hostile neighbour (the late Roman empire), not to mention much later Iranian traditions with the usual problems of distortion and colouring. Inscriptions play an important part in offsetting the dearth of other kinds of written testimony in the cases of Persia and Egypt. These texts are not, of course, without problems of their own: Egyptian funerary inscriptions address eternity; official inscriptions of the Achaemenid or Sasanian rulers belong to the field of royal representation and must be understood as such. As for material remains, for one of the contributions, on Alexander, they are simply not available: modern knowledge of the physical setting of Alexander's court is dependent on written descriptions. For the other ancient societies studied in this volume there is, indeed, archaeological evidence, although the modern tradition of archaeological exploration is much stronger for some parts of what was once the ancient world, such as Egypt, than for others, such as the Sasanian empire (respectively Spence and Wiesehöfer in this volume). Eighteenth Dynasty Egypt and Achaemenid Persia are particularly remarkable for the survival of a rich body of 'royal' art depicting the ruler and the court; these to some extent compensate for the absence of much (Egypt) or anything (Achaemenid Persia) in the way of indigenous written observations about the ruler's court.

The chapters in the book illustrate this diversity of ancient source-material and also show how this diversity limits, in different ways, our attempts to analyse ancient courts. At one extreme, that of Sasanian Persia, simply to delineate the court in broad brush-strokes, on the basis of a fragmentary and problematic palette of evidence, is an achievement. At the other extreme, the court of the fourth- and fifth-century Roman emperors is attested by a copious body of evidence across a wide range of media. The varying nature of the surviving evidence inevitably makes for difference in the length of chapters in this book. The one on Sasanian Persia, a first attempt to document the Sasanian court, is relatively brief. The length of the chapter on the later Roman empire (Rowland Smith), by contrast, is justified by the richness of the evidence and the consequent complexity of the topic.

What can be said to have emerged from this book? Some general remarks can first be made about the Eliasque approach and its relevance to ancient courts. In terms of the physical arenas for courtly behaviour, none of the ancient courts studied here turns out to have been like Versailles in the sense

of being housed in a palace which also provided lodgings for elite courtiers.[19]
Partly this seems to have been a function of the absence of a tradition of
domestic attendance on ancient rulers by high-status members of the elite –
except in the case of Achaemenid Persia and Macedon (both societies, significantly, without large slave populations). But there were certainly court
capitals like Persepolis, early imperial Rome, the palace-cities of the Han,
or Akhetaten. Another practice of Versailles, the system of entrées which
controlled the admission of members of the elite to the ruler's presence first
thing in the morning, has ancient parallels (Paterson). This has long been
noticed, and may be understandable in broadly similar terms: 'attendance
on the prince's first public appearance has a sound practical reason: to find
out what he intends to do, to try to remain in his company and hope to enjoy
its attendant advantages'.[20] The disproportionate influence at court of low-
status household attendants, especially those whose personal services made
them intimates of the ruler, turns out to be a recurrent feature of courts
both ancient and modern. Imperial freedmen and eunuchs in Roman and
Chinese antiquity (Paterson; Smith; van Ess), royal valets at Versailles:[21] the
amalgam of private household and 'stateliness' which constituted the ruler's
court had the effect of politicising quite lowly domestic roles if they conferred frequent access to the ruler. The ruler's promotion of such people
has also been seen as structural rather than a function (as contemporaries
claimed) of personal 'weakness': a device, that is, to offset over-reliance
on an entrenched military and political elite (Smith). Along with eunuchs,
the harems of some ancient courts offer a dimension to court life which
is obviously missing from more recent European courts. This undoubtedly
real difference might seem to limit the applicability of an Eliasque approach
to ancient courts (van Ess), although even this is debatable. Harems and
eunuchs were also very much a part of the Achaemenid Persian and the
late Roman courts, which Brosius and Smith in this volume both see, albeit
from different perspectives, as complex court societies 'in something like
the sense Elias proposed for Versailles' (Smith).

Looking at the chapters more closely, Brosius argues that the hierarchical
practices of the Achaemenid court were rooted in the tribal social structure
of the Persian people. The quest for legitimacy and stateliness prompted the
arriviste Persian monarchy to absorb and adapt the older courtly traditions of
ancient Mesopotamian kingship. As the rulers of a territorially vast empire,

---

[19] Although it is now recognised that even in an early modern context Versailles was atypical in
this respect.
[20] Baillie 1967: 171–2.   [21] Da Vinha 2004.

the Achaemenid kings evidently felt the need for a strong representation of power and stability at the centre of the state. To this end, ceremonial, palaces and royal image harmonised a presentation of the ruler's person as the divinely ordained embodiment of the imperial polity. In Achaemenid Persia, far more strongly than in the other ancient monarchies considered in this book, one arguably has the sense of the 'King of Lands' as anticipating Jean-Marie Apostolidès' early modern vision of 'le roi-machine', a ruler whose physical body was somehow understood as the symbolic incarnation of the state.[22] As the place where the king and his entourage resided, the Achaemenid court seems also to have constituted the chief physical setting for playing out the relationship between the king and the Persian nobility, the elite group which provided the dynasty with its ascriptive pool of top-level 'helpers', mainly as satraps and generals. This politically pivotal relationship was continually being renegotiated through gift-giving, household office, participation in ceremonial, and royal activities such as feasting and hunting.

At the other end of Iranian antiquity, Josef Wiesehöfer breaks new and difficult ground by surveying the evidence for the court of the Sasanian kings. Although very fragmentary, it is sufficient to show a generally well-known correlation between the social prestige of the ruler's court and the ebb and flow of monarchical authority. The relative weakness of the Sasanian kings down to the late fifth century AD is reflected in the very limited integration of the great landowners as courtiers. The monarchy became much stronger for a time in the fifth and sixth centuries AD. During this period the prestige of the court grew correspondingly, as shown, for instance, by its control over sartorial distinctions of rank.

The borrowing of one monarchy's court culture by another monarchy returns as a theme in the next chapter, by Tony Spawforth, on Alexander the Great. In a manner not so different from Cyrus the Great, founder of the Achaemenid empire whom he professed to admire, the Macedonian conqueror presided over a vast territorial expansion of a hereditary kingdom. This in turn prompted him to adopt the court culture of the former ruling power (the Achaemenids) as a device of representation and elite-integration in the altogether new and unprecedented circumstances in which, as Macedonian king, he now found himself. The approach of Elias permits a much more realistic assessment of ceremonial at Alexander's court as a mechanism for ranking and integrating the multi-ethnic elites of the empire and also of Alexander's measured use of magnificence – especially his imposing royal tents. It also becomes much clearer how Alexander's courtly practices

---

[22] For this formulation see Apostolidès 1981.

have been distorted by the classical (especially Greek) critique of monarchical splendour as barbaric which colours the surviving literary accounts of Alexander.

In his chapter on the creation of an imperial court under Augustus and his dynastic successors, Jeremy Paterson argues that the changed arrangements of power resulting from the transition from monarchy to empire made the emergence of a court in imperial Rome more or less inevitable. He delineates the negotiation of new types of relationship between the Roman elite and the emperor as the former adapted their traditional quest for power, status and wealth to the new political circumstances and the latter experimented with different approaches to monarchical representation. In economic terms the emperor's court is seen as the centre of distribution and brokerage, where the emergence of a courtly discourse characterised by flattery and lack of frankness was an inevitable consequence of the intense elite competition for rewards (see also Spawforth on the 'Alexander-flatterers').

In the period studied by Rowland Smith (*c.* AD 300–*c.* AD 450), the available sources across a range of media consistently present the emperor's court as a much more formal and ritualised institution in ways which cannot be explained away as simply a subjective matter of shifting perceptions within the upper-class literary milieu. This change is attributed in the main to the third-century decline in imperial reliance on the senatorial class, and the rise of a new and numerically greatly expanded 'service aristocracy' as a result of the administrative reforms of Diocletian and his successors. On the one hand the late antique emperors were freed from the dictates of *civilitas* – the pretence of equality which the old senatorial class had valued so highly. This removed earlier constraints on the ceremonial elevation of the person of the emperor and enhanced the importance of the court as the focus of imperial ceremonies. On the other, the creation in effect of a new aristocracy enhanced the role of the court as the chief place where social ranking was displayed and the complex hierarchy of office and honour integrated. Borrowings by one court culture from another – in this case the Sasanians – may also have helped to give the late Roman court its distinctive timbre, as did its militarisation (although a strong military identity crops up in other ancient courts, e.g. Spawforth and Spence in this volume).

Powerful dynastic women and household servants were also elements of continuity in the configuration of the imperial court from early to late antiquity. In the fifth century, Roman empresses combined with child-emperors, eunuchs and generals to rule the empire in a way strikingly similar to the picture of the later Han Chinese emperors in the analysis of van Ess. In Han China, a sacralised, hereditary emperor as often as not reigned rather than ruled, especially in Later Han times. Van Ess argues that the Later Han court survived for as long as it did because it acted as a kind of quasi-constitutional fulcrum, serving to balance the complementary interests of powerful clans related to the imperial women on the one hand, and of the imperial bureaucracy on the other. As Smith suggests for the fifth-century Roman imperial court, an important role of the court in this kind of arrangement of power may have been to maintain "'the set of symbolic forms expressing the fact that [a governing elite] is in truth governing'" (quoting Clifford Geertz). In his description of the Han court and its physical setting, van Ess also draws attention to the story of the founding emperor of the Han line, Han Kao-tsu, a man of humble origins, who has to be told by a supporter why the emperor needs to build imposing palaces: 'Without great and elegant [buildings], you will not [be able to display] your authority and majesty.' This appears to be one of the rare items of evidence for the ancient rationalisation of monarchical display, to be compared with the claim of Louis XIV in his *Mémoires*: 'The people over whom we rule, unable to see to the bottom of things, usually judge by what they see from outside.'[23]

The final chapter, by Spence, takes us furthest back in time, to ancient Egypt, with its focus the later Eighteenth Dynasty (*c.* 1390–1295 BC). Spence traces the origins of a court-style institution to the predynastic period. Echoing Brosius on the social roots of ranking at the Achaemenid court, she sees a link between the innate stratification of ancient Egyptian society and the pharaonic court, a place where the ranking of the elite was put on display and where a sacred ruler was marked off ritually from lesser humanity. The Egyptian court generated culturally specific royal ceremonial, of which the use of the Window of Appearance for rewarding courtiers, studied here by Spence, is a distinctive feature of the reign of Akhenaten. More generally, prostration formed part of the ritual of approaching the ruler in Egypt as, later, it did in Achaemenid Persia. Like Persia, Egypt probably borrowed features of its court culture from the even older royal traditions of the ancient Near East. It is tempting, indeed, to see something of a courtly *koine* in this part of the ancient world, with shared features including sacred monarchy (the Achaemenid ruler seems to have been a quasi-sacred figure, albeit not divine as such), a common language of gesture, and practices such as sartorial distinctions for courtiers based on royal gifts. Under Philip and Alexander, this style of court culture penetrated further westward than it had ever done previously, and it did so again in late (Roman) antiquity.

---

[23] *Mémoires* II, p. 15, ed. Dreyss; Elias 1983: 117–18.

As is becoming clear, the religious underpinnings of ancient monarchy, along with their expression in court art and ceremonial, is another recurrent theme of this volume. If they have not received more emphasis in the Introduction, this is because the advance in the scholarly understanding of this phenomenon over the last quarter-century has been considerable, certainly where Greco-Roman antiquity is concerned. It is perhaps not facetious to say that ancient historians have at last caught up with the eighteenth-century French chancellor d'Aguesseau, who took the sanctity of supreme power so much for granted that he saw 'régimes de droit divin' even in republican Holland or Venice.[24]

The Newcastle project never aimed for comprehensive coverage of the courts of the ancient world – an impossible task between one set of covers. The courts of the Greco-Macedonian dynastic states which between them came to rule over the tri-continental imperial state of Alexander the Great have received considerable scholarly attention in the past and are not accorded separate treatment here. But two important studies published independently of each other at much the same time, and explicitly acknowledging Elias, must be mentioned. Gabriel Herman (Herman 1997) used the contemporary Greek historian Polybius (second century BC) as the basis for a penetrating study of the social formations which grew up around the Ptolemies in Egypt and the Antigonids in Macedon and which clearly reproduce features of a complex court society. In this period the political dominance of monarchy within the enlarged Greek world created by Alexander's conquest is shown by the appearance of terms for 'court' and 'courtiers' in contemporary Greek writers.[25] Herman is mainly concerned with diagnosing the type of the courtier in the leading members of the royal entourage, the ruler's so-called 'friends', entrepreneurial individuals, overwhelmingly Greek, who were entirely dependent on his favour, served him in various capacities as a governing elite in return for material rewards, and belonged socially to larger networks connecting the court to Greek cities within and beyond the kingdom's frontiers. An entourage constituted in this way in important respects was anticipated by the court of Alexander and, indeed, that of Philip before him (Spawforth in this volume). Herman shows that competition for royal favour among the 'friends' was intense, and seeks to demonstrate that these entourages generated their own rules of behaviour or 'etiquette' which allow them to be identified as 'court societies' in the Eliasque sense.[26]

---

[24] Quoted by Antoine 1989: 170.   [25] E.g. Men.897; *FGrH* 81 F 44 = Athen.142b.

[26] Herman 1997: 204, 219, 223–4, although it is not clear that the behaviours adduced are not sometimes simply the normal standards of civility in upper-class Greek society of the time.

In a long chapter which appeared in the same year, Gregor Weber covered similar terrain, likewise basing himself on the written sources and concentrating on the social structure and styles of communication within the Hellenistic courts, with recognition, but only a brief discussion, of their representative function (Gregor 1997). Weber emphasises the evolution of the forms of interaction between kings and courtiers from the ethos of equality and informal friendship in the opportunistic atmosphere of the early Hellenistic courts, to the formal hierarchies of 'friends' ranked as 'first', 'second' and so on which emerged in the second century BC. In this period, the Hellenistic kingdoms were contracting territorially and from an Aegean point of view were no longer the lands of opportunity of earlier times. In this harsher climate, honorific titles at court were part of the struggle to retain the loyalty – no longer guaranteed – of the leading figures serving in the royal army and administration. This 'frozen formalism' (Herman 1997: 223) characterised the Hellenistic courts which survived into the period from the later second century BC, and influenced the households of leading Roman aristocrats when they began to resemble courts in miniature, with their segregation of callers into 'first' and 'second' friends.[27]

The summaries offered above of the chapters which follow hardly do justice to their depth or richness. The contributors hope that the variety of modern approaches and ancient evidence, and the broad span of both places and periods, will offer the opportunity to observe a range of ancient courts, and stimulate debate on the usefulness of 'the court' as an analytical category in the study of ancient monarchy.

---

[27] Sen.*de Ben.*6.34.2, cited by Gregor 1997: 71 n. 192. See Paterson in this volume.

1 | New out of old? Court and court ceremonies in Achaemenid Persia

MARIA BROSIUS

Introduction

The need for a systematic study of the courts of ancient Near Eastern monarchies, including the court of the Achaemenid empire, is only now becoming clear.[1] Amélie Kuhrt identified these courts as elements of Near Eastern kingship and the expression of power (Kuhrt 1995). Briant (1996, 2002) offered a descriptive account of the Achaemenid court, although he fell short of providing a historical context or adopting a theoretical approach to the court as a political institution in the sense first defined by Norbert Elias. Most recently Wiesehöfer (in press (c)) has discussed the Achaemenid palace and its importance for the king.[2]

Elias' analysis asked how the social position of monarch was perpetuated over numerous generations and dynasties and over considerable time periods. He identified the court as a grouping of people who played a key part in this phenomenon and had an immediate interest in preserving the monarch. King and court existed in a relation of interdependence, in which each used the other constantly to reaffirm their position within a strict hierarchical order. Both the king and the court used court ceremonies and court etiquette as vehicles for expressing this interdependence. While the king used them to emphasise his unique position and his social distance from his courtiers, the courtiers used them to display their own position within the hierarchical order of the court. This system led to the creation of a self-perpetuating 'court society'. This chapter attempts to identify a court and court society in Achaemenid Persia, operating on the principles of interdependence between king and court as argued for by Norbert Elias.

In the case of Achaemenid Persia, it needs pointing out that to a large extent our knowledge depends on classical, and chiefly Greek, sources. Archaeological evidence from the Achaemenid empire sheds light on the material

---

[1] For one such study of palace institutions in the first millennium BC see now Nielsen (2001). As far as I am aware, as yet there is no systematic discussion of ancient Near Eastern courts and court societies. But see Spence and Wiesehöfer in this volume; also Joannès 2004: 94–8 on the Assyrian court.

[2] I wish to thank Josef Wiesehöfer for making his article available to me before publication.

manifestations of the Achaemenid court and kingship. But no Achaemenid
literature survives which would allow us to study the problem from a Persian
perspective. To an overwhelming degree the Greek sources were hostile to
Achaemenid Persia. Their accounts of Achaemenid court society are often
ideologically imbued, serving to construct the lifestyle of the king, and by
extension all Persians, as opulent and decadent.[3] The Greek sources therefore need careful handling if we are to use them to identify the elements of
a court society and to explain the workings of the Achaemenid court. This
deficit in the literary sources is offset to a limited extent by the administrative texts from the Persepolis archive.[4] These provide independent evidence
for the hierarchy of administrative officials and their interaction with the
Persian king.

Any discussion of an ancient court must begin with the problem of
definition. How are we to define the 'court' of the Achaemenids? In the
introduction to the volume *Hof und Theorie*, Butz and Dannenberg (2004:
4) distinguish between the court as a social grouping and as an institution.
Thus, 'court' describes on the one hand the people surrounding the king,
and on the other the institutional context within which the king operates,
that is, the centre of his political, administrative, judicial and military power.
A further ambiguity of the term 'court' becomes apparent from the fact that
it refers to a social configuration of groups of people extending beyond the
king's household – those people, that is, who permanently accompany the
king, wherever he is. In order to distinguish between these different groups
who can all be considered a part of the court entity, scholarship differentiates
between the close or inner court and the wider or outer court (Butz and
Dannenberg 2004: 12). This distinction allows us to separate out those
members of the court who constitute the permanent entourage from the
rest.

This chapter investigates the personnel and the institutional character of
the Achaemenid court and the appropriateness for the Achaemenid monarchy of this distinction between an inner and outer court. Before doing so, we
should remember that 'court' refers not only to the 'Personalverbände' structured around the king, but also to a physical space within which ceremonies
and forms of etiquette are performed. The palaces and palace complexes
of the Achaemenid kings bear witness to the importance of a designated
space within which the court – meaning the groups of people around the

---

[3] On the problem of the Greek sources see Wiesehöfer 2001: 11–12; Sancisi-Weerdenburg 1987:
   33–45; Briant 1989a: 33–77.
[4] See Hallock 1969, 1978.

king – operated. The importance of the palace as a 'court' is also mirrored in the design, size and splendour of the royal tent which accommodated the court on its journeys between royal residences and on campaigns (see also Spawforth in this volume).

Historical background

When the Persians settled in eastern Elam, in the province of Persis (modern Fars), around 1000 BC, their society was tribal. Each tribe consisted of a number of clans, which in turn were made up of extended families. It can be assumed that the heads of these families formed a hierarchy among themselves and thus created a natural ranking order within each tribe. Family hierarchies may have been based upon the number of generations in a family lineage; or on a family's size, gauged by the number of children, especially sons, on whom depended a family's chances of extending its influence over others; or on a family's wealth, in terms of livestock and land. The shaping of these hierarchies may also have been influenced by the qualities of the head of the household as a leader, qualities revealed by success in the political and military sphere. Two social issues were the particular concern of the head of a family: the protection and welfare of his family, including the betterment of its way of life; and, beyond the family, the welfare of his tribe. Self-preservation; natural ambition within one's social environment; a way of life characterised by an awareness that an individual's actions affected the well-being of the tribe as a whole; and protection from outside threat: all these factors contributed to the profile of the head of a family and shaped his ambitions for himself, and for his sons and daughters. They also contributed to his family's standing within the tribe, in turn affecting the tribe's standing among other tribes.[5]

Herodotus knew of nine Persian tribes, the leading Pasargadae, Maraphians and Maspians, the settled tribes of the Panthialaeans, the Derusians and the Germanians, and the nomadic tribes of the Mardians, Dropicians and Sagartians (Hdt.1.125). The tripartite division of these tribes already reflects a ranking order, within which the Pasargadae were identified as the most notable. They had been the leading tribe for three generations, when in the fourth generation Cyrus II the Great (559–530 BC) emerged as the leader of the Persians and the founder of the Persian empire.[6]

---

[5] For the importance of the family in Persian society see for example DB IV: 60–1.

[6] The first Persian leader attested in the sources is Teispes (*c.* 650–620 BC), who was succeeded by Cyrus I (*c.* 620–590 BC) and Cambyses I (*c.* 590–559 BC) (see Cyrus Cylinder line 21).

The identification of several Persian tribes allows the assumption that the concept of a social ranking order was in place at the time of the emergence of the Persians as a political power. It may thus be postulated that the elements of a hierarchically structured court society in their earliest form went back to the extended-family formation of the tribe. Protection of a group, aspiration to leadership and competition among equals affected the head of the family, the leader of the tribe, the leader of the dominant tribe and, on the ultimate level, the king and his nobility. Within this structure a key aspect of court society can be detected: namely, the group's support for an individual and that individual's reciprocal dependence on the group to maintain his status (cf. Elias 1983: 3; Herman 1997: 200). The relationship between the individual and the group of supporters evolved from the group's support for the head of a tribe, then for the head's son and successors, before moving from this lineage of tribal chiefs to a dynasty of kings.

The kings of the first Persian dynasty, the Achaemenids, named after the eponymous founder of the empire, Achaemenes, ruled their empire from 560 to 330 BC. Despite succession struggles[7] and internal revolts, royal power remained with the Achaemenid dynasty throughout this time. They controlled the empire through vast provinces, so-called satrapies, which were made up of conquered kingdoms and territories. Each province was governed by a satrap, who was installed in office by the king, and who was often a close relation of the king, especially in important satrapies such as Bactria (roughly modern Afghanistan) and Egypt. Owing both to their familial link with the king and to the importance of the office itself, satraps were members of the royal court. They represented the king at local level and had their own palaces, satrapal parks and estates, as well as their own courts modelled on the royal court. Their office gave them a key role as intermediaries between the king and his subjects (cf. Herman 1997: 200). One of the most significant political achievements of the Persian monarchy was the creation of the satrapal system, which proved an effective means of government for over two centuries, and was even adapted by the Macedonian successors of the Achaemenids, the Seleucids.[8]

External influence on the establishment of the Persian court

Persian court society was not generated solely by the internal structure of Persian tribal society. It was also subject to external influence from the other

---

[7] Especially following the murders of Xerxes and his heir Darius in 465, of Xerxes II in 424 and of Artaxerxes III in 338.

[8] On satraps and the satrapal division of the empire see Wiesehöfer 2001: 59–62; Jacobs 1994; Tuplin 1987. On the Seleucid empire see Sherwin-White and Kuhrt 1993.

Near Eastern monarchies which helped to shape Persian kingship. These kingdoms included Elam, as well as those of Media and Urartu, Lydia, Babylonia and Assyria. Since the formation and the development of a court society go hand in hand with monarchy and the expression of kingship, it is more than likely that the courts of these neighbouring monarchies influenced the court society of Achaemenid Persia. The fact that their political and cultural influence can be traced on other levels adds weight to the idea of a Persian adaptation of their court organisations. But it is difficult to assess the extent of this influence, since the evidence for their own court societies is scarce. Their influence on the development of the Persian court can be grasped only to a limited extent.

The Neo-Elamite kingdom gave the Persians their first encounter with the concept of kingship and a political entity headed by the king and his court. Elam was centred on two royal capitals, Susa, west of the Zagros mountains, and Anshan, east of the Zagros, in the province of Persis. An ancient civilisation, Elam had a history of monarchic rule dating back to the third millennium BC.[9] Owing to the scarcity of historical sources for Elam, however, it is well-nigh impossible to grasp Elamite court life. Given the duration of Elamite royal rule, the existence of a court society supporting the kingship can certainly be assumed. In Elam there is evidence for a dynastic succession, for the expression of kingship in the representation of the royal couple on reliefs and in sculpture, as also in the construction by kings of public and religious buildings, as attested by numerous building inscriptions. Local dynasts, too, expressed their kingship in rock reliefs depicting scenes of prayer or religious processions composed of selected(?) groups of retainers, led by the king.[10] The reliefs clearly reflect a need to express kingship visually for the benefit of a (court) society of high-ranking individuals close to the king.

Following the destruction of Susa in 646 BC by the Assyrian king Assurbanipal, the Elamite kingdom came under Assyrian control until the fall of Nineveh in 612 BC. A Neo-Elamite dynasty arose briefly in Susa; meanwhile the Persians gradually established their power in the region of Anshan, eventually annexing Susa under Cyrus II (see Vallat 1998: 311). Anshan was, if not the actual, then certainly the ideological centre of the Persian rulers, who claimed to be the political heirs of the Elamite kings.[11] There is no doubt that the early Persian kings adapted aspects of Elamite kingship, as well as

---

[9] On the history of Elam see Potts 1999; Vallat 1998; Carter and Stolper 1984.

[10] The reliefs at Kul-e Farah III (*c.* 1100–1000 BC) are an example of the visual expression of a king performing a (religious) ceremony in the presence of a group of people (see Potts 1999: pl. 7.9).

[11] This is most apparent in the Persian adaptation of the Elamite royal title, according to which the Persian kings were called 'king of Anshan' (see Cyrus Cylinder lines 20–1).

taking over administrative and possibly military practices from Elam. It is likely, then, that the court of the Elamite kings likewise influenced the palace organisation of the early Persian kings.

Other influences might have come from neighbouring Media and from Urartu,[12] though in both cases we know almost nothing about their courts. The Medes, like the Persians, were an Iranian people. They had settled in north-west Iran around the same time as the Persians, and soon became a political and military force to be reckoned with by their Mesopotamian and Lydian neighbours. Median political organisation appears to have been a loose federation of kings centred on different cities.[13] Out of this grouping a dominating dynasty emerged under Deioces of Ecbatana. Herodotus credited him with the introduction of court etiquette and court procedures:

It was Deioces first who established the rule that no-one should come into the presence of the king, but all should be dealt with by the means of messengers; that the king should be seen by no man; and that it should be in particular a disgrace for any to laugh or to spit in his presence. He was careful to hedge himself with all this state in order that the men of his own age (who had been bred up with him and were nobly born as he and his equals in manly excellence), instead of seeing him and being thereby vexed and haply moved to plot against him, might by reason of not seeing him deem him to be changed from what he had been.

(Hdt.1.99)

Even if the historicity of Herodotus' Median *logos* must be regarded with caution, the portrayal of the king's recognition of his unique position, which set him apart from people who had been formerly his peers, reflects a credible historical development from tribal or military leader to kingship. The idea that the king had to distance himself from his subjects is echoed in Xenophon's description of Cyrus' court:

Cyrus conceived a desire to establish himself as he thought became a king, but he decided to do so with the approval of his friends, in such a way that his public appearances should be rare and solemn and yet excite as little jealousy as possible . . . So Cyrus stationed a large circle of Persian lancers about him and gave orders that no-one should be admitted except his friends and the officers of the Persians and the allies. (Xen.*Cyr*.7.5.37, 41)

Limited access to the king meant that the person of the king was exalted above other members of the court. In order for the king to maintain his

---

[12] For evidence on Urartu and its court see Kuhrt 1995: 559–60.
[13] On the question of the Median kingdom see Sancisi-Weerdenburg 1988. See also Kuhrt 1995: 653–6; Rollinger 2003.

extraordinary position, he could not seem to be one of the nobles: he had to be a singular figure, removed from the nobility. Those who were admitted to the royal presence were privileged above all others. This access to the king set them apart from the majority who were denied it. Thus a noble's closeness to the king meant closeness to power, which in turn affected his standing among his peers. For most, access to the king was not direct: anyone seeking an audience had to be announced and accompanied by an intermediary. This was the royal messenger, or staff-bearer, who was one of the most important officials at the court, holding a key position between the king and his subjects.[14]

The Babylonian and Assyrian courts

A building text of Nebuchadnezzar II (604–562 BC) gives us a glimpse of Babylonian court society. The text lists a number of functionaries in the royal household (Bab. *mašennu*), including the chief baker, the chief of the *kāṣiru*, the superintendent of the palace, the major-domo, the *mašennu* of the House of the Palace Women, the scribe of the House of the Palace Women, the master of ceremonies(?), the chief barber(?),[15] the overseer of slave-women, the cup-bearer, the chief singer, the secretary of the crown prince, the chief of cattle, the chief of boat-men, and the chief of the king's merchants. These are followed by a list of names of the 'great ones', i.e. the governors, then by a list of officials, and finally by a list of the royal city officials including the city kings of the Levantine coast (*ANET* 307–8; cf. Kuhrt 1995: 605–7).

The social groups revealed by the text in turn point to the existence of a court hierarchy. First come the officials immediately serving the king; then the officials responsible for the women's quarters in the palace. All these attendants operated in the immediate vicinity of the king. Distinct from them are the holders of political office – the governors (Bab. *šaknu* and *pīhātu*) in the land of Akkad, who are referred to as 'the great ones'. They in turn are placed at the top of the administrative structure, above officials of smaller districts and governors of the cities and towns. Their status made them members of the court, but, unlike the first group, they belonged to the outer court, i.e. to the grouping of courtiers who were not constantly in the royal vicinity.

The principal elements of kingship and court organisation are already apparent in the court of the Assyrian empire. The Assyrian king resided in

---

[14] On the royal staff-bearer see Lewis 1977: 16; Briant 2002: 259.
[15] Or 'chief engineer', or 'chief of couriers'.

the palace complexes of the royal capitals. Royal inscriptions attest to his concern for religious buildings as well as the beautification of the city. Palace reliefs demonstrate his prowess in war, his military excellence and his skill with weapons, both on horseback and in a chariot. The king was depicted honing his military skills as a successful hunter of wild beasts, including lions and panthers. Dynastic concerns found expression in the king's nomination of an heir from among his sons; also in the staging of his funeral – the heir's first duty was to observe his father's funerary rites.

The existence of an order of rank amongst members of the Assyrian court emerges in a text in which the loyalty of the courtiers is being questioned:

> [Will any of the] 'eunuchs' (and) the bearded (officials), the king's entourage, or (any) of his brothers or uncles
> [his kin], his fa[ther's line], or junior members of the royal line, or the 'third men', chariot drivers (and) chariot fighters,
> [or the recruitment officers, or] the prefects of the exempt military, or the prefects of the cavalry, or the royal bodyguard, or his personal guard,
> [or the keepers] of the inner gates or the keepers of the outer gate, or the ... 'eunuchs',
> [or . . .], or the palace superintendents, the staff-bearers (and) the wa(tch)men, or the mounted(?) scouts (and) the trackers,
> [or the lackeys, tailor]s, cup-bearers, cooks, confectioners, the entire body of crafts-men,
> or the Itu'eans and the Elamites, the mounted bowmen (?), the Hittites (or) the Gurreans, or the Aramaeans, [or the Cimmerians, o]r the Philistines, or the Nubians (and) the Egyptians or the Shabuqeans, [or the 'eunuchs' who b]ear [arms], or the bearded (officials) who bear arms and stand guard for the king.
> (*SAA* 4 no.142; Kuhrt 1995: 529–30)

As Kuhrt has pointed out, the high-ranking officials operating around the king enjoyed considerable wealth and social standing at court (cf. Kuhrt 1995: 531; Joannès 2004: 96). They were given freehold and tax-exempt estates, and are attested as landowners across the empire.[16] Apart from the household staff, there is also evidence for the presence at court of scholarly advisors who counselled the king on matters of science, religious ritual and astronomy.

As in Babylonia, a household for royal women also existed at the Assyrian court. The kings were polygamous and there is slight evidence that at least some royal women descended from the Assyrian nobility. Presumably there was some kind of ranking amongst them, with the highest rank probably assigned to the mother of the designated heir. Beyond that, their family

---

[16] See Kuhrt 1995: 531 for the example of the chief reinholder of Assurbanipal.

background may well have had a bearing on their standing within the group. An important observation can be made regarding the status of these royal women, which in turn provides a clue as to the palace organisation. Assyrian queens owned estates and controlled large households. They had residences in the royal capitals (cf. Kuhrt 1995: 526–7; Joannès 2004: 96). At the head of the queen's household was the *šakintu*, a female official who herself controlled considerable wealth, and her deputy. Other members included a female scribe of the queen's household, a cook, and a male and female confectioner, as well as a woman referred to as *sekretu*, 'enclosed woman of the house' (Akk. MUNUS.ERIM.É.GAL). This was either a term used for women of the palace other than the king's wives, or a reference to female servants.

As all the evidence shows, a court society was well established in Mesopotamia and northern Iran at the time of the Achaemenids' rise to power. Even though there is no clear proof that the Persian king modelled his court on the Assyrian and Babylonian examples, the extant sources allow us to note different components within the court societies of Mesopotamia and northern Iran. The following discussion will explore how far these same components, including the different levels of personal attendants, a hierarchy of officials holding political and administrative office in the vicinity of the king, a court of the royal women, and a wider royal court, can be identified in the organisation of the court of the Achaemenids.

The Achaemenid court

Achaemenid royal inscriptions give a term for the palace, OP viθ-(Bab. *bitu-*/ Elam. *ulhi*) (cf. Wiesehöfer, in press). The term is ambiguous, as Wiesehöfer notes: 'When Darius asks the god [*Ahuramazda*, M. B.] to protect the Persians and his 'house' he is, of course, not referring to viθ- as a building, but to the people living and working in the royal household' (Wiesehöfer, in press; cf. DB I: 61–71). In other inscriptions, the buildings of Persepolis are referred to as *halmarraš* (DPf), with individual palaces more specifically identified as *taçara* ('suite of rooms') (DSd) and *hadiš* (DSj) 'seat of power' (cf. Wiesehöfer, in press).[17] In Greek terminology we find terms such as *ta basileia* (e.g. Hdt.1.30, 98, 178, 181) and *ta oikēmata* (Ctesias, *FGrH* 688 F 9.13). These terms are equally ambiguous, denoting both a building complex and also the people operating within it.

---

[17] Wiesehöfer points out that the Babylonian term used for these buildings is *bitu-* rather than *ekallu*.

In the first instance the king's court was defined by a group of attendants and officials whose duties kept them permanently in the immediate vicinity of the king. Together with members of the king's immediate family they formed the inner court. The king's attendants included his personal servants, ointment bearers, the cup-bearer, the king's parasol-bearer, the royal charioteer and the stool-bearer. Members of this group took care of the king's daily needs, prepared and served his meals, and were in attendance wherever the king happened to be – not just within the palace complex, but during his migrations between royal capitals and on campaign. Some were eunuchs, and Greek sources emphasise that eunuchs held particular positions of trust at the court. According to Xenophon Cyrus II appointed eunuchs as his personal attendants because of their loyalty;[18] and Xerxes I was said to have entrusted the safe return of his sons to his 'most honoured' eunuch Hermotimus (Hdt.8.104).

Among the king's personal attendants depicted in the palace doorways of Persepolis we find parasol bearers and attendants variously holding the fly-whisk above the king's head and carrying perfume, ointment bottles and towels. The very fact of their depiction in these prominent locations suggests the importance attached to the presentation of the king within his own court. These courtly scenes showed the king in his own palace, 'performing' ceremonies connected with court life and court ritual.

Other attendants were responsible for ensuring the king's comfort on foot, on horseback or in the royal chariot. Their depiction on the reliefs of the staircases leading up to the Throne-Hall shows that the king regarded them and their functions as an expression of his kingship.

The attendants carried carpets and rugs, ready to place before a king whose foot was never supposed to touch the ground:

Through their (*the bodyguards'*) court also the king would go on foot, Sardis carpets, on which no-one else but the king ever walked, having been spread on the ground. And when he reached the last court he would mount his chariot, or sometimes his horse; but he was never seen on foot outside the palace. (Athen.12.514c)

The king's stool-bearer ensured that the king never mounted or descended from his chariot without the aid of a stool, which in turn always stood on a

---

[18] 'As for servants, he considered the most trusted as well as the most loyal men to be eunuchs: he selected eunuchs for every post of personal service to him, from the door-keepers up' (Xen.*Cyr.*7.5.65). Ctesias seems to confirm Xenophon's assertion that eunuchs were among the courtiers close to the king. They enjoyed the king's trust, and were given vital tasks, such as supervising the return of the king's body to Persepolis (Ctesias, *FGrH* 688 F 13). On eunuchs at the Persian court see Briant 2002: 268–77; in the (late) Roman and Han Chinese courts: Smith and van Ess in this volume.

special rug. According to Dinon:

whenever the king descended from his chariot ... he never leaped down, although the distance to the ground was small, nor did he lean on anyone's arms; rather, a golden stool was always set in place for him, and he descended by stepping on this; and the king's stool-bearer attended him for this purpose. (Dinon ap. Athen.12.514)

Given their frequent and close access to the king, complete trust and loyalty was required from these servants. To ensure this, they were recruited chiefly from among the members of the Persian nobility.[19] Non-Persians could also serve in these posts, as shown by the well-known example of the biblical Nehemiah, who served as Artaxerxes' cup-bearer. Eunuchs too were frequently recruited from a non-Persian background (cf. Hdt.3.92, 97; Athen.12.514d). The allocation of these seemingly servile tasks was probably done in such a way as to create a hierarchy among the Persians and non-Persians involved.[20]

At the second level up were those Persians who held a court office which gave them immediate access to the king. These people included the king's spear-bearer, his bow- and axe-bearer, the heads of the king's bodyguard (*hazarapatiš*), palace administration and royal treasury, the chief scribe, the keeper of the gate, and the priest(s), along with the Persian nobles serving as the King's Councillors, as Royal Judges, and as the King's Eye. In a separate category were the royal physicians, required to be permanently in attendance on the king and his family, but who were of non-Persian origin.

The king's spear-bearer and the axe- and bow-bearer occupy a prominent position behind the king in the reliefs at Bisitun and Naqsh-i Rustam, as well as on the audience relief from Persepolis. These positions were held by high-ranking Persian nobles who enjoyed the king's trust. In the Naqsh-i Rustam relief they are identified as 'Gobryas, the Patischoraean, spear-bearer of Darius the king' (DNc), and 'Aspathines, the bow-bearer, (who) holds the king's axe' (DNd).[21] Both were members of the Persian nobility, and Gobryas

---

[19] See for example Patiramphes son of Otanes, who was Xerxes' chariot driver (Hdt.7.40); see Briant 2002: 310.

[20] It is hard to know whether to classify the attendants of the king as courtiers or merely as members of the household staff. While they may not have been courtiers in the sense of holding an official position of authority and being able to take part in the decision-making process, the fact that they were of noble descent must mark them as members of the court. Historically, personal service by nobles is a hallmark of the courtier; cf. the Macedonian court under Philip and Alexander (Spawforth in this volume).

[21] Aspathines is thought to have succeeded Ardumaniš in office soon after Darius' accession to the throne. It would be interesting to know whether Gobryas and Ardumaniš held their positions as the king's spear-bearer and bow-bearer/axe-bearer at the time of Darius' accession, and should therefore be identified on the Bisitun relief. Darius himself had been a spear-bearer of Cambyses II in Egypt (Hdt.3.139.2).

Figure 1.1 Staircase of the *Apadana* (after F. Krefter)

had been a fellow-conspirator in Darius' coup in 522 (see below). The *haza-rapatiš* was the head of the king's personal bodyguard, the One Thousand, also known as the Apple-bearers after the golden apples on the butts of their dress-spears.[22] This elite guard can probably be identified with the rows of spear-bearing soldiers on the reliefs decorating the staircase of the Throne-Hall in Persepolis (Fig. 1.1). They formed a part of the 10,000 Immortals, household troops forming a constant presence around the king.[23] According to Heracleides of Cumae, a court in the palace complex was named after the One Thousand as the 'Court of the Apple-bearers'. The same writer says that these troops were all Persian by birth (Heracleides, *FGrH* 689 F 2; ap. Athen.514b). Pseudo-Aristotle sums up the appearance of these courtiers and bodyguards in the Achaemenid palace as follows:

The king himself, they say, lived in Susa or Ecbatana, invisible to all, in a marvellous palace (*basileion oikon*) with a surrounding wall flashing with gold, electrum and ivory; it had a succession of many gate-towers, and the gateways, separated by many stades from one another, were fortified with brazened doors and high walls; outside these the leaders and most eminent men were drawn up in order, some as personal bodyguards (*doryphoroi*) and attendants (*therapontes*) to the king himself, some as guardians of each outer wall, called Guards (*pyloroi*) and Listening-Watch (*ōtakoustai*), so that the king himself, who had the name of Master and God (*despotēs kai theos*) might see everything and hear everything.

(Ps.-Aristotle, *de Mundo* 398a; cf. Wiesehöfer, in press)

While the *hazarapatiš* headed the military presence at court, there was also a head of the administration. Under Darius I this official was Parnaka son of Arsames, an Achaemenid and the uncle of the king (cf. Lewis 1977: 7–8). Parnaka oversaw the administration of Persepolis and its province, Persis.[24] His position at court gave him direct access to the king and he received orders from the king in person relating to the distribution of foodstuffs from the royal storerooms. On Parnaka's authority, the king's orders were recorded in writing before being carried out. A typical letter-order would begin with the formula 'Tell PN, Parnaka spoke as follows', followed by a reference to

---

[22] Rendered *chiliarch* in Greek, the term was once thought to designate a second-in-command, but, as D. M. Lewis has demonstrated, the term describes a military office (Lewis 1977: 17–20; cf. Hdt.7.41.1).

[23] Cf. Xen.*Cyr*.7.5.41. Cyrus II is credited with the creation of the 10,000 Immortals (Xen.*Cyr*.7.5.66–8).

[24] Neither Parnaka nor Ziššawiš is known to have borne a title. The idea that Parnaka may have been the satrap of Persis or the 'grand vizier' of Persepolis must be rejected (see Lewis 1977: 8–9). As the Persepolis texts reveal, Parnaka was permanently based at Persepolis, and so must be regarded as the chief administrator of the royal capital. On the subordinates of both Parnaka and Ziššawiš see Lewis 1977: 10–12.

the king having given the order (see below, p. 34). Parnaka's command was then sealed with his personal seal. The officials addressed by Parnaka were the chiefs of departments heading different sections of the administration: the chiefs of the workers (Elam. *kurdabattiš*), of the cattle (Elam. *kasabattiš*) and of the wine (Elam. *W.GEŠTIN. kutira*). The high status of the head of administration was reflected in the amount of daily rations he was entitled to receive from the royal storehouse: 90 quarts of wine, 180 quarts of flour, and 2 sheep.[25]

Among his subordinates Ziššawiš can be identified as Parnaka's chief assistant. He carried out similar administrative tasks, including the issuing and recording of orders to other officials.[26] Other officials serving under Parnaka were the palace scribes. They wrote in Elamite, Babylonian and Aramaic, and themselves were probably headed by a chief scribe.[27] The royal messengers needed the king's permission (Elam. *halmi*) before they could travel the empire in his name; probably only a few had direct access to the king. Besides Parnaka, there was a chief treasurer (Elam. *kapnuškira*), operating the financial section of the palace administration, who also may have had access to the king.

King's Councillors, Royal Judges and the King's Eye

Members of both the royal family and the nobility acted as political advisors to the king. They formed an unspecified group of Persians of unknown size; nor do we know when and how often they advised the king. Its members were probably not treated as a homogeneous group, but were ranked individually according to the importance of their services to the king (Lewis 1977: 22). Royal Judges were consulted in legal matters.[28] Their number, it seems, was uneven, possibly to ensure a majority vote in a judgement (Diod.15.10.1). The Royal Judges held permanent office at the court. Their level of jurisdiction was different from that of the legal personnel of the satrapies and sub-districts, where local judges, bailiffs and magistrates dealt with everyday legal affairs. Permanently on call, the Royal Judges, like the Royal Councillors, belonged to the inner court of officials in the king's immediate service.

As his title suggests, the King's Eye was charged with intelligence-gathering, reporting to the king. No doubt there were many informants in the king's service. They probably reported to the chief informant, the

---

[25] See PF 665, 662, 668.

[26] On the identification of Ziššawiš with Tithaios (Hdt.7.88.1) see Lewis 1977: 592.

[27] Plut.*Al.*18.8 refers to a 'chief of correspondence'; see Briant 2002: 258.

[28] Note also the king's consultation of the admirals of his fleet before Salamis (Hdt.8.67).

King's Eye, who uniquely had access to the king.[29] Their task was to gather information on any signs of seditious activity in the empire which could jeopardise the Persian peace, whether by individuals or groups.

The most important group in the inner court was the king's immediate family. This included the king's mother and his wife or wives, the heir to the throne, other royal sons and daughters, and those royal siblings who resided at the court. The king's mother and wife and the heir to the throne held the highest rank at court. They were allowed to dine with the king (cf. Plut.*Art.*5.3) and to be present during royal audiences. Owing to their familial closeness to the king, the royal women were able to act as mediators between the king and members of the nobility (see Brosius 2002: 116–19).[30]

The audience relief from Persepolis shows the heir to the throne taking up a position immediately behind the king's throne (Fig. 1.2). The relief offers a spatial expression of the position of the heir as second-in-command. That such a position formally existed is suggested by an inscription from Persepolis, in which Xerxes, the crown-prince, describes his rank as 'the greatest after the king'. As he puts it: 'Other sons of Darius there were, but it was the desire of Ahuramazda that my father Darius made me the greatest after himself' (XPf §4). A similar position could be awarded to the king's brother. Ariamenes, a brother of Xerxes, was discouraged from his plan to challenge his brother's succession with the promise of lavish gifts and the position of 'the greatest at court' should Xerxes become king (Plut.*Mor.*173B–C).[31]

A court for royal women?

A more difficult question to answer is whether the women of the royal family and the nobility formed a court in their own right. As well as female royalty and noblewomen, this grouping would have included their attendants; royal concubines; and administrative personnel. As noted above, an institution called the 'House of the Palace Women' is attested at the courts of the Assyrian and the Babylonian kings. Was this tradition continued at the Persian court? Comparison of the status of Persian royal women with their Assyrian and Babylonian counterparts is certainly justified. As in Mesopotamia, the mother of the king (Bab. *ummi šarri*, Elam. **sunki ammari*) and the king's wife (Bab. *aššat šarri*; Elam. *sunki irtiri*) held the highest positions at court, followed by other royal wives, their daughters and the concubines.

---

[29] On the King's Eye see Wiesehöfer 2001: 62; 266.

[30] For the importance of Assyrian women in court politics see Brosius 2002: 105–19.

[31] See also Sancisi-Weerdenburg's interpretation of Masistes as the 'greatest after the king' (Sancisi-Weerdenburg 1980: 48ff; 122ff).

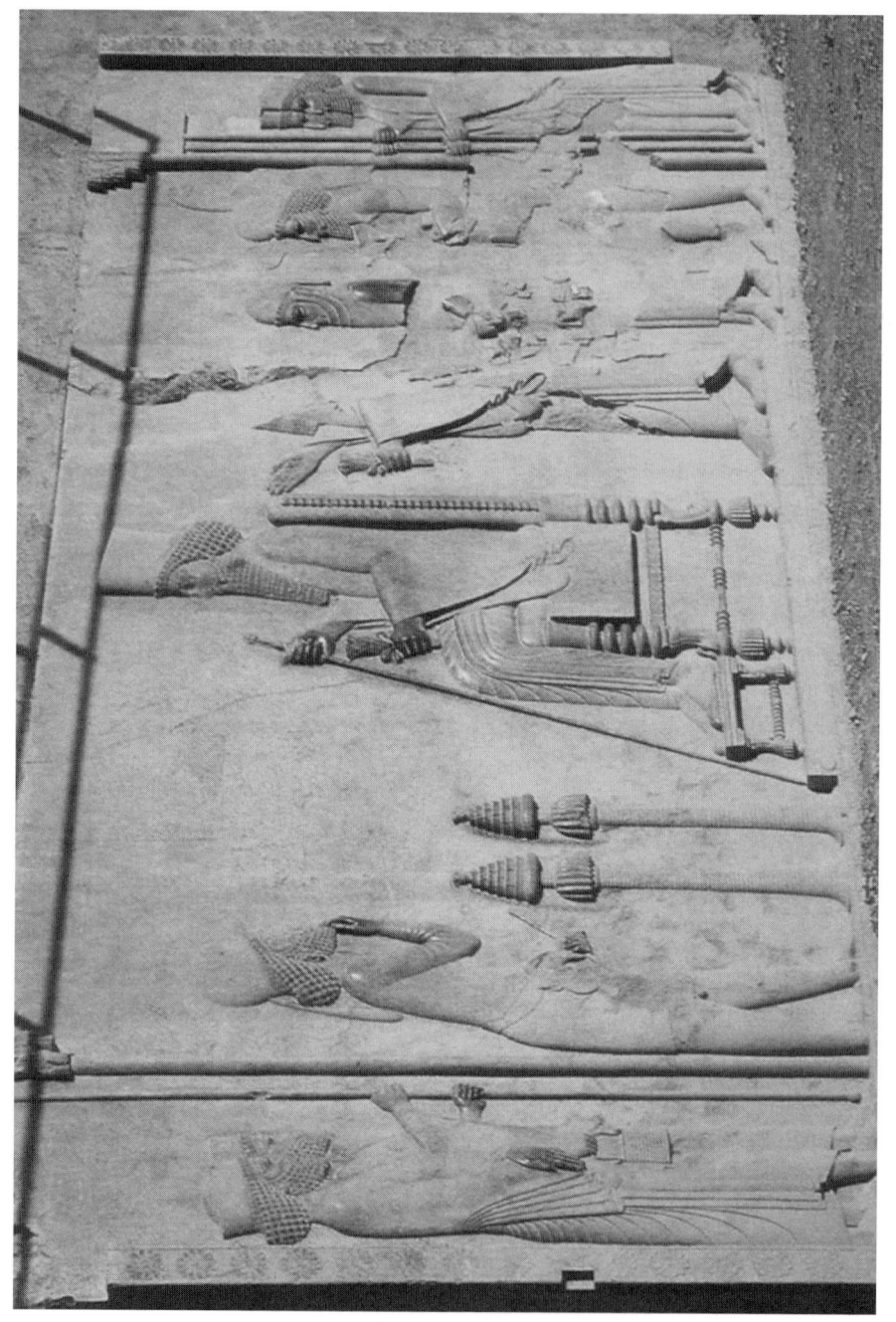

Figure 1.2   The audience relief, Persepolis (photo: M. Brosius)

They were part of the royal entourage accompanying the king on his travels to the royal capitals and on campaigns. Women were part of Xerxes' army (Hdt.9.76.1) and accompanied the train of Darius III (Arr.*An*.2.11.9–10; Curt.3.8.12; Plut.*Al*.24.1).[32] When they travelled with the king, separate tents were put up for them in a designated area of the camp (see Spawforth in this volume). Like the royal women in Mesopotamia, Achaemenid royal women controlled considerable wealth. As the Near Eastern and Greek sources certify, they owned estates, land and workshops across the empire, and controlled their own workforce. Administrators acted on their behalf, and their personal seals show that royal women were able to give orders in their own right.[33]

So far no structure has been identified at Persepolis which could have served as the women's quarters. This makes it difficult to give a firm answer to this question of a separate court for the women.[34] It is certainly wrong to speak of a 'harem' – a term implying that the women were secluded and their freedom of movement restricted. But some kind of designated space for the royal women, comparable to the Assyrian expression 'House of the Palace Women', seems likely. Greek sources frequently refer to the women's quarters at the Persian court. It is possible that an appropriate space was set aside for formal appearances by the royal women, just like the king's more public rooms, where visitors were received and banquets held. Literary and archaeological evidence shows that royal women had the right both to attend the king's audiences and to hold audiences of their own. Seals dated to the Achaemenid period show audience scenes in which high-ranking women receive a female visitor.[35] There can be no doubt as to their typological association with the royal audience scene from the Persepolis reliefs. The Bible shows that the king's wife could attend royal audiences (Neh.2:6), and

---

[32] See also Brosius 2002: 87–91.

[33] Two officials are known to have acted as administrators for Irdabama, a princess: Rašda and Uštana were responsible for distributing rations to her workforce at Shiraz (see Brosius 2002: 134). Both Irdabama and Irtašduna/Artystone are known to have used their own seals (PFS 51 and PFS 38 respectively).

[34] See Root 1979: 101–3. The identification of one building on the royal terrace as a 'harem' is tenuous, and has to be discarded completely if we accept the theory that the royal terrace was in fact not used to accommodate the court (see below pp. 44, 47).

[35] A seal from Persepolis, PFS 77* (Garrison and Root (forthcoming)), crafted in Neo-Elamite style, depicts a woman with a bobbed hairstyle seated on a throne. She is attended by a female servant holding a fly-whisk. In front of her, standing before an incense burner, is a female visitor, dressed and coiffed similarly. The audience scene on a chalcedony cylinder seal depicts a woman seated on a throne wearing a Persian dress and a mural crown, a veil hanging from it at the back. Her feet rest on a footstool. She is approached by a female attendant offering a bird and a lotus flower – perhaps gifts brought by the Persian woman standing behind the attendant. This woman's crown, veil and a Persian dress similar to the seated figure identify her high rank (see Spycket 1980: fig. 7).

also mentions separate feasts celebrated by the women of the court (Esther 1:9–12).[36] The Persepolis Fortification texts record the distribution of wine and foodstuffs for the king's wife by order of the king, showing that the king footed the bill for the queen's entertainments. The quantities involved – some 2,000 litres of wine and 100 sheep – indicate occasions involving several hundred guests:

Tell Yamakšedda the wine-carrier, Parnaka spoke as follows: '2,000 quarts of wine are to be issued to Artystone (Elam. *Irtašduna*) the *dukšiš* (princess). It was ordered by the king.' Month 1, year 19. Ansukka wrote the text. Maraza communicated the message. (Fort.1795)

Tell Harrena the cattle chief, Parnaka spoke as follows: 'Darius the king ordered me, saying: "100 sheep from my estate are to be issued to Artystone the *dukšiš*."' And now Parnaka says: 'As the king ordered me, so I am ordering you. Now you are to issue 100 sheep to Artystone the *dukšiš*, as was ordered by the king.' Month 1, year 19. Ansukka wrote the text. Maraza communicated the message. (Fort.6764)

The court ranking of royal women was determined by degrees of kinship to the king. Persian noblewomen at court were ranked by the standing of their male relations, unless they had married into the royal family.

Royal physicians

The king employed the most eminent physicians from Egypt and Greece. They, too, were members of the court. One of the earliest known was the Egyptian Udjahorresnet, who attended Cambyses II:

His Majesty assigned to me the office of chief physician. He caused me to be beside him as a companion administrator of the palace. I made his royal titulary, his name being the King of Upper Egypt and Lower Egypt Mesuti-Re (*Son of Re*).

(Brosius 2000: no. 20)

Greek physicians such as Democedes of Croton, Apollonides of Cos and – according to his own testimony – Ctesias of Cnidus lived at the court and attended the king and members of the royal family. Greek historians credit them with close and frequent access to members of the royal family, and they enjoyed a high status at court. For example, Democedes received rich gifts after successfully treating Darius I, including a house, and was invited to join the King's Table (Hdt.3.132.1). Quite clearly, non-Persians whose skills

---

[36] The depiction of a funerary banquet on a stele from Dascyleium, showing a female in Persian style dress seated on a stool next to a man reclining on a couch, both holding cups, is evidence for the continuation of a motif known from the Assyrian court (see Boardman 2000: fig. 5.61; cf. Winter 1986): Assurbanipal reclines on a couch, with his queen enthroned beside him, both holding drinking cups (Strommenger 1962: pl. 241).

benefited the king were granted the same privileges as the Persian nobles. Apart from foreign physicians, the king also made substantial gifts to Greek political exiles, among them the Spartan king Demaratus (Hdt.6.70), the Athenian tyrant Hippias (Hdt.5.96) and the Athenian statesman Themistocles (Thuc.1.138.5). That said, their non-Persian ethnicity may have ranked these Greeks rather low in the hierarchy of the court.

The outer court

The outer court included individuals and groups of people who belonged to the court on either a permanent or a temporary basis, but who did not normally operate in close physical proximity to the king. These courtiers can be separated into several different groups. First, there were the members of the extended royal family: that is, royal kin holding high office in the satrapies, along with their families. They resided in the satrapal centres, but joined the king when official occasions required their presence at the royal court. Both their descent and their high rank gave them access to the king. Satraps who were members of the royal family held a higher rank within the aristocracy than those who were merely members of the nobility, though there will have been distinctions even among these last – some nobles, for example, could claim closer affinity with the king than others, thanks to a marriage alliance with a member of the royal family.[37] The hierarchy among the satraps also had a bearing on their position at the King's Table, and in the king's entourage.

Among the most important members of the outer court were the satraps, governors of the lands of the empire. They could be members of the immediate and extended family of the king: brothers, sons, illegitimate sons (i.e. Darius son of Artaxerxes I, who was satrap of Hyrcania before succeeding to the throne as Darius II), or brothers- and sons-in-law; or members of the nobility with no known family tie to the royal house. Appointment to high office was intended to give employment to close members of the royal family, and also to share power with Persian nobles linked to the royal court by marriage. In this way a complex network was established which helped to create a court society. If a hierarchical order existed amongst the satraps, it was probably based on family ties to the king. This, of course, was subject to change: that is, when the king decided to honour a satrap with the marriage of one of his daughters, as is attested in the case of

---

[37] Forms of greeting conveyed differences of rank. According to Herodotus, Persian peers kissed each other on the mouth, Persians of different ranks kissed each other's cheeks, while a much greater social disparity required the one to bow before the other (Gr. *proskynesis*) (Hdt.1.134.1). Cf. Spawforth in this volume.

the satraps Pharnabazus (Plut.*Art*.27.7), Tissaphernes (Diod.14.26.4) and Orontas (Xen.*An*.2.4.8; 3.4.31).

Satraps represented the king in the royal provinces. They had to execute the king's law, ensure the collection of royal taxes, administer the province and levy troops at the king's request. They were also responsible for the celebration of royal ceremonies at local level and the observation of the royal religious cult of Ahuramazda, as well as of other Persian gods. Major political and military ventures were subject to the king's approval. Satraps who had successfully fought the king's cause could expect rewards of various kinds.

Local officials and dynasts of the cities under Persian control were not able to approach the Persian king directly but had to go through the satraps. One of the best examples of the satrap's role as intermediary is the case of Artaphernes, satrap of Sardis, who negotiated the Persian campaign against Naxos on behalf of Aristagoras of Miletus (Hdt.5.31–2). After Darius had approved the campaign, Artaphernes assembled a naval force of 200 triremes under the command of his cousin Megabates, while Aristagoras, the ruler of Miletus, levied the infantry (Hdt.5.33.1). Other cases highlight the satrap's authority to act in lieu of the king. For example, when Sparta and Athens began investigating the possibility of Persian support to resolve the Peloponnesian war, it was the satraps of Lydia and Phrygia who negotiated the possible alliance with one or the other;[38] and when Evagoras of Salamis rebelled against Persian rule, the king ordered the satraps of those provinces closest to Cyprus to deal with the matter (cf. Diod.15.2.2). As this policy reveals, the king delegated political and military issues to the satraps. On his command, and with his consent, they were required to quash rebellions at local level.[39]

The second group of the outer court included the Persian nobility, defined as the families of the six nobles who had joined Darius I in 522 BC against the usurper Bardiya/Gaumata (DB IV: 80–6). According to Herodotus, these nobles were given the privilege of direct access to the king's chambers (Hdt.3.84). In principle the Persian nobles were permanent members of the court, though how much time they spent in the king's immediate vicinity must have depended on what office they held within the imperial

---

[38] For a narrative of the negotiations between Sparta and the Persian satraps between 412 and 411 see Lewis 1977: 88–107.

[39] Only in exceptional cases did the king take part personally in military campaigns. After Darius' punitive campaign against Athens ended in failure, Xerxes personally led his army against Athens. After several failed attempts to recover Egypt for the empire after the second rebellion of 400, a campaign led by Artaxerxes III returned Egypt to Persian control in 343/2. Finally, it took the defeat of the Granicus and the dawning recognition of Alexander's military power before Darius III led his army in person at Issus and Gaugamela.

and satrapal organisation.[40] But noble rank did not of itself secure the Persian noble's position at court. On the contrary, this position was always subject to the king's scrutiny. Behaviour judged improper by the king could lead to punishment and loss of status; rebellion resulted in exile or death for the noble himself as well as other male members of his family. This created a complex hierarchy among the nobility, in which the standing of individual nobles could shift to reflect particular deeds of loyalty, or the extension of royal favours and privileges. For example, among the six nobles around Darius I, Otanes and his family were honoured with special gifts and a lifelong position of privilege which placed them above all other nobles (Hdt.3.83.3).

In the Bisitun Inscription Darius lists these nobles in the following order: Intaphernes, Otanes, Gobryas, Hydarnes, Megabyxus and Ardumanish[41] (DB IV: 80–6). Intaphernes, the first Persian named in Darius' list, had been appointed commander of an army to quash the rebellion of Arakha in Babylon (DB III: 76–92). He was one of Darius' trusted officials, expressed in the Old Persian term *bandaka* which may be translated as 'bondsmen' or 'dependants'.[42] According to Herodotus, Intaphernes fell out of favour at court and was suspected of rebellion when he made use of his right to enter the king's chamber directly: 'He desired to enter the palace and speak with the king; for this was the law, that the rebels should come into the king's presence without announcement given, if the king were not with one of his wives' (Hdt.3.118.2). His entry was regarded as a breach of trust and Intaphernes was charged with treason. He and the male members of his family were punished with death.

Gobryas, Darius' spear-bearer, held a high rank at court, judging from his daily ration of 100 quarts of wine (PF 688), which places him above

---

[40] Speaking through Cyrus' general Chrysantas, Xenophon describes the role of the nobility at the time of Cyrus II as follows: 'They [*the Persian nobles*] passed a resolution that the nobles should always be in attendance at court, and be in readiness for whatever service Cyrus wished until he should dismiss them. And as they then resolved so even unto this day those who are the subjects of the great king in Asia continue to do – they are constantly in attendance at the court of their princes . . . Accordingly, the nobles came to Cyrus' court with their horses and their spears for so it had been decreed by the best of those who with him had made the conquest of the kingdom' (Xen.*Cyr.*8.1.6–8).

[41] Ardumaniš would soon be replaced by Aspathines, who appears on Darius' relief at Naqsh-i Rustam. Herodotus names him as one of the conspirators of 522. His order of nobles differs from the one in DB. According to Herodotus (3.70), Otanes first recruited Aspathines and Gobryas, and then Intaphernes, while Gobryas roped in Megabyxus, and Aspathines Hydarnes.

[42] See Wiesehöfer 2001: 34. The *bandaka* included loyal 'king's men' as well as mere subjects of the king. Briant suggests that those loyal to the king were initiated into the circle by an official ceremony in which the candidate swore an oath of allegiance to the king (see Briant 2002: 325).

Parnaka.[43] According to Herodotus (7.2.2) Darius had married a daughter of Gobryas (she remains unnamed) before he became king, while Gobryas himself was given a sister of Darius in marriage (Hdt.7.5.1). Their son, Mardonius, married Darius' daughter Artazostre (cf. PFa 5, Hdt.6.43.1). Thus we find Gobryas' family linked to the king in a triple alliance. This was part of a deliberate royal policy of establishing family alliances. The marriages served to perpetuate royal links with this noble family beyond the first generation. Gobryas held high office under Darius, while Mardonius was to become a commander in the Persian army, serving in Ionia after the rebellion of 499/8–493/2. Their case provides a splendid example of the way in which the nobility was bound to the king and thereby to the royal court.

The Gobryas family was by no means unique. In a similar fashion Darius established close ties with Otanes, who may himself have been the son of the Achaemenid Pharnaspes. Darius married a daughter of Otanes, Phaidyme, when he succeeded to the throne (Hdt.3.88.4), while a sister of Darius was married to Otanes himself (Hdt.7.82). A daughter, Amestris, was to become the wife of Darius' son and heir Xerxes (Hdt.7.61.2). Like Gobryas and his family, the house of the Persian noble Otanes was inextricably linked to the royal family. His own status as the father of the wife of the heir to the throne will have put him among the leading grandees at court.[44]

Whether or not similar marriage alliances were concluded with the nobles Megabyxus and Hydarnes, they certainly remained closely connected with the court. The homonymous son of Hydarnes was a commander of the guards under Xerxes (Hdt.7.83.1) and later became satrap in Phrygia. Artaxerxes II (424–404) was married to a daughter of the younger Hydarnes, Stateira (Ctesias, *FGrH* 688 F 15), while the royal sister Amestris was married to Hydarnes' son Teritouchmes. Tissaphernes, the satrap of Sardis, most likely also a member of this family, married one of Artaxerxes II's daughters (Diod.14.26.4). Megabyxus' son Zopyrus held military office under Darius I, and his grandson, also called Megabyxus, was one of Xerxes' chief marshals. He, too, was given a royal daughter in marriage called Amytis (Ctesias, *FGrH* 688 F 13). Under Artaxerxes I he commanded the Persian troops in Egypt during the revolt of 460–454 BC.

These alliances point to a royal policy aimed at establishing and maintaining the support of the Persian nobles. Do they give us an indication of a ranking order amongst the families? Certainly Gobryas and Otanes, and possibly Ardumaniš/Aspathines too, were ranked highest during the reign

---

[43] As the highest official at Persepolis, Parnaka received 90 quarts daily (see above). The amounts of the daily rations of wine and grain or flour are an indicator of the status of the recipient (see above, p. 30).

[44] On the marriage alliances see Brosius 2002: 52–4, 60–3.

of Darius, and the military offices held by the sons of all these nobles show the efforts made by the kings to keep the families closely linked to the court. As Artaxerxes II's marriage to the daughter of Hydarnes (II) indicates, the family of Hydarnes (I) also was considered of sufficiently high rank for their daughter to be elevated to the status of the king's wife.

It was a special honour when the king bestowed the status of a King's Friend.[45] This status was expressed through royal gifts including land, estates and cities. Other gifts were weapons (daggers), jewellery (bracelets, torques, earrings), horse bridles and a special robe. The design and quality of the metal and precious stones used to produce these items, and the colour and embroidery of the textiles used, as well as the quality of craftsmanship, all identified the gift as a royal one, singling out its recipient among his peers.[46] In some cases, the gift took the form of an offer of marriage to a royal daughter. A King's Friend was a member of the court and allowed to join the King's Table, that is to say, he was privileged to dine with the king at the king's invitation. It is important to note that even within the group of the King's Friends a social ranking order existed (Wiesehöfer 1980: 13).[47]

Structures of communication

It was one thing to be a member of the court, but quite another to have direct access to the king. As the analysis so far has revealed, the limitation of access to the king was a prerequisite of kingship, and, at least under Darius I, only the six Persian nobles were exempt from it. The physical separation of the king from those permitted to dine at the King's Table also suggests that only a select few members at court were allowed to address the king. In this light, Plutarch's claim that the king's wife and the king's mother, as well as the heir to the throne, were allowed to dine with the king gains considerable significance, highlighting the importance of these few members as mediators between the king and the royal and noble courtiers.

Arguably only a few members of the close court were allowed to address the king directly. As we saw, information was filtered through to the chief officials who were entitled to approach the king. Those permitted to come into the presence, be they satraps, high administrators, councillors, commanders

---

[45] There was a distinction between a King's Friend and a King's Benefactor, though it seems that the Greeks did not always comprehend it (see Wiesehöfer 1980: 10–11). The status of a Benefactor was bestowed upon individuals and groups of peoples in recognition of acts of loyalty (Wiesehöfer 1980: 15). In my view Benefactors were not members of the court.

[46] See Wiesehöfer 1980. On the creation of a 'service aristocracy' of the king see Wiesehöfer 2001: 37. On gift-giving see Sancisi-Weerdenburg 1989.

[47] Not least in the distinction between Persians and non-Persians.

of the royal bodyguard and of the army, probably had to follow a strict protocol, only speaking with the king's express permission. Thus, for example,
Nehemiah, the king's cup-bearer, expressed his concerns only after the king
invited him to speak (Neh.2:2). The head of the administration, Parnaka,
who took direct orders from the king, may only have spoken directly with
the king when summoned or after requesting an audience through a royal
messenger.

Those who wanted to approach the king from outside the palace depended
on the keeper of the gate to be admitted. A well-known case is that of Syloson
of Samos, who took up his place at the palace gates to obtain an audience
with Darius I (Hdt.3.140), which was duly granted. However, in the case
of Intaphernes' wife, who requested a royal audience so as to intercede on
behalf of her brother, communication with the king was conducted via the
royal messenger (Hdt.3.119).

The hierarchy of office determined a courtier's chances of taking part
in political, administrative and military decision-making. Members of the
royal family, especially the king's mother and the king's wife, are described as
being able to pass judgement with the king's permission (cf. Ctesias, *FGrH*
688 F 14). Satraps were authorised to make decisions at local level, but
matters of state could only be decided in consultation with the king. In fact,
the satraps were the crucial link between the king and his subjects (Herman
1997: 200). However, it is hard to reach a clear-cut view of the courtiers'
participation in political decision-making, mainly owing to the fact that
the hierarchy of offices did not necessarily coincide with that of rank. For
instance, in the hierarchy of the court, where are we to place Parnaka, who
was the head of administration, but who also was the uncle of the king?
Equally, lineage could make high office quasi-hereditary. This happened in
the case of the satrapy of Phrygia, which remained within the dynasty of
Pharnabazos. On the available evidence, it is hard to determine how these
two strands – official status and court ranking – interacted. In addition, the
hierarchies of office and of rank were in constant flux as the king conferred
or withdrew special favours and positions in individual cases. Overall the
courtly hierarchy was clearly very complex.

Royal representation and royal centre

The self-presentation of the sovereign within his court was intimately bound
up with the people – the courtiers – with whom the king chose to surround
himself. The presence of these courtiers was therefore required at all official
events, including the funerary rites for a dead king, the royal investiture, royal

audiences, and the king's migration between the different royal capitals. The death of one king and the accession of another were the most important events of any reign, requiring the presence of the Persian nobility as an affirmation of their loyalty to the king and the Achaemenid dynasty. At the death of a king, it was his successor's duty to proclaim the official empire-wide mourning period. The king's body was returned to Persepolis and prepared for burial in one of the tombs of the Achaemenid dynasty at nearby Naqsh-i Rustam.[48] Carved in the rock face, the cross-shaped façades held a varying number of tombs. The proximity of these tombs to the royal centre, the fact that the king's body had to be returned to Persepolis, and equally, the consistent burial of the later Achaemenid kings at the same site, together show that the royal funeral was a central event for the royal dynasty, requiring the presence of the court to perform the necessary ceremony and ritual.

Equally, the ceremonial investiture of the new king demanded the presence of the courtiers so that they could confirm their allegiance to the new king. From the time of Darius I on, the royal investiture was celebrated at Pasargadae – thus paying homage to the founder of the empire, while also offering a reminder of the humble origins of the Persians. Before the king could don the royal robe, tiara and other paraphernalia of kingship, he had to put on the ancient robe worn by Cyrus before he became king, eat terebinth and drink sour milk (Plut.*Art*.3.1–2). Only then would he receive his royal staff, special shoes, the king's seal and the lotus flower (Polyaen.7.7.17).[49] The ceremony was observed by the king's family as well as by the courtiers, the king's bodyguard, the nobility and the Immortals.

It is usually assumed that the proclamation of the heir was marked by an official celebration. At this point, the heir would adopt an official throne-name and be presented with the *kitaris* and the lotus flower as symbols of his status. He was also now allowed to stand behind the king at official audiences, as discussed above (see Brosius 2006).

Among other events which doubtless required the presence of the court was the official celebration of the king's birthday.[50]

Royal banquets and royal hunt

Feasting and hunting enjoyed a long history as royal pursuits in the courts of ancient Mesopotamia and are well attested in archaeological and literary

---

[48] On the royal tombs see Schmidt 1970.   [49] See Wiesehöfer 2001: 32; Brosius, 2006.

[50] See Hdt.1.133: 'The day which every man most honours is his own birthday. On this he thinks it right to serve a more abundant meal than on other days; before the rich are set oxen or horses or camels, or asses, roasted whole in ovens; the poorer serve up the lesser kinds of cattle.'

sources. Private and official banquets were an expression of kingship, as was the display of foodstuffs, tableware of precious plate, and the luxurious couches on which the king and dignitaries reclined. An invitation to the royal banquet was an official declaration of royal favour, high rank and privilege. Dining with the king was a privilege for any member of the court who was invited; when the king was on campaign, it also became a privilege for the generals and commanders, who were invited to the royal table (see Sancisi-Weerdenburg 1989: 133–5). According to the *Cyropaedia*, on campaign the king took his meals with his army: that is, he was not isolated from the men, but shared the same food and had his tent pitched in the middle of the encampment, surrounded by the tents of his army.

And for himself Cyrus had a tent made big enough to accommodate all whom he might invite to dinner. Now he usually invited as many of the captains as he thought proper, and sometimes also some of the lieutenants and sergeants and corporals; and occasionally he invited some of the privates, and sometimes a squad of five together, or a squad of ten, or a platoon, or a whole company in a body. And he also used to invite individuals as a mark of honour, whenever he saw that they had done what he himself wished everybody to do. And the same dishes were always placed before those whom he invited to dinner as before himself. (Xen.*Cyr*.2.1.30)

According to Heracleides of Cumae the king's dinner was a court ceremony following a strict protocol:

All who attend upon the Persian kings when they dine first bathe themselves and then serve in white clothes, and spend nearly half the day on preparations for dinner. Of those who are invited to eat with the king, some dine outdoors, in full sight of anyone who wishes to look on; others dine indoors in the king's company. Yet even those do not dine in his presence, for there are two rooms opposite each other, in one of which the king has his meal, in the other the invited guests. The king can see them through the curtain at the door, but they cannot see him. Sometimes, however, on the occasion of a public holiday, all dine in a single room with the king, in the great hall. And whenever the king commands a symposium (which he does often), he has about a dozen companions at the drinking. When they have finished dinner, that is, the king by himself, the guests in the other room, these fellow-drinkers are summoned by one of the eunuchs; and entering they drink with him, though even they do not have the same wine; moreover, they sit on the floor while he reclines on a couch supported by feet of gold; and they depart after having drunk to excess.

In most cases the king breakfasts and dines alone, but sometimes his wife and some of his sons dine with him. And throughout the dinner his concubines sing and play the lyre; one of them is the soloist, the others sing in chorus ... For one thousand animals are slaughtered daily for the king; these comprise horses, camels, oxen, asses, deer, and most of the smaller animals; many birds are also consumed, including Arabian ostriches . . . geese and cocks. (Heracleides, *FGrH* 689 F 2; ap. Athen.4.145)

People invited to dine with the king were by no means a limited group of nobles. According to Xenophon the king used the seating order as a means of singling out and honouring individual guests:

Cyrus thus made public recognition of those who stood in his first esteem, beginning even with the places they took when sitting or standing in his company. He did not, however, assign the appointed place permanently, but he made it a rule that by noble deeds any one might advance to a more honoured seat, and that if anyone should conduct himself ill he should go back to one less honoured. And Cyrus felt it a discredit to himself, if the one who sat in the seat of highest honour was not also seen to receive the greatest number of good things at his hands. (Xen.*Cyr*.8.4.5)[51]

Royal feasts were no small matter: they catered for several thousand guests. According to Polyaenus (*Strat*.4.3.31–2) Alexander found the following list of foodstuffs for the king's breakfast and dinner inscribed on a bronze pillar:[52]

400 *artabai* – a Median *artabe* is an Attic *medimnos* – of pure wheat flour,[53] 300 a. of second-grade flour, 300 additional a. of third-grade flour: a total of 1,000 a. of wheat flour for dinner. 200 a. of pure barley flour, 400 of second-grade and 400 of third-grade: a total of 1,000 a. of barley flour. 200 a. of rye, 10 a. of the finest barley flour made for a drink. X a. of ground cardamon, sifted fine. 10 a. of peeled barley. $\frac{1}{3}$ a. of mustard seed.

400 male sheep, 100 oxen, 30 horses, 400 fatted geese, 300 turtle doves, 600 small birds of all kinds, 300 lambs, 100 young geese, 30 gazelles.

10 *maries* – a *maris* is ten Attic *choes* – of fresh milk, 10 m. of sweetened whey. A talent by weight of garlic. $\frac{1}{2}$ t. by weight of pungent onions, 1 a. of *phyllon* (silphium fruit?), 2 mnai of silphium juice, 1 a. of cumin, 1 t. by weight of silphium, $\frac{1}{4}$ a. of oil of sweet apples.1 a. of posset from sour pomegranates, $\frac{1}{4}$ a. of oil of cumin, 3 t. of black raisins, 3 mnai of anise flowers, $\frac{1}{3}$ a. of black cumin, 2 *kapeties* of seeds of *diarinon*, 10 a. of pure sesame, 5 m. of *gleukos* from wine, 5 m. of cooked round radishes in brine, 5 m. of capers in brine, from which they make sour sauce, 10 a. of salt, 6 m. of Ethiopian cumin, 30 mnai of dried anise, 4 k. of celery seed, 10 m. of sesame oil, 5 m. of cream, 5 m. of terebinth oil, 5 m. of acanthus oil, 3 m. of sweet almond oil, 3 a. of dried sweet almonds, 500 m. of wine.

When he was in Babylon or Susa, half was palm wine and half grape wine. Two hundred waggon loads of green wood, 100 waggon loads of wood (*hule*), 100 square

---

[51] See also Wiesehöfer, in press.
[52] See Spawforth in this volume for Alexander's imitation of Persian royal dining.
[53] a. = artabe (about 52.5 litres); m. = maries (about 33 litres); t. = talent; k. = kapeties (about 1.1 litre); mna (about 437 grams).

cakes of liquid honey, weighing 10 mnai. Whenever he was in Media he distributed the following items. Three artabes of safflower seed, two mnai of saffron. These items were used for drinks and for breakfast.

He distributed 500 a. of pure wheat flour, 1,000 a. of pure barley flour, 1000 a. of second grade barley-meal; 500 a. of semidalis, 500 m. of groats made from *olyra*, 20,000 a. of barley for the animals, 10,000 waggons of chaff, 5,000 waggons of straw, 200 m. of sesame oil, 10 m. of vinegar, 30 a. of finely chopped cardamon. All these things listed he distributed to the soldiers(?). This is what the king consumes in a day, including his *ariston*, his *deipnon*, and what he distributes.

(Polyaen.*Strateg*.4.3.31–2; see Lewis 1987: 82–5)

The preparation of a royal feast is depicted on the ceremonial staircases leading up to Darius' palace, the *taçara*. Servants carry dishes, wineskins and animals, sheep and goats: the victuals for the royal feast (see Sancisi-Weerdenburg 1989: 133). This fact alone, by the way, must make us wary of accepting the notion of a 'private palace' in the case of Darius, or indeed Xerxes and Artaxerxes I. The structures often identified as such are perhaps better seen not as living quarters, but as the private dining space of the king, where he ate in isolation from his guests at the King's Table. Greek sources frequently state that the king dined alone or with his immediate family, while guests dined in a separate room. The palaces of the Achaemenid kings must have provided a dining space for the royal family which met these requirements.

The king's banquets were imitated by the satraps who represented the king at local level. Banquet scenes depicted on reliefs, funerary stelai, ivories and seals found in many different parts of the empire show that the representation of the dignitary *en couchant*, accompanied by his wife, was a recognised artistic motif for the expression of the courtly life.[54]

Like banqueting, hunting too was a royal Achaemenid pursuit, as in other ancient court societies studied in this volume (see the chapters by Spawforth, Wiesehöfer, van Ess and Spence). Hunting took place in royal enclosures stocked with wild beasts and tended by gamekeepers, or in the wild, where royal endurance and physical and mental toughness were tested even more. With its reliance on lances and the bow, hunting was seen as a form of military training. Fighting against the most ferocious animals, such as boars, lions, panthers and bears, as well as hunting game like gazelle, deer and birds such as ostriches, exercised the skill of the participants and displayed it to one's peers:

When the king goes out hunting, he takes out half the garrison; and this he does many times a month. Those who must take the bow and arrows, and, in addition

[54] See above, n. 36.

to the quiver, a sabre or scimitar, they carry along also a light shield and two spears, one to throw, the other to use in case of necessity in hand-to-hand encounter . . . and as their king is their leader in war, so he not only takes part in the hunt himself but sees to it that the others hunt too. The state bears the expense of the hunting for the reason that the training it gives seems to be the best preparation for war itself.

(Xen.*Cyr.*1.2.9–10)

Participation in the royal hunt was hedged with etiquette. The chief rule was that the king reserved to himself the right to strike the first blow. When the king's son-in-law (Megabyxus: see above, p. 38) disobeyed this rule in good faith, thinking that the king was about to be attacked by a lion, he was banned from the court and stripped of his court privileges. Only the intervention of the king's mother Amestris, and the king's daughter Amytis, Megabyxus' wife, secured his pardon, eventual return to the court and restoration of his privileges – he was permitted once more to join the King's Table (Ctesias, *FGrH* 688 F 40–1).[55] It is likely that, on occasion, the women of the court joined the hunting party.

The royal entourage

Members of the court, obviously enough, formed an essential part of the king's entourage. Whenever the king travelled across the empire, migrating between his royal capitals or on campaign, the court travelled with him. The royal entourage was an expression of kingship, conveying power, order and control. The precise order in which the entourage travelled was carefully planned. This emerges from the order of march described in three sources: Xenophon's *Cyropaedia* (for the order of the entourage of Cyrus II), Herodotus (for the army of Xerxes in 480 BC), and Curtius Rufus (Curt.3.3.8–16), who listed the order of the train of Darius III as follows:

1. fire carried on 2 silver altars in front
2. magi
3. 365 men in purple robes
4. white horses pulling the chariot of Ahuramazda
5. 1 horse of the sun
6. 10 chariots
7. horsemen of 12 nations
8. 10,000 Immortals

---

[55] But compare this to Plut.*Mor.*173d: '[Artaxerxes] was the first to issue an order that any of his companions in the hunt who could and would might throw their spears without waiting for him to throw first.'

9. 15,000 royal kindred (*cognati*)[56]
10. spear bearers (*doryphoroi*)
11. the king's chariot
12. 10,000 lancers
13. 200 king's relatives on right and left
14. 30,000 infantry
15. 400 king's horses
16. the chariots of the king's mother and king's wife
17. the women of the queen's household on horseback
18. the king's *harmamaxa* for children and eunuchs
19. 365 concubines
20. 600 mules, 300 camels
21. the wives of the King's Relatives and Friends
22. the troops of sutlers and batmen
23. the band of light-armed troops.

Centrally positioned, the king was surrounded by spear bearers and lancers, *cognati* and kin, the 10,000 Immortals and 10,000 lancers. These were complemented by the cavalry and 400 of the king's horses. Then there followed the royal women, children and concubines, as well as the wives of the King's Relatives and Friends.

The physical space of the court: Pasargadae, Persepolis and Susa

The physical manifestation of the court chiefly took the form of the palaces in the royal capitals of the Achaemenid kings. The palace was an expression of kingship, royal power and political control.[57] Spaciousness and monumental architecture were as important as luxurious building materials, artistic style, and interior and exterior design. Cyrus II recognised that monarchical power could be physically expressed in the foundation of a new royal capital – an idea with a long Near Eastern tradition. The creation of new settlements,[58] along with a new royal palace with its buildings projecting the royal image, was the visual expression of a monarch's command of resources.

---

[56] For these, see Spawforth in this volume.

[57] On the Persian 'royal house' (OP *viθ-*) and the palaces of Darius and Xerxes see above, pp. 25–6; also Wiesehöfer, in press.

[58] For an excellent analysis of Near Eastern cities see van de Mieroop 1997, who cautions against seeing royal power as the sole determinant of civic government. As he points out, we need to distinguish between the king's roles as a 'national' leader and as head of the palatial organisation, his own household (1997: 119).

In support of his role as national leader the king could rely on an elaborate palatial organization that provided him with administrators and warriors. Palaces were among the most prestigious buildings of all Mesopotamian cities, and the palatial sector was at times of utmost prominence in society. (Van de Mierrop 1997: 120)

The palace with its extensive building complexes was the dominating feature of the royal city thanks to its position within the city, which was normally both elevated and fortified, though not necessarily central. The royal palace was a manifestation of the unique position of the king, of his exalted position above all other levels of society, yet at the same time it asserted his presence among his subjects. A new royal complex required the creation of a whole palatial organisation, from the king's personal attendants to other kinds of royal servant, along with officials, administrators and guards. As the palace became a manifestation of kingship, so did the royal court and its society.

The conquest of Media in 559 BC provided Cyrus II with his first opportunity to manifest his power in this way, with the foundation of the first Persian royal capital, Pasargadae (Elam. *Batrakataš*). Named after Cyrus' tribe, the city was testimony to the value placed on the pre-eminent Persian tribe. Its location in the plain of Marv Dasht in Persis was said to commemorate the historic battle between the Median king Astyages and the army of Cyrus II.

The full extent of Pasargadae is unknown and will only be revealed by further excavation. However, the recent suggestion of R. Boucharlat deserves serious consideration, namely, that the city's inhabitants may have continued to live traditionally as nomadic pastoralists, erecting their tents around the official buildings.[59] These buildings, intended for royal representation, were built in stone and decorated with black and white marble. One was Cyrus' 'private' palace, a hypostyle hall based on a rectangular plan and set within a royal garden, hidden from the public palace, where the king held audiences. The visitor was admitted to the palace complex via a gate. Here guards controlled access and only allowed visitors to enter the royal compound after approval by a courtier. If admission was granted, the visitor would be guided to the royal audience hall (Fig. 1.3).

As for their architectural design, the buildings at Pasargadae show their artistic debt to the kingdoms conquered by Cyrus. Median influence can be detected in the construction of columned halls.[60] But in the construction of his palaces at Pasargadae, Cyrus II went further than merely acknowledging

---

[59] www.achemenet.com/recherche/sites/pasargades/pasargades.htm; Boucharlat 2001a and 2001b.

[60] Our earliest archaeological evidence for these comes from Godin Tepe and Nush-e Jan; see Stronach 1987 (with figs. 6 and 7 for plans of Godin Tepe and Nush-e Jan).

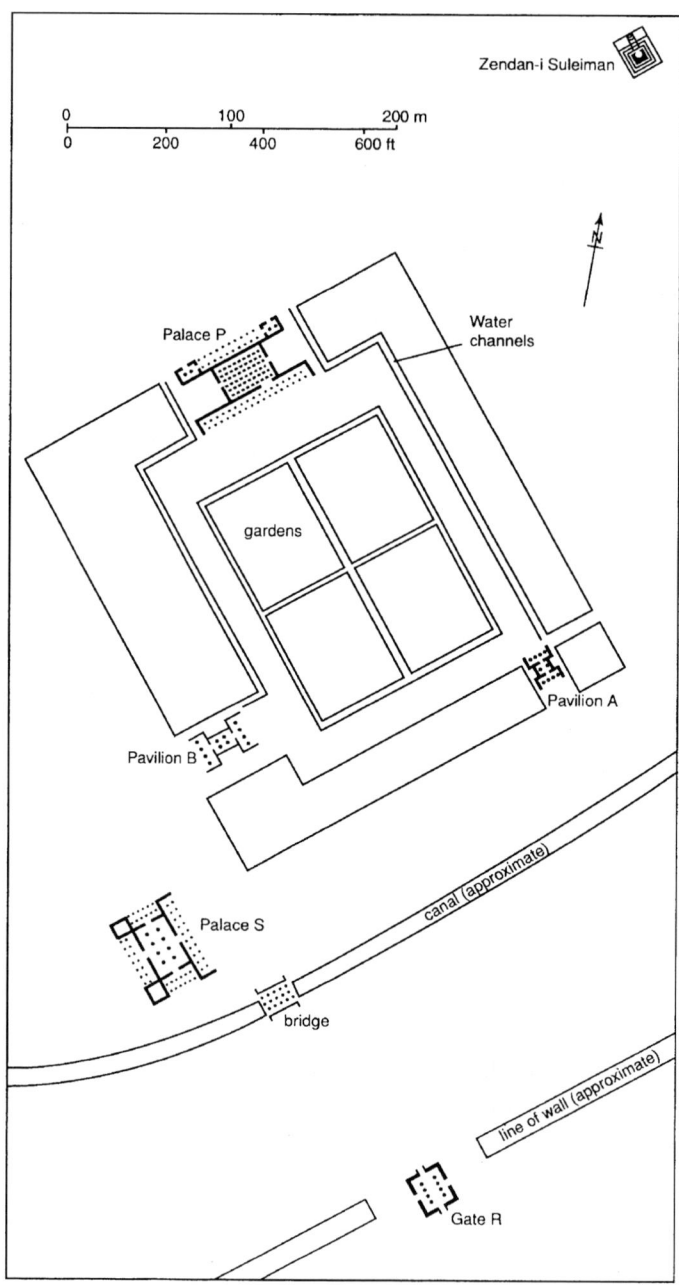

Figure 1.3 Plan of Pasargadae (drawing by Marion Cox)

a Median connection. The remaining wall decorations of the palaces, carved in relief, show an adherence to the style of decoration of the Assyrian and Babylonian palaces. Though the reliefs at Pasargadae are only partly preserved, we can still identify the Assyrian smiting-god and lion demon, as well as the Assyrian fish-garbed man and the bull-man, though the pairing of these last two departs from Assyrian tradition (see Stronach 1997: 44). The entrance gate to the royal compound depicts one of the most intriguing figures in Persian art, the winged genius: a figure commonly depicted in the art of the Levantine coast, with two pairs of wings, clothed in Elamite dress and an Egyptian headdress. While the figure of the winged genius ultimately derives from Assyrian models known from the palace relief at Dur-Sharrukin (Khorsabad),[61] the Elamite dress is a reminder of the Persian link with Elamite culture (cf. Stronach 1997: 43).[62]

The achievement of Cyrus at Pasargadae cannot be emphasised too strongly. He (and his advisors) integrated architectural features from the lands which the king had conquered to create his royal capital. In one space it offered a visual expression of Cyrus' conquest of the western kingdoms. It was this space which gave a visitor – whether a foreign ambassador, a local petitioner or a satrap – access to the king. Cyrus' idea was innovative: the physical seat of monarchy embodied the power of the king and reflected the triumph of his conquests. It was simultaneously an expression of kingship, of power, of control and of political integration. Darius I and his successors were to base their concept of kingship on Cyrus' ingenious idea. It found physical expression in the royal terrace of Persepolis and the tombs at Naqsh-i Rustam.

What does the palace complex at Pasargadae reveal about the king and kingship and about the establishment of the Persian court? Primarily, the construction of this walled palace complex with its entrance gate established an important feature of kingship: controlled access to the king. This vetting of access to the king turned him into a figure remote from his subjects. From leader of his tribe, from first among equals, Cyrus II had established his royal power through the conquests of kingdoms. Subsequently he took on the trappings of kingship and of monarchical representation. The audience hall was separate from the private palace of the king, itself set apart by a structured garden and accessible, we can assume, only to the king's attendants, his bodyguard and members of his family.

---

[61] The city was founded by Sargon II (721–705 BC).   [62] See Herrmann and Curtis 1998.

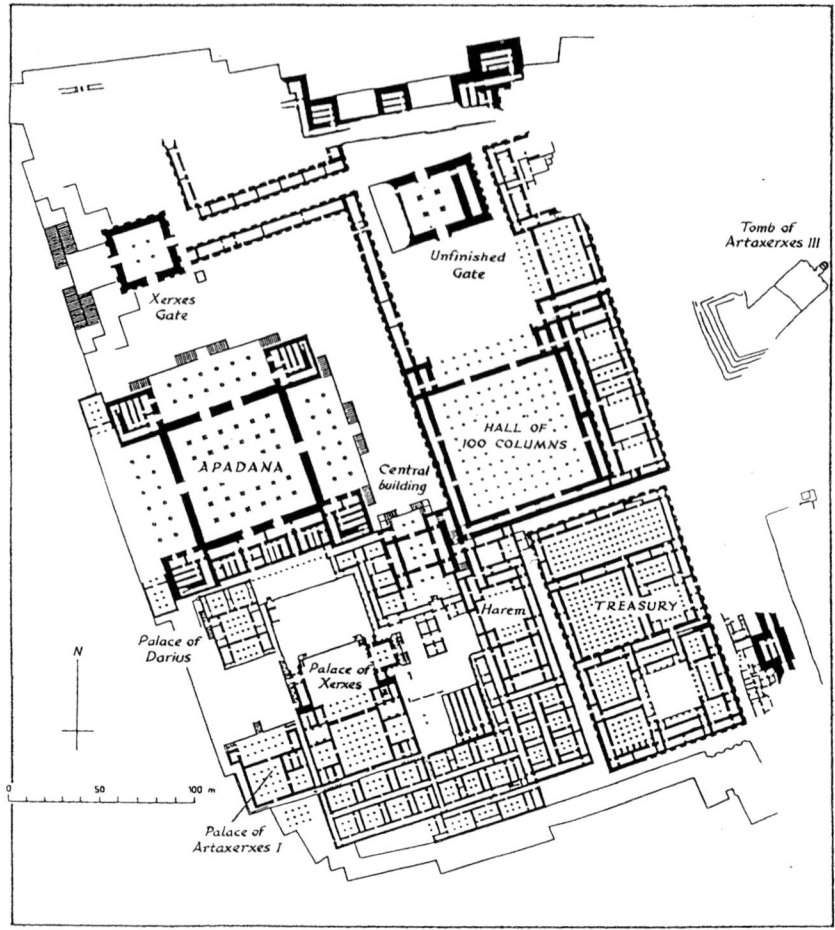

Figure 1.4 Plan of Persepolis

Persepolis and Susa

The palace complex of the city of Persepolis, called Parsa by the Persians, epitomises royal power and Achaemenid kingship (Fig. 1.4).[63]

The city itself has not yet been excavated, the archaeological focus so far being the royal terrace. Exploiting the natural rock of the Kuh-e Ramat, which was extended by a retaining wall of massive masonry, the royal terrace towered 18 metres above ground level. The complex is surrounded by a fortification wall which incorporates the hill of Kuh-e Ramat as well. Access to the terrace was provided by a large double staircase which led to the Gate

[63] For Persepolis see Schmidt 1953, 1957; Root 1979.

of all Lands. Its broad, shallow steps ensured two things: first, a visitor could progress only by slow steps onto the royal terrace. Second, the steps allowed the ascent and descent of horses, and possibly even chariots. Doubtless this would have been a privilege permitted only to an exceptional few – perhaps to the king alone. Once on the terrace, the visitor entered the Gate of all Lands, a square building with four columns at its centre. Here, the visitor had to sit and wait – stone benches were provided for this purpose – until a guard or royal messenger had announced his arrival to the king and permission was given to advance onto the terrace.[64] As in Pasargadae, the entrance gate controlled access to the king. Its attendants, guards and royal messengers ensured that no one could enter the palace complex unnoticed or unannounced.

The first buildings constructed by Darius I included the palace of the king, the so-called Treasury and the administrative complex. The most important one, however, is the vast Throne-Hall, the *Apadana*. Elevated from the ground level of the rest of the complex by a further 3 metres, the *Apadana* was built on a square ground plan, with thirty-six columns arranged in rows of six, each 20 metres high, their bull-headed capitals supporting a cedar-wood roof. The two double staircases with the famous reliefs depicting the inner court and the Immortals, as well as the peoples of the empire, led to the hall. The visitor would be led up to the audience hall via one of these two staircases.[65]

Darius' successors completed his public and administrative buildings and added their own palaces also. Under Artaxerxes I (465–424 BC) the complex underwent a significant change. A new gate was added, giving access to a new court in turn leading to a second throne-hall, the Hall of One Hundred Columns. This was not raised up in the manner of the first throne hall, and the only public access was through a porticoed entrance. But there can be no doubt as to the representational function of the hall, which processions would reach from the Gate of all Lands by means of the new gate and across a courtyard.

As Cyrus II had done in Pasargadae, Darius I incorporated many architectural elements into the design of the palaces and halls of Persepolis inspired by the regional traditions of the empire. But unlike the mere borrowing of

---

[64] See above, pp. 39–40.

[65] It would be intriguing to know whether the two staircases implied a hierarchy amongst those who used it. Who was allowed to ascend which staircase? Was one reserved for the king only, the other for visitors? As for the double staircase itself, the reliefs imply that courtiers and bodyguards used one side, gift-bearers of the lands the other. But we cannot be sure that the staircase reliefs depict a reality or an ideal.

stylistic elements at Pasargadae, Darius and his advisors created a coherent new royal style, which was consistently adhered to in the construction of all royal palaces and copied in the satrapal centres of the empire. This style combined Assyrian, Babylonian, Median, Urartean, Egyptian and Greek elements in the construction of columns and column bases, gateways, window frames and blind windows. This was a deliberate decision to create a palace complex articulating in its architecture the idea of an all-inclusive empire. It finds clear echoes in Darius' building inscription from Susa, listing the origins of the building materials used in the construction of the palace there, along with the multi-ethnic workforce.

The cedar timber was brought from a mountain called Lebanon. The Assyrian people brought it to Babylon. From Babylon the Carians and Ionians brought it to Susa. The *sissoo*-timber was brought from Gandara and from Carmania. The gold which was worked here was brought from Sardis and from Bactria. The precious stone lapis lazuli and carnelian which was worked here was brought from Sogdiana. The precious stone turquoise, which was worked here, this was brought from Chorasmia. The silver and the ebony were brought from Egypt. The ornamentation with which the wall was adorned was brought from Ionia. The ivory which was worked here was brought from Ethiopia, and from India and from Arachosia. The stone columns which were worked here were brought from a village called Abiradu, in Elam. The stone-cutters who worked the stone were Ionians and Sardians. The goldsmiths who worked the gold were Medes and Egyptians. The men who worked the wood were Sardians and Egyptians. The men who worked the baked brick were Babylonians. The men who adorned the wall were Medes and Egyptians. (DSf §4)

The same palatial configuration of an entrance gate, throne-hall, palace and administrative rooms was copied at Susa, where Darius I began construction soon after his accession. Passing through the entrance gate (40 × 28 m), the visitor entered the elevated royal complex; with the palatial buildings opposite, he then had to turn right into the courtyard to approach the *Apadana*. As at Persepolis, this was based on a square plan,[66] though at Susa neither the throne-hall nor the palace was raised above ground-level. The palace itself was rectangular, with three courtyards leading to royal apartments.[67] The surviving architecture of the palace complex of Persepolis

---

[66] Each side was 109 metres long, with three columned porticoes. Six row of six columns 20 metres high held up the wooden ceiling. The throne was probably placed on the stone foundation in the northern row (Boucharlat 1997: 59).

[67] Royal palaces were also built in Ecbatana and Babylon. Current excavations at Ecbatana have not yet revealed an Achaemenid palatial space; but the Achaemenid palace at Babylon is well attested (see Kuhrt 2001).

and the other royal cities nowadays only hints at the former splendour of the Achaemenid court, its rituals and its ceremonies.

Ways of recruitment

The question as to how courtiers were recruited is not easily answered for the Achaemenid court. Clearly, many came from the extended royal family itself; as we have seen, male relations of the king held high office as satraps, administrative heads and military commanders. Holders of other offices in the inner and outer court were appointed by the king, and while some offices acquired a hereditary character, others were always filled by the king when they fell vacant. At this point a number of factors influenced the king's patronage, such as the desire to promote a specific noble in return for loyal deeds bringing him to the royal notice. The same factors could influence the appointment of non-Persian officials too. It is likely too that children of the nobility were educated at the court, although we have no detailed information about this practice.[68]

It is clear enough, however, that the Achaemenid court was an institution of considerable complexity. Different hierarchies of tribe, rank and high office were interwoven to create a court organisation. Importantly, these hierarchies did not exist independently of one another: a flexible system allowed changes within and between them. The king controlled these changes as the fount of court patronage. Court life was a system of inclusion and exclusion, of separate groups around the king who enjoyed closer or lesser proximity to the king. Court life gained complexity because within each group, be it the members of the King's Table, or the King's Friends, among the councillors and military leaders, a ranking order existed. While, on the one hand, this created a clear structure, on the other it created competition, ambition and strife among courtiers eager to maintain and improve their position. Servile opportunism and flattery were undoubtedly part of everyday life at court.

This complex grouping of courtiers became a unity through ceremony and ritual, which included royal feasts, hunting, birthday and New Year celebrations, investiture, royal funerals and commemorative rituals. For some, if not all, courtiers, this unity was also a matter of sharing the same court

---

[68] For an overview of Persian education see Briant 2002: 327–30.

language, Old Persian, and the celebration of the cult of the Persian royal gods, especially Ahuramazda.

Manifestation of social ranking through royal gifts

This leads us to the final questions. How did the court work? Why was the system, set in place by Cyrus II, so successful over so many reigns? Elias' judgement on the French court applies here, too. A court society is not an anonymous group of people, but a figuration of individuals (see Elias 1983: 8; Herman 1997: 200). It is likely that the establishment of court ceremony and ritual created a highly stratified ranking order among attendants, the military, the administrators, the royal household, the women and the nobility. Each individual would then have identified closely with his or her role within this ranking order. Rank was recognised and acknowledged among the Persian nobles themselves (see Hdt.1.134). Even the satrapal rebellions in Asia Minor, which disrupted the '*pax Persica*' during the mid-fourth century, could not overturn the kingship. Why? The answer, in my view, lies in the king's emphasis on the individual. Everyone involved in court life was related or known to the king, marriage alliances were carefully constructed, and high positions were filled by individuals trusted by the king. Loyalty had to be proven, and was rewarded with royal gifts, land and estates, with appointment to high office, and sometimes with the honour of intermarriage with the royal family. Within this highly personalised meritocracy, one aspect was of vital importance: the ruler's personal knowledge of each subject whom he honoured:

And whenever Cyrus wished to honour anyone it seemed to him proper to address him by name. Furthermore it seemed to him that those who were conscious of being personally known to their general exerted themselves more to be seen doing something good and were more ready to abstain from doing anything bad.

(Xen.*Cyr.*5.3.47–8)

Showing a similar concern for the army, Xerxes is said to have addressed his soldiers before the army's march to Greece as follows:

Riding in a chariot past the men of each nation he questioned them, and his scribes wrote all down, till he had gone from end to end of the infantry and cavalry. This done . . . Xerxes alighted from his chariot into a ship of Sidon, sitting wherein under a golden canopy he was carried past the prows of the ships, questioning of them in the manner as of the army and making the answers to be written down. (Hdt.7.100)

The key to the successful workings of the Achaemenid court was personal recognition by the king and his bestowal of gifts to reward service. According to Xenophon, the importance of gift-giving as a political instrument was already recognised by Cyrus II:

And besides this he used to reward with gifts and positions of authority and seats of honour and all sorts of preferment others whom he saw devoting themselves most eagerly to the attainment of excellence; and thus he inspired in all an earnest ambition, each striving to appear as deserving as he could in the eyes of Cyrus.

(Xen.*Cyr*.8.1.39)

The king had created a system of royal favour and patronage in which the constant royal scrutiny of the achievement of individual courtiers gave them in turn the chance to increase their wealth and status and to enhance their official position and degree of personal closeness to the king. Terms like 'the greatest after the king', the 'most honoured' and the 'most trusted' allow a glimpse of the pyramidal formation which characterised the different courtly ranks. Importantly, the system never stagnated, but was in constant flux, with royal favour and gift-giving acting as a continuous spur to individual ambition. Equally, privileges could be revoked, and therefore, time and again, the nobles had to reaffirm their loyalty in order to confirm their worth and status. Failure to do so led to the withdrawal of royal favour. No court official was exempt from punishments for disloyalty, running from loss of status and landed wealth to banishment from the court, and even death (potentially for all the male members of his family too). Thus the ethos of this 'service aristocracy' was based not only on personal ambition, but also on fear of loss of status. Accordingly, it fostered loyalty on the one hand, but also intrigue and rivalry on the other, with ambitious nobles and royal scions becoming allies in the plotting of potential palace coups.[69]

Each noble, satrap and commander was an integral part of the monarchy. This is at the heart of the Achaemenid king's creation of a court society. The king was an absolute monarch, but he reigned with the support of his courtiers, who had an active interest – stimulated by both ambition and fear – in maintaining the stability of empire. As satraps they had a share of political power, since they represented the king in the provinces – where the

---

[69] Herman's observation about Hellenistic courts seems equally valid for Achaemenid Persia: 'Within the court were taken the decisions which shaped the destiny of the kingdom, and within it were found the most formidable groupings both of the king's supporters and of his opponents' (Herman 1997: 200).

court system was repeated on a smaller scale – and formed the link between the king and his subjects. As nobles in high office close to the king, they contributed to creating and maintaining the king's exalted position, while their relative proximity to the monarch gave them prestige and status among their peers.

Importantly, members of the non-Persian elite were also integrated into the system, being selected for (high) office both at the court and – more frequently – at provincial level. Drawing the circle even wider, the peoples of the lands of the empire, too, were assigned an integral place in the presentation of kingship. At any rate, this is the message conveyed on the door-jambs of Artaxerxes' palace at Persepolis and on the tomb reliefs of Naqsh-i Rustam. The king, enthroned, is held up by an even mightier throne, supported by the peoples of the empire. Royal consideration for the individual who honoured the king, however humble his background,[70] underlay the court system with its intricate human networks, and this system in turn helped maintain the stability of the empire.

Conclusion

The court had long been an integral part of monarchical rule in the ancient Near East. Concepts of court, court ceremony and court ritual therefore were well established when the Persians rose to power, and the Achaemenids were able to integrate these older court styles into the existing tribal and military structure of their own society. That said, it remains hard to identify major changes in the court structures of the ancient Near Eastern monarchies over time, and we have no means of knowing whether aspects such as admission to the court, appointment to high office and the ranking procedures among courtiers changed in the course of Achaemenid rule.

With the establishment of Persian kingship, the creation of a highly organised court became a necessary element of royal self-representation. The interdependence of king and court revealed itself as the king felt obliged to emphasise his unique position, becoming remote from his peers and his subjects, while at the same having to remain a highly visible figure. The court society responded to both these aspects of Achaemenid kingship: as

---

[70] See the story told of Artaxerxes' attitude towards gifts: 'it was no less the mark of a king and lover of his fellow men to accept small gifts graciously and with a ready goodwill; and so, on a time when he was riding by, and a simple labourer, possessed of nothing else, took water from a river in his two hands and offered it to the king, he accepted it pleasantly and with cheerful smile, measuring the favour by the ready goodwill of the giver, and not by the service rendered by the gift' (Plut.*Mor.*172B).

an institution it emphasised the king's exalted status, while the courtiers themselves became intermediaries between the king and his subjects. The king needed the court as a 'theatre of power' which emphasised his unique position through pomp and court ceremony. The stability of the empire, or at least the impression of a stable empire, depended on the king and his court.[71]

[71] In my view, this becomes evident in the breakdown of the relationship between king and satrap under Alexander the Great, who adapted the political structure of the satrapies, but failed to recognise the need to honour individuals and integrate them in his court. See Brosius 2003; also Spawforth in this volume, with a different interpretation of Alexander's court politics.

2 | King, court and royal representation in the Sasanian empire

JOSEF WIESEHÖFER

Introduction[1]

With the exception of the (late) Roman imperial court,[2] theoretical and historical approaches to the princely court as 'the most general arrangement of power in pre-modern society'[3] are mostly a phenomenon of medieval and early modern, rather than ancient, history.[4] As for the civilisations of the ancient Near East, here we are more or less treading on virgin ground.[5] Yet the monarchies of the Assyrians, Babylonians, Egyptians, Persians, Parthians and Sasanians stand absolute comparison with their early modern European counterparts in terms of their impact on their subject-populations and neighbours. This does not mean that no scholar until now has ever studied the life, institutions and modes of communication in ancient Near Eastern courts.[6] But such work has seldom been based on a theoretical model or comparison with the court phenomenon in other societies or cultures.[7] As for the Sasanian empire, we do not even possess detailed descriptions or antiquarian studies of the court as a centre of decision-making and governance, as the focus of social networks, as a stage for royal or aristocratic representation, as a centre of consumption, or as a control centre for transregional communication.[8] Nor has any expert in the Iranian languages ever addressed the question as to whether there was a Middle Persian or Parthian equivalent of Latin *curia*, English *court* or German *Hof*.

Unfortunately, the specific nature of the Sasanian source material (see below) makes it extremely difficult to rise above the merely descriptive and antiquarian approach. Despite the difficulties, this chapter aims to provide

---

[1] I would like to thank Tony Spawforth for his kind invitation to take part in the courts workshop at Newcastle and all my fellow-participants for helpful comments on a first draft of this chapter. A short outline of Sasanian history and culture can be found in Wiesehöfer 2001.

[2] See Smith in this volume; Winterling 1998, 1999; Scholten 1995.

[3] Duindam 2003: 302.   [4] But see Winterling 1997b; Herman 1997.

[5] The proceedings of a Copenhagen colloquium on 'Palace, King and Empire', held in 2000, are still in press (Larsen, in press).

[6] See, e.g., Briant 2002: *passim* for the Persian empire.

[7] But see now Brosius and Spence in this volume.

[8] There is some relevant material in Wiesehöfer 2001 (with the older literature).

an initial 'problematisation' of the following aspects of Sasanian arrangements of power:[9] the social constitution of the 'court' and the fluctuating
presence there of various different groups of people; structures of communication at court (court politics in other words), as well as the problem
of order and conflict at court; the function of the court in royal decision-
making and as a site of royal (and aristocratic) representation (including the
exemplary role of the court in matters of manners and culture); methods of
recruiting the people closest to the ruler and of safeguarding their loyalty;
the 'stateliness' of the court, and its importance as a setting for the display
of social ranking.

The chapter does not pretend to answer all these questions. But it strives
to cut a swathe through the source material for the court so as to improve
our understanding of power and 'state-building' in Sasanian Iran.

A short history of the Sasanian empire

As with the Parthians, we have only patchy evidence for the aims of Sasanian
foreign policy and military campaigning. The focus of this material is the history of Sasanian encounters, friendly or bellicose, with western neighbours.
Under Ardashir (AD 224–241/2), the founder of the Sasanian empire, all
the former Parthian provinces except Armenia fell into the Sasanids' hands.
Under the same king, an offensive policy against Rome is also discernible.
Shabuhr I (240–271/2) was more successful than his father: his campaigns
not only saw the conquest of Armenia, but shook the Roman empire to
its foundations. Sasanian armies overran Syrian Antioch and Cappadocia,
and for the first time a Roman emperor (Valerian) fell into the hands of
the enemy. Despite later setbacks (e.g. the successful resistance of Odaenathus of Palmyra), Shabuhr left an empire extending from Mesopotamia
in the west to Peshawar in the east. Quarrels for the throne and Diocletian's
equally aggressive eastern policy caused the Sasanians to lose Armenia and
even some of their territories east of the Tigris. It was only Shabuhr II in
the fourth century who was able to set aside the terms of the ignominious
treaty of Nisibis (298). Shabuhr not only fended off the Roman emperor
Julian in a battle outside the Sasanian royal residence of Ctesiphon, but
also made successful use of diplomacy and warfare to wrest much of the

---

[9] For these 'Weberian' constituents of a court see Winterling 2004. Although originating in
attempts to define the ideal type of the early modern European court, Winterling's typology has
proved helpful for the analysis of the Sasanian court undertaken in this chapter. Other useful
concepts: Duindam 2004; Butz and Dannenberg 2004.

lost Sasanian territory from the Roman emperor Jovian, Julian's successor (AD 363). These wars were marked by harsh persecutions of the Sasanian empire's Christian subjects, who were regarded by the Christian emperors to the west as under Roman protection, and by the Sasanian authorities as a pro-Roman fifth column. In 387 the eastern part of Armenia again became a Sasanian province.

Over the next century the Hephthalites ('White Huns') gave the Sasanians much more trouble than the Romans, with whom the kings of Iran came to a mutual agreement around 400. The Hephthalites were a kindred people of the steppes who had gradually penetrated central Asia, conquering Sogdia, Bactria, the western parts of the Tarim basin and north-west India. They not only inflicted two crushing defeats on the Sasanian king Peroz (465/484), but were also able to force tributary status on the Sasanian empire. Together with famines, these defeats brought the empire to the verge of ruin. Under the influence of the ethical and religious ideas of one Mazdak, the peasants rebelled, weakening the landowning aristocracy, to whom the vast majority owed services and obligations. At first supporting these ideas, King Kawad and his son Husraw ended by brutally suppressing them. However, they both tried to take advantage of this weakening of the nobility to initiate fundamental social, economic and military reforms. On the basis of a general land survey, a new system for exacting the land-tax was devised. Together with agricultural reforms, this system aimed to support small farms from which taxes could easily be extracted, and to prevent the growth of huge estates with powerful owners who could resist the royal tax-collectors. In addition, the empire was divided into four military districts, and special forces were raised for the purpose of surveillance and border control.

With domestic stability re-established, Husraw I reopened hostilities with Rome (Byzantium) by breaking the 'eternal peace' (540). Military success on the western and south-Arabian fronts meant that he was eventually able to raise the level of Byzantine tribute-payments to Iran. In the east, Husraw destroyed the Hephthalite empire with the help of the Western Turks (c. 560).

His reign also constituted the cultural climax of Sasanian civilisation. Under Husraw, known as the 'wise king', Iran became the hub of a reciprocal transfer of knowledge between east and west. But as early as the reign of his son Ohrmezd (Hormizdas) IV, the conflict between king and aristocracy resurfaced (after 579); serious attacks by the Turks worsened the situation. Matters seemed to improve when Ohrmezd's son Husraw II was able to put down the rebellion of Wahram Chobin, a general descended from the ousted Arsacid dynasty; in a war with Byzantium he succeeded in campaigning as far into Byzantine territory as Egypt (619) and the vicinity of Constantinople itself (626). But a counter-attack of the emperor Heraclius forced Husraw to give up his newly conquered territories, and the king himself was overthrown by a rebellion of nobles, and eventually killed (628). After an ensuing phase of anarchy marked by frequently changing regencies, the noble faction of Rustam put Yazdgerd III on the throne. However, the last Sasanian king proved unequal to the task of defending his empire against the Muslim armies, weakened as it was by particularism and by the dissolution of the pro-Sasanid Lakhmid 'buffer state' in Arabia. After heavy defeats at Qadisiyya in Iraq (636) and Nihawand in Media (642), Yazdgerd retreated to eastern Iran, where he was killed at Merw (651). His empire was soon incorporated into the caliphate.

The sources[10]

Dealing with the Sasanian court as a centre of communication and a place of representation is not an easy undertaking. Most of our information is not of a documentary character. Instead, the sources from the centre of the empire, like the royal inscriptions, the works of royal art (rock reliefs, silver bowls, etc.) and the extant works of Middle Persian literature, present an ideologically biased image of the king and court society. They normally stress the exemplary role and behaviour of both parties, sometimes describing the fatal consequences when courtly norms were transgressed. By contrast, Christian and Manichaean writers and the Romano-Byzantine authors present the Sasanian kings and their officals either as persecutors of their faiths or as military opponents. The early Islamic historians situate pre-Islamic Iran into the larger 'history of salvation' which started with Muhammad's mission. Finally, many late Middle and New Persian or Arabic texts preserve allegedly authentic proclamations by Sasanian rulers or reports of Sasanian court life. But in reality these are later (Islamic) views of a glorious early Sasanian past, or belong to the 'legendary cycles' of the semi-official 'Iranian National History'.

As a result of this configuration of source-material, two moments in the history of the Sasanian court and Sasanian royal representation are much better attested than others. The first is the age of the empire's founders Ardashir (Artaxerxes) I, Shabuhr (Sapor) I, Wahram (Bahram) I and Narseh (third century AD), the second the reigns of the reformer king Husraw

---

[10] For an overview see Wiesehöfer 2001: 153–64, 283–7. See also Abka'i-Khavari 2000 and Cereti 1997.

(Khusro/Chosroes) I and his successors Ohrmezd (Hormezd/Hormizdas) IV and Husraw II (sixth and seventh centuries AD).

For the early Sasanian court, the royal inscriptions are the most important source. First, some mention the major officials and dignitaries of the empire and at court.[11] Second, the way in which they present the kings with their titles and pronouncements embodies a specific idea of kingship as the quasi-divine authority interceding with the gods, in particular Ohrmezd (Ahura Mazda), on behalf of the king's subjects. Third, some royal inscriptions are in effect records of royal achievements or *res gestae*, serving as a corrective to the Roman and the late Arabic sources. Of course, these inscriptions must be viewed as extremely one-sided evidence for the royal patron's self-image. In their original versions on rock façades and buildings at sacred sites, they were meant to proclaim the king's intimate relationship with his putative ancestors and with the gods. In the now-lost copies which once circulated, they aimed to prove the legitimacy of Sasanian royal rule to the outside world.

In a well-judged choice of site, Shabuhr I had his *res gestae* inscribed on an ancient building (Ka'ba-i Zardusht) of Achaemenid date at Naqsh-i Rustam in the vicinity of Istakhr and Persepolis, in front of the rock-cut tombs of the Achaemenid kings. Emulating these earlier Persian kings, he had his deeds inscribed in three languages: Middle Persian, Parthian and Greek.[12] For Roman historians, the *Res Gestae Divi Saporis* (ŠKZ) are mainly interesting as evidence for Shabuhr's campaigns against the Roman east. But they are not just a record of the deeds of the 'King of Kings of Eran and Non-Eran': they also provide an insight into the royal court of the third century AD and its numerous governmental and court offices.

In a bilingual (Middle Persian and Parthian) inscription on the Paikuli monument in Iraqi Kurdistan (NPi), Shabuhr's son Narseh describes at length the military challenge to his succession from his rival and great-nephew Wahram III, and his subsequent recognition and coronation by the great men of the empire.[13] Like his father's *res gestae*, Narseh's inscribed achievements also list royal dignitaries and functionaries and mention numerous titles and offices.

Highly hagiographic in character, the Manichaean texts concerning the death of Mani in a Sasanian state prison give some further details about modes of communication at the court of the early Sasanians.[14] The royal

---

[11] For a prosopography of the early Sasanian empire see the current online project of Weber.

[12] Huyse (1999) offers an excellent edition of the *Res Gestae Divi Saporis*.

[13] Edition with commentary: Humbach and Skjærvø 1978–83.

[14] See Sundermann 1981 (edition and commentary); Weber, s.v. 'Kerdīr, Sohn des Ardawān' (for the traditions concerning Mani's death).

reliefs are closely linked to the royal inscriptions both as to find-spots and subject-matter.[15] They combine cosmic with worldly events, and have a compound and cumulative character. They offer eloquent witness to the self-representation of the Sasanian rulers, to their efforts to establish their legitimacy, and to their relations with the gods, foreign enemies (the Roman emperors), and family-members and dignitaries.

Our most important evidence for the court of Husraw I and his successors comes from the Byzantine and Islamic historical tradition, the latter depending heavily on late Sasanian works – notably the *X^w adāy-nāmag* ('Book of Lords'), a semi-official and semi-legendary history of Iran from the first world king Gayomard to the time of Husraw II, compiled under Yazdgerd III, the last Sasanian monarch.[16] As well as these 'historical' texts, there existed in Sasanian times a number of works dealing with institutions, court protocol and etiquette, the arts and entertainment – *Ā'īn-nāmag(s)* ('Book(s) of Rules (of Propriety)') – which from an early date were being translated into Arabic. Other genres of Middle Persian literature are normative or didactic works, *andarz* ('wisdom') and courtly (partly epic) texts. Only a small part of the literature of late Sasanian times has come down to us.[17] The main problem with what survives is the difficulty of separating historical from legendary material and the descriptive from the prescriptive.

In order to construct as full a picture as possible, in this chapter I shall deal with the court society, royal representation and courtly life of both early and late Sasanian times. For the reigns of Shabuhr I and Narseh, the surviving epigraphic and artistic evidence puts the stress on court society and royal representation. For the sixth and seventh centuries, the emphasis of the available evidence shifts to court ceremonial, etiquette and entertainment, and also to the normative styles of courtly communication.

The Sasanian court

The constitution of the court

And also here, by means of this inscription, we founded: a fire (temple), Husraw-Shabuhr by name, for Our soul and (Our) glory; 1 fire (temple), Husraw-Adur-Anahid by name, for the soul and glory of Adur-Anahid, the Queen of Queens, Our daughter; 1 fire (temple), Husraw-Ohrmezd-Ardashir by name, for the soul and

---

[15] Most of the reliefs have been published in the excellent series 'Iranische Denkmäler' (Berlin: Reimer).

[16] See Yarshater 1983; see also Huyse, in press.

[17] An excellent short history of Middle Persian (Pahlavi) literature was published by Cereti 2001.

glory of Ohrmezd-Ardashir, the Great King of the Armenians, Our son . . . And we ordered that (the following) should be done [i.e., offerings be made]: for our soul 1 lamb, 1 *grīw* (and) 5 *hōfan* bread, 4 *pās* wine; for the souls (of) Sasan, the Lord; and Pabag, the King; and Shabuhr, the King, the son of Pabag; and Ardashir, the King of Kings; and X^war(r)anzem, the Queen of the Empire; and Adur-Anahid, the Queen of Queens; and Denag, the Queen; and . . . (*ŠKZ* mpI 22–5)

The pre-eminence of the royal family within the Sasanian court is always apparent. The *res gestae* of both Shabuhr I (*ŠKZ*) and Narseh (NPi) contain lists of court personnel graded by rank. These give first place to the members of the royal family, including queens and other 'ladies' (mpI *bānūg*).[18] The genealogical section of *ŠKZ* is in three parts. The first (mpI 23–4/paI 18–19/grI 39–43) is reserved for Shabuhr himself, his daughter Adur-Anahid, the 'queen of queens' (*bāmbišnān bāmbišn*), and his three sons Ohrmezd-Ardashir (the later king Ohrmezd I), Shabuhr and Narseh. The second (mpI 25/paI 20/grI 46) names the royal ancestors: Sasan, the founder of the dynasty, the kings Pabag, Shabuhr and Ardashir (I), and X^war(r)anzem, the 'queen of the empire' (*šahr bāmbišn*), probably Ardashir's wife. The third section (mpI 25–7/paI 20–2/grI 47–52) lists the living members of the royal house, again starting with Adur-Anahid and ending with the consorts of Narseh. In this second list of King Shabuhr's descendants, members of the royal house are not graded by rank, but probably by age. It has rightly been stressed that social, not family, status dictated a man's or a woman's ranking both in the royal genealogy and in the royal household. Female members of the royal family appear on the royal reliefs as well as on coins; they are also immortalised on gems and seals of their own. These artworks, together with the ranking of queens, consorts and princesses attested in the inscriptions, show the social prominence of the royal women. It is not surprising to find women even ascending the throne shortly before the fall of the empire: this was the case with Boran and her sister Azarmigdukht (in the absence of male candidates, it must be admitted).

In addition, the rule of succession was strictly patrilineal and restricted to members of the Sasanian family. The succession crises of the third century AD (Narseh against Wahram III), the fourth century AD (Ardashir II against Shabuhr III), and the sixth century AD (Wistahm against Husraw II) all demonstrate the difficulty of circumventing this rule. But birth and selection by the preceding sovereign were only two of the necessary prerequisites for rulership. There is also the idea that the future king should have divine grace (*xwarrah*), best understood in modern terms as the 'charisma' of

---

[18] Many of these people are now included in Weber's online prosopography.

kingship.[19] In the inscriptions of the early kings, legitimacy can also be claimed by emphasising kinship with preceding rulers: Shabuhr refers to his father Ardashir, his grandfather Pabag, the eponymous Sasan, and even to the former great kings of Iran (the legendary Kayanids?).[20]

Third, the title *māzdēsn bay kē čihr az yazdān* ('Mazdean divine Lord, whose origin [is] from the gods') borne by the reigning *šāhān šāh* ('King of Kings') in *ŠKZ* shows that the Sasanian kings stressed the Mazdean quality of their royal power and their own divine nature – although this differed from that of the *yazdān*, i.e. Ohrmezd and the other gods.[21] Other royal males do not share this title with the kings.

Fourth, Shabuhr I founded fire temples 'for his own soul and glory' (*pad amā ruwān ud pannām*) and for the souls and the glory of his relations and deceased ancestors, endowing their upkeep. These endowments served social functions, providing material help for relations and friends and a special 'pension' for the founder's descendants. But they were also meant to confer prestige on their royal donor, to foster his subjects' trust and loyalty and to reinforce the existing social order. Deceased members of the royal family also became objects of organised worship, in a manner similar to the Greek cult of dead heroes.[22] The fire temples were normally named after their founders and benefactors. Thus the fire temple founded by Shabuhr I for his own soul and glory was given the name *Husraw-Shabuhr* ('Glorious is Shabuhr').

Finally, the Sasanians practised close-kin marriage (*xwēdōdah*), deemed meritorious by the Zoroastrian theologians. This served not only to keep property within the family, but also to retain kingship within the clan.[23] However, not all royal marriages were incestuous: exogamy for political reasons is also attested.

As both the royal inscriptions and Manichaean texts show, not all members of the royal household were permanent members of the royal court. In particular, the king's adult sons and other important relations were in personal proximity to the ruler only when their administrative duties or exceptional events, such as festivities or wars, required their presence at court, or if the 'travelling king' with his entourage happened to visit a prince's province. Thus, we may distinguish a nuclear or inner court of permanent members from an extended or outer court of temporary courtiers. In early

---

[19] Cf. Gnoli 1999.

[20] For different attempts to identify these 'ancestors' and 'forefathers' see Daryaee 1995, 2001–2; Shahbazi 2001; Wiesehöfer 2002; Huyse 2002; Kettenhofen 2002.

[21] Panaino 2003: 276–83.   [22] Macuch 1992, 1994; Stausberg 2002: 219–20.

[23] Wiesehöfer 2001: 180, 291.

Sasanian times the inner court mainly seems to have comprised members of the royal family and the royal household. The great aristocratic landowners and magnates belonged to the outer court, since they were mainly preoccupied with managing their estates and their dependants, the peasants and tenant farmers (see below).

Social ranking in the Sasanian empire and court and the recruitment of 'courtiers'

This is the range of the arrow shot by Us, the Mazdean divine Lord Shabuhr, the King of Kings of Eran and Aneran, whose origin is from the gods, the son of the Mazdean divine Lord Ardashir, the King of Kings of Eran, whose origin is from the gods, the grandson of the divine Lord Pabag, the king. And when we shot this arrow, we were shooting before the kings (landholders (*šahrdārān*)), the princes (*wispuhrān*), the grandees (*wuzurgān*) and the nobles (*āzādān*). (*ŠH* 1–6)

In his inscription at Hajjiabad,[24] Shabuhr I mentions four groupings of aristocrats in order of political prominence and prestige and according to the dictates of lineage. His son Narseh also refers to these groups in his Paikuli inscription, showing that they were the most important people to require royal acknowledgement. Members of the first group were called by the (singular) title *šahrdār* in Middle Persian and 'ruler of the peoples' (*despotēs tōn ethnōn*) in Greek. They comprised local dynasts and those sons of the 'King of Kings' to whom he had entrusted the government of key parts of the empire. The group ranked second (mpI *wispuhrān*, grI *hoi ek basileōn*) comprised members of the royal clan who did not belong to the ruler's immediate family ('princes of the blood' in more recent parlance). The third grouping (mpI *wuzurgān*) was made up of the heads of the seven most important noble families – the Waraz, the Parthian clans Suren and Karin, the Spahbed, Mihran, Spandiyad and the 'lords of Andegan'. Last came the *āzādān*, or rump of the Iranian nobility.[25]

Since these groups shared with the king the obligation to sacrifice for the souls of both the living and the dead, Shabuhr's *res gestae* list their membership at the time of inscription both by name and, if appropriate, by court or governmental function. But we need to bear in mind that in *ŠKZ* a mighty king is making his report on the state of his empire and court. On the other hand, the Narseh inscription makes clear that the 'King of Kings' and

[24] The inscription describes an archery contest between the king and his suite, in which Shabuhr 'broke a record'.

[25] The ranks of nobility are also mentioned in *ŠKZ* 22/17/39f. and NPi 2–3 (85).

the aristocracy were linked by a network of mutual obligations and common interests; but also that a ruler in need of political and military support had to respect aristocratic privileges and was heavily dependent on noble consent and cooperation. In other words, in early Sasanian times social ranking certainly manifested itself at court. But, as far as the nobility was concerned, it was not only the king who dictated rank: lineage could be as important as royal favour. The Sasanians did not create these 'structures of standing' themselves, but inherited them from the Parthians – while at the same time enhancing the rank of the Persian, i.e. south-west Iranian, aristocracy. This is shown by the ending of the 'formula' for presenting the different groups of nobility in the Paikuli inscription: 'The landholders and the princes, the grandees and the nobles and the Persians and the Parthians.'[26] Loyal Parthian clans had not had to give up their leading position, but were now complemented by Persian clans. At a later period, other 'clans' rose into the rank of the magnates.

As a result of their high social, political and economic standing, the leading families were also made to play an advisory and validating part in the proclamation of a new king: for Narseh and his predecessors, we can assume a token consultation of the highest dignitaries of the empire. This affirmed the nobility's ancient role in determining, or at least confirming, the succession.[27]

While this was going on at the court of Constantine . . . Antoninus [a Roman deserter] was led into the winter residence of the king [Shabuhr II, J.W.] and was received there with open arms. He was distinguished with the dignity of the tiara, an honour by which you may sit at the royal table and by which deserving men among the Persians are allowed to give advice and voice their opinions at assemblies.

(Amm.Marc.18.5.6)

As the extract clearly shows, under a powerful king outsiders and new men had a good chance of promotion to a prominent position in the inner court by arbitrary acts of royal patronage. An outstanding example is the ambitious Zoroastrian 'priest' Kerdir. In the period from the reign of Shabuhr I to that of Wahram II, he rose to great prominence at court and was even in a position to advertise his promotion by means of inscriptions. These were carved onto the façades or walls of important royal sites and monuments, as in this example: 'The King of Kings Ohrmezd [i.e. the son of Shabuhr I, J.W.] bestowed on me the tiara (*kulāf*) and the belt (*kamar*), and he raised

---

[26] NPi 3 (§5) e.a.

[27] See Skjærvø in Humbach and Skjærvø 1983: 13 and Sundermann 1983: 84ff. A 'king's council' is mentioned in NPi §68, the 'sham consultation' in NPi §§73 and 75.

Figure 2.1 Relief of Shabuhr I at Naqsh-i Rajab near Persepolis

my position (*gāh* ['throne', i.e. the place near the king, J.W.]) and my dignity' (*pthšly*).[28] Kerdir is the clearest instance of a dignitary who rose from being a rather humble 'courtier' to the highest position. He owed this success to his special talents and to his skill in making himself indispensable to each new king in turn. Close proximity to the king (i.e. the position of one's *gāh* at royal pronouncements, audiences and banquets) and function announced a person's standing at the early Sasanian court, and distinctive dress then advertised this position to a broader public. Among the most prominent markers of status were the tiaras (*kulāf*), with certain colours and heraldic symbols indicative of particular ranks or distinctions. Belts (*kamar*) studded with gems and earrings played a similar role.[29]

For the Iranian aristocracy, however, for a long time the real criterion of social grandeur was less a title or royal distinction than lineage, and in times of crisis or under 'weak' kings the higher nobility could even force a ruler to put lineage first. The Byzantine historian Procopius shows this happening in the crisis-prone reign of King Kawad (fifth–sixth century), father of the famous Husraw I: 'He [Kawad] was mindful of the rule that did not allow the Persians to transfer any offices (*archai*) to strangers, but only to such

[28] KKZ 4/KNRm 9f. /KSM 5 (Edition: Gignoux 1991).   [29] Peck 1992.

men who were entitled to the respective position of honour (*timē*) through their lineage.'[30]

Next he [Husraw/Khusro I] ordered the heads of the leaders of the Mazdakites to be chopped off and their possessions to be shared out among the poor and needy. He killed a large number of those people who had confiscated other people's possessions, and restored these possessions to their original owners . . . He decreed that, where those responsible for the upbringing of the children of leading families had died, he himself would be responsible for them. He married the girls among them to their social equals and provided them with their bridal outfit and necessities out of the state treasury; and he gave the youths in marriage to wives from noble families, presented them with money for dowries, awarded them sufficient riches, and ordained that they should be members of his court so that he might call upon them for filling various of his state offices . . . He made enquiries about the cavalrymen of the army (*al-asāwira*), and those lacking in resources he brought up to standard by allocating to them horses and equipment, and earmarked for them adequate financial allowances . . . He selected good administrators, tax officials, and governors, and gave the persons appointed to these functions stringent orders.

(Tabari 1.897.1ff., trans. C. E. Bosworth)

As we saw, the rank of a Parthian or Persian nobleman remained more or less independent of royal favour until the end of the fifth century AD. Down to that time, the unruly heads of the great noble houses (the Suren, Karin, Lords of Andegan, and others) admitted only a nominal allegiance to the central power. In their hereditary territorial domains they were virtually independent of the king, and royal power and influence depended to a large degree on effective control of the provincial governors – mostly members of the royal clan – and on the active support of the majority of the higher nobles. This state of affairs changed only in the late Sasanian period. Symptomatic is the way in which the wearing of belts, rings, clasps and other sartorial distinctions now required royal approval. As the Byzantine author Theophylactus (1.9) maintains, official rank now acquired greater prestige than lineage.[31] This strengthening of royal power resulted from the great crisis of state and empire starting in the mid-fifth century.[32] Crucial elements in the crisis were the disastrous defeats of Peroz I (AD 459–484)

---

[30] Procop.*Pers*.1.6.13; cf. 1.13.16 (Mihran is in fact the name of a noble clan, J.W.).

[31] 'Since it is a well-known habit of Persians to bear names according to distinguished positions, as if they disdained to be called by their birth names'. See Procop.*Pers*.1.17.26–18 (a Mihran is punished by being deprived of a golden hairband): 'For in that country no one is allowed to wear a ring or a belt, a clasp or any other object of gold without royal bestowal.' For other examples see Tabari 1.990.16f. de Goeje; Theophyl.Sim.3.8 and Dinawari 85,6f. Guirgass.

[32] That the fifth and sixth centuries AD were crucial times in Sasanian history is proved by the many important developments in domestic politics during that era, such as the emergence of a

against the Hephthalites in the east, resulting in tribute-payments to the Hephthalite 'state', and several years of drought and famine. Meanwhile, the twofold burden imposed on the peasants by landlords and state taxes on the one hand, and by the Hephthalite occupation of parts of the kingdom on the other, prompted a rural exodus and peasant revolts. The peasants drew religious and moral inspiration for such actions from the social teachings of Mazdak, especially his call for communal ownership. The nobility had also been weakened by war casualties, encroachments by the poor, and internecine strife over how best to handle the crisis. History leaves unclear whether the chief victims of these uprisings were the great landowners or the lower nobility.[33] Whatever the case, the subsequent reforms by Kawad I and his son Husraw I were fundamental.[34] They extended direct taxation to the estates of the landed aristocracy. By establishing a new order for the nobility and the army, they also tried to change the empire's social structure and the position of the ruler vis-à-vis the aristocracy: both the restoration to the nobility of its old lands and the reassignment of unclaimed estates were measures carried out at the behest of the king. In addition, new noble groups were created. The 'knights' (mp *aswārān*) were a military nobility obliged to follow the king on campaign. They seem to have been meant to replace the old units of aristocratic retainers (who had borne their own arms and had never really been at the king's disposal). Arab authors also introduce a new (or newly emerged) lower nobility, the *dehkānān*, who as the richest local landowners – sometimes owning entire villages – took over the administration of a village. They owed their elevation to the king, who had granted them land, money and other assistance. They were to serve as local counterweights to the high aristocracy, who were critical of royal policy, and the potentially rebellious peasantry, and could also, if necessary, offer the king military support.[35] Tabari's report of Husraw's reforms, quoted above, states unambiguously that the late Sasanian court changed too. As we saw earlier, the inner court had previously consisted of members of the king's personal household (family members and domestic staff), with other higher nobles being included only as temporary visitors to the (outer) court. But Husraw's inner court now comprised both his relations and members of a kind of service nobility (*Dienstadel*). Hand-picked and promoted by the ruler himself, these last were more loyal to him than to their clans of origin.

clerical hierarchy in Zoroastrianism modelled on the state hierarchy, and a new emphasis in dynastic legitimation on the mythological Kayanid link, etc.

[33] For the Mazdakite movement see Sundermann 1977; Guidi and Morony 1991; Wiesehöfer 2007a.

[34] Rubin 1995. A rather different picture is drawn by Howard-Johnston 1995.

[35] For the 'knights' and *dehkānān* see Altheim and Stiehl 1954: 129–74; 1957: 57–81.

It is this kind of court which is mirrored in most of the Middle Persian literary works (see below).

Under Husraw's immediate successors, however, tensions between king and high aristocracy reappeared. It has been suggested that the king rapidly lost control of the knights, who reverted to being retainers of the great – and virtually independent – landowners. And right from the start the king's supreme military commanders must have been powerful territorial lords.[36] As the political influence of the great landowners revived, they began to re-create their own armed retinues of fighting men and to make their own domains fiscally independent. As in early Sasanian times, these powerful and ambitious nobles once more became only occasional visitors to the court. By contrast, members of the king's inner court risked losing their political clout under a 'weak' ruler and becoming 'courtiers' in the strict sense of the word. Briefly checked in their ambitions by Husraw II's centralising of the financial administration, the landed and military aristocracy still managed to conspire against him, reproaching the king for his tyrannical treatment of the nobility, his ruinous exaction of land taxes and his bloody wars against Byzantium. After Husraw's death, kingship became the instrument of different factions of the aristocracy. The rapid advance of the Muslim army and the sudden collapse of Sasanian sovereignty in Iran are eloquent testimony to the paralysis induced by the particularist interests of the leading classes of the empire in this last phase of Iran's pre-Islamic history.

The 'stateliness' of the court and structures of communication at court

(Offerings shall be made for the benefit of the souls of those who live under the reign of Shabuhr, the King of Kings:) For Ardashir, king of Adiabene; for Ardashir, king of Kerman; Denag, the queen of Meshan, the *dastgerd* of Shabuhr; Hamazasp, the king of Iberia; Walakhsh, the prince (*wispuhr*), the son of Pabag; Sasan, the prince, brought up (in the house of) Farragan; Sasan, the prince, brought up (in the house of) Kadugan; Narseh, the prince, the son of Peroz; Narseh, the prince, the son of Zadsprakhm; Shabuhr, the 'viceroy' (*bidaxš*: 'second in command'); Pabag, the chiliarch (*hazāruft*); Peroz, the 'master of the cavalry' (*aspbed*); Ardashir (from the house of) Waraz; Ardashir (from the house of) Suren; Narseh, the lord of Andegan; Ardashir (from the house of) Karin; Wohnam, the 'commander-in-chief' (*framadar*); Frig, the satrap (*šasab*) of Weh-Andiyok-Shabuhr; Sridoy (with the surname) Shahmust; Ardashir (with the surname) Ardashir-Shnom; Pachihr (with

---

[36] Rubin 2000: 657.

the surname) Tahm-Shabuhr; Ardashir, the satrap of Goyman; Chashmag (with the surname) New-Shabuhr; Wohnam (with the surname) Shabuhr-Shnom; Tirmihr, the commander-in-chief of the fortress of Shahrkerd; Zig, the master of ceremonies (*ayēnīg*, grI *deipnoklētor*: 'caller to the meal'); for Ardawan (from) Demawend; Gundifarr, the son of Ewag (?); Pabig (?) (with the surname) Peroz-Shabuhr, the son of Shanbid; Warzan, the satrap of Gay; Kerdsraw, the 'viceroy'; Pabag, the son of Wisfarr; Walakhsh, the son of Seluk; Yazadbed, the 'adviser' (*handarzbed*) of the queens; for Pabag, the 'sword-bearer' (*šafšēlār*); Narseh, the satrap of Rind; Tiyanag, the satrap of Hamdan; Wardbed, the 'master of the servants' (*paristagbed*); Djoymard, the son of Rastag; Ardashir, the son of Wifr; Abursam, the son of Shabuhr, the 'head of the palace guards' (*darīgān sālār*); Narseh, the son of Barrag; Shabuhr, the son of Narseh; Narseh, the 'master of supplies' (*grastbed*, grI *ho epi tēs annōnēs*); Hormezd, the 'master of scribes' (*dibīrbed*), the son of Hormezd, the 'master of scribes'; Nadug, the 'master of the state prison' (*zēndānīg*); Pabag, the 'master of the gate' (*darbed*); Pasfal, the son of Pasfal; Ewakhsh (?), the son of the 'commander of the fortress' (*dizbed*); Kerdir, the 'priest' (*ēhrbed*); Rastag, the satrap of Weh-Ardashir; Ardashir, the son of the Viceroy; Mihrkhwast, the 'treasurer' (*ganzwar*); Shabuhr, the 'commander' (*framādār*); Ashtad, the 'scribe of contracts' (*dibīr ī Mihrān*) from Ray; for Sasan, the eunuch (*šābestān*), the son of Sasan; Wiroy, 'the supervisor of exchange' (*wāzārbed*); Ardashir, the satrap of Niriz; Baydad, the son of Wardbed; Kerdir, the son of Ardawan; Zurwandad, the son of Bandag; Winnar, the son of Sasan; Sasan, the judge (*dādwar*); Wardan, the son of Nashbed (?); Gulag, the 'master of the wild boars' (*wārāzbed*). (*ŠKZ* mpI 31–5)[37]

In his *res gestae*, Shabuhr I lists the dignitaries, officials and aristocrats of his empire whose proximity to the ruler, if only as occasional members of the outer court, entitled them to have offerings made on behalf of their souls. Other inscribed lists of this kind have come down to us, one of them in the *res gestae* of the second Sasanian king, and several more in Narseh's Paikuli inscription. They are all similarly arranged, starting with the members of the royal house, followed by members of the (seven) most important noble clans and ending with other dignitaries and officials. As far as Shabuhr's list (*ŠKZ*) is concerned, the arrangement of names seems to result from a particular combination of personal and political considerations. In other words, the list is evidence both for the dignitaries' personal relationship to the king and for Shabuhr's appointment of people to office on the basis of decisions of character and/or talent.

Ardashir, the king of Adiabene, heads the sixty-seven dignitaries of Shabuhr's court. As he is only mentioned in *ŠKZ*, we cannot be sure if he owed his outstanding position to a personal relationship with the king

---

[37] Many of these individuals appear in Weber's prosopography.

or to the importance of his province at that time – or both. The consolidation of royal power under the first two Sasanids probably explains the considerable increase in the size of the outer court. The court of King Pabag (Shabuhr's grandfather) had consisted of a mere eight members; Ardashir I appointed thirty-one dignitaries; Shabuhr I doubled their number. In other words, empire-building generated greater complexity in the court.[38]

He [the prophet Mani, J.W.] went to Belabad (Bēṯ Lāpāṭ/Wēh-Andiyōk-Šābuhr), the place of suffering ... They [the Magi, J.W.] ... charged him (Mani) before Kardel [Kerdir, the *mowbed*, J.W.]. And Kardel told it to the *synkathedros*. Then they both went to see the counsellor to the king (*magistōr*) and told him about the charges. And the *magistōr* brought them forward to the king. After he had heard about them ... he sent for my lord. On Sunday, Mani entered Belabad. On Monday, he was accused. On Sunday, the king gave out an order and sent for him.

(Manichean Homilies, 45.9–23 Polotsky)

And he [Wahram I, J.W.] stood up from his meal; and, putting one arm around the queen of the Sakas and the other round Karder [Kerdir, J.W.], the son of Ardawan, he came to the Lord [Mani, J.W.].   (Manichean Text from Turfan M 3.15–20)

Although we cannot be sure about the exact functions implied by the terms *synkathedros* and *magistōr*, it is clear from this passage that in order to get an audience with the king in early Sasanian times, people had to go through the proper channels. King Wahram, who is dining with two close 'friends' (as shown by the royal gesture of embrace), orders Mani to wait. At the end of the meal, he goes over to the waiting 'prophet' and makes clear that he is not welcome.

An elaborate courtly protocol was also part of late Sasanian diplomatic procedures.[39] In their self-representation, the two great powers of Iran and

---

[38] Sadly there is no documentation for the Arsacid court comparable to these early Sasanian lists. If there were, we might be able to recognise the special Sasanian traits of court office and court society. Even more regrettably, we lack a comparable account of the inner and outer court of late Sasanian times: Byzantine historians give detailed reports of Persian diplomatic missions to the Roman emperor (see Constantin.Porphyr.*de Caeremoniis* 1.89f. Bonn), but show little interest in the diplomatic traffic in reverse. Even Menander the Guardsman, who has much to say about Byzantine–Sasanian diplomacy, gives no description of Husraw's court. And the Iranian reports either are of literary rather than historiographical character (the contemporary works of Middle Persian literature, see below), or are New Persian or Arabic adaptations of late-Sasanian works (Firdausi, *Shahnameh*, etc.). These have to be approached with great caution, since they are not simply translations, but in fact are epic or historiographical texts recast in the idiom of their time of composition and with distinctive Islamic touches (Abka'i-Khavari 2000, a useful collection of sources, is quite uncritical in this respect).

[39] For late Sasanian diplomacy see Güterbock 1906; Sako 1986; Winter 1988; Lee 1993; Wiesehöfer, 2007c.

Rome/Byzantium rhetorically stressed their respective superiority. In practice both sides had to recognise their equal might and achieve a modus vivendi. Unsurprisingly, peace treaties between the two powers were drawn up with particular ceremony. In the preamble to a Sasanian document of ratification 'the divine, good, father of peace, ancient Chosroes [Husraw I], king of kings, fortunate, pious and beneficent, to whom the gods have given great fortune and a great kingdom, giant of giants, formed in the image of the gods' calls his Roman opposite number 'Justinian Caesar, our brother'. Even if the titulature given to the Byzantine emperor is clearly briefer than his own, the form of address ('brother') nevertheless reveals the 'king who reigns over kings' and the 'victor of wars' conceding to the 'lord of all things and of the world' (Amm.Marc.19.2.12) equal rank in a diplomatic context. This emerges with particular eloquence and colour in the words which Byzantine authors such as Petrus Patricius and John Malalas ascribe to Sasanian kings and their diplomats. The two empires are described as two lights, which, 'like eyes, are adorned by each other's light' (Petr.Patr. fr. 13 Müller), or as two divinely ordained centres of civilisation, 'the moon of the west' and 'the sun of the east' (Ioh.Mal.18.44 (p. 449) Thurn). Equally, Rome/Byzantium granted parity of rank and dignity to the Sasanians, even though many Romans in fact wished total annihilation on the eastern foe (Amm.Marc.23.5.19), not least because its existence challenged Roman pretensions to universal empire. It was also customary for the two great powers to announce new reigns to each other by means of a special envoy, and to respond with messages of congratulation,[40] as well as exchanging gifts and asking after the well-being of the royal 'brother' when each received the other's embassies in solemn audience.[41]

Royal representation: manners and the cultural example of the court

When Ardashir was 15 years old, news reached Ardawan [the last Parthian king, later on deposed by Ardashir] that Pabag had a son who was accomplished in the chivalrous arts . . . [Ardawan asks Pabag to send him his son, and the latter does not dare disobey the command]. When he [Ardawan] saw Ardashir, he rejoiced, held him in esteem, and ordered that he should go hunting and to the ball game [polo] with his sons and knights every day. Ardashir did so. With god's help he became

---

[40] Ioh.Mal.18.34, 36 (pp. 445, 448) Thurn; Men.Prot. fr.9.1 Blockley; Th.Sim.3.12; Theophan.*Chron.*250 de Boor; *Chr.Pasch.*735 Dindorf.

[41] Petr.Patr. *apud* Constantin. Porphyrogen., *de Caeremoniis* 1.89, 90 Bonn; Procop.*Pers.*1.24; gifts of the Augusta to the Persian queen: Ioh.Mal.18.61 (p. 467) Thurn.

more competent and more clever than all of them in the ball game, in riding, in chess and in backgammon. (Kārnāmag ī Ardaxšīr ī Pābagān 2.5, 10–12)

The 'Ardashir romance', written in the late Sasanian period and subsequently revised,[42] retrojects the social conditions of its date of composition into the period of the empire's founder. For this reason it is sometimes seen basically as a description of the court of the last Sasanians.[43] It is certainly true that after Husraw's reforms and the creation of a service nobility, there was a new stress on good breeding in the social milieu of the king, where the sons of this nobility spent time both as hostages for their father's loyalty and as 'courtiers'. Obedience, elegant manners, culture, games and hunting were expected and practised. It is unsurprising, then, that late Middle Persian *andarz* texts ('wisdom literature') or their Arabic translations include works which employ royal utterances and speeches from the throne to discuss or prescribe the proper character, behaviour and appearance at court (at meals, special festivities, audiences, etc.) not only of the king, but also of his subjects (*bandagān*). In their original form these works were probably meant to foster belief in a divinely sanctioned political and social hierarchy in the empire generally and, more specifically, at the royal court. The unique position of the king[44] manifests itself in his dress, jewellery, headgear, crown and throne, in his luxurious habits[45] and, last but not least, in the splendour and architectural plan of his residential palaces. It is clear from Arabic translations that the Arab conquerors of Iran in the seventh century AD were hugely taken with the enormous crown of Husraw II[46] and with the giant royal carpet known as 'Khusro's spring' in the winter palace at al-Mada'in.[47]

Middle Persian texts like the famous *Husraw ī kawādan ud rēdag-ē* ('Husraw and his page')[48] present the court of Husraw I and his successors as the home of *savoir vivre*. Waspuhr, a poor and unemployed young man, presents himself to the king, asking to be tested on his knowledge of luxurious living, which embraced fine cuisine, including the preparation of jellied meats, ragouts, preserves and stewed fruit; music; flowers and their

---

[42] For an excellent edition with a French translation and commentary see Grenet 2001.

[43] For late-Sasanian court culture see Altheim 1962: 195–212.

[44] For the titulature of the kings see above.

[45] For the respective sources see Abka'i-Khavari 2000.

[46] For the famous crown of Husraw II see Tabari 1.2446.11ff. de Goeje.

[47] Tabari 1.2452.7ff: 'Sixty times sixty yards as a single carpet by the dimension of its surface, on which the paths formed figures, the separating parts rivers, the intervals between them hills. On its border earth sown with spring growth out of silk against branches of gold, and its blossoms of gold, silver and the like.' See Morony 1989.

[48] Edition: Unvala 1921. For the character of the text (and other similar texts) see Cereti 2001: 178–84.

Figure 2.2 The deer hunt from the relief of Khusro II at Taq-i Bustan

scents; and connoisseurship of women and steeds for riding. This text also itemises the various different arts of warfare, every kind of board game, and seventeen different types of quarry on the royal hunts.[49] This last list includes game birds, showing that the 'sport' *par excellence* of the Iranian rulers served not just as a test of strength, but also as a source of victuals.[50]

Husraw's interest in foreign games like chess[51] relates to his promotion of scholarship and the arts, a well-known aspect of royal self-representation.

Chosroes [Husraw I] has been praised and admired quite beyond his deserts not just by the Persians but even by some Romans. He is in fact credited with being a lover of literature and a profound student of philosophy and somebody is supposed to have translated the works of Greek literature into Persian for him. It is rumoured

[49] This interesting list comprises bulls, wild asses, stags, boar, young camels, calves, buffaloes, gazelles, hares, rabbits, partridges, pheasants, larks, cranes, bustards, ducks and peacocks.

[50] For the royal hunt see the famous hunting reliefs of the Taq-i Bustan grotto near Kirmanshah (Tanabe 1983).

[51] The Middle Persian text *Wizāriśn ī čatrang ud nihišn ī nēw-ardaxšīr* tells the story of chess's introduction to Iran (edition and commentary: Panaino 1999; see also Daryaee 2002).

moreover that he has absorbed the whole of the Stagirite [Aristotle] more thoroughly than the Paeanian orator [Demosthenes] absorbed the works of the son of Olorus [Thucydides], that his mind is filled with the doctrines of Plato the son of Ariston and that not even the Timaeus, bristling as it does with geometrical theorems and scientific speculations, would elude his grasp, nor for that matter the Phaedo or the Gorgias or any other of the polished and more intricate dialogues, as for instance the Parmenides. Personally, I could never bring myself to believe that he was so remarkably well-educated and intellectually brilliant.

(Agathias 2.28.1–3.1, trans. J. D. Frendo)

In a spirit of hyper-patriotism Agathias challenged the admiration for the enemy king found in Syriac literature, where Husraw was described as a 'wise king' or one 'who has read all the books of the philosophers'.[52] He also calls into question the claims and motives of Husraw himself, as found in the royal *res gestae* (*kārnāmag*):

We have made inquiries about the rules of the inhabitants of the Roman empire and the Indian states . . . We have never rejected anybody because of his different religion or origin. We have not jealously kept away from them what we affirm. And at the same time we have not disdained to learn what they stand for. For it is a fact that to have knowledge of the truth and of sciences and to study them is the highest thing with which a king can adorn himself. And the most disgraceful thing for kings is to disdain learning and be ashamed of exploring the sciences. He who does not learn is not wise. (Ibn Miskawaih 206.4ff. Caetani)

Despite the unmistakable note of self-praise here, the king's efforts to promote higher learning are undeniable. Agathias himself (2.30f.) reports that Husraw offered a welcome to the Neoplatonic philosophers, homeless after the closure of their school in Athens. When their disappointment with Iran and its inhabitants led them to return home, he insisted on their exemption from punishment by the Romans during his peace negotiations with Byzantium.[53] The king's discussions with Zoroastrian, Christian and other experts about questions of cosmogony and the end of the world, about God, primary matter and the elements are famous.[54] Husraw's interest in the east is shown by his commissioning a translation of the Indian book of fables, the *Panchatantra*, which the physician Burzoy had brought from India.[55] Besides philosophy, theology and statesmanship, Husraw was also interested in foreign contributions to law and medicine. In medicine, Iranian and Indian as well as western traditions were assimilated – they are reported

---

[52] Barhebraeus *Chron.Eccl.*3.91.8f. Abbeloos-Lamy; Michael Syr.366 v. 11f. Syr; 2.339 trans. Chabot. See Cameron 1969/70, esp. pp. 172–4.

[53] Cf. Hartmann 2002.   [54] Wiesehöfer 2001: 217, 299.   [55] de Blois 1990.

by Burzoy, himself a physician from Nishapur, in his introduction to the collection of fables. According to one Arabic source, Husraw I even wrote a medical book himself, a compilation based on Greek and Indian works. Through Sasanian–Middle Persian mediation not only medical and pharmaceutical literature from both east and west, but also Romano-Byzantine agricultural writings and the *Almagest* of Ptolemy, found their way into Arabic literature.[56]

In general, the late Sasanian period witnessed a literary renaissance, much of it sponsored by the royal court. In particular, Husraw I Anushirwan and his successors are credited with the promotion of literature: Weh-Shabuhr, the head of the Zoroastrian clergy under Husraw I, is said to have published the twenty-one *nasks* of the Avesta; in addition the $X^w ad\bar{a}y$-$n\bar{a}mag$ ('Book of Lords'), the semi-official 'Iranian National History', evidently acquired an initial authoritative form under Husraw, before being repeatedly revised (and continued) in later times.[57] Finally, numerous compilations of *andarz* texts, as we have seen, are attributed to Husraw and his entourage, and even the composition of such texts by the king himself.

Conclusion

Sadly the Sasanian empire and monarchy are still neglected by ancient historians.[58] Although the source material, as we have seen, is unbalanced and difficult to handle, this preliminary contribution aims to show that the Sasanian court has a part to play in the further development of ancient court studies. Sasanid Iran shaped Near Eastern history and cultures for more than four hundred years as the great opponent and neighbour of Rome and Byzantium. It also heavily influenced neighbouring cultures to both east and west, and in turn was greatly influenced by them. Earlier studies of Sasanian 'feudalism' all too often drew unjustified and inappropriate

---

[56] For the intermediary role of Sasanian Iran in law and science see Gignoux 2006; Ullmann 1978; Richter-Bernburg 1998, 1999, 2000.

[57] It was from a New Persian prose translation of the 'Book of Lords', collected by Zoroastrians in eastern Iran and compiled by Abu Mansur Ma'mari, secretary of the municipal head of Tus, that Abu'l-Qasim Mansur Firdausi drew his material when, between the years 975 and 1010, he decided to collect the stories about pre-Islamic Iran into an epic poem, the *Shahnameh*. However, although the poet's Sasanian kings are particularly vivid and complex characters, and although the *Shahnameh* gives detailed information about king, court and royal representation in the Sasanian empire, we have to see it not as a historical source for Sasanian institutions and conditions, but as a complex mix of reality and fiction, of historical information and contemporary attitudes towards the past.

[58] Cf. Wiesehöfer 2006.

parallels between Sasanian Iran and the medieval European monarchies. Nonetheless, the theoretical parameters of modern court-studies, based on late medieval and early modern courts, have proved useful in rationalising the source material for the Sasanian court and power and 'state-building' in Sasanid Iran. However, much remains to be done. On the problem of the sources, we urgently need a fresh analysis of the Arabic and New Persian texts in the light of the extant late Sasanian, Byzantine and Syriac literature. The possibility of the mutual influence of Iranian and Byzantine court institutions merits closer examination (see Smith in this volume). The etymological fields 'court', 'rank' and 'dignity' in Middle Persian and Parthian deserve more research. And finally, more archaeological research on palace architecture and royal representation is needed.

Table 2.1. Rulers of the Sasanian dynasty

Number	Date AD	Name	Indigenous name	Genealogy	Commentary
1	224–241/2	Artaxerxes (Artaxares) I	mp Ardašīr	Son of Pābag	Founder of the Sasanian empire
2	239/40–270/2	Sapor(es) I	mp Šābuhr	Son of 1	Co-regent with 1 until 241/2
3	270/2–273	Hormisdas (Hormizdes) I	mp Ohrmezd-Ardašīr	Son of 2	
4	273–276	Wahram (Va(ra)ranes) I	mp Wahrām	Son of 2	
5	276–293	Wahram (Va(ra)ranes) II	mp Wahrām	Son of 4	
6	293	Wahram (Va(ra)ranes) III	mp Wahrām	Son of 5	Contest for the throne with 7
7	293–302	Narses	mp Narseh	Son of 2	Contest for the throne with 6
8	302–309	Hormisdas II	mp Ohrmezd	Son of 7	
9	309–379	Sapor(es) II	mp Šābuhr	Son of 8	
10	379–383	Artaxerxes (Artaxares) II	mp Ardašīr	Son (brother?) of 9	
11	383–388	Sapor(es) III	mp Šābuhr	Son of 9	
12	388–399	Wahram (Va(ra)ranes) IV	mp Wahrām	Son (brother?) of 11	
13	399–421	Yazdgird I (Isdigerdes)	mp Yazdgerd	Son of 12	
14	421–439	Wahram (Va(ra)ranes) V	mp Wahrām (Gōr)	Son of 13	
15	439–457	Yazdgird II (Isdigerdes)	mp Yazdgerd	Son of 14	

16	457–459	Hormisdas III	mp Ohrmezd	Son of 15	
17	459–484	Peroz(es)	mp Pērōz	Son of 15; brother of 16	
18	484–488	Balas (Blases)	mp Walaxš	Son of 15; brother of 17	
19	488–496; 499–531	Kabades I	mp Kawād	Son of 17	
20	496–498	Zamasphes (Zames)	mp Zamāsp	Son of 17; brother of 19	
21	531–579	Chosroes I	mp Husraw (Xusrō)	Son of 19	Epithet Anōširwān
22	579–590	Hormisdas IV	mp Ohrmezd	Son of 21	
23	590–628	Chosroes II	mp Husraw (Xusrō)	Son of 22	Epithet Abarwēz
24	590–591	Wahram (Va(ra)ranes) VI	mp Wahrām Čōbīn		Rival claimant to the throne of 23
25	628	Kabades II	mp Kawād	Son of 23	
26	628–630	Artaxerxes (Artaxares) III	mp Ardašīr	Son of 25	
27	630	Shahrbaraz	mp Šahrwarāz		
28	630	Chosroes III	mp Husraw (Xusrō)	Nephew of 23	
29	630–631	Boran	mp Pūrān	Daughter of 23	Queen
30	631	Azarmidukht	mp Azarmīgduxt	Daughter of 23; sister of 29	Queen
31	631–632	Hormisdas V	mp Ohrmezd	Grandson of 23	
32	631–633	Chosroes IV	mp Husraw (Xusrō)	Grandson of 23	
33	633–651	Yazdgird III (Isdigerdes)	mp Yazdgerd	Grandson of 23	

3 | The court of Alexander the Great between Europe and Asia

TONY SPAWFORTH

Introduction

In a book on ancient courts, this chapter[1] arguably is an oddity, since alone of the contributions its focus is a single ancient ruler, who himself was scarcely typical, given not only the freakish scale of his conquests, but also his plans, novel in a Greek context, for stabilising his dominion over them. But Alexander is simply too important a figure to leave out. Partly this is a matter of the ancient evidence. Given the ancient preoccupation with Alexander's military achievements, it can come as a surprise to find that he is the only Macedonian or Hellenistic ruler about whose 'court' ceremonies we have some detailed knowledge (Weber 1997: 43). This evidence leaves us in no doubt that Alexander attached real political significance to 'holding court'. It is clear too that, like his father, Philip II, or Augustus in a later age, Alexander was a consummate 'master of self-representation'.[2] Here a reappraisal is offered of the evolving role which Alexander assigned to his 'court' and its ceremonies in the period after his invasion of the Persian empire (334 BC), with particular emphasis on a neglected topic, namely, the physical space constituted by the royal quarters, including his feasting- and audience-tent (*tente d'apparat*). The underlying assumption throughout is that Alexander from the outset was intent on retaining his conquests in Asia. This is shown by his maintenance of Persian structures of control and exploitation as soon as Persian territory began to fall into his hands (Arr.1.17.1): that is to say, whatever his ultimate aims may have been when he first invaded, he was consciously engaged from the start in what modern historians would call 'state-building'. It is in this light that the role of his 'court' seems worth reappraising.

---

[1] This chapter has been immeasurably improved by interaction with participants at the Newcastle workshop 'The Court and Court Society in Ancient Monarchies' in May 2004. I am particularly grateful to Maria Brosius, Simon Hornblower and John Moles for discussion and comments on earlier drafts. Responsibility for the final content, of course, is mine alone.

[2] Carney 2000a: 275, of Philip.

Issues of definition

It is nothing new for modern scholarship on Macedonian kings to refer to 'the court' and to 'courtiers', although it is fair to say that the assumptions underlying these usages tend not to be spelt out. The only detailed study of Alexander's 'court' is that of Helmut Berve, who assigned to 'der königliche Hof' the first third of his tripartite study of the institutions of Alexander's empire (1926, I: 3–100). Since he came too early to be influenced by the more theoretical and sociological approaches to court studies triggered ultimately by Norbert Elias, his study may now seem to lack conceptual rigour (Herman 1997: 201). That said, and quite apart from the fact that his researches provide the basis for all further work, Berve also took for granted the historical importance of the 'court' in Alexander's monarchy. This is by no means always the case in Alexander-studies. There is a long-standing tendency, reaching back to antiquity indeed, to sound a negative note in confronting the aulic side to Alexander's reign. Symptomatic is the dismissal of Chares, Greek author of a lost history which took a marked interest in Alexander's 'court', as a 'trifler' by one distinguished historian of Alexander (Tarn 1948, II: 70).[3] This viewpoint seems to reflect the traditional censoriousness of modern historiography in the face of the nowadays 'moribund' social formation of the court (Elias 1983: 8; Winterling 1997: 151–2). For rather different reasons, the court as an analytical category was omitted from the most exhaustive study of Macedonian royal institutions yet published (Hatzopoulos 1996), whose author was committed to a 'constitutional' view of the Macedonian monarchy.[4] In the long-running modern debate about the nature of Macedonian kingship, Hatzopoulos' position runs counter to the tendency in recent years, with which this chapter is in essential agreement, to emphasise the informal nature of royal power, the absence of much in the way of 'constitutional' checks and balances, and the conduct of day-to-day politics as a 'power game' between the king, the Macedonian elite and the people (Völcker-Janssen 1993: 33; Errington 1996). On this view, the king was 'basically an autocrat limited principally by his relative power vis-à-vis the Macedonian nobility' (Anson 1985: 316; cf. Carney 2000b: 6). A focus on the court of the Argeads, as Alexander's dynastic lineage was known, may offer a new perspective on this debate, given that historically 'court culture has often been associated with absolutism' (Asch 2003: 80).

---

[3] The implicit criticism seems to be of the subject-matter which Chares focused on. As a recorder of fact, Chares was certainly not above criticism: see Badian 1981: 50–1.

[4] See the reviews of Archibald 1999 and, more critical of the main thesis, Borza 1999 and Lévy 2001.

So far I have preferred to use scare-quotes around 'court'. How appropriate, in fact, is a court-centred analysis to the study of the fourth-century Macedonian monarchy, and in particular to Alexander and his (after 334 BC) usually roving entourage? Few would dispute that fourth-century BC Macedon was a state in which power and decision-making were centred on the ruler's house (or tent when, as commander-in-chief, the king led the Macedonian army to war). Alexander's royal entourage in Asia exhibits most, if not all, the characteristics of a court, as defined in modern theory (Winterling 2004: 89–90). It can be divided into an inner and an outer court (Butz and Dannenberg 2004: 12), the first centred on the 'service' (*therapeia*) which followed him in Asia and the other on people with whom he socialised on a daily basis (see below). The second comprised high-status individuals within the empire who were not normally a physical part of this immediate entourage, such as members of the royal family left behind in Macedon, or elite-administrators (his provincial governors or satraps, notably). It also included visitors of standing – increasing in numbers, no doubt, as Alexander's successes mounted – such as the numerous 'people sojourning' (*parepidēmountas*) who were included by Alexander in the wedding festivities at Susa (Appendix, especially B, 7). Some of these visitors were prominent members of communities under Alexander's sway, such as the arms-dealer (*hoplophulax*) Gorgus, a leading citizen of Greek Iasos in south-west Asia Minor, said to have 'passed time (*diatribōn*) with Alexander' at Ecbatana in 324 BC, when he successfully brokered a deal on behalf of his Iasian fellow-citizens.[5] A privileged category (to which Gorgus may or may not have belonged) comprised Alexander's 'ritualised friends' (*idioxenoi*), who were given seats of honour at the Susa weddings (Appendix, A, 1–2). These high-status people were non-Macedonian (Berve 1926, I: 62–3), and were likely to include non-Greeks as well as Greeks (Herman 1987: 12), and in the nature of this particular type of social relationship their home-communities would be far away (Herman 1987: 31).

In the classic fashion of rulers' courts, Alexander's close court incorporated representatives of the upper classes of his kingdom among his personal servants. The 'royal boys' (*basilikoi paides*), drawn from the leading

---

[5] *SIG*[3] 312.7–8; Bosworth 1988: 253 with refs.; Herman 1987: 85–6. I take this meaning of *hoplophulax* to be implied by his alleged offer to Alexander of ten thousand suits of armour, along with catapults and other weapons, at Ecbatana in 324 BC, which presumably Gorgus intended to provide from his own resources: Ephippus, *FGrH* 126 F 5 = Athen.12.538b. His huge wealth obviously reflects the vast fortunes to be made from supplying Alexander's war-machine. Heisserer (1980: 170) took the post to be an official one in Alexander's army.

Macedonian families (at least one royal prince, the future Amyntas II, was said to have taken his turn: Ael.*VH* 12.43), performed a mix of domestic services, such as waiting on the king at table, and outside duties, notably attendance on the royal hunt, which, taken together, justify the conventional equation with the royal pages of more recent European monarchies. The institution was clearly intended to promote ideals of personal service and loyalty to the monarch, as suggested by its function 'as a kind of seminary' for Macedonian officers and generals (Curt.8.6.6).[6] Under Alexander, and possibly earlier Macedonian monarchs, domestic servitors of the king included adult members of the Macedonian elite (see below, on Ptolemy). It needs stressing that service of this kind, glossed in Ptolemy's case as 'distinguished and honourable',[7] was profoundly alien to the Greeks and later the Romans, for whom the pages were comparable to, or even mistaken for, chattel slaves (Ael.*VH* 12.43; Curt.8.6.2).

The other key group in this inner court comprised the Hetairoi ('Companions'), Macedon's traditional officer class, since Philip's time recruited by the king personally, but continuing to include members of established families whose lineages and, perhaps, landed bases gave them a certain independence from the king.[8] Socially this group dominated the daily entourage of the king. It furnished him with his personal bodyguard, under Alexander a hand-picked and particularly favoured group normally seven-strong, transformed by their privileged access to the king into brokers of royal graces – Hephaestion, Alexander's childhood friend, is the chief exhibit here (refs. at Berve 1926, I: 63).[9] The Companions also provided the pool from which Alexander selected his daily companions at the royal table (below). Since these two, socially interconnected, groups of royal pages and Companions provided the chief internal opposition under both Philip and Alexander, it is likely that their incorporation into the inner court served a monarchical strategy of promoting the personal allegiance of the Macedonian elites to the king. On one level, Alexander in particular seems to have used the routines of his domestic and social life to try to manage these groups in a manner reminiscent of the Eliasque reading of the Bourbon court – thus a

[6] Hammond 1990; Bosworth 1995: 90–3.

[7] See Athen.4.171b–c citing Artemidorus: *epiphanēs kai entimos hē chreia*, of the post of *edeatros* held by Ptolemy (see below).

[8] Kienast 1973: 258; Völker-Janssen 1993: 32–7.

[9] Note too the courting of Alexander's 'friends' with rich gifts by Orsines, satrap of Persis, in 325/4 BC (Curt.10.1.24). Such brokers already existed at Philip's 'court' in 336 BC, when a Macedonian (almost certainly), his name lost, was honoured by the Athenians for 'taking care of Athenians visiting Philip': Tod 1948: no. 181 lines 12–15. I am grateful to Simon Hornblower for this reference.

royal invitation to dinner could serve to dissemble a leading Companion's imminent fall from grace.[10] On another level, Alexander's relations with his retinue conform to the revisionist model of early modern courts, which emphasises how 'the exercise of authority [at court] was always in some sense a negotiation' (Adamson 1999b: 38). This observation seems borne out in Alexander's case by his habit of sounding out the opinion of leading Macedonians on controversial issues over food and wine; in this way the royal table served as 'the ground on which one's relationship with the king and others was constantly being tested'.[11] As will be seen in the 'obeisance' affair (below), Alexander did not always have his way.

The communicative structure typical of relations between an absolutist ruler and his courtiers was a feature of Alexander's entourage. On the one hand an ancient tradition presents 'frank speaking' or *parrhēsia* as a convention in relations between Macedonian kings and their subjects,[12] and this convention is evident in exchanges between Alexander and individual Companions.[13] On the other, praises, flattery and submissiveness were increasingly the norm under Alexander (Plut.*Al*.23.4; Arr.4.8.2–3), and the type of the courtier, entirely dependent on his sovereign, is well captured in Alexander's alleged reproof of his favourite, Hephaestion (a Companion), as 'a fool and a madman for not knowing that without Alexander's favour he was nothing' (Plut.*Al*.47.6). The uneasy concurrence of two such antithetical styles of communication reflects a transformation under Philip and Alexander in the character of the Companion-elite from people with a fair degree of social and economic independence from the Macedonian monarch into courtiers,[14] in the Polybian sense of *hoi peri tēn aulēn*, 'at the nod of the king . . . at one moment universally envied and at the next universally pitied' (5.26.3, cited by Herman 1997: 205). This change had less to do with the moral defects of individuals, *pace* the ancient writers, than the way in which, under Alexander above all, the huge aggrandisement in royal power created competition for the ruler's graces on a scale previously unknown in Macedon, as is suggested by the cohort of 'Alexander-flatterers', as they were known (Chares, *FGrH* 125 F 4 = Athen.12.538f), who were in the habit of giving Alexander 'extravagant presents'. The favour-currying mentality behind such gifts is suggested by the tale of Hagnon of Teos in western Asia Minor, a Companion of Greek extraction who sought to please

---

[10] Curt.6.8.16 (Philotas).
[11] Borza 1983: 54; Völker-Janssen 1993: 46–7; cf. Davidson 1997: 286–8 ('power dinners').
[12] Polyb.5.27.6; see Anson 1985: 314–15; Murray 1996.
[13] E.g. Coenus at the Hyphasis river: Arr.5.27.2–9.
[14] On this change see Völker-Janssen 1993: 32–48.

Alexander by 'writing to him that he wanted to buy Crobylus, whose beauty was famous in Corinth, as a present for him'.[15]

Off the battlefield, Alexander's 'court' was the chief site of the representation or image-management which contributed to creating his outward identity as a monarch (Butz and Dannenberg 2004: 24). In another classic function of courts, it was also the place where the ruler used ceremonial to construct and display the relative ranking of elite groups within the state. These two aspects of Alexander's 'court' receive particular emphasis in this chapter, where their role in Alexander's state-building enterprise is re-examined.

Other features of courts are missing or not strongly present under Alexander, in part as the result of his itinerancy. There was no central palace, although this feature of the court phenomenon was present in Macedon at least from the reign of Archelaus (413–399 BC); and by the time of Philip II at the latest was physically fixed at Pella (Nielsen 1994: 81). But even under Philip the 'court' must have often been migratory, since he was famous for campaigning throughout the year (Dem.9.50); Alexander's use of elaborate royal tents may well have gone back to Philip (see Appendix). By the same token the sustained physical proximity of Alexander to the Macedonian officer class during the campaigns in Asia should not be seen as completely without precedent. Even so, Alexander's city of tents must have gone much further in developing the features of a centre of governance as well as power; the presence of the royal archive, housed in the tent of Alexander's secretary (Plut.*Eum*.2), is surely suggestive here. The women of the royal family, in particular Alexander's mother and full sister, did not accompany him into Asia, although they can be considered a part of the outer court (above), and in the case of Olympias brought influence to bear (or sought to) by letter (Berve 1926, I: 63; II: no. 581); on the other hand, new royal women entered Alexander's household in Asia, including two wives and a harem (below).

The ancients themselves probably did not see Alexander's peripatetic entourage as qualitatively different from the fixed power-centres of other ancient monarchs. At any rate, aulic language was certainly applied by later ancient writers to describe his household, as in 'the Macedonian courtiers' of

---

[15] Plut.*Al*.22.2. Plutarch's Alexander indignantly rejects the offer, although, as has been pointed out (Berve 1926, I: 10–11), such an offer (if historical) must have been thought likely to win royal approval. In passing, to see relationships of reciprocity between Alexander and his entourage (so Hatzopoulos 1996, I: 335–6) seems misguided: the essence of reciprocity, at least as the ancient Greeks understood it, lay in the approximate parity not only of the gifts' value but also of the donors' status: G. Herman, *OCD*[3], s.v. 'reciprocity (Greece)'.

the king, *hoi peri tēn aulēn Makedones* (Diod.Sic.17.101.3), or the malefactor whom Alexander expelled 'from his *aulē*' (Plut.*Al*.70.3); these usages conceivably go back to the primary sources on which these later writers drew. From a comparative perspective, finally, this itinerant retinue meets all the criteria of the early modern court: the place where the ruler lived; the seat of governance; and 'the venue where the ceremonial and ritual that surrounded the prince could be properly observed' (Adamson 1999a: 10).

In sum, it seems safe to drop the scare-quotes and refer straightforwardly from now on to the Macedonian, and specifically Alexander's, court.

Bias in the ancient evidence

When approaching the ancient writers on Alexander, a basic truth must first be acknowledged. The Alexander which they have bequeathed to us to a considerable extent is a 'Roman' Alexander. Their construct, to be sure, is based on earlier accounts, albeit to an extent, and by routes, which remain hotly contested.[16] But this material, acquired by whatever means, had to be recast so as to hold the interest of Roman-period audiences, living at a time when monarchy was the dominant state-form of the Greco-Roman world and when the past could serve as a discreet vehicle for discourse about 'good' and 'bad' rulers and the vicissitudes of court life. In the case of Quintus Curtius, writing in Latin under the Caesars, his portrayal of Alexander is the most obviously coloured by Roman-elite concerns about the exercise of imperial power (Spencer 2002; see Paterson in this volume). Beyond that, all these texts are cast in a consciously literary vein, so that their artfulness, or 'craftedness', can hardly be overestimated.[17]

When it comes to court life, Alexander is presented paradoxically in these sources. On the one hand, and especially in those texts aimed chiefly at a Greek readership, he is made to resemble a well-behaved Athenian gentleman in his personal disdain for royal luxury and his self-control in the face of sensory temptations such as Darius' beautiful wife, or Asiatic gastronomy.[18] On the other hand, as a matter of record he adopted more and more of the imposing ceremonial of the Persian court from 330 BC onwards, and his court eventually became a byword for conspicuous consumption, as shown by a long section 'concerning the luxury (*truphē*) of Alexander'

---

[16] For example, Hammond 1983, esp. 1–11.

[17] See, for instance, Moles 1985, on the intertextuality in just one passage (admittedly, the important 'second preface') of Arrian.

[18] Especially in Plutarch: e.g. *Al*.20.8; 21.4; 22.4.

included by the third-century AD Greek writer Athenaeus of Naucratis in his *Deipnosophists* (537d–540a). Ancient writers themselves were aware of the paradox. The preferred solution, which suited the moralising tendency in classical historiography as well as reflecting the unwillingness or inability of most ancient writers on Alexander to rationalise royal splendour, was to personalise the issue in terms of Alexander's corruption by his eastern conquests.[19] This was a particularly tempting line of explanation in Alexander's case, since it allowed Greek and Roman writers to play with the classical stereotype of 'oriental/barbarian monarchy' (e.g. Hall 1989), to which the 'corrupted' Alexander could be assimilated when he was not being preferred to the ancient reader as its morally superior – because 'Greek' – antithesis.[20]

Our fullest accounts of ceremonial at Alexander's court come in the form of anecdotal material deriving ultimately from Chares and (probably) Ephippus (App.) and relating to his stay at Susa (324 BC). Detailed descriptions survive of his use during this time of a palatial tent-complex to celebrate the 'mixed marriages', as well as for his routine public audiences. As a reminder of the extremely partial coverage in the ancient sources generally of ceremonial at Alexander's court, it is instructive to compare the coverage of these events in the anecdotal tradition about Alexander on the one hand and in the primary Alexander-narratives on the other. These last make no mention at all of Alexander's audience-giving at Susa. As for the marriage feast, its setting goes unreported by either Diodorus (17.107.6) or Arrian (7.4.4–8); Plutarch notes it sparingly (*Al.*70.2, with a few details); the coverage of Susa by Curtius, who might have entered into more detail, is lost (it probably fell in the lacuna at the end of 10.1). To judge from this one example, it is a reasonable assumption that the aulic aspects of Alexander's reign are generally under-reported in the surviving ancient tradition about Alexander. One explanation for this state of affairs may well have to do with the predominantly apologetic presentation of Alexander, at least in Plutarch and Arrian: thick description of 'barbarian' display and pageantry would have tended to undermine the case which they make for Alexander's heroic Greekness. The dangers of this ancient bias for modern historians are suggested by modern evaluation of the splendours of Susa. Illuminated as these splendours are by the chance spotlight of the anecdotal material, did they really constitute a significant ratcheting up of Alexander's use of pomp and circumstance in 324 BC, as has been assumed (Bosworth 1980: 8)?

---

[19] E.g. Arr.4.7.4; Diod.Sic.17.77.4; Curt.6.6.1–3; Justin 12.3.8–12.

[20] Briant (2002) gives an insightful discussion of narratological sub-texts to the classical portrayal of Alexander.

The court of Philip II

Before looking further at Alexander's court, something more must first be said about that of his father, Philip II. The evidence is poor, but makes clear nonetheless that the Macedonian court even before Alexander's conquests was developing along new lines. Philip II (360/59–338 BC) was a hereditary ruler who succeeded after a prolonged period of dynastic weakness. Politically and militarily Philip had laid the foundations for Alexander's achievements by transforming Macedon from a minor Balkan kingdom into a multi-ethnic empire or 'Vielvölkerstaat', one which united Macedonians, Thracians and Greeks under Philip's personal rule in a fashion not so unlike that of Macedon's giant imperial neighbour, the 'supraethnic' Achaemenid Persian state (Kienast 1973: 248). The centre of this new state-entity was Philip's court at Pella, and most scholars are agreed that Macedon's new-found power under Philip was linked to important changes at court, both in its organisation (Kienast 1973: 251–68) and more broadly in 'the public presentation of monarchy in Macedonia' (Carney 2000a: 275).

On this last point, it is clear that Philip, well before Alexander started to do so, was increasing the association of royal power with display and ceremonial. The Macedonian court has acquired a rather homespun image in modern scholarship as a place where the 'women of the royal family made the daily meals and wove the clothing of their menfolk' (Hammond 1989: 31). But display had been an adjunct of monarchy in Macedonia at least since the reign of King Archelaus (413–399 BC), said to have hired Zeuxis, a leading Greek painter, to decorate his palace.[21] Since Greek authors were disinclined to view royal luxury, in Macedonia any more than in Persia, as 'une marque et un symbole de la splendour royale' (Briant 2002: 356), Philip's conspicuous consumption is reported in negative terms ('insatiable and extravagant', *aplēstos kai polutelēs*: the hostile Theopompus, *FGrH* 115 F 224 = Athen.4.167a).[22] But his lavish hospitality impressed Athenian ambassadors in 346 BC,[23] and Philip may well have devised the 'hundred-seater' dining tent which Alexander is found using at Dium as early as 335/4 BC, scarcely two years into his reign (Appendix). As his son would

---

[21] Ael.*VH* 14.17; Nielsen 1994: 81.

[22] The evidence of the 'Tomb of Philip' at Vergina for the lifestyle of the Macedonian court is left out of this discussion, since doubts continue to surface about the dating and the identity of the occupants (Palagia 2000: 189–98). The question in the end may only be decided, if at all, with the full publication of the finds, pottery included.

[23] Hammond 1989: 142 citing Aeschin.2.41–2; 47; 51–2.

be later, Philip was an impresario of monarchy, as shown by the spectacular royal wedding which he organised at Aegeae in 336 BC. This included a procession of statues of the twelve gods made for the occasion, 'wrought with great artistry and wondrously adorned with the brilliance of wealth', to which, with a showman's touch, Philip boldly added his own statue, 'suitable for a god' (Diod.Sic.16.92.5).

Two details in the evolving ceremonial at Philip's court are of particular interest because they raise the question of Persian influence at Pella prior to Alexander's succession. When Arrian is describing the duties of the 'royal boys' he includes their mounting the king on his horse in 'the Persian style' (Arr.4.13.1). The clear implication of the passage is that this custom went back to Philip (rather than being an innovation of Alexander). Bosworth (1995: 92–3) rightly saw the custom as a 'mark of honour for the reigning king'. The straightforward inference would be that Philip took over this Persian royal practice from knowledge of customs at the Persian court (see below). Bosworth however denied this, on the grounds that the practice was known earlier in the fourth century BC to the Athenian Xenophon, who recommends it for the old and infirm. But there is no obvious reason why the custom should have been imported to Pella via the Greeks rather than directly from the Persian empire. And it was presumably the royal Persian associations which made 'the Persian style' an appropriate way of honouring the Macedonian king; so a direct Macedonian borrowing from the Persian court is probably in question here.

Secondly, by 336 BC at the latest, Philip had taken to using a special chair to signify his elevated rank, a *thronos* or 'throne', on public occasions. The evidence comes from a fragmentary reference to 'the Macedonians around the throne' (*peri thron[ou]*) at the moment of his assassination in the theatre at Aegeae.[24] It is therefore not quite true that the royal throne was 'unknown as such to the Macedonians' (Fredricksmeyer 2000: 159), although this seems to be its first firmly dated appearance.[25] It is tempting to see the practice as another innovation which Philip borrowed from the Persian court, the throne having for long been the 'primary symbol of royalty in the Near East' (2000: 159).[26]

---

[24] P. Oxy.15.1798; Hammond 1991: 401; re-edition by Grzybek 1999.

[25] A lavish marble throne was discovered at Vergina in the 'Tomb of Eurydice'. It is probably a royal tomb, with a firm *terminus post quem* of 344/3 BC, but both the sex and the identity of its occupant are disputed: Carney 2000b: 242–3 with refs.

[26] Alexander's use of a golden throne, certainly after his return from India, is well documented: Fredricksmeyer 2000: 152, 159–60, 161. For the Persian capital crime of sitting on the king's throne, and Alexander's changing attitude to this taboo: ibid.

More generally, Dietmar Kienast (1973) has argued that many of Philip's reforms at court and in the administration were inspired by neighbouring Persia. Even if this argument can be contested here and there in the detail,[27] the general thesis of Persian influence should hardly be controversial, unless, as Kienast observes ironically, one believes that the only outside influence on fourth-century Macedon came from Greece (1973: 269). Even the Athenians were susceptible to their hereditary enemy Persia's culture and way of life (Miller 1997). When it came to monarchy, the paramount prestige of the Persian court made it an inevitable model for lesser courts on its periphery.[28] Macedon in addition had a long history of Persian links. For thirty years in the fifth century BC it had been a Persian vassal state (Kienast 1973: 269); under Philip there was continued contact, including the Persian envoys famously entertained in his father's absence by the young Alexander (Plut.*Al.*5.1), and the prolonged presence at the court for seven years of a high-ranking Persian satrap, Artabazus, along with his entourage.[29] As the substance of royal power increased under Philip, there was a parallel elaboration of its trappings, in conformance to the sociological proposition that 'the most real way of asserting one's rank is by documenting it through an appropriate social appearance' (Elias 1983: 64). If this view of Philip is essentially correct, then two striking characteristics of Alexander's reign, his interest in the appearances of power and his imitation of the Persian royal court, can be situated on a larger trajectory rooted in his father's 'Macedonian revolution'.

Alexander's court before 330 BC

Although Alexander's court in this period is ill attested, there is enough evidence to show that his adoption of Persian court ceremonial in 330 was far from being a Damascene conversion to royal pomp. His early understanding of conspicuous consumption as a facet of royal prestige is shown by the festival which he staged in Macedonian Dium on the eve of his expedition (335/4 BC), including a sumptuous feast. 'He erected a tent to hold a hundred couches and invited his friends and officers, as well as the ambassadors from the cities, to the banquet. Employing great magnificence, he entertained great numbers in person besides distributing to his entire force sacrificial animals and all else suitable for the festive occasion, and put his

---

[27] Bosworth 1995: 92–3; Briant 2002: 924–5.
[28] Briant 2002: 670–3, on the Xanthian dynasts of Lycia.
[29] Berve 1926, II: no. 152; Kienast 1973: 270–1.

army in fine humour' (Diod.Sic.17.16.4). Such events formed a key part of that distinctly non-Greek 'culture of generosity' whereby, 'through lavish gift-giving and hospitality', Macedonian kings 'obliged men into their service' (Dalby 1996: 153–4). In the first few years of the expedition, when its success hung in the balance, Alexander used display to make a show of force. His progress was marked by a series of armed parades at Ephesus (334 BC), Soli (333 BC) and Memphis (332/1 BC), presumably aimed at local audiences likely to include Persian spies, but no doubt intended to promote cohesion and team-spirit among the men themselves (Arr.1.18.2; 2.5.8; 3.4.5); as will be seen later, this military dimension would remain fundamental to Alexander's evolving self-representation in Asia. We begin to hear of more elaborate feasts as the victories accumulated: after Issus, a dinner in the magnificent state tent of Darius, now Macedonian booty (Curt.3.11.21; 3.12.2; Plut.*Al.*20.6–21.1); lavish feasts laid on by the Babylonians after Gaugamela (Diod.Sic.17.64.4); and then the junketing at Persepolis (Diod.Sic.17.22.1; Curt.5.7.2). Throughout this period Alexander also gave audience to envoys, such as the Lycians in 334/3 BC (Arr.1.24.5), or the 'many embassies from Greece' at Memphis in 332/1 BC (Arr.3.4.5); but there is as yet no hint in the sources that these occasions were particularly marked by pomp.

Alexander's initial adoption of Persian court ceremonial (330 BC)

The sources are in agreement that Alexander began to hold court with new splendour after the sack of Persepolis (early 330 BC), and they associate the first moves in this direction with his passage through the adjacent regions of Hyrcania and Parthyaea in northern Iran, later in the same year. Alexander's feasting- and audience-tent, of which more shortly, makes its first alleged appearance in Hyrcania (Polyaen.*Strat.*4.3.24); his personal adoption of a form of Persian royal dress is placed by Plutarch (*Al.*45.1) a little later (autumn 330 BC), when he had moved on into Parthyaea (Bosworth 1980: 5–6). Prior (*prōton*) to this sartorial innovation, according to Diodorus Siculus (17.77.4–7), he had already introduced Asian ushers (*rhabdouchoi*) at court and given himself a new Persian bodyguard, including Darius' brother Oxyathres. Later (*eita*), along with his own assumption of a new royal costume, he gave purple cloaks to the Companions and Persian harnesses for their horses, as well as acquiring a harem[30] with its accompanying

---

[30] Accepted e.g. by Bosworth 1980: 5; Fredricksmeyer 2000: 155.

staff of eunuchs (Curt.6.6.8). Both the cloaks and the harnesses were Persian status-indicators; the former were worn by the Persian king's courtiers.[31] The ushers marked the introduction of Persian court etiquette, which stressed the mystique and deference surrounding the king, and required in turn the maintenance of order and policing of behaviour on formal occasions; in 328 BC these ushers were the object of a complaint to Alexander that 'Macedonians had to beg Persians in order to approach the king' (Plut.*Al*.51; see below). Their appearance in 330 probably also heralds Alexander's appointment of an 'introducer' (*eisangeleus*), a chamberlain who managed official receptions and audiences, his duties modelled on those of Persian counterparts.[32] The only *eisangeleus* known by name was a Greek, Chares of Mytilene (Plut.*Al*.46).

More elaborate tented accommodation, not to mention the harem, would have added considerably to Alexander's baggage train, and on the face of it their acquisition at this juncture is at odds with the claim in one ancient source (Curt.6.6.15–17) that the king burnt his transport carts before the next leg of his march, towards Bactria (modern Afghanistan). Although accepted by some moderns (e.g. Bosworth 1988: 99), this claim is dubious, however, not least because the same episode is assigned a different date in other ancient writers.[33] Indeed, Pierre Briant (2003: 361–5) has questioned whether such a measure was ever taken, pointing to the exemplary, moral and rhetorical context of these passages, which implicitly contrast Alexander's commitment to military discipline with the luxurious practices on campaign of the Persian kings. Whatever the case, it seems clear that Alexander's army remained heavily encumbered during the Bactrian campaigns. Already in 328 BC the 'royal service' (*basilikē therapeia*) was sufficiently important to be in the charge of a leading Companion, Pithon son of Sosicles, and large enough to have to be left behind while Alexander campaigned against Spitamenes (Arr.4.16.6; Berve 1926, I: 25).

Alexander's tented quarters

It is time now to consider Alexander's tented accommodation in more detail (the ancient evidence is set out in the Appendix). One of his tents was an ancient marvel, repeatedly described by ancient authors at least until the third century AD (Appendix, A, nos. 1–3). In the early Principate

---

[31] Bosworth 1980: 5; Savalli-Lestrade 1998: 300–1; Fredricksmeyer 2000.
[32] Berve 1926, I: 19–20; Jacoby, *FGrH* 125 F 2, commentary.
[33] On the eve of the invasion of India, 327 BC: Plut.*Al*.57.1; Polyaen.*Strat*.4.3.10.

two of its tent-poles were thought worthy of display outside the imperial palace at Rome (Appendix, A, no. 10). The fullest descriptions of this tent, going back to the lost Alexander-historians Chares and (probably) Ephippus (Appendix, B, nos. 1, 3), describe its use by Alexander at Susa in 324 BC. Here the tent's magnificence arose from its sheer size as well as its copious use of precious materials, including costly embroideries, precious stones, and gold and silver; on this occasion it formed a tripartite complex comprising the *oikos* or 'house', a vast forecourt (*aulē*), and a surrounding enclosure wall (*peribolos*).

Alexander's use of imposing tents can be traced further back. A luxurious tent had been with the king in India, where he used it (or elements from it) in 326/5 BC as a luxurious *andrōn* for feasting local leaders (Appendix, A, no. 9). This or another tent appears earlier on the Indian campaign. Following a life-threatening wound while storming a town of the Malli people, Alexander had displayed himself by having 'his tent' (*tabernaculum*) set up on two ships lashed together for this purpose on the River Hydraotes (Appendix, A, no. 8). That this tent was an imposing affair seems confirmed by its appearance earlier, at the battle of the Hydaspes river (326 BC): Alexander 'ordered his tent (*tabernaculum*) to be pitched . . . the unit usually in attendance on him to stand guard before it, and all the sumptuous trappings of royalty (*omnem apparatum regiae magnificentiae*) to be deliberately flaunted before the enemy's eyes' (Appendix, A, no. 7). Two years earlier, in Bactria, the erection and striking of a royal tent on the banks of the Oxus river in 328 BC required the oversight of a dedicated Macedonian official with specialist tent-pitchers (*ho epi tōn strōmatophulakōn*), whose excavations for the tent-poles dug deep enough to strike oil.[34] The existence of a royal tent for audience-giving by this date is alleged by Polyaenus, a second-century AD Macedonian writer, according to whom Alexander 'had it made' for use as a courtroom 'when deciding cases among the Bactrians, Hyrcanians and Indians'. Although this author's reputation for veracity is mixed, some of the entries in his collection of stratagems being 'historically valuable, others fictitious',[35] the particular of this tent's use as a 'courtroom' (*dikastērion*) is not self-evidently the invention of Polyaenus (see below). As it happens, the mention of Hyrcania fits with the text of Diodorus, who implies – as already noted – an initial introduction of court ceremony in two phases late in 330 BC, with an earlier phase preceding Alexander's part-adoption of Persian dress in Parthyaea.

---

[34] Appendix, A, no. 6 = Plut.*Al.*57.4; cf. Arr.4.15.7; Berve 1926, I: 18.
[35] J. B. Campbell in *OCD*[3], s.v.

As for the origin of the Susa tent, scholars have often assumed that it was the same tent as the one used by Alexander at Dium in 335/4 BC,[36] since both are described as 'one-hundred couch tents' (Appendix, A, nos. 1–5). This tent in turn may well have been a legacy from Philip, who perhaps acquired it during his years of intensive campaigning in Thrace. It could well have accompanied Alexander to Asia in 334 BC: his dinners and symposia on campaign are attested as early as the following winter (Plut.*Al.*17.5 (Phaselis in Lycia)), and tented accommodation for them must have been anticipated. On the other hand, in key respects Alexander's Susa tent sounds decidedly Persian: the richly embroidered tapestries and rugs, reminiscent of the tent of Mardonius (Hdt.9.82.1); the sky-like canopies (*ouraniskoi*), obviously derived from the circular *ouranos* of Persian royal tents (Appendix, A, nos. 3, 11); and the fifty supporting columns, recalling the hypostyle halls of Susa or Persepolis (Miller 1997: 51). Its Persian character is most straightforwardly explained on the view that it was, in fact, a Persian royal tent (so Miller 1997: 51): if not one of those captured after Issus in 333 BC (below), then another, perhaps the tent which accompanied Darius on his final, fatal, march in 330 BC (Curt.5.19.3); or, if not, then an older, Macedonian, royal tent was, at the least, now transformed by the incorporation of Persian elements (a version which would better accommodate the account of Polyaenus). As a temporary structure made up of different components, this tent could have been assembled in different ways, and its fittings could easily have seen further evolution – for instance, its linen hangings in 324 BC (Appendix, A, no. 1: *othonia*) recall the earlier gifts to Alexander of Indian linen (Curt.9.8.1, *linea vestis*).

Nowadays the well-documented tents of the Ottoman Turks perhaps best convey just how luxurious Alexander's royal tents may have been (Miller 1997: 50). Like the ancient Persians, the Turks in origin were Asian nomads, and in both societies the rulers' tents seem to have developed strikingly similar forms. The imperial tents of the sultans likewise depended for their imposing effect on size and magnificent decoration, including rich embroideries using precious metals. According to a European writer, in 1673 six hundred camels were needed to carry the sultan's two campaign tents. There are specific similarities to Alexander's Susa tent: the sultans' tents were also surrounded by a screen wall; they too were used for audiences, banquets and other festivities.[37]

---

[36] C. Bradford Welles in the Loeb Diodorus at 17.16.4; Murray 1996: 16; Savalli-Lestrade 1998: 299 n. 38.

[37] For pictures of Ottoman Turkish tents see www.turkishculture.org/tents/tents.html (with accompanying notes by Professor Nurhan Atasoy) (visited June 2004). Note in particular the

It remains to ask whether these various royal tents known to have been used by Alexander between late 330 and 324 BC were one and the same. The camp of Darius III at Issus (333 BC) included a complex of at least three royal tents (cf. Curt.3.13.11): one, in which Alexander took a bath, was for Darius' personal use (Plut.*Al.*20.6); another, 'worthy of admiration for its size and height', was used for feasting (Plut.*Al.*20.6); a third, next door, was for the use of Darius' wife and mother (Curt.3.12.3), and had its own forecourt (3.12.8; 10). It is argued below (pp. 99–101) that, in a development parallel to Alexander's initial adoption of Persian court ceremonial, from late in 330 BC his feasting style also underwent a Persian-style elaboration. Alexander also, from this date, was accompanied by a Persian-style harem (above). The whole spatial arrangement of Alexander's royal quarters must have undergone reorganisation and enlargement to accommodate these changes. It makes sense to assume no longer just one, but a whole complex of royal tents, some or all of them in some sense Persian in origin. It is conceivable that Curtius reflects this development when, after describing Alexander's initial adoption of Persian ceremonial in 330 BC, he thereafter invariably describes Alexander's itinerant accommodation with a new and more imposing term, '*regia*' or 'royal quarters', of which Alexander's personal tent was just one component.[38]

Feasts and audiences

What use did Alexander make of his feasting- and audience-tent in particular? One scholar has recently expressed surprise that Alexander 'chose to organise his festivities in a tent even though the Persian palaces were still standing' (Briant 2002: 258). This paradox is starkest for the tent's most famous outing at Susa in 324 BC, for the celebration of the 'mixed marriages': seemingly odd because Susa possessed a perfectly good royal palace which Alexander had left unscathed in 331 BC (Fredricksmeyer 2000: 148). In this particular case, an explanation will be canvassed later. But

---

miniature 'Tents at Okmeydani, Surname-i Vehbi, 1720', illustrating the imperial tent complex for a circumcision festivity: a hierarchy of imperial tents forming a complex, including four of graded size enclosed by circular screen walls. The largest has a separate entrance-tent.

[38] For Alexander's personal *tabernaculum* within the *regia* note 8.1.47; 2.5; 9.5.22 (the Cleitus episode at Maracanda, although Arr.4.8.9 and Plut.*Al.*51.4; 6 place this within a building); 9.5.22; 30 (Alexander's Mallian camp in 326 BC). In fairness, it cannot be excluded that Curtius' switch to '*regia*' is rhetorical, to emphasise the more 'royal' demeanour of Alexander which Curtius had just described disapprovingly (6.6.1–9) before the word makes its first appearance to describe Alexander's quarters (the Philotas episode in Drangiana: 6.7.6–8.23 *passim*).

the tent's purpose must anyway be seen in the broader chronological context of the use to which Alexander had put it since (on the view argued above) late in 330 BC. Its hundred-couch capacity made it suitable for his daily dining, which normally took place in the company of sixty or seventy of his inner circle, mostly Companions (Berve 1926, I: 13). As for state functions, one of these, certainly, was feasting, for which it had been used in India; this last was a special diplomatic event, noted as such by Curtius (Appendix, A, no. 9).

In addition, and no less importantly, Alexander used the tent for an activity denoted in the ancient sources by the Greek verbs *chrēmatizein*, 'transacting business', and *dikazein*, 'sitting in judgement'. The former verb is used in ancient descriptions (Appendix, A, nos. 3–5) of the tent's use for audiences at, once again, Susa in 324 BC. The use of the imperfect tense (*echrēmatizen*) suggests the volume of business which Alexander transacted on this occasion alone. It is unlikely that Susa was exceptional in this regard. At Babylon in the following year, according to Ephippus (*FGrH* 126 F 4 = Athen.12.537d), he also transacted business (*echrēmatise*), this time in a royal park[39] – again in state, sitting on a gold throne, flanked by couches with silver legs for the Companions. Berve (1926, I: 12) assumed that this 'business' mainly meant military affairs. But Plutarch (*Al.*23.2) paired 'attending to military business' (*suntattōn ti tōn polemikōn*) with 'judging' (*dikazōn*) in his description of Alexander's daily routine when not at war, and it was the requirements of 'judging', specifically among 'barbarians', which for Polyaenus explained the audience-tent's creation.

By 'judging' we should probably understand, as well as administrative activity specific to the field of 'laws', the whole gamut of administrative business which must have been put before Alexander for a decision. 'Petition-and-response' is a model of rule applied to the Roman imperial monarchy: 'the whole nature of the imperial entourage, with its remarkably limited resources and increasingly peregrinatory character, was shaped by the pressure to respond to initiatives from below' (Millar 1977: 617). This model seems to be applicable, at least to some extent, to the Persian empire too. Audience-giving was a fundamental aspect of royal governance under the Achaemenid kings, to the extent that the image of the king in audience has been claimed as the summation of Achaemenid rulership. Whenever they left their palaces, the Persian kings were the targets of petitioners.[40] Since what was taking place as Alexander progressed through the eastern provinces of the former Persian empire was nothing less than the replacement of one

[39] For the location note Arr.7.25.3.   [40] Briant 2002: 191 citing Xen.*Cyr*.8.3.19–23.

sovereignty with another, Alexander is likely to have found himself, willy-nilly, the heir to this traditional role of the Persian king. These audiences – one can hypothesise – would have given Alexander the opportunity to cultivate the local elites of central Asia, to exchange presents, and to present the public face of the new ruler, based on a carefully crafted self-image incorporating the tent and his newly adopted Persian royal ceremonial, along with heavy military show (below). That Persian royal audiences provided a specific model for Alexander, finally, is suggested by a (hostile) fragment of the Greek historian Ephippus. For Alexander's audience-giving he records the use of scented wine and unguents to perfume the floor, of incense, and a 'holy stillness (*euphēmia*) and silence' (*FGrH* 126 F 5 = Athen.12.538a). Censers placed before the enthroned monarch were a feature of Persian royal audiences (Briant 2002: 240), and it is likely enough that all these practices which Ephippus records were taken over from Persian court etiquette. The picture presented by Polyaenus, then, of Alexander 'deciding cases among the Bactrians, Hyrcanians and Indians', in spite of its Roman colouring,[41] has the ring of truth.

Upgrading the royal table

Another aspect of Persian rule which Alexander seems to have imitated from 330 on was the Persian king's famously lavish table. Despite the alleged simplicity of his personal eating habits, paradoxically Alexander became renowned for the magnificence of his dinners (Plut.*Al*.23). As we have seen, the tradition of lavish royal dining in Macedon went back to Philip. But under Alexander its lavishness reached new heights by an incremental process, the outlay 'increasing with his successes until it reached the sum of 10,000 drachmai' per dinner (Plut.*Al*.23.6). Dating the stages of this elaboration is hard. It was marked by the increasing numbers involved in preparation and service: we hear of 'officials in charge of the bakers and meat-cooks' (Plut.*Al*.23.3) and waiters under the orders of a *trapezokomos* or *trapezopoios* (Berve 1926, I: 41 with n. 6). Luxury in terms of expanding numbers of domestics was already marked among Alexander's Companions before the end of 330 BC, as shown by the masseurs and chamberlains acquired by Philotas before his execution (Plut.*Al*.40; Berve 1926, I: 42), and in these matters Alexander surely led rather than followed.

---

[41] Polyaenus, a syndic in the imperial courts at Rome, makes Alexander sound a bit like a Roman proconsul on his assize tour.

Other signs suggest that this increasing elaboration of the royal table coincided with Alexander's adoption of Persian court ceremony late in 330 BC. There is slight evidence for honorific positions in the king's table-service held – in the fashion of more recent courts, as already noted – by members of the Macedonian elite. As well as a 'chief cup-bearer', attested in 324/3 BC in the person of a young son of Alexander's viceroy in Europe (Plut.*Al*.74), we also hear of the *edeatros* or taster of royal dishes (Chares, *FGrH* 125 F 1 = Athen.4.171b–c). He in fact was a kind of lord high steward in charge of the whole service of the table.[42] This post was held by none other than Ptolemy, Alexander's childhood friend. Since Chares mentioned this appointment relatively early on in his history of Alexander, in the third of at least eleven books, it is reasonable to suppose, with Jacoby,[43] that the appointment belonged to Alexander's initial elaboration of his court in 330. Finally, Plutarch (*Al*.50.2) describes the arrival of 'some people bringing Greek fruit from the coast' in 328 BC when Alexander was in Maracanda (Samarkand). By this date at the latest, we can see the establishment of an aspect of the luxury of Alexander's table on which elsewhere Plutarch comments generally: the supply for royal delectation of 'the rarest fruits or fish from the coast' (*Al*.23.5–6).

This aspect of Alexander's dinners is strongly reminiscent of the dining practices of the Persian court. Greek contemporaries certainly saw similarities between the two styles of royal dining, and relative costs were explicitly compared (Ephippus, *FGrH* 126 F 2 = Athen.146c–d). Other details suggest conscious imitation: on one occasion at least (Susa) Alexander graded his guests at a feast according to royal Persian protocol: the more favoured ate inside, the less favoured in the courtyard;[44] the circular seating at the Opis feast in the same year was likewise a Persian arrangement (below). The office of *edeatros* was believed in later antiquity to render by a Greek word what in fact was a Persian usage.[45] Reasonably, then, some have seen here a Persian office,[46] or, if not, the reinvention of a traditional Macedonian office along Persian lines (Berve 1926, I: 39–40). Going back to the rare foodstuffs offered to Alexander, likewise the Persian king was supplied with food and drink

---

[42] Artemidorus of Tarsus (first century BC) cited by Athen.*Deipn*.; Aelius Dionysius (p. 151 Schwabe) cited by Eust.1403.40; Berve 1926, I: 39–40.

[43] *FGrH* 125 F 1 and F 4, commentary.

[44] Appendix, A, nos. 1–2; B, no. 7; Athen.12.538c; Briant 2002: 258. See below.

[45] *to men onoma Hellēnikon, hē de chreia Persikē*, according to the second-century AD grammarian Aelius Dionysius (p. 151 Schwabe), cited by Eust.1403.40; see Jacoby, commentary to *FGrH* 125 F 1.

[46] Briant 2002: 263; Berve 1926, I: 39–40 for the view that only its titular quality under Alexander was Persian-inspired.

from all over the empire: subjects 'anxious to curry regal favour would deliberately send delicacies to tempt the royal palate' (Strong 2002: 8). Plutarch's evidence, cited above, could at a pinch be argued to show that Alexander became heir to this Persian royal tradition, although Plutarch mentions only one part of the empire, the Greek 'coast' (*thalassa*), by which presumably he meant the seaboard of Asia Minor. Recent scholarship has emphasised the political and symbolic overtones of the Persian king's dinner: 'the supply of food and drink from all over the empire highlighted and embodied the domination of the king over his subjects' (Sancisi-Weerdenburg 1993: 298). Was Alexander aware of, and did he also seek to perpetuate, this ideological dimension to Persian royal dining? It is possible. At any rate, when Alexander decided to create a Persian-style court, he evidently decided – and for the same reasons – to re-create some of the display and aulic deference characteristic of the Persian royal style of dining as well.[47]

Timing and context of the adoption of Persian ceremonial

This section takes fuller stock of Alexander's timing in the initial elaboration of his court on Persian lines from late 330 BC onwards. The standard view is that the decision was a rational one, prompted by the murder of Darius III and the news shortly afterwards of the usurpation of the Persian throne by Bessus, an Achaemenid (Bosworth 1980). The political decision by a ruler to adopt an imposing court as a state-building device has parallels in other periods and places (see van Ess in this volume); for what it is worth (since Roman colouring may have crept in), ancient sources express the view that Alexander on this occasion was motivated by state interest (Plut.*Al.*47.3; Arr.7.29.4). What needs stressing is how far he took this elaboration of the trappings of his court. As well as the adoption of Persian ceremonial, Alexander's use of imposing Persian-style tents dates from this time, from which seems to date, as well, the growing splendour, Persian-style, of his table. Taken together, these initiatives seem more than a 'limited gesture' (Bosworth 1980: 8): they suggest a major turning point in Alexander's evolving strategy of state-building in Asia.

On the specifics of timing, if weight can be placed on the language of Diodorus, Alexander had already begun to introduce these changes *before* he adopted Persian-style dress in Parthyaea; and if Polyaenus is taken *au pied de*

---

[47] On the practical level, captured specialists from the service of the Persian king were available to help (Athen.12.608a).

la lettre, his feasting- and audience-tent was already in use in Hyrcania. The point may seem a small one: but these scraps can be construed to show that Alexander's decision was not only bigger in scope but also more premeditated than is sometimes allowed: at any rate, it was not just a contingent response to the news, arriving in Parthyaea, of Bessus' usurpation of Darius' throne (as argued by Bosworth 1980: 5–6). The true catalyst seems to have been the discovery of the murder of Darius some six weeks earlier, and Alexander's decision, made public soon after, to pursue the conquest of the eastern parts of Darius' empire (Bosworth 1988: 96–7). But it is hard to credit that he and his friends had never discussed future plans rather earlier: it had been over a year ago, following his victory at Gaugamela (331), since Alexander had taken a new royal title, 'king of Asia' (Fredricksmeyer 2000), and over a year since he had appointed his first non-western satrap of a newly conquered province (the Persian Mazaeus, put in charge of Babylonia: Arr.3.16.4) – the first step in a sustained attempt by Alexander to develop a hegemonic relationship with the ruling elite of the Persian empire (of which more shortly).

Social ranking, court ceremonial and obeisance

In a monarchical state with a pyramidal social structure, one recognised function of courts is 'rank allocation' at the top end of the social hierarchy. At public ceremonies, strict rules governing the order of precedence in such matters as seating served to display, and indeed construct, the relative ranking of the highest social strata (Winterling 1997: 153). From 331 BC Alexander's entourage had started to incorporate a tiny but growing number of high-status Persian/Iranian collaborators. This number was increased from late in 330 BC by Alexander's recruitment of high-ranking Persians to form a guard of honour at court.[48] Participation by high-ranking Persians in the daily life of the court is revealed in the ancient accounts of the drinking party at which Alexander attempted to introduce obeisance in 327 (Arr.4.12.2; Curt.8.7.22; see below). Indeed, the social, as well as political, dimension to Alexander's admission of Persians to his court should not be underestimated, given that 'Macedonian and Persian nobles had in common an aristocratic way of life . . . and values';[49] long ago Berve estimated that 'the number of leading orientals taking part in the campaigning must

[48] Fredricksmeyer 2000: 151 and 152 n. 45; see above.
[49] Briant 1985: 183 cited by Gregor 1997: 35 n. 31.

have been very important' (1926, I: 80). Once Persian ceremonial had been introduced at court late in 330, it could serve to display the relative ranking of these Persians alongside the Companions and other elite groups within the hegemonic class of his empire. As it happens, the clearest instance of ceremonial functioning in this way comes in 324 BC at the vast banquet for 9,000 diners (Arr.7.11.9) which Alexander celebrated at Opis on the Tigris river. On this occasion, according to Arrian, dining couches were organised in concentric circles centred on Alexander himself: the nearest circle comprised his 'Macedonians', the next 'Persians', the third 'any persons from the other peoples who took precedence for rank or any other high quality'.[50] In this hierarchical seating plan, the order of precedence radiated outwards from Alexander, with the 'Macedonians' assigned the places closest to him and thus the highest rank. Two points about these arrangements need more emphasis than they normally receive. First, feasting in concentric circles seems to have been a Persian custom, which Alexander on this occasion (and no doubt others, if we were better informed) had taken over. After Alexander's death, in 317/16 BC, it appears again in the detailed description of a feast at Persepolis hosted by Peucestas, the Macedonian satrap of Persis famed for his adoption of Persian ways.[51] Second, not only did the seating arrangements at Opis, as others have noticed, single out the Persians in Alexander's entourage by assigning them highest ranking after the 'Macedonians', but they also conferred no special distinction on Greeks *qua* Greeks; high-status Greek guests on this occasion (with the exception, no doubt, of ethnic Greeks among the Companions) sat in an undifferentiated mass with the 'other peoples'.[52]

Alexander's concern to honour the Persians, on this occasion over and above 'even' the Greeks, invites reappraisal of a more problematic episode which had occurred three years earlier: Alexander's attempted introduction of 'obeisance' (*proskunēsis*). This much-discussed episode (Bosworth 1995: 68–90) took place at a drinking party at court in spring 327 BC, when Alexander, in collusion with sympathetic members of his entourage, experimented with the introduction of this Persian custom at court for performance by his Macedonian and Greek, as well as his Persian, courtiers. 'Obeisance' (*proskunēsis*) was a term used by Greek authors to describe two quite different things (which the Greeks then confused). First, it denoted the gesture (or range of gestures) of veneration which Greeks performed before *agalmata* or images of deities in temples. Second, it embraced a variety of

---

[50] Arr.7.11.8–9; Badian 1958: 429–30.   [51] Diod.Sic.19.22.1–3.
[52] As noted by Brunt 1983: 240–1 nn. 7–8.

Persian gestures of greeting which differed according to the relative rank of those involved (Hdt.1.134). In this second context, for Greeks the word evoked above all the obeisance offered by subjects before the Persian king. Persian evidence confirms that obeisance was an essential preliminary to a royal Persian audience (Briant 2002: 222–3). The later Greek tradition took Alexander's attempted introduction of obeisance as a bid to be worshipped as a god; not only this, but at least one Greek on the spot, Alexander's official historian Callisthenes, refused to perform obeisance on this occasion, and there are grounds for assuming that his objection was religious.[53] Some powerful modern voices share this ancient Greek view, which has effectively hijacked the debate, both ancient and modern, about Alexander's intentions on this occasion.[54] On an alternative view, 'it is plausible to suppose that Al[exander] sought to introduce the practice among all his courtiers, only in order to create a greater measure of equality between Persian and western notables and thus to conciliate the Persians'.[55] Here two points are emphasised. First, even if Alexander was aware of the religious significance of obeisance for Greeks (as opposed to Macedonians), it is scarcely credible that Greeks were his first priority in 327. As the whole logic of his adoption of Persian court forms in 330 suggests, and seating arrangements at Opis confirm, Alexander was chiefly concerned in these years to use rank allocation to honour Persian nobles (and Asiatic elites more generally: see below on the Susians) who chose to collaborate with the invader. Moreover, this innovation was certainly more than a 'a purely technical reform' (Badian 1981: 52, paraphrasing the view of others): it went to the heart of the evolving representation of his state-building enterprise since late in 330 (more of this in the concluding section). Although the experiment took place in the relative informality of a routine drinking party, Alexander (on this argument) intended the act, if accepted, to be performed mainly on formal occasions, such as audiences, as in the old Persian court, when the implied parity of standing between Macedonian and Persian notables would have been witnessed by people outside the court.

The second point concerns the Macedonian (as opposed to the Greek) view of obeisance in the third quarter of the fourth century BC. The Macedonian Companion Leonnatus, who is cited as 'off-message' on this occasion, mocked the act – not an obviously religious reaction.[56] It is worth asking, then, how readily fourth-century BC Macedonians would have seen

---

[53] Badian 1981: 51–2.   [54] Badian 1981: 51–2; Bosworth 1995.

[55] Brunt 1976–83, I: 539; other refs.: Badian 1981: 40.

[56] Leonnatus in Arr.4.12.2; Polyperchon (wrongly) in Curt.8.5.22–4 (Badian 1981: 52 n. 38).

obeisance in religious (as opposed to more broadly cultural) terms. The case for a widespread Macedonian adherence at this date to the veneration of religious statues remains to be proven.[57] Major temples to house such images are conspicuously absent in the fourth-century BC homeland, not least at Dium, the pan-Macedonian religious centre (Spawforth 2006a: 34). Macedonian cult-buildings which pre-date Philip's reign have been excavated at Vergina and Dium. All three are small and, to judge from the remains as published, architecturally modest. The 'temple of Eukleia' at Vergina comprised a porch and a small inner building with bases for statues in each of the two far corners; the position between these on the central axis, where by this date a principal *agalma* would normally be found in a Greek temple, was reserved for an offering table (Andronicos 1984: 49–51). Two structures comparable in size and plan to the 'temple of Eukleia', dated to the late sixth century BC, have been found at Dium in a sanctuary of Demeter near that of Zeus; 'inside were wooden benches on which were placed dedications'; no traces of *agalmata* are reported from either building (Pandermalis 1997: 17–18; 1999: 61–2). None of these three buildings supports the view that the familiar Greek triad of *naos*, *agalma* and *bōmos* (see Burkert 1985: 50) was central to Macedonian religion before Alexander.[58] Turning to the sanctuary of Zeus at Dium, Polybius (4.62.2) implies that at the time of the Aetolian sack in 219 BC the roofed elements were limited to stoas; the excavations have uncovered a huge altar, but no sign of a temple. The enthroned Zeus on Alexander's coinage 'was most certainly not a particular statue' (Price 1991, I: 30), although here, if anywhere, one might expect to find the Zeus of Dium, had such a statue existed at the time.[59]

In sum on this point, the planners of the attempted introduction of obeisance in 327 BC certainly seem to have anticipated Macedonian objections, but they may not necessarily have expected these to be on religious grounds, if, as suggested here, Macedonians in 327 had not been in the habit of performing *proskunēsis* before *agalmata* back home. From a court perspective,

---

[57] For this Greek religious phenomenon see Scheer 2000.

[58] Pandermalis 1999: 44–51. Philippson claimed a temple for Dium, but cited no evidence: *RE* V.1 (1903) col. 833.

[59] A life-sized Demeter, an Artemis and a Core, said to be fourth-century BC, were found in the sanctuary of Demeter near Lete in 1936, but the precise archaeological context is unknown, and until or unless they can be shown to pre-date Philip and to have been what are traditionally called 'cult-statues' (as opposed, e.g, to offerings), their existence does not refute the argument presented here (Hatzopoulos 1994: 48, 123–7). The implications of this argument, if any, for Macedonian Hellenism cannot be pursued here; but Dodona, another *ethnos*-sanctuary on the Greek periphery, was likewise slow to adopt the cult of statues (Mee and Spawforth 2001: 379, 382). Whatever one makes of Philip's play with *agalmata* at Aegeae in 336 BC, he was chiefly concerned to impress the Greeks present on that occasion (Diod.Sic.16.91.6).

the issue for the Macedonians arguably boiled down to status: the implied equality with the defeated Persian nobility, to be displayed before the world on formal occasions, turned out to be an unacceptable assault on their sense of their social worth.

Conclusion: court and state-building

In assessing the increasingly symbolic weight which (on the view presented here) Alexander assigned to his court and its trappings from late 330 BC, one can sense the realities of the Macedonian position, or at least Alexander's perception of them, once the death of Darius highlighted his camp and army as the real centre of power for most of the former Persian empire. More than ever, Alexander from now on was engaged in the process of state-building even as he continued his conquest of the remaining Persian satrapies and sought out the 'usurper' Bessus. He was succeeding a monarchy which traditionally relied heavily on the projection of its claims to domination through a lavish court (Brosius in this volume). The compulsion on Alexander to present his newly evolving successor-régime in comparable terms must have been strong. The projection of 'stateliness', another classic function of monarchical courts, seemed to be required at this juncture, to be achieved in Alexander's case by a new level of aulic display, which placed before Asian observers images of military might, royal luxury and the ruler's symbolic pre-eminence, this last constituted by 'trappings' and by the ceremonial deference of a high-status entourage, including leading Persians. Anthropology has recognised this political dilemma: 'The state is invisible: it must be personified before it can be seen, symbolized before it can be loved, imagined before it can be conceived.'[60] One might go further and argue that the increasing resemblance of Alexander's court to that of the Persian kings was a function of the pressure to adopt a similar approach to the challenge of 'ruling' huge territories with rudimentary technologies of control, so that hill-tribes such as the Uxii in the Zagros mountains, under Alexander as much as under the later Achaemenids, may never have been properly subdued.[61] The Persian monarchy had evolved central symbols, ceremonial and a supporting ideology which together projected a royal image of divinely ordained omnipotence (Briant 2002). In some ways Alexander's self-representation from late 330 BC increasingly headed in a similar direction, at least in its use of display and ceremonial

---

[60] Clifford Geertz, cited by Muir 1997: 230.   [61] Note Badian 1985: 441–2 n. 2.

to create 'a strong impact on the senses' aimed at 'convey[ing] the essence of power' to the gamut of spectators, local and from further afield, at these courtly performances (Duindam 2003: 183).

In warming to the Persian model, Alexander's longer-term political conditioning was surely also a factor. He had grown up in an increasingly cosmopolitan court, and watched his father come to rule with the help of a multi-ethnic Companion elite (Theopompus, *FGrH* 115 F 224 = Athen.4.167b) over a state structurally similar to the Persian empire in that both were an agglomeration of 'peoples' (Kienast 1973: esp. 247–51). From the outset, Alexander may well have been unable to imagine his rule over Asia except in broadly similar terms.

As is well established, Alexander certainly had good political reasons for seeking to coopt the Persian nobility – a process begun in 331 BC with his appointment of Mazaeus (above). The Macedonians were a tiny minority in the former lands of the Persian king and some kind of consensual rule based on the winning over of the central and regional elites of the old empire was the only long-term hope for the stabilisation of the Macedonian conquest. The message implicit right from the start of his adoption of Persian court ceremonial in 330 was made explicit in 324 BC, when Alexander used a court festivity (the Opis banquet again) to proclaim publicly 'harmony and partnership in rule' (*homonoia kai koinōnia tēs archēs*, Arr.7.11.9) between Macedonians and Persians (Bosworth 1980).

The adoption of Persian court ceremonial not only offered people a sensory representation of Alexander's commitment to this ideal of 'partnership in rule'. Along with Alexander's adoption of an increasingly Persian style of feasting, it also sent out the clear signal that Persians were welcome at Alexander's court. The evidence for high-ranking Persians in his entourage has already been noted. Their physical presence was important if Alexander was to be in a position to imitate the famed 'open-handedness' or *poludōria* of the Persian kings, which served as a fundamental lubricant in the Persian court system (Brosius in this volume). Alexander was famously generous (Plut.*Al.*15.3; 39–41; 63), to the extent that he supposedly defined royal friendship as the acceptance of his gifts ('he could not regard as his friends those who wanted nothing of him', Plut.*Phoc.*18.4); his recorded gifts include land, houses, incense, apparel and gold plate, not to mention appointments. Alexander certainly used gift-giving for specific political ends: he was said to have 'conciliated with gifts' the Macedonians who disapproved of his adoption of Persian customs (*tais dōreais etherapeuen*, Diod.17.78.1). It is inconceivable that Persian nobles who attended his court were not rewarded, and seen to be rewarded, in this way, even if the specific evidence (except in the case of appointments) is hard to come by. Alexander's definition of friendship, if true, suggests that his generosity also had a symbolic value in creating, or cementing, ties and obligations with his elites (Asiatics included). One might compare early modern courts, where gifts were 'a means of enhancing the status of the recipient and of creating a social bond between ruler and the noblemen attending his court' (Asch 2003: 88–9).

Alexander's increasing remoteness as a result of the introduction of Persian court ceremonial surely also had a practical purpose. Access to Alexander had never been free. Routinely, it seems, rank-and-file Macedonians had to wait outside Alexander's tent to be escorted in by a Companion (in 330 BC: Curt.6.7.17), or by the duty bodyguard from the select group of seven mentioned earlier (in 326 BC: Arr.4.13.7). The Companions seem to have had a general right of access (Arr.5.28.3); but this privilege was probably linked to official duties, since even as high-ranking a figure as Philotas was said to visit the royal tent only twice daily at the time of his arrest (Arr.3.26.3; Berve 1926, I: 19). The adoption of Persian court ceremonial late in 330 BC clearly transformed the rules of access. This development was sufficiently marked by 328 BC that a leading Companion (Cleitus), as noted above, could complain that Macedonians had to beg Persians in order to approach the king (Plut.*Al.*51): the reference was to Alexander's Persian ushers. By 324 BC, it could be claimed, 'the number of his friends and servitors being so great, no one dared approach Alexander; such was the majesty associated with his person' (Phylarchus, *FGrH* 81 F 44 = Appendix, A, no. 3). In absolutist monarchies well-defined mechanisms controlling admission to the royal presence have served historically as a coping mechanism in the face of pressure from courtiers seeking access to the ruler. As the empire of which he was the human centre inexorably expanded, along with the business which it generated, including, crucially, the increasing numbers hoping to benefit from his favour (cf. Winterling 2004: 80), Alexander would have faced similar problems. The volume of business for his audiences suggested by the imperfect *echrēmatize* at Susa has already been noted. One result was (with little doubt) an increase in the brokering role of Alexander's inner circle (p. 85 above). Another was to compel the introduction of greater controls in the organisation of audience-giving. That Alexander (and his chamberlains) were doing just this is shown by the 'ingenious and methodical arrangements', as Bradford Welles called them, for Alexander's audiences at Babylon in 324. Diodorus alone preserves these interesting details: a schedule (*apographē*) was drawn up, according to which the king heard (*echrēmatise*) the embassies in order of subject matter: religion first;

then bearers of gifts; then disputes with neighbours; and so on. Significantly, although many embassies came from places outside Alexander's dominions, many communities from territory under Alexander's direct rule were also represented, including Macedonian envoys and ones from 'the peoples and cities, as well as the local rulers, of Asia'. That is to say, notwithstanding the administrative division of the kingdom into satrapies and (as Macedon effectively was) a viceroyalty, Alexander's subjects expected to approach their king in person.[62]

Going back to Alexander's Persian-style tents, their acquisition reflects the functional attractiveness of Persian 'court nomadism', which provided a very specific, and apt, model for Alexander and his itinerant centre. When the Persian king was on the move, 'the royal tent . . . became the centre of power', and in his travels the king 'showed off the might and wealth of the court and army' (Briant 2002: esp. 186–91).[63] All this was precisely what Alexander seems to have tried to do from late in 330 as he moved further east. Indeed, one reason for accepting Polyaenus' implied date for the creation of the feasting- and audience-tent is that it answers the question: where was Alexander's new court ceremonial performed? It required a setting of commensurate grandeur and stateliness which nonetheless could be conjured up in an army camp: a state tent *à la Perse* was the obvious solution. As Polyaenus, with more than a touch of Greek condescension, puts it: a 'brilliant courtroom suitable for a general, astonishing the barbarians . . . by [its] appearance' (Appendix, A, no. 4).[64]

This emphasis by Polyaenus on Alexander 'the general' specifically glossed the marked projection of military authority in the audience-tent ceremonial which he had just described. Since it was embedded in an army camp, Alexander's itinerant court inevitably had a pronounced military character; and anyway the routine presence of bodyguards at Alexander's feasts (Arr.4.8.8–9; Plut.*Al*.51.5–6) reminds us that the physical security of the king was a traditional aspect of the Macedonian royal court – quite apart from any additional measures felt necessary in the context of Asia. But the ancient accounts of the audience-giving at Susa reveal the extent to which a formidable display of the powers of coercion at Alexander's disposal had become integral to his 'image-management'. This is hardly surprising: army processions, as noted earlier, were already a feature of Alexander's progress through Asia Minor

---

[62] Diod.Sic.17.113.1–4, citing the editor on p. 453, n. 3 of the Loeb edition.

[63] Nurham Atasoy (above n. 36) makes similar points about Ottoman imperial nomadism.

[64] Alexander's itinerant use of this tent for audiences and feasts, on the reconstruction offered here, affords a rather more dynamic picture of his interaction with the Iranians from that put forward in the most recent discussion of Alexander and the Persians (Brosius 2003).

and Egypt; and right from the start Alexander had openly proclaimed the spear as the legitimation of his assault on Persian territory (Diod.Sic.17.17.1–2). By the time of Susa, Alexander's command of the military resources of Asia allowed for a more nuanced symbolism. The array of elephants, to be sure, may have had straightforward overtones of 'shock and awe'. But the parading of Persian and other Iranian troops in and around the audience-tent conveyed a consensual, multi-ethnic feel to Alexander's army, one which chimed both with local memories of the ethnically composite army of the Achaemenid kings, and also with Alexander's self-proclaimed quest for 'harmony and partnership in rule' with the Persians in particular (above). Finally, although the military parade at Susa reflected the increasing momentum of Alexander's enrolment of Iranian manpower in the last years of the reign, his first recruitment of a Persian guard of honour went back (as seen earlier) to late 330 BC, and presupposes the ceremonial deployment of these troops from that time onwards.

The broad aims of Alexander's adoption of court ceremonial are easier to evaluate than its consequences. It is clear, for a start, and this is a key point which the chapter seeks to make, that Alexander did not waver in the importance, indeed centrality, which he attached to his court ceremonial as a political tool in this respect. He delayed until 327 BC the attempted introduction of obeisance (above), which, on the view taken here, was intended as a ceremonial representation of the *koinōnia* or commonality of the Macedonian and Persian components in Alexander's new imperial elite. This delay presumably reflected Alexander's heedfulness of the hostility to the Iranian rapprochement in some Macedonian quarters, and the consequent need for a graduated approach (cf. Diod.Sic.17.77.7). After the obeisance episode Alexander proceeded to the invasion of India, returning to the central regions of his empire in 325/4 BC. The use of the court as a medium for cultivating the Iranians now resumed. In 324 BC he conferred on 'select Persians' the title of 'kinsman' (*sungenēs*), a Persian distinction, along with the equally Persian privilege of kissing the king.[65] But the weddings between Alexander and the Macedonian Companions and brides of royal and noble

---

[65] Arr.7.11.1; 6–7; Fredricksmeyer 2000: 156–7. The usual view that 'Kinsman' was a title taken over from the Persian court has been questioned by Savalli-Lestrade 1998: 395–8, who rejects the authenticity of the alleged 15,000 '*cognati regis*' in Darius III's army in 333 BC (Curt.3.3.14) on the grounds that they were too many to be real kinsmen. But this number of royal kinsmen generated by a polygamous lineage in power by this date for over two centuries is not inherently improbable when compared with the estimated 73,418 members of the Chinese imperial clan in 1915, after nearly three centuries of Qing rule: Rawski 1998: 94. Briant (2001: 108) does not agree that the passage should be 'evacuated from the Achaemenid dossier'.

Persian stock, celebrated at Susa with a great feast in the state tent, are the eye-catching item here.[66]

It is on this occasion that we are given a unique glimpse of the integrating function of the court at the level of Asian local, rather than central, elites. On this occasion Alexander made gifts of purple clothing to 500 men of Susa – local notables presumably – and assigned them places in the audience-ceremonial (Appendix, A, no. 4). In passing and in the same connection, one would dearly like to know more about Alexander's hunts in Asia, where boar (Curt.8.6.7) and lions were among his quarry. The royal lion-hunt was a traditional symbol of royal power both in Macedon and in Asia.[67] In other periods and places, rulers' hunts have been an aspect of central negotiation with local elites, providing lower-ranking notables with opportunities to come into close contact with the ruler and his court by following the hunt themselves.[68] Was this a traditional aspect of Persian royal hunts, and was it one which Alexander's hunts in Asia took over?

In sum, it is arguably hard to find a much clearer affirmation from classical antiquity of the political importance attached by a clear-sighted monarch to his court as an instrument of power. In a book on courts, it would be useful to be able to point to a clear consequence of this emphasis by Alexander on the court. It is clear that, in the years immediately prior to his death, circumstances had led him to reduce – at least for the time being – his use of Iranian satraps (Bosworth 1980: 9, 13). However, whether in some larger sense his construction of his state as a joint Macedonian and Persian project had 'succeeded' or 'failed' at the time of his death is sufficiently unclear in the sources for modern historians to have opposing views. Just to canvass some recent scholarship, on one view '[h]is success was particularly remarkable with Medes and Persians' (Hammond 1989: 226); on another, 'the vision of a new empire based upon a Macedonian–Persian elite failed'.[69] What is

---

[66] Alexander's avoidance of the Persian royal palace when holding court at Susa (above), and preference on this occasion for his state tent, may perhaps be explained by his lingering weather eye on Greek opinion, since for Greeks Susa had always been far more a symbol of the old Persian power than Persepolis.

[67] Palagia 2000: 181–4; Briant 2002: 297–9.

[68] Compare Rawski 1998: 22 on contacts between the lower-ranking members of the Inner Asian elites and the Qing emperors during imperial hunts. The same point could be made about Bourbon royal hunts in the Île-de-France.

[69] Brosius 2003: 192. This position is in danger of becoming a topos, not always in accordance with the evidence. For instance, the mixed Macedonian/Persian marriages at Susa have been claimed as at best a 'limited success' (2003: 176–7). But of the 'around eighty' Iranian noblewomen married off to Macedonian Companions in this way (Arr.7.4.6), precisely one (Amastris: Berve 1926, II: no. 50) is certainly known to have been abandoned by her Macedonian husband (Craterus), although, since she ended up as the wife of Lysimachus,

undeniable is that within seven years of the first introduction of Persian court trappings Alexander was dead. Historiographical justice probably requires that we register a *non liquet* as to how his state-building would have fared had he ruled for as long as, say, his great predecessor in Asia as imperial conqueror, Cyrus the Great – around twenty-seven years.

Appendix: Alexander's state tents

A. The ancient texts

[1] The wedding tent. Chares, *FGrH* 125 F 4 = Athen.538b-539a (late third century BC):

Χάρης δ ἐν τῇ δεκάτῃ τῶν περὶ Ἀλέξανδρον ἱστοριῶν 'ὅτε,' φήσιν, 'εἶλε Δαρεῖον, γάμους συνετέλεσεν ἑαυτοῦ τε καὶ τῶν ἄλλων φίλων, ἐνενήκοντα καὶ δύο θαλάμους κατασκευασάμενος ἐν τῷ αὐτῷ τόπῳ. ἦν δὲ οἶκος ἑκατοντάκλινος, ἐν ᾧ ἑκάστη ἦν κλίνη κεκοσμημένη στολῇ γαμικῇ εἴκοσι μνῶν ἀργυρᾶ· ἡ δὲ αὐτοῦ χρυσόπους ἦν. συμπαρέλαβεν δὲ εἰς τὸ συμπόσιον καὶ τοὺς ἰδιοξένους ἅπαντας καὶ κατέκλινεν ἀντιπροσώπους ἑαυτῷ τε καὶ τοῖς ἄλλοις νυμφίοις, τὴν δὲ λοιπὴν δύναμιν πεζήν τε καὶ ναυτικὴν καὶ τοὺς πρεσβείας καὶ τοὺς παρεπιδημοῦντας ἐν τῇ αὐλῇ. κατεσκεύαστο δὲ ὁ οἶκος πολυτελῶς καὶ μεγαλοπρεπῶς ἱματίοις τε καὶ ὀθονίοις πολυτελέσιν, ὑπὸ δὲ ταῦτα πορφυροῖς καὶ φοινικοῖς χρυσουφέσιν. τοῦ δὲ μένειν τὴν σκηνὴν ὑπέκειντο κίονες εἰκοσαπήχεις περίχρυσοι καὶ διάλιθοι καὶ περιάργυροι. περιεβέβληντο δὲ ἐν τῷ περιβόλῳ πολυτελεῖς αὐλαῖαι ζωωτοὶ καὶ διάχρυσοι, κανόνας ἔχουσαι περιχρύσους καὶ περιργύρους. τῆς δ αὐλῆς ἦν τὸ περίμετρον στάδιοι τέσσαρες.'

Chares in the tenth book of his *Histories of Alexander* says: 'When he overcame Darius, he concluded marriages of himself and of his friends besides, constructing ninety-two bridal chambers in the same place. The structure was large enough for a hundred couches, and in it every couch was adorned with nuptial coverings, and was made of silver worth twenty minae; but his own couch had supports of gold. He also included in his invitation to the banquet all his personal friends and placed them on couches opposite himself and the other bridegrooms, while the rest of his forces, both land and naval, he entertained in the courtyard with the foreign embassies and tourists. Moreover the structure was decorated sumptuously and magnificently with

another of Alexander's Macedonian Companions and subsequently a king (Brosius 2003: 177 n. 13 with refs.), even she is hardly evidence for a failed experiment.

expensive draperies and fine linens, and underfoot with purple and crimson rugs interwoven with gold. To keep the pavilion firmly in place there were columns thirty feet high, gilded and silvered and studded with jewels. The entire enclosure was surrounded with rich curtains having animal patterns interwoven in gold, their rods being overlaid with gold and silver. The perimeter of the courtyard measured four stadia.' (Loeb translation by C. B. Gulick, 1933)

[2] The wedding tent. Aelian, *Varia Historia* 8.7 (early third century AD):

Ἀλέξανδρος ὅτε Δαρεῖον εἷλε, γάμους εἱστία καὶ ἑαυτοῦ καὶ τῶν φίλων. ἐνενήκοντα δὲ ἦσαν οἱ γαμοῦντες καὶ ἰσάριθμοι τούτοις οἱ θάλαμοι. ἦν δὲ ὁ ἀνδρὼν ὁ ὑποδεχόμενος καὶ ἑστιῶν αὐτοὺς ἑκατοντάκλινος· καὶ ἑκάστη κλίνη ἀργυρόπους ἦν, ἡ δὲ αὐτοῦ χρυσόπους, καὶ κεκόσμηντο πᾶσαι ἁλουργοῖς καὶ ποικίλοις ἱματίοις ὑφῆς βαρβαρικῆς μεγατίμου. συμπαρέλαβε δὲ εἰς τὸ συμπόσιον καὶ τοὺς ἰδιοξένους καὶ κατέκλινεν ἀντιπροσώπους ἑαυτῷ. ἐν δὲ τῇ αὐλῇ εἱστιῶντο αἵ τε ἄλλαι δυνάμεις, αἱ πεζαὶ καὶ αἱ ναυτικαὶ καὶ οἱ ἱππεῖς, καὶ αἱ πρεσβεῖαι δὲ εἱστιῶντο καὶ οἱ παρεπιδημοῦντες Ἕλληνες.

When Alexander captured Darius he celebrated his own marriage and that of his friends. The number of people marrying was ninety, and the bridal chambers equal in number. The hall for the reception and banquet had one hundred couches. Each couch had silver feet, except his own, which had gold; they were all decorated with purple or embroidered cloth, of a weave much prized among the barbarians. He took his personal guests from foreign states to the banquet and had them seated facing him. In the courtyard there was a feast for the other forces, the infantry, marines, and cavalry. Ambassadors and Greeks resident locally were at the feast. (Loeb, translation by N. G. Wilson, 1997)

[3] The audience tent. Phylarchus, *FGrH* 81 F 44 = Athen.141f–142f (third century BC):

τὰς δὲ χρυσᾶς πλατάνους καὶ τὴν χρυσῆν ἄμπελον ὑφ' ἣν οἱ Περσῶν βασιλεῖς ἐχρημάτιζον πολλάκις καθήμενοι . . . ἐλάττω φησὶν ὁ Φύλαρχος φαίνεσθαι τῆς καθ' ἡμέραν ἑκάστοτε γινομένης παρ' Ἀλεξάνδρῳ δαπάνης. ἦν γὰρ αὐτοῦ ἡ σκηνὴ κλινῶν ρ', χρυσοῖ δὲ κίονες ν' κατεῖχον αὐτήν. οἱ δὲ ὑπερτείνοντες οὐρανίσκοι διάχρυσοι ποικίλμασιν ἐκπεπονημένοι πολυτελέσιν ἐσκέπαζον τὸν ἄνω τόπον. καὶ πρῶτοι μὲν Πέρσαι φ' μηλοφόροι περὶ αὐτὴν ἐντὸς εἰστήκεσαν πορφυραῖς καὶ μηλίναις ἐσθῆσιν ἐξησκημένοι· μετὰ δὲ τούτους τοξόται τὸν ἀριθμὸν χίλιοι, οἱ μὲν φλόγινα ἐνδεδυκότες, οἱ δὲ ὑσγινοβαφῆ, πολλοὶ δὲ καὶ κυάνεα εἶχον περιβόλαια. προεστήκεσαν δὲ τούτων ἀργυράσπιδες Μακεδόνες πεντακόσιοι. κατὰ δὲ μέσην τὴν σκηνὴν χρυσοῦς ἐτίθετο δίφρος, ἐφ᾽ οὗ καθήμενος ἐχρημάτιζεν ὁ Ἀλέξανδρος τῶν σωματοφυλάκων πανταχόθεν ἐφεστηκότων. ἔξωθεν δὲ κύκλῳ τῆς σκηνῆς τὸ τῶν ἐλεφάντων ἄγημα διεσκευασμένον ἐφειστήκει καὶ Μακεδόνες χίλιοι Μακεδονικὰς στολὰς ἔχοντες, εἶτα μύριοι Πέρσαι, τό τε τὴν πορφύραν ἔχον πλῆθος εἰς πεντακοσίους ἦν, οἷς Ἀλέξανδρος ἔδωκε φορεῖν τὴν στολὴν ταύτην. τοσούτην δὲ ὄντων καὶ τῶν φίλων καὶ τῶν θεραπευόντων οὐδεὶς ἐτόλμα προσπορεύεσθαι Ἀλεξάνδρῳ τοιοῦτον ἐγεγόνει τὸ περὶ αὐτὸν ἀξίωμα.

Moreover, the famous plane-trees of gold, even the golden vine under which the Persian kings often sat and held court ... appeared to be of less worth, says Phylarchus, than the expense lavished daily on all occasions at Alexander's court. For his pavilion alone contained a hundred couches and was supported by fifty golden uprights. The canopies stretched over the upper part to cover the whole were elaborately worked with gold in sumptuous embroideries. Inside, all round it, stood first of all five hundred Persians, Apple-bearers, with gay uniforms of purple and quince-yellow; after them bowmen to the number of a thousand, some dressed in flame-colour, others in crimson; but many, too, had mantles of dark blue. At the head of these stood five hundred Silver-Shields, Macedonians. In the centre of the pavilion was placed a golden chair, sitting on which Alexander held court with his bodyguard stationed close on all sides. Outside the tent the elephant-division was posted near in a circle with full equipment, also a thousand Macedonians in Macedonian uniform, next ten thousand Persians, and the large body, amounting to five hundred, who wore the purple; for Alexander had granted them the privilege of wearing this garment. And the number of his friends and servitors being so great, no one dared to approach Alexander; such was the majesty associated with his person. (Loeb translation by C. B. Gulick, 1933)

[4] The audience tent. Polyaenus, *Strategemata* 4.3.24 (mid-second century AD):

Ἀλέξανδρος ἐν μὲν τοῖς Μακεδόσιν ἢ ἐν τοῖς Ἕλλησι δικάζων μέτριον καὶ δημοτικὸν ἔχειν τὸ δικαστήριον ἐδοκίμαζεν, ἐν δὲ τοῖς βαρβάροις λαμπρὸν καὶ στρατηγικόν, ἐκπλήσσων τοὺς βαρβάρους καὶ τῷ τοῦ δικαστηρίου σχήματι. ἐν γοῦν Βάκτροις καὶ Ὑρκανίοις καὶ Ἰνδοῖς δικάζων εἶχε τὴν σκηνὴν ὧδε πεποιημένην. ἡ σκηνὴ τὸ μέγεθος ἦν κλινῶν ἑκατόν· χρύσεοι κίονες ὑπετίθεντο αὐτῇ πεντήκοντα. ὑπερτείνοντες οὐρανίσκοι διάχρυσοι,

ποικίλμασιν ἐκπεπονημένοι, τὸν ἄνω τόπον ἐσκέπαζον. Πέρσαι μὲν πρῶτοι πεντακόσιοι μηλοφόροι περὶ τὴν σκηνὴν ἐντὸς ἵσταντο πορφυραῖς καὶ
μηλίναις ἐσθῆσιν ἐξεσκημένοι. μετὰ δὲ τοὺς μηλοφόρους τοξόται τὸν ἴσον
ἀριθμὸν ἔχοντες ταῖς ἐσθῆσι διήλλαττον· οἱ μὲν γὰρ αὐτῶν φλόγινα, οἱ δὲ
κυάνεα, οἱ δὲ ὑσγινοβαφῆ περιεβέβληντο. τούτων προστάντο Μακεδόνες
ἀργυράσπιδες πεντακόσιοι τῶν μεγίστων ἀνδρῶν. κατὰ δὲ τὸ μέσον τῆς
σκηνῆς ὁ χρυσοῦς ἔκειτο θρόνος, ἐφ'οὗ προκαθήμενος ἐχρημάτιζεν· οἱ σωμα-
τοφύλακες ἐφεστήκεσαν ἑκατέρωθεν τοῦ βασιλέως δικάζοντος. ἐν κύκλῳ τῆς
σκηνῆς τὸ τῶν ἐλεφάντων ἄγημα διεσκευασμένον ἐφεστήκει καὶ Μακεδόνες
χίλιοι στολὰς Μακεδονικὰς ἔχοντες. ἐπὶ δὲ τούτοις πεντακόσιοι Σούσιοι
πορφυροσχήμονες, καὶ μετὰ τούτους ἐν κύκλῳ πάντων Πέρσαι μύριοι (Περσῶν) οἱ κάλλιστοι καὶ μέγιστοι, κεκαλλωπισμένοι παντὶ κόσμῳ Περσικῷ,
πάντες ἀκινάκας ἔχοντες. τοιόνδε ἦν Ἀλεξάνδρου τὸ δικαστήριον ἐν τοῖς
βαρβάροις.

When deciding legal cases among the Macedonians or Greeks, Alexander preferred to have a modest and common courtroom, but among the barbarians he preferred a brilliant courtroom suitable for a general, astonishing the barbarians even by the courtroom's appearance. When deciding cases among the Bactrians, Hyrcanians and Indians he had a tent made as follows: the tent was large enough for one hundred couches; fifty gold pillars supported it; embroidered gold canopies, stretched out above, covered the place. Inside the tent five hundred Persian Apple Bearers stood first, dressed in purple and yellow clothing. After the Apple Bearers stood an equal number of archers in different clothing, for some wore flame-coloured, some dark blue, and some scarlet. In front of these stood Macedonian Silver Shields, five hundred of the tallest men. In the middle of the tent sat the gold throne, on which he sat to give audiences. Bodyguards stood on each side when the king heard cases. In a circle around the tent stood the corps of elephants Alexander had equipped, and one thousand Macedonians wearing Macedonian apparel. Next to these were five hundred Susians dressed in purple, and after them, in a circle around them all, ten thousand Persians, the handsomest and tallest (of Persians), adorned entirely with Persian decorations, and all carrying short swords. Such was Alexander's courtroom among the barbarians. (translation by P. Krentz and E. Wheeler)

[5] The audience tent. Aelian, *Varia Historia* 9.3 (early third century AD):

αὐτῷ δὲ Ἀλεξάνδρῳ ἡ μὲν σκηνὴ ἦν κλινῶν ἑκατόν, χρυσοῖ δὲ κίονες πεντήκοντα διειλήφεσαν αὐτὴν καὶ τὸν ὄροφον αὐτῆς ἀνεῖχον, αὐτὸς δὲ ὁ

ὄροφος διάχρυσος ἦν καὶ ἐκπεπόνητο ποικίλμασι πολυτελέσι. καὶ πρῶτοι μὲν Πέρσαι πεντακόσιοι οἱ καλούμενοι μηλοφόροι περὶ αὐτὴν ἐντὸς εἰστήκεσαν πορφυρᾶς καὶ μηλίνας ἠσθημένοι στολάς· ἐπ' αὐτοῖς δὲ τοξόται χίλιοι, φλόγινα ἐνδεδυκότες καὶ ὑσγινοβαφῆ· πρὸ δὲ τούτων οἱ ἀργυράσπιδες πεντακόσιοι Μακεδόνες. ἐν μέσῃ δὲ τῇ σκηνῇ χρυσοῦς ἐτίθετο δίφρος καὶ ἐπ' αὐτῷ καθήμενος Ἀλέξανδρος ἐχρημάτιζε, περιεστώτων αὐτῷ πανταχόθεν τῶν σωματοφυλάκων. περῄει δὲ τὴν σκηνὴν περίβολος, ἔνθα ἦσαν Μακεδόνες χίλιοι καὶ Πέρσαι μύριοι. καὶ οὐδεὶς ἐτόλμα ῥᾳδίως προσελθεῖν· αὐτῷ πολὺ γὰρ ἦν τὸ ἐξ αὐτοῦ δέος ἀρθέντος ὑπὸ φρονήματος καὶ τύχης εἰς τυραννίδα.

Alexander's own tent could accommodate a hundred beds. Fifty gold pillars divided it and supported the roof, which was gilded and expensively embroidered. Inside it stood in line first of all five hundred Persians, called the apple bearers, wearing cloaks of purple and quince yellow; then came a thousand archers dressed in flame colour and scarlet. In front of these were the five hundred Macedonians with silver shields. In the middle of the tent was a golden throne, on which Alexander sat to transact business, surrounded on all sides by bodyguards. An enclosure wall around the tent was manned by a thousand Macedonians and ten thousand Persians. No one dared approach him without good reason, as he aroused great fear; his pride and good fortune had raised him to the position of a tyrant. (Loeb, translation by N. G. Wilson, 1997)

[6] Alexander's tent on the River Oxus, 328 BC. Plutarch, *Life of Alexander* 57.4 (around AD 100):

ὁ γὰρ ἐπὶ τῶν στρωματοφυλάκων τεταγμένος ἀνὴρ Μακεδών, ὄνομα Πρόξενος, τῇ βασιλικῇ σκηνῇ χώραν ὀρύττων παρὰ τὸν Ὦξον ποταμὸν ἀνεκάλυψε πηγὴν ὑγροῦ λιπαροῦ καὶ πιμελώδους·

The Macedonian, namely, who was set over those in charge of the royal equipage, Proxenus by name, as he was digging a place for the king's tent along the river Oxus, uncovered a spring of liquid which was oily and fatty (etc.). (Loeb translation by B. Perrin, 1949)

[7] The royal tent at the Battle of the river Hydaspes, 326 BC. Curtius, *History of Alexander the Great* 8.13.20 (?first century AD):

Alexander in diversa parte ripae statui suum tabernaculum iussit assuetamque comitari ipsum cohortem ante id tabernaculum stare et omnem apparatum regiae magnificentiae hostium oculis de industria ostendi.

Alexander ordered his tent to be pitched elsewhere on the river bank, the unit usually in attendance on him to stand guard before it, and all the sumptuous trappings of royalty to be deliberately flaunted before the enemy's eyes. (translated by J. Yardley, 1984)

[**8**] A royal tent afloat on the River Hydraortes, 326 BC. Curtius, *History of Alexander the Great* 9.6.1 (?first century AD):

duobus navigiis iunctis, statui in medium undique conspicuum tabernaculum iussit.

[Alexander] ordered two ships to be lashed together, and his tent to be set up in the centre.

[**9**] A royal tent used in a banquet for Indian tribes, 326/5 BC. Curtius, *History of Alexander the Great* 9.7.15 (?first century AD):

Invitatis deinde ad epulas legatis gentium regulisque, exornari convivium iussit. c aurei lecti modicis intervallis positi erant, lectis circumdederat aulaea purpura auroque fulgentia, quidquid aut apud Persas vetere luxu aut apud Macedonas nova inmutatione corruptum erat, confusis utriusque gentis vitiis, in illo convivio ostendens.

Alexander then invited the ambassadors and petty kings of the two tribes to a banquet and had a sumptuous feast prepared for them. A hundred gold couches were set out a short distance from each other, around which he had set tapestries glittering with purple and gold. In that banquet he put on show all the decadence that had long existed among the soft-living Persians or had been recently acquired by the Macedonians, thus combining the vices of the two peoples. (translated by J. Yardley, 1984)

[**10**] Elements of the tent in Rome. Pliny, *Historia Naturalis* 34.48 (first century AD):

Alexandri quoque Magni tabernaculum sustinere traduntur solitae statuae, ex quibus duae ante Martis Ultoris aedem dicatae sunt, totidem ante regiam.

It is also said that the tent of Alexander the Great was regularly erected with {four} statues as tent-poles, two of which have now been dedicated to stand in front of the temple of Mars the Avenger and two in front of the Royal Palace. (Loeb, translation by H. Rackham, 1952; 'four' is not in the Latin)

[11] The *ouranos* of Persian royal tents. Photius, *Lexicon*, s.v. οὐρανός (ninth century AD):

Πέρσαι δὲ τὰς βασιλείους σκηνὰς καὶ αὐλὰς, ὧν τὰ καλύμματα κυκλοτερῆ, οὐρανούς.

In Persia the royal tents and courts, with circular ceilings, (like) skies.

B. Commentary

1. Chares, Alexander's chamberlain (*eisangeleus*), from whom Aelian's account [2] patently derives, described in the tenth book of his *Histories* the tent used for the wedding feast at Susa in 324 [1]. Phylarchus, Polyaenus and Aelian (again), based ultimately on a primary source which is lost, described Alexander's audience tent [3–5]. The two tents were one and the same, as seen long ago (Jacoby's commentary to Chares, F 4).

2. The use of the imperfect ἐχρημάτιζε of Alexander holding audience shows that the original text which passages 3–5 reflect was not describing a specific audience, but a specific run of audiences. The five hundred Susians (Polyaenus) were presumably recruited during Alexander's stay at Susa in 324. So this is a description of Alexander's audience-giving while at Susa, as seen by Bosworth (1980: 8).

3. Jacoby (ibid.), following Droysen, assumed that book 10 of Chares' lost history was the source for the descriptions of *both* tents. If so, Chares must have described the tent's fittings at Susa twice in the same book: once in his account of the wedding, and once in a description of Alexander's audience-giving. Anything is possible, but this repetition seems a bit odd. Moreover, while Chares gives the height of the tent's columns but not their number, the description drawn on by Phylarchus, Polyaenus and Aelian does the reverse. Therefore this description probably derived from another author. The obvious candidate is Ephippus, who also described Alexander giving audience at Babylon (*FGrH* 126 F 4). Its predictable association with tyranny in Aelian's version, if not his own interpretation, would suit this attribution, given Ephippus' marked hostility to Alexander (Pearson 1960: 63). By contrast, the Macedonian patriotism of Polyaenus seems to have toned down this judgement.

4. Polyaenus includes two details about the audience-tent not found in Phylarchus or Aelian: (1) that Alexander had it specially made, and (2) that it served as his 'court-room' among 'the Bactrians, Hyrcanians and Indians'. Here Polyaenus refers sketchily to the years 330–326 BC, during which Alexander did indeed campaign in Hyrcania (330 BC), Bactria

(329–327 BC) and India (327–326 BC). Plutarch (*Al.*45.1) places his initial adoption of Persian court-ceremonial in autumn 330, immediately after his campaign in Hyrcania and during his stay in Parthyaea (Bosworth 1980: 5–6). The acquisition of the tent at this juncture would then have coincided with Alexander's initial elaboration of his court. Miller (1997: 51) pointed out that the Susa tent 'so well parallels the Achaemenid tradition in palace architecture that it may have been the tent of the Persian king'. For the several Persian royal tents which fell into Alexander's hands, see above, pp. 96–7.

5. Bosworth (1980: 8) doubted whether 'such a mammoth structure could have accompanied Alexander on all his travels'. The whole point about tents, however, is that they can be disassembled. Moreover, the royal baggage train did not follow Alexander everywhere. Later in 330, for instance, in the campaign against the Tapuri, he separated from 'the waggons and the baggage-train' (Arr.3.23.2); and in 328 BC, during the second invasion of Sogdiana, 'the royal service' (*basilikē therapeia*) was left behind at Zariaspa (Arr.4.16.6; Berve 1926, I: 25). On the other hand, the 'royal equipment' (*basilikē paraskeuē*), along with women, children and transport animals, was sufficiently indispensible that it followed Alexander on his gruelling march across the Gedrosian desert in 326/5 BC (Arr.6.25.5).

6. Polyaenus illustrated the use of the audience-tent in 330–326 BC with a description specific to 324 BC. In this sense, at any rate, 'his information is garbled to some extent' (Bosworth 1980: 8). One would like to know whether this was the only detailed description of the audience-tent to which he had access. The tent itself may have been refurbished after the return from India, especially if it had formed part of the royal baggage train 'swept away' by flood-water in the Gedrosian desert (Arr.6.25.5). As suggested above (p. 89), it was not necessarily the case that the ceremonial for the audiences at Susa was more impressive than in the early days of the tent's use, although the associated show of military force had now evolved to include large numbers of Persian troops in parade-uniforms, as well as Indian elephants. Then again, there were any number of eye-witnesses at Susa, Greek as well as Macedonian. The source of Polyaenus' information, both the detailed description and the tent's prior history, is uncertain. Wöfflin (1860; cited by Krentz and Wheeler 1994) thought of Phylarchus. But the specificity of Polyaenus' 'Susians', where Phylarchus simply has a 'large body', suggests that Polyaenus was closer to the original than Phylarchus. Polyaenus was himself a native of Macedonia, where interest in Alexander was marked in the early Roman empire (Spawforth 2006b: 17–18), and presumably he had access to a fair amount of the earlier Greek literature on the king. Aelian's version, while simplified, has a detail not found in the other two, namely,

the *peribolos* or screen wall which enclosed the tent, a fact which seems to exclude his direct use of Athenaeus (*pace* N. G. Wilson, Loeb, p. 285, note a). Since the same material about the luxury of the Companions precedes the tent description in both authors (Athen.539b–d; Ael.*VH* 9.3), both may have adapted an unknown, earlier, anthology (see N. G. Wilson, pp. 10–11 of the Loeb).

7. Gulick translated *tous parepidēmountas* of Chares as 'tourists', noted Aelian's version ([2]), and (p. 434 note) took these 'tourists' to be 'the Greeks who happened to be visiting the city' (i.e. Susa); Wilson has 'Greek residents locally'. Berve (1926, I: 80–1) correctly saw that these were visitors, not to Susa as such, but to Alexander's court, including them among his 'voluntary courtiers'; *pace* Aelian, their Greekness should not be assumed. Berve took ἐν τῇ αὐλῇ with τοὺς παρεπιδημοῦντας alone, 'the visitors to the court' (in the abstract sense). But *aulē* here has its concrete meaning, serving to locate Chares' list of additional diners not eating in the tent (as in Gulick's translation). The word returns later in the same extract, when Chares gave the dimensions which explained the courtyard's huge capacity. Aelian's version mistakenly took ἐν τῇ αὐλῇ with the feasting troops only, leaving the ambassadors and Greek visitors, by implication, to feast elsewhere.

8. The ancient texts may give some clues as to the shape of the tents. Ancient etymology derived 'tabernaculum' [8–9] from 'taberna', a structure built from boards or *tabulae* (Lewis-Short, s.v. 'tabernaculum', citing Festus). Thus 'tabernaculum' is assumed to indicate a rectangular tent (e.g. Perron 1990: 220). The gold-threaded *ouraniskoi* or 'little skies' [3–4], constituting the feasting- and audience-tent's ceiling, evoke the circular canopies or *ouranoi* which were a feature of Persian royal tents [11] and which Alexander evidently imitated (Lavagne 1988: 96–7). Modern scholars have speculated that this tent was 'au dôme d'or' (Lavagne 1988: 96–7); that the *ouraniskos* was a central feature in an otherwise rectangular tent (Perron 1990: 220); and that it formed the canopy of a royal dais or baldachino, supported by the statue-like columns of which four were known to Pliny [10], with the royal throne placed underneath (Goukowsky 1978, I: 191–2; Perron 1990: 220 n. 16). A cosmic meaning has been assumed: 'symbole céleste d'une domination universelle' (Goukowsky 1978, I: 191–2).

4 | Friends in high places: the creation of the court of the Roman emperor

JEREMY PATERSON

Introduction

The end of the first century BC witnessed a profound transformation of the Roman *res publica* from a political system in which power was diffused across a range of democratic and aristocratic institutions to one where power was seen to reside primarily in the hands of one man. This period of change and experiment provides a unique opportunity to see a court and court society coming into being, a process of interest not just to Roman historians but also to all those who seek to understand the nature of court societies.

The first impetus for the creation of any court society is the recognition of the ruler as the monopoly, or near-monopoly, possessor of power. I would argue that *all* societies in which power becomes the monopoly of the ruler create the conditions for the emergence of some form of 'court society'; in other words this is a truly sociological, or even anthropological, phenomenon.[1] Norbert Elias' famous study of court society (Elias 1983) starts by claiming a specifically sociological approach as opposed to a historical one; however, he ends up by representing his chosen court society, that of Louis XIV in France, as a stage in the formation of the modern state, which is in essence a historical argument.[2] In claiming that the court is a sociological phenomenon I am not suggesting that all court societies develop in the same way or in accordance with some law of nature.[3] The evolution of a court and court society around the Roman emperor has many features historically specific to that period of Rome's development. For example, although Romans were influenced by the model set

---

[1] See Herman 1997: 206: 'The emergence of court societies has more to do with universal social configurations than with concrete historical circumstance: it is a sociological rather than a historical phenomenon.'

[2] See the critique of Elias by Duindam (1995: *passim*). For a major new attempt to bring rigour to theorising about courts see now the contributions in Butz, Hirschbiegel and Willoweit 2004, which exploit a range of approaches well beyond the Weberian analytical techniques of Elias, including New Institutional Economics.

[3] See Savalli-Lestrade (1998: 289), who notes that the existence of a group of faithful followers is a characteristic of all absolute monarchs; but the particular form it takes in any one place and time can be in any of a great many different configurations.

by the Hellenistic rulers they encountered in the eastern Mediterranean, there were significant differences, most notably the fact that, whereas in the Hellenistic monarchies all political institutions were centred on the figure of the ruler, in Rome the senate and magistracies, which already existed before the emergence of the Principate, to some extent continued to provide potential sources of power and influence not entirely dependent on the emperor.

In reality no monarch can rule alone. The Roman emperor was no exception to this. He needed trusted and reliable helpers, who expected rewards for their loyalty. For their part his subjects queued up to represent themselves as worthy recipients of rewards, favours and careers. It follows from this that the court and court society are a negotiation between the ruler and the subject; the court is not simply imposed by the ruler.

Courtly behaviour is the 'language' of this dialogue; it becomes the medium through which loyalty, favour, deference and respect are expressed both by the ruler and by his courtiers. Above all, as will be highlighted later, the conventions and customs of the court provide an element of reassurance and confidence in a relationship which is inherently unstable and fraught with uncertainty. The early Roman Principate was an age of experiment, in which ruler and ruled combined in a lively contemporary debate about the consequences of the identification of power with the emperor and his household. Contemporaries had a variety of models to work with. There was the tradition about the early kings of Rome. There were also the archaic Greek model of the tyrant (Greek: *turannos*), the traditions about the kings of Persia (see Brosius in this volume), and the near contemporary encounters with the Hellenistic monarchs of the Greek east. The interesting point about all these models is their ambivalent nature, depending on whether the tyrannical and autocratic aspects or beneficial rule, respect and civility are emphasised. The relationship between the ruler and his subjects could be characterised as either that between master and slave or that between father and child.[4]

Whereas problems about the legal powers of the Roman emperor have absorbed the attention of generations of modern scholars (though less so in the past thirty years), contemporaries of the emperors tended to take the emperor's all-encompassing power as a given and were concerned far more on the one hand with the behaviour of the emperors, their lifestyle, attitudes, social values and relationships with others, and on the other with the etiquette and appropriate behaviour of the subject who is seeking to gain

---

[4] See the useful discussion of Roller (2001: 213–87).

office, reward or benefit from the emperor – in other words with the issues which are central to all court studies.

Power is a reality, but it is also invisible, like the wind.[5] But the emperor needed to be *seen* to have power. For their part courtiers also had to be able to demonstrate to the rest of the world that they had access to, and benefited from, the ruler's power. Hence the ceremonies, the etiquette of courts, and the honours granted to and by grateful subjects ought to be interpreted as ways of making power manifest. It follows that the emperor's court should be at the heart of our understanding of the Roman Principate. So it is all the more surprising that Brian Jones in an excellent brief section on the nature of the imperial court in his biography of Domitian could comment as recently as 1992 that 'detailed discussions of the imperial court are rare' (Jones 1992: 202 n. 3). In fact the subject has not been ignored so much as simply taken for granted as being largely unproblematic.[6] One reason for this comparative neglect is that the ancient sources themselves at first sight do not contain any full-blown study of the emperor's court. It has been suggested that the reason for this is the secrecy which the historian Cassius Dio (53.19) argued surrounded the decision-making processes in the Principate.[7] But this is to miss the point. It is true that the processes by which the emperor came to major decisions were often obscure because the debate, if there was any, was usually behind closed doors, or informally among close friends of the emperor. But under most emperors the court was relatively open and accessible, certainly to the majority of those who chose to write the history of Rome in this period.[8] It is much more likely that the sources tended to take for granted the everyday ceremonial and courtesies which from the start were part of their life at court, and concentrated instead on the examples of exceptionally arrogant or demeaning behaviour. We do not have a Saint-Simon for the Roman Principate. However, once we get our eye in and know what we are looking for, it is clear that commentary on the court

---

[5] The comparison of power with the wind and ceremonial with snow was made by David Cannadine (Cannadine and Price 1992: 1).

[6] See Wallace-Hadrill (1996: 285) and also the lively, useful, but under-theorised study by Turcan (1987). It is interesting to note that the situation until recently has been the same with regard to the historical study of the Hellenistic kings. For Alexander see now Spawforth in this volume; for the Hellenistic kings, Herman (1997) presents a ground-breaking study explicitly influenced by Elias and briefly discussed in this volume's Introduction.

[7] Wallace-Hadrill 1996: 284; it is important to note that Dio's primary concern in the passage is a historical one about the reliability of the information in his sources.

[8] Pliny the Younger in his panegyric of the emperor Trajan states, 'Your meals are always taken in public and your table open to all' (*Pan.*49.5), and Pliny himself (*Ep.*6.31) recalls with pride his attendance at informal dinners with the emperor after a hard day's work in his council (*consilium*).

and court life is everywhere in our sources – from Tacitus' concerns about
the servility shown by many senators and the rise in the public influence of
freedmen from the imperial household, for example, to Suetonius' anecdotes
about the manners, conversation and public appearances of emperors.[9] The
discourses of Epictetus on 'How should we behave towards tyrants?'(1.19)
and 'On Freedom' (4.1) certainly draw on a long, conventional literary and
philosophical tradition about the nature of flattery and the distinction of
the flatterer from the true friend – one might compare Plutarch on 'Having many friends' (*Mor.*93B–95B) and on 'How to distinguish a flatterer'
(*Mor.*48F–74E).[10] In the case of Epictetus, they take on an added resonance
and contemporary significance once it is realised that the author, as a slave
in the service of an influential freedman at the court of Nero, was writing as
a court 'insider'.[11] All these sources come alive once it is realised that they
reflect a vital contemporary debate about how an emperor should behave
and how his subjects should behave towards him – that is, in large measure,
a debate about the court and court life.

ptMuch of our source material about courtly society in the early
Principate comes from people who, to a greater or lesser extent, were part of
that society. Tacitus, Pliny the Younger and the Greek historian Cassius Dio
were senators with successful public careers which depended on the favour
of emperors. What men like this had to do to rest easy at night was above
all to concoct an interpretation of events which saw monarchy in Rome as
an unavoidable consequence of the failure of Romans to govern themselves
collectively under the late Republic.[12] On this view there was no alternative
to monarchy and this in turn justified the members of the elite in their participation in public life and in their willingness to adopt courtly behaviour
to solicit the emperor for office and favours. They had to believe that it was
possible to have a successful public career and take part in the life of the
court, while avoiding degrading servility or compromising their integrity.
Tacitus saw a model in Marcus Aemilius Lepidus, the consul of AD 6.
Lepidus was described by a contemporary as a man who stood 'very close to
the name and fortune of the Caesars' (Velleius Paterculus 2.114.5); indeed he
had a very distinguished Republican ancestry and was related to the emperor
Augustus himself. According to an anecdote, the emperor on his deathbed

---

[9] Another reason for the neglect of the court as a subject may be the modern scepticism about
anecdotes as historical evidence (see Saller 1980). However, Laurence and Paterson (1999: 195)
discuss the ways in which sayings by and about emperors may be used to illustrate
contemporary perceptions of the emperor's role, despite the impossibility in many cases of
confirming their historicity.

[10] See Fraisse 1974: 409–11.   [11] Millar 1965 and Starr 1949.   [12] Syme 1986: 439–54.

had pronounced Lepidus 'fully capable of becoming emperor (*capax imperii*) but considering the position beneath him'. All the more surprising then that a cynical historian like Tacitus should pick such a man out as the archetype of the good courtier. In Tacitus' opinion Lepidus was a serious and wise man, who enjoyed consistent influence and favour with the emperor Tiberius; but he was no toady – rather he used his influence to do good by successfully countering the savage proposals against individuals made by flatterers of the emperor.[13] This assessment leads Tacitus on to wonder whether success in winning the emperor's favour was a matter of luck or whether a person could make their own luck by behaving with integrity and 'by steering a path, clear of intrigue and danger, between the perils of open defiance and the degradation of servility'. Tacitus here reflects the central preoccupation of the Roman elite under the Principate, which was to expect the emperor to create the conditions in which they could acknowledge the fact of his pre-eminence without feeling uncomfortable, and could maintain their belief that their success and favour with the emperor was the natural recognition of their true abilities, rather than the mere accident or whim of the ruler.[14] So the insiders in their histories praise emperors who make life easy for men of their kind by not lording it over them in too obvious a manner. The elite also expected reasonable and direct access to the emperor. Tacitus and others reserve their fiercest criticisms for the members of the imperial household, who were their social inferiors but because of their position within the court could come between the senator and the emperor, such as Claudius' freedmen.

Suetonius and Epictetus were 'insiders' in a somewhat different sense. They had careers within the imperial households. They were part of the administrative system of the emperor that kept the Principate going. Suetonius, in particular, tended to judge the effectiveness of the emperor and the court by the practical criteria of the extent to which they got the job done successfully. He was largely unencumbered by sentimental longing for the lost Republic or touchiness about the issue of 'freedom'.

The ultimate 'insider', of course, was the emperor himself. For all the remarkable insights within the *Meditations* of Marcus Aurelius, there is comparatively little on the court. He recognised that life in court was potentially corrupting for the monarch. Yet he insisted that 'in a court too it is still possible to live well' in accordance with his chosen Stoic philosophy.

---

[13] Tac.*Ann*.4.20.

[14] Pliny *Ep*.8.6.13 on the emperor honouring those who 'deserved reward' (*praemia merentes*), a passage discussed by Brunt (1988: 39).

Of his teacher, Sextus of Chaeronea, Plutarch's nephew, he said, 'Simply to be in his company was more delightful than any flattery, while at the same time those who enjoyed his company looked upon him with greatest reverence' (*Med.*1.9.1) – it was an ideal model for a philosopher king. Marcus (*Med.*1.17.3) thanked the gods that he had learned that it was possible to live in court yet do without the trappings and pomp of bodyguards, spectacular costumes, torch-lit parades, statues and the like (an interesting list of what could in the second century AD constitute court ceremonial). In short, Marcus sought to avoid becoming 'Caesarified' (*Med.*6.30).

A poet like Statius has been categorised as a sycophantic insider because of the half dozen poems to Domitian in his collection, *Silvae*. It is true that Statius was always keen for signs of imperial favour – quite naturally given that this was the route to success and reward; but it would be wrong to dismiss his poem on being invited by Domitian to a large formal dinner in the palace (*Silvae* 4.2) as mere flattery. A man who does not walk the corridors of power regularly is unlikely to be blasé or cynical about attendance at a banquet in the presence of the emperor. On the contrary he would expect, indeed would exult in, a level of dignity, pomp and splendour – otherwise what is the point of being part of the occasion? And if the emperor condescended to mingle with his diners, so much the greater would be the impact of the occasion. Formal court poetry it may be; but it reflects a reality.

It is important to realise that our sources are not going to give a single, clear and consistent account of the experience of being part of courtly society. It depends very much on who the source is.

When it comes to the analysis of the court of the Roman emperor, for once in the study of Roman history Theodor Mommsen did not succeed in setting the agenda for future generations. He concentrated on the internal organisation of the emperor's household and the access of his friends to the court. But he offered little by way of dynamic analysis; indeed his main account ('Hof und Haushalt') is startlingly brief and is fundamentally flawed by a false distinction between the 'state' aspect of the emperor's court and the court as the emperor's private household.[15] The account to which all studies since have been indebted is that of Ludwig Friedländer in his monumental study of Roman life and manners, originally published in 1862 (Friedländer 1921). He also details the bureaucrats, freedmen and slaves who made up the imperial household along with the emperor's friends and companions; but his most important innovative contribution was his study of court ceremonial, which has only recently been superseded. Aspects of the

---

[15] Mommsen 1887 Bd II 2, 3, 833–9. For a wide-ranging study of the earlier research on the Roman imperial court see Winterling (1999: 12–38).

Roman court continued to receive close study, for example the members of the emperor's household (e.g. Weaver 1972), but rarely, if ever, were they set in a more general discussion of court society. The grand synthesis of Millar (1977) contains vast amounts of material of relevance, but significantly the term 'court' does not appear in the index. Wallace-Hadrill (1996) cites Elias in his account of the imperial court for the *Cambridge Ancient History*, but this is really almost the first sign that ancient historians were beginning to take account of the emergence of aulic studies among historians of the early modern period, which had followed the publication of Elias. As a result ancient historians are bound to be indebted for a long time to come to the scholarship of Winterling (1999; and for the later Roman period Winterling 1998). He is at the heart of the groups of European scholars who are in the process of bringing intellectual rigour to the theories about the nature of court society, though their focus has been largely, but not exclusively, on the courts of early modern Europe.

In all this it may be salutary, for a moment, to listen to the occasional note of scepticism about whether the reason historians have not explicitly dealt with the court and court society of the Roman emperors is that there was in reality no court of the Roman emperors. Gagé (1971: 191ff) questions whether we should talk about an imperial court – at least in the period down to the Severi. It is of interest that his principal reason is that Roman senators and their families did not live permanently in the imperial palace. In other words he takes Versailles under Louis XIV as the defining template for a court. However, in other court societies, such as the Habsburg court in Vienna, the nobility were not constantly present at court. In any case, in Rome it was a regular expectation that senators, unless excused, attended the morning greeting (*salutatio*) of the emperor at the palace on the Palatine. Nevertheless, Gagé's doubts force us to attempt to define what is meant by the court of the Roman emperor.

Language can often be a key indicator of change. A clear sign that there was a new phenomenon comes from the appearance in Latin of the term '*aula*' for the court. It scarcely appears during the Roman Republic.[16] But it becomes the normal noun for the imperial court from at least the mid-first century onwards. The term is Greek in origin and its primary meaning is the hall or courtyard of a house. It was borrowed from the Hellenistic world, where it was regularly used both for the physical palace of a monarch and for the collective members of that court (see this volume's Introduction). It is an indication that the Romans had models of Hellenistic kingship in

---

[16] Only in Cic.*Fam*.15.4.6 (where significantly it is used of the court of the Hellenised king of Cappadocia).

their minds when the Roman Principate came into being, because the Greek term became current rather than its Latin equivalent, 'atrium'. The Greek terms 'to basileion' or 'ta basileia' for palace in the same way came to mean not just the palace as a building but the more abstract 'court'. In this case, however, the Hellenistic term was not adopted, perhaps because of its too overt reference to kingship (Greek: basileus); instead Palatium, the name of the hill on which Augustus' residence was located, came to mean 'palace' and also by extension those within the palace.[17] Hence Dio (53.16) explained: 'The royal residence (ta basileia) is called Palatium, not because it was ever decided that it should be called this, but because Caesar lived on the Palatine and had his headquarters there . . . Even if the emperor resides somewhere else, the place where he stops is called the Palatium.' The palace is wherever the emperor is.

Another indication of a changed world is the way words in the new context can take on a significance they did not have previously. The emperor Tiberius publicly rebuked someone for addressing him as dominus ('master') (Suet.Tib.27 and Tac.Ann.2.87). In this, as in so much else, he was following the precedent of Augustus (Suet.Aug.53.1). In private life, the term 'dominus' was a formal, respectful address between social equals (roughly equivalent to 'my lord'). 'Vale domine frater' ('Farewell, master and brother') is the way a correspondent signs off a letter found at Vindolanda near Hadrian's Wall in the North of England.[18] Pliny the Younger regularly addressed Trajan as 'domine' in his official correspondence with the emperor.[19] But in public in the context of the court this form of address became problematic, because 'dominus' is also the term regularly used for the owner of slaves – a connotation which emperors would be anxious to avoid.[20] Forms of address become critical and difficult issues. In the context of court life 'the path of language is narrow and slippery' (angusta et lubrica oratio), as Tacitus (Ann.2.87) so memorably put it.

The genesis of the emperor's court at Rome

To leave on one side for the moment the question of exactly who constituted the emperor's court, it is illuminating to consider how and why the court came into being in Rome. In so far as they have considered the matter at

---

[17] See K. Ziegler, RE XVII.3, col.6ff.   [18] Tab.Vindol.II 295; cf. Tab.Vindol.II 234 and 248.
[19] Pliny Ep.10 passim.
[20] This is well discussed by Roller (2001: 254–8). A full discussion of dominus by M. Bang in Friedländer 1921: 82–8.

all, historians have tended to take one of two approaches. The first, which may be dubbed 'from Haus to Hof', is to emphasise the continuity from the Republic to the Principate by identifying many of the features of the imperial court as already existing in some form in the houses and house-holds of the great members of the Roman Republican elite. So the palace and court of the Roman emperor are different in scale but not in kind from these precedents.[21] The alternative is to see the courts of the Hellenistic kings as providing conscious models for the construction of a system which was essentially novel for Rome and in some respects offensive to the traditions of the Roman Republic. The solution suggested here is that both elements play a role.[22] However, our understanding of the nature of the Roman impe-rial court is fundamentally aided by concentrating on those features of the Principate which contemporaries considered novel:

1 Power and patronage were perceived as residing ultimately in the person of one man.
2 As a consequence those immediately around the emperor – his family, household and close companions – were perceived as deriving power and influence in their own right from the emperor.
3 One result of this was that in some cases individuals from outside the social and political hierarchy were recognised as having abnormal power and influence, e.g. women, imperial freedmen, some of the slaves attendant on the emperor, and eunuchs in the later empire; while court societies frequently reinforce already existing social hierarchies, they also can have this subversive effect.
4 Access to and recognition by the emperor became the key to a successful and secure public life for the elite.
5 The obverse was, if anything, even more important: exclusion from the court frequently spelt political, social and often actual death (either by suicide out of despair at the end of one's career or as a result of being attacked in the courts by opponents who were encouraged to do so as a result of the emperor's indication of the withdrawal of his favour).[23]

---

[21] Wallace-Hadrill 1996: 290.

[22] Anticipated in a slightly different context by Crook (1955: 21), in his discussion of the friends of emperors: 'The institution of *amici principis* derives from two sources, the purely Roman political tradition of the Republic and the hierarchy of the Hellenistic courts. It is important not to overemphasize one at the expense of the other.'

[23] So, for example, Sextus Vistilius, who had been accepted into the entourage (*cohors*) of the emperor Tiberius, fell out of favour after the emperor took offence over something he was accused of saying, and committed suicide after being excluded from the emperor's company (*convictu principis prohibitus*) (Tac.Ann.6.9).

6 A set of conventions or norms emerged which governed the social interaction between the emperor and those around him.[24]

7 Flattery as a form of behaviour became important and prevalent, even
   though emperors may have protested against it and subjects found it
   demeaning.

'The Roman senate was an assembly of kings.' Such it is claimed (though
with variations in our sources) Cineas reported back to Pyrrhus, Hellenistic
king of Epirus, after an abortive attempt to negotiate peace with Rome in
280 BC.[25] The remark is most likely apocryphal. At the heart of the Roman
Republic there was a body of families who, particularly in the last two centuries BC, accumulated extraordinary levels of wealth. Once the Roman elite
encountered the Hellenistic world on a regular basis, they began to take on
the trappings of the Hellenistic kings. As provincial governors, their pro-
gresses around their provinces could seem very like the arrival of a Hellenistic
dynast, and the provincial communities responded by using the language
and etiquette which they had previously used about their Hellenistic rulers,
praising them as founders, god-like, and establishing festivals in their honour (see Rawson 1975). Back in Italy and Rome the elite sought to make
their houses the equivalent of the Hellenistic palaces they had encountered
in the east. They raided the great libraries of the Hellenistic rulers.[26] Their
entourages included poets and scholars. They filled their houses and their
gardens with the statuary of the Greek world.[27] The need for their houses
to have large public reception rooms was discussed in a famous passage
of Vitruvius (6.5), where he emphasises their requirements for vestibules,
atria and peristyles on a grand scale, which befitted their rank (*ad decorem
maiestatis*).[28] The reason for this was that parts of the *nobiles'* houses were
essentially public places, the setting for councils and for judicial activities
associated with the holding of the magistracies.

According to Seneca (*Ben.*6.34), it was Gaius Gracchus and, a little later,
Livius Drusus the Younger who adopted the practice of classifying their
callers at the morning *salutatio* (*segregare turbam suam*), by receiving some
in secretum, others in company and the rest *en masse*. This was an overt

---

[24] On the importance of norms and rules of conduct in the creation of a court society see Asch
and Birk 1991.

[25] Plutarch *Pyrrhus* 19, or 'a city of kings' according to Justin *Epit.*18.2.

[26] See Aemilius Paullus (Plut.*Aem.*28.6), Sulla's appropriation of Aristotle's library (Strabo
1.1.54), and Lucullus' great collection (Plut.*Luc.*42) (Rawson 1985: ch. 3).

[27] Flamininus in 194 BC (Livy 34.52), Marcellus after the capture of Syracuse in 211 BC, and most
notoriously Mummius after the sack of Corinth in 146 BC.

[28] See the nuanced discussion of Wallace-Hadrill (1994: 10ff).

adaptation of the practice at Hellenistic courts.[29] The practice of receiving friends at the morning salutation in groups was continued by the emperors, although some tried to modify or even abolish it (see Talbert 1984: 68–70). Winterling (1999: 121) has argued that the practice may have been no more than a practical arrangement of dividing those who came between different rooms which the master of the house then toured. But whether or not the head of the household, or later the emperor, intended a ranking or privilege, they were unable to prevent it from being taken in that way.[30]

Thus many of the features of the courtly society under the Principate are found in some form in the Republic. However, despite the competitiveness of the Roman Republican elite, social norms, often expressed in terms of morality, sought to keep all the members of the elite on a par. When power fell into the hands of a single individual with Julius Caesar and the coming of the Principate, a continuous debate was initiated among the elite as to just what was fitting and reasonable in terms of deference, display and behaviour towards the monarch.

The ruler's court is not the creation of the ruler alone or even his initiative. It is as much the means by which the subjects come to terms with the fact that power is now the monopoly of the ruler, and the way they create a *modus vivendi* with that ruler. Some strands of this can be seen in the aftermath of the civil war in the 40s BC and the dictatorship of Julius Caesar. An extraordinary range and scale of honours were granted Caesar in 46 and 45 BC.[31] They included the right to special dress, the use of a gilded chair, a bodyguard of senators and *equites*, the renaming of the month of his birth, quadrennial games in his honour, the creation of a cult in his honour and much else (many of these can be traced to Hellenistic precedents). But they were all initiated by the senate, usually in Caesar's absence. They represent less Caesar's manoeuvring to create a new role for himself, and much more the attempt by the senators and others to come to terms with the new realities of power. Cases like this raise the more general issue of who created court ceremonial – the emperor, the courtiers, or both? In the Roman context the initiative should more often be ascribed to the courtiers rather than to the ruler, whose main role was to attempt to restrain novel, excessive flattery.

The extraordinary honours granted to Julius Caesar raise another more general issue. There has been an endless and largely inconclusive debate from

---

[29] For the ranking at the court of Ptolemy V Epiphanes of the king's 'first friends', etc. see Mooren (1975 and 1977).

[30] See e.g. *ILS* 1320, an inscription, now lost, of C. Caesius Niger, an *eques* who is described as '*ex prima admissione*' in the time of Augustus or Tiberius.

[31] See Gelzer 1968: 307, 315–16.

antiquity to the present about what Julius Caesar's intentions really were and what the motives behind the grants of honours were. However, the reason why such investigations are bound to be inconclusive lies in the difficulty of interpreting the significance of any ceremonial practice. Whatever the motives of the proposers of these honours and whatever the intentions of Caesar in accepting them, it was impossible for anyone, ruler or courtier, to restrict the meaning of any practice. Consider the notorious events of the Lupercalia (15 February 44 BC). At this religious ceremony Julius Caesar, recently designated *dictator perpetuus*, appeared in public seated on a gilded chair on the Rostra and for the first time wearing the ceremonial dress of the early Roman kings (purple toga and gold wreath).[32] It is Valerius Maximus (1.6.13) who acutely points out that these honours had been granted to him by the senate and that Caesar wore them on this occasion so as not to offend the senate! The Luperci, priests dressed in goatskin loin-cloths, were led in their run round the Palatine by the consul, Mark Antony, who on his return to the Forum, mounted the Rostra and attempted to place on Caesar's head a diadem (a characteristic feature of the dress of Hellenistic kings). Caesar refused, had the diadem taken to the Capitol to be dedicated to Jupiter Optimus Maximus, and ordered that it should be placed on public record that on that day Caesar had refused the kingship offered to him. The refusal of honours offered is a key aspect of the dialogue between ruler and subject. So Augustus in his account of his reign, the *Res Gestae* (5, 6 and 10), lists the honours and posts he had been offered, but had refused. Our sources for the Lupercalia incident have every possible interpretation of what happened and its meaning.[33] Depending on the source, the people either applauded or groaned when Antony tried to put the diadem on Caesar's head, and again when Caesar refused it. The event has been interpreted either as staged by Caesar to test the waters, or as an initiative by Antony as an act of flattery, or as an attempt to get Caesar publicly to renounce his worrying ambitions (Dio 46.17 and 19), or even with more sinister intent – 'You [Antony] signed Caesar's death warrant at the Lupercalia' (*tu . . . illum occidisti Lupercalibus*, Cic.*Phil*.13.41). This is not just a problem of our source material; it is rather that the event could have at the same time any or all of these meanings depending on who you were. What matters here is not 'what was happening', but 'what was thought to be happening' by the participants and other observers.

---

[32] Cic.*Div*.1.119.

[33] Cic.*Phil*.2.85–7 – and elsewhere in the Philippics; Dio 44.11; Suet.*DJ* 79.2; Livy *per*.116; Nicol.Dam.F130, 71–5; Vell.2.56.4; Plut.*Caes*.61; *Ant*.12; Appian *BC* 2.456ff; Florus 2.13.91.

In a perceptive comment, Cicero considered the possibility that Caesar wanted to restore a Republican constitutional government, but he saw that he would not be able to because he had bound himself to so many.[34] The dictator was the prisoner of his entourage – those who had joined him in the civil war in the hope of personal advancement and who had no interest in the return of a republic. Elias (1983) sought to represent the court as a mechanism created by the ruler to control the noble courtiers. But in his critique of Elias, Duindam (1995) demonstrated that the development of a court and court society was not necessarily an effective means of controlling noble-born courtiers, that the court can be a source of power and influence for its noble courtiers, and that the ruler can be as much in the effective control of the court as vice versa. Further, Caesar's successors would have noted that among his assassins were those whose hopes of advancement had been disappointed.[35]

In the last years of Julius Caesar's life many features later associated with emperors appear. Here was a court in the making. He was accompanied in his tours by a huge entourage – 2,000 (probably mainly soldiers) by Cicero's estimate in a famous account of Caesar's visit to him in Campania (*ad Att.*13.52). Caesar himself became the focus of a deluge of petitions and requests, a circumstance which itself could cause problems. On a visit to Caesar's house to present a petition, Cicero was kept waiting. According to Matius, a Caesarian supporter, Caesar remarked, 'Can I doubt that I am utterly loathed when Marcus Cicero has to sit and wait?'(*ad Att.*14.1.2 and 2.3). The creation of regular procedures is essential for a ruler to avoid this sort of offence. The ceremonial and etiquette which developed in the Principate may have been irksome to some, but to most was a confirmation of their status and privilege.[36] It was essential that the courtier knew what his position was, how to approach the ruler, what to do and say to win favour. Finally, there was the issue of Caesar's *clementia*, his willingness to forgive opponents and allow them to resume their public lives. *Clementia* was an attribute of monarchs, so that the soliciting of forgiveness and the granting of it were acts which acknowledged and confirmed the primacy of the ruler. Hence Cato's ostentatious suicide as an act of refusal to recognise any dependency on Caesar's good will. But the majority, who were not prepared to take such a drastic line, had to modify their behaviour in order to achieve

---

[34] Cic.*ad Fam.*9.17.2. Cf. Cicero's similar assessment of Octavian in *ad Att.*14.12.2.

[35] Among them the great-grandfather of the emperor Galba, who despite serving as a legate with Caesar in Gaul ascribed his defeat in the consular election to Caesar's failure to support him and so out of pique joined the conspiracy against him (Suet.*Galba* 3).

[36] Cf. Elias 1983: ch. 5.

their goals in the face of the new situation in which Caesar had the power. Thus at a meeting the whole senate appealed to Caesar to forgive M. Marcellus, the consul of 51 BC (*ad Caesarem supplex accederet*), while Marcellus' cousin, Gaius, threw himself at Caesar's feet (*se ad Caesarem pedes abiecisset*) (Cic.*ad Fam*.4.4.3). Caesar gave in. But such behaviour was recognition of where power now lay. Again, Cicero in his speeches before Caesar himself on behalf of Q. Ligarius and later King Deiotarus chose to plead directly for mercy rather than mount a full defence: 'I take refuge in your clemency. I seek mercy for the offence. I beg forgiveness' (*Lig*.30); 'Forgive, forgive, Caesar' (*Deiotar*.12) This was the sort of plea (*deprecatio*) which was to become the norm, but which Quintilian (*Inst*.5.13.5) recognised had no real role previously in a Republican advocacy. Courtly behaviour is more a creation of the ruled than an imposition by the ruler.

Modelling monarchy and the Dictator's Dilemma

In the few years of the 40s BC in which Julius Caesar dominated Roman public life, some of the characteristics of a court society were already emerging as a negotiated response to his pre-eminence. More significantly indeed, in the years that followed his assassination the attempt to restore the Republican system was essentially a sideshow to the main struggles, which were about who would be the next Caesar. Julius Caesar had opened up the possibility of getting things done in a new way. He should be seen not as representing the end of the Republican system, but as the beginning of the Principate.

Julius Caesar did not create a court around him; nor, I suggest, did the early emperors. But a court grew up, and it is important to look at the factors which encourage the creation of a court around autocrats. Weber's model of court society as 'patrimonial' in pre-modern societies – that is, centred upon the palace and personal household of the ruler, rather than on a bureaucratic machinery of government – has obvious relevance to the court of the Roman emperors.[37] Elias' work (1983) is essentially a Weberian sociological study which concentrates on the connections between power and social structures and values. It offers a picture of the French *ancien régime* in which the elites are offered distinction and privilege as compensation for the loss of control of power. He posits an unavoidable interdependence between king and court. But these sociological approaches do not tackle fully the fundamental question about why court societies arise around autocrats

---

[37] For the lack of bureaucratic machinery see Garnsey and Saller 1987: ch. 2.

in the first place. One answer centres upon the recognition that autocrats are often more effective redistributors of wealth than other political systems.[38] According to Suetonius (*Aug.*101), Augustus declared that no more than 150 million sesterces would come to his heirs, even though he had received 1,400 million during the last twenty years of his reign simply from the wills of his friends, 'because he had spent nearly all of it along with his two paternal patrimonies and other inheritances for the benefit of the state (*in rem publicam*)'. On the basis of these figures Augustus retained about 10 per cent of this part of his income. This gets into context the issue of the emperor's expenditure on buildings, show, personal luxury, etc., which could from time to time excite adverse comment. It is an example of what may be termed the 'Imelda Marcos shoe syndrome' – her extraordinary expenditure on shoes excited much comment and was powerful propaganda against her, but was only ever a small part of the wealth that came to the Marcoses. If the emperor is seen essentially as a redistributor rather than an accumulator, then rent-seeking becomes centred on the emperor. Access to him becomes essential for maintaining and increasing wealth, privilege and position for the elite. The courtiers, however, also become brokers, interceding to win favours for their clients (cities, communities and individuals), an essential part of the redistribution system.[39]

In this way the court and court society becomes the context for this process of brokerage, and the means by which this system is organised and maintained. But there is one more central factor which structures the dynamics of the relationship between ruler and court – this is 'the Dictator's Dilemma'.[40] The autocrat can never be entirely sure that his subjects' words and actions are truly motivated by loyalty and respect. As a result the position of autocrat carries with it an inherent sense of insecurity, which cannot be relieved either by the use of fear and repression or by the distribution of rewards. No Roman emperor could be unaware of this, given the assassination of Julius Caesar, which ushered in the Principate. The dilemma was also felt by the subject: 'Praise a tyrant and he takes no pleasure in it. For he thinks that those who praise him feel otherwise' (Dio Chrysostom *Orat.*6.59).

---

[38] For modern models of the economics of autocracy see Wintrobe 1998. He includes discussion (not always accurate) of Roman emperors. He argues that 'dictatorships tend to redistribute income more than democracies do' (149–60). See also Paterson 2004.

[39] On this see Kettering (1986) on seventeenth-century France, cited as a useful comparison for the Roman empire by Wallace-Hadrill (1989: 81ff).

[40] See Wintrobe (1998: 20–39) for a detailed analysis of the dilemma.

The dilemma was recognised in antiquity and analysis of it tends to centre on discussions of how to distinguish the true friend from the flatterer.[41] In terms of rational-choice theory the ruler and his subjects have a mutual 'signalling' problem. Essentially the problem is how either party can make 'credible' commitments in situations when there is gross inequality between the two, and promises and obligations on either side are unenforceable. The ruler can never be sure that the subject is speaking frankly and the subject has no means of holding the ruler to his word. Furthermore the dilemma is inescapable. It is a fundamental feature of autocracy.[42] 'Grant to every one who wishes to offer you advice on any matter whatever, the right to speak freely and without fear. For if you are pleased with what is said, it will benefit you greatly, and if you are not persuaded, you have not suffered any harm.' Such was the advice to Augustus put in the mouth of Maecenas by the historian Dio (52.33.6). Indeed, both rulers and subjects frequently stated the need for free and frank discussion; but the situation they found themselves in made this end unattainable. When the ruler holds the power to advance you or hold you back, include you or exclude you, even ultimately decide whether you lived or died, then as a subject your actions and words inevitably became something of a 'performance' put on for the benefit of the ruler to convince him of your worthiness and loyalty.[43] This involved an element of second-guessing what the response to your words or actions might be from the ruler and modifying your own behaviour so as to generate a particular response. This is why consistency and predictability are so prized in rulers. Hence the criticism of Gaius Caligula – what was frightening about him was that no one knew what he would do next: this puts the courtier in an impossible position where he cannot calculate the emperor's reaction to his words or actions. Cassius Dio, a successful courtier, has some thoughtful comments on the difficulty facing courtiers when dealing with Tiberius, who had a reputation for never saying what he really meant.[44]

The competitiveness of court life also ensured that the courtiers were bound to employ flattery. They were playing for big stakes: 'It is not Caesar himself that anyone fears, but death, banishment, prison, loss of property, deprival of civic rights. Nor does anyone love Caesar himself, unless he happens to be a man of great worth; but we love riches, a tribunate, a

[41] See Fraisse 1974: 409–11; Savalli-Lestrade 1998: 345ff; Plutarch *Mor.*93B–95B ('On having many friends') and *Mor.*48F–74E ('How to recognise the flatterer').
[42] Kuran (1995) analyses the disjunction between 'private beliefs' and 'publicly expressed opinions' of subjects under an autocracy. See also Scott (1990) and Goffman (1967: 47–95).
[43] The 'theatricality' of court life has been splendidly analysed by Bartsch (1994).
[44] Dio 57.1.

praetorship, a consulship. When we love and hate and fear these things, those who have the disposal of them must necessarily be our masters' (Epictetus *Disc.*4.1.60 (On Freedom)). So no one could afford to opt out from the use of flattery, because they could not ensure their rivals for rewards would not use it. Indeed, the tendency will be to seek ever more extravagant and novel forms of flattery in order to outdo competitors for the favours of the emperor. Although philosophical critics tended to emphasise the degrading nature of flattery, it was not simply a mark of servility; it was also a powerful tool in the hands of the courtier to achieve his ends.[45]

There are two main strategies open to the ruler for trying to deal with the dilemma: repression and reward.[46] These can be set out as the two axes of a graph and the position of any ruler represented as a point which marks the particular combination of repression and reward that is used. Repression can be effective; but its primary limitation is that it does not solve the Dictator's Dilemma; rather it engenders it – the more the ruler represses, the more he increases his fear, because he cannot be sure of what his subjects are really thinking and planning. From the start of the Principate, with the precedent of the assassination of Julius Caesar before them, emperors had to take measures to protect themselves – so bodyguards, occasional wearing of armour under the toga at public events, and personal searches became the norm. But emperors had to balance this against the expectation of being open and accessible to people. They faced a further problem, summed up in an aphorism ascribed to Domitian (Suet.*Dom.*21): 'He used to say that the lot of emperors was a most miserable one, because no one ever believes in any conspiracy they discover unless it has resulted in their deaths.'[47] So the suppression of plots, such as that of Piso in AD 65, can lead to the creation of martyrs, whose reputation posthumously may be exploited to foster and maintain opposition to the emperor. But the existence of men, often of influence and access to the emperor, who are ready to plot the emperor's death, raises problems for the rest of the elite. Is ostentatious and violent opposition to tyranny the most desirable model for their own behaviour? Should they feel guilty, or morally deficient, if they refuse to join in the opposition and, indeed, seek to continue their careers even under repressive tyranny? These problems are neatly illustrated by Tacitus' own unsympathetic account of the

---

[45] Scott 1990: 34: 'We get the wrong impression . . . if we visualize actors perpetually wearing fake smiles . . . To do so is to see the performance as totally determined from above and to miss the agency of the actor in appropriating the performance for his own ends.'

[46] Wintrobe 1998: 33ff.

[47] Transferred to Hadrian by *SHA Avidius Cassius* 2.4, on which see Laurence and Paterson (1999: 192f).

Piso conspiracy (*Ann.*15.48), in which he challenges the motives, behaviour and bravery of most of the participants. The reason for his attitude is revealed in his biography of his father-in-law, Agricola (*Agr.*42), where he represents Agricola as the model of an honourable man, who with *moderatio* and *prudentia* steered a successful career under Domitian and did not provoke the vengeance of the emperor upon him by defiant and futile parades of independence (*libertas*). Tacitus declares: 'Let those, whose habit is to admire disobedience, recognize that men can be great even under bad emperors, and that *obsequium* and *modestia*, if allied to industry and energy, can reach that peak of praiseworthiness, which most men attain only by following a perilous course, winning fame, without benefiting the state, by an ostentatious martyrdom.' Tacitus was speaking for most of those around him who sought to live out honourable lives under the Principate. Here is the true credo of the courtier. The continued survival of the Principate as a system was dependent upon Tacitus' viewpoint being the general one.

Reward is a key strategy for rulers, or rather *over-reward* – that is, the use of a price premium to stimulate loyalty and build trust. This can be done by the distribution of rents, direct gifts to enable individuals to gain or maintain status, the support for individuals' public careers, the granting of office, etc. There are innumerable examples of the Roman emperor's giving of rewards and gifts both large and small.[48] The need to appear generous, to reward lavishly, remained despite the fact that the Roman emperors tended to become the monopoly providers of most major goods (high office, funding for major projects, etc.). Emperors could ill afford a reputation for stinginess. According to Suetonius (*Tib.*46) Tiberius was '*pecuniae parcus et tenax*' – although it might be questioned whether this was necessarily a criticism – and Galba had a reputation for avarice (*Galba* 12). On the other hand, excessive lavishness and generosity were equally the subject of criticism, because it was recognised that the emperor would need to fund this through additional exactions from the people (Suetonius *Gaius* 38). The fact that the outcome of trials was often the confiscation of wealth and property, which frequently came directly or indirectly into the funds controlled by the emperor, created the view that the primary motivation for such trials was to benefit the coffers of the emperor.

There is another key feature of rewards. They need to be given with the prospect that they will be repeated in the future. The expectation of future reward is a powerful incentive for the courtier to remain loyal (see Brosius in this volume on the politics of gift-giving at the Achaemenid court). It is part

---

[48] Millar 1977: 133ff and Kloft 1970.

of the process of building up trust on both sides, the creation of confidence, and the building of a reputation for not 'cheating' on the unspoken contract between ruler and ruled, despite the fact that such a contract was essentially unenforceable by either party. This is the fundamental explanation behind much of the court routine and ceremony – the invitation to the *salutatio*, to the *convivium*, the daily greeting of senators and *equites*, and the formal kiss of the emperor. All these help to promote a regular way of demonstrating continuing confidence on both sides in the relationship.

Finally, it is in the interest of the ruled to persuade the ruler to take a long-term view of his rule. A ruler who only expects to be in power for a short time is more likely to take all opportunities to enrich himself and his supporters at the expense of the immiserisation of his subjects, because he does not care about the longer-term consequences. On the other hand the ruler who seeks to remain in power is more susceptible to implementing policies designed to encourage long-term loyalty, including being seen to be of benefit to his subjects. This is why from the very beginning of the Principate the succession to the Roman emperor is seen as a key issue not just for the ruler but also for the ruled. The annual oath of loyalty sworn by all communities was to the emperor and his family. By transferring allegiance to the heir of the emperor, his subjects fostered the emperor's willingness to take a long-term view. Equally, among the Roman elite the succession of the emperor's legitimate heir held out the prospect of the continuation of favours currently enjoyed and, perhaps more importantly, prevented the possibility of power falling into the hands of a rival member of the elite. As Elias (1983: 177–8 no. 15) notes, hereditary succession 'assured each of the leading groups that [the king] was not too one-sidedly bound to the interests of an opposing group since, unlike a usurper, he had not needed to seek allies among the conflicting social groups in order to come to power. The lawful origin of the kings distanced them equally from all the social groups in the country.' In the case of the Roman emperors there was the interesting variation of the current emperor designating a successor by adopting from within the Roman elite, normally when no natural heir was available.[49] It is far from clear that adoption was obviously more acceptable to Roman senators than the continuation of a dynasty. Tacitus' attitude is difficult to discern, as commentators have noted (see Chilver 1979: 76–7 and Hammond 1959: ch. 1), and he also gives Mucianus a speech later which forcefully rejects this approach (*Hist.*2.76–7). The undesirability of any alternative to the legitimate inheritance of the position of *princeps* was amply illustrated

---

[49] On Galba's adoption of Piso see Tac.*Hist.*1.14ff; on Nerva's of Trajan in October 97: Pliny *Pan.*8.

on those occasions when the system broke down – the civil wars of the 30s BC and of 69 AD and 194 AD.

Imperial circles

Elias (1983: 122ff) notes that in crises charismatic leaders (in a Weberian sense) emerge. They need to foster a cohesive group around them who are prepared to suppress their jealousies and rivalries to work to promote their leader. In such situations talent and ability rather than lineage and nobility are essential for the members of such a group. So such situations can offer considerable opportunities for advancement which are not normally available. However, once the monarchy has been established, then the absolutist patrimonial monarch really wants to promote jealousies and rivalries within his court in order to ensure the fragmentation which helps to prevent the emergence of rivals. This model neatly fits the emergence of the Principate. Augustus' inner circle originally consisted of 'new men' rather than Republican nobility (the thesis of Syme 1939). Such men owed their careers entirely to Augustus. On the other hand, one of the notable features of the succeeding reigns is the number of trials in which the Roman elite sought to destroy the careers of rivals – a situation fostered and encouraged by emperors with rewards for successful prosecution and frequently the addition of confiscated property to the imperial holdings.

Around the emperor there grew up a series of concentric circles containing groups and individuals who gained power and influence for themselves by their perceived proximity and access to the emperor: the imperial family (*domus*), close confidants, the imperial household (*familia*) and 'friends' (*amici*). These made up the bulk of the 'court'. As noted above, the Hellenistic term '*aula*' was adopted and widely used for the court surrounding the emperor. The term covers both the sense of the physical environment – the palace itself – and the people who surrounded the emperor. So the *aula* could be said to favour a person (Tac.*Hist.*1.13: *prona in eum aula* – said of Otho). What is less clear is how far the court extends. Marcus Aurelius (*Med.*8.31) described the court of Augustus as consisting of 'wife, daughter, descendants (*eggonoi*), members of his parents' generation (*progonoi*), sister, Agrippa, kinsfolk (*suggeneis*), members of the household (*oikeioi*), friends, Areius [court philosopher], Maecenas, physicians, haruspices (*thutai*)'. So the court usually covers family and household, but also at least some 'friends' – those who were regularly in the company of the emperor, particularly at leisure times. Suetonius (*Vit.*4), for example, describes Aulus Vitellius as holding a prominent place at court (*praecipuum in aula locum tenuit*). He was the *familiaris* of three emperors (Gaius, Claudius and Nero), because, according to Suetonius, he shared Gaius' passion for charioteering and Claudius' obsession with gaming, and flattered Nero's lyre-playing.

At the heart of the court was the emperor himself. Proximity to power endows individuals with power and influence in their turn. Thus the imperial *domus*, the family, frequently acted as power-brokers in their own right. The most notable evidence of this phenomenon is the appearance under the Principate of powerful women (the mothers, wives, daughters and mistresses of emperors) wielding an unprecedented public influence. Livia under Tiberius is a case in point. There was her notorious support for Plancina, Piso's wife, now confirmed by the inscription recording the trial and punishment of Piso (Tac.*Ann*.3.15). Then there was the consul of 29, Gaius Fufius Geminus, who, according to Tacitus, was good at attracting women (*aptus adliciendis feminarum animis*) and owed his success to the favour of Livia (*gratia Augustae floruit*). All the members of the imperial family attracted supporters and an entourage.[50] Within the family group there is an interesting subset – the children of particular favourites who live and are brought up alongside members of the imperial household. For example the future emperor, Titus, son of Vespasian, who was closely associated with Narcissus, the powerful freedman at Claudius' court, was brought up *in aula* with Claudius' own son, Britannicus, and had the same schooling, with the same masters. He was sitting next to Britannicus at the fateful dinner when Britannicus collapsed and died (Suet.*Tit*.2). Even more interesting were the sons of foreign kings brought up in the court – they are sometimes misleadingly described as 'hostages'. They are a group which deserves further study.[51]

Close to the emperor there was a small number of individuals of varying status, who acted as trusted confidants, and whose whole career rested upon their intimate connection with the *princeps* rather than any official office they held. Maecenas and, above all, M. Agrippa under Augustus and Sejanus under Tiberius provide the model for these *socii laborum* – 'partners in my labours'. They too came to wield influence and power.[52] The fact that these individuals' influence was based entirely on their connection with the emperor and their being seen as the recipient of special favours from him is shown by the protests of senators after the fall of Sejanus. They

---

[50] See an excellent study of the circle around Antonia under the reign of Tiberius: Kokkinos 1992.

[51] I owe much on these last two groups to discussion with Andrew Lipinski, my postgraduate student.

[52] For a detailed discussion of how the influence of such people was gained and employed see Roddaz (1984).

were anxious that their public demonstrations of favour towards him might be the source of accusations now that he had been removed from power. Tacitus (*Ann.*6.8) has M. Terentius admitting that he was Sejanus' friend, 'that he had sought him out and had been delighted when his friendship was accepted'; but he had done so because he had seen the honours and favour which Tiberius had bestowed on him. 'We thought it marvellous if Sejanus' freedmen and doorkeepers recognised us.' Friendship with Sejanus opened the way to friendship with Tiberius (*ut quisque Seiano intimus ita ad Caesaris amicitiam validus*). It was not Sejanus Terentius and others honoured, but Tiberius, who had shown Sejanus such favour. It was not their role to reason why: 'The gods have given you, Tiberius, supreme control, to the rest of us is left the glory of obedience (*obsequii gloria*).' The whole passage is a powerful illustration of the processes at work in the imperial court.

Around the emperor grew up the *familia*, the household of slaves and freedmen, some of whom also gained influence from their proximity to the central power.[53] The *familia* included the domestic staff of the imperial residences, the doorkeepers, litter-bearers, ornamental gardeners, tasters, chefs, court jesters, doctors, astrologers and the like. Most of these were slaves; but once again proximity to the emperor could endow the individual with influence in his own right. The post of *cubicularius* (controller of the bedchamber), for example, had considerable influence on access to the emperor. Gaius' *cubicularius*, Helicon, is described by Philo (*Leg.*175) as 'playing ball with Gaius, exercising with him, bathing with him, sharing meals, and was with him when he went to bed'. It was a matter of concern to Philo's Alexandrian embassy that Helicon sided with their Greek opponents in their dispute. People of course objected to the role which such individuals played as 'gatekeepers' to the emperor. 'How should a man become wise all of a sudden when Caesar puts him in charge of his chamber-pot?', remarked Epictetus.[54] Epictetus, a court insider, himself a one-time slave of Epaphroditus, Nero's freedman *a libellis*, recalled how his master sold another slave because he was useless, only to find the same man installed as shoe-maker to the emperor. Whereupon, 'if only you could have seen how Epaphroditus honoured him now!' It was not the emperor specifically who gave such minor post-holders power and influence inconsistent with their low social status. Rather it was the courtiers who perceived the person as potentially influential and as someone who might give them access to the

---

[53] On all of these see the excellent study by Weaver (1972).
[54] Epictetus *Disc.*1.19.7 (How should we behave towards tyrants?). See also Millar (1965) and Starr (1949).

emperor. While the court in some ways reflected and reinforced the structure of Roman society, in these ways it could also be perceived as subverting it.

The *familia* also included the slaves and freedmen who carried out the day-to-day administrative tasks, dealing with funds, imperial property, etc. The hierarchy ran from what Weaver designates as 'sub-clerical' functionaries, up through 'clerical grades' to the senior administrative posts staffed under the Julio-Claudians by freedmen. Again the posts could be a source of power and influence. The most notorious examples were the freedmen of Claudius, Pallas, Narcissus and their like, whose very real power (for example representing the emperor on campaign) and access to the emperor were deeply resented by the elite. That their influence was real is shown by the fact that these posts came to be held by *equites* in the second half of the first century. Members of the *familia Caesaris* attracted a much higher proportion of wives of freeborn status than the rest of slave-born society, according to Weaver's analysis. At the pinnacle the offices could be the cause of great social mobility – at least for a few. Augustus granted the equestrian gold ring to his physician Antonius Musa (Dio 53.30.3). Under Claudius, Narcissus received *ornamenta quaestoria* by senatorial decree and Pallas the *ornamenta praetoria*. Under Vespasian, Hormus was advanced into the equestrian order for the leading role he had played in the Flavian takeover (Tac.*Hist*.3.12: '*is quoque inter duces habebatur*', and 4.39).

Then there were the *amici* ('friends'). 'Good *amici* were the most valuable instrument of good government' (Tac.*Hist*.4.7). However, these are a very difficult group to define. In a sense everyone of roughly the same social status as the emperor, that is, of the senatorial and equestrian orders, could expect to be considered an *amicus*, unless the emperor specifically renounced that friendship. Emperors regularly described individuals in letters or decrees as 'my friend', both as a courtesy and to emphasise to others that the person had his backing. The important thing was that 'Caesar knows you'. Thus Epictetus (2.14.1): 'What else could anyone imagine you need? You are rich; you have children, possibly also a wife and many slaves. Caesar knows you. You have many friends.' When the emperor was in Rome, it became the custom for senators and *equites* to go to greet him daily (these are the *cotidiana officia*). These were separate from the more general *salutatio*. A call to the palace, a meeting with the emperor, the ceremonial kiss, all were sufficient to confirm an individual as a 'friend'. However, it is clear that a closer group of companions (*comites*) and advisors formed an important sub-category of 'friends' – the *cohors amicorum*, the entourage of the emperor. One of the things which distinguished them from other *amici* was that they would travel with the emperor when he was away from Rome. The choice of such

companions as advisors and officials was one of the most fraught decisions
any emperor had to make. It is no surprise that discussion of such decisions
takes up by far the greatest part of the debate on how to run the empire, which
is put in the mouths of Agrippa and Maecenas by the senatorial historian
Dio.[55] The general principle advocated by Dio and others was to pick the
'best' citizens. By 'best' was meant those of the highest social classes, but
there was also recognition to be given for ability and talent. However, there
was no escape from the emperor's dilemma: 'The ruler who grants such gifts
in the correct way clearly makes it his primary goal to weigh the merits of
each individual. In this way he honours some and passes over others, with
the result that some have another reason for pride and others feel a new
resentment, each being conscious of their own worth. If, however, the ruler
tries to avoid this result and tries to distribute these honours in a haphazard
way, then he will fail completely' (Dio 52.12.5). The *comites*, then, are those
amici who are called regularly to advise the emperor, to form his *consilium*,
to dine informally with him, and to enjoy relaxation and entertainment with
him. Such men rarely lived in the palace. They were called into the presence
of the emperor. The Elder Pliny would visit Vespasian before daylight (Pliny
Ep.3.5.9) before going on to carry out his official duties. It is clear that being
a *comes* was frequently a very demanding position.[56] There were complaints
that it diverted them from their other duties – particularly advocacy. Cn.
Cornelius Lentulus Augur, the wealthy confidant of Augustus, complained
that Augustus 'had not heaped on him nearly so much as he had lost by
surrendering the practice of eloquence' (Sen.*de Ben*.2.27.2). Pliny (*Ep*.4.24)
remarked of a contemporary that: 'Friendship of the emperor has taken
him away from his civil duties.' The duties of 'those who were occupied
in the emperor's entourage' (*hi qui circa principem sunt occupati*) could be
accepted as a legitimate excuse for not being able to fulfil a legal obligation
(*Dig*.4.4.11.2).

It was exclusion from friendship which could be viewed as so serious.
When Vespasian gave offence to Nero by his lack of attention at Nero's performances in Greece, he found himself excluded not just from the emperor's
entourage (*contubernium*) but also from the public *salutatio*, as he discovered to his consternation (*trepidum*) when a doorkeeper (*quidam ex officio
admissionis*) put him out and told him to go to hell! He retired to a country
estate, where he was described as in hiding and terror until a grant of office

---

[55] Dio 52.1–40. The debate, which reflects the views of Dio at the beginning of the third century
AD, has been described as 'the most remarkable treatise on politics that survives from the
principate' (Brunt 1988: 40).

[56] Crook 1955: 26.

signalled he was back in favour (Suet.*Vesp*.4 and 14). When Nero forbad
Thrasea Paetus from attending with the rest of the senate to congratulate
the emperor on the birth of his daughter, according to Tacitus Thrasea
took this as 'the announcement of his imminent death' (*Ann*.15.23). Again
Plutarch (*Mor*.508A, 'On talkativeness') describes a certain Fulvius, whose
indiscreet gossip to his wife about Augustus caused the emperor embar-
rassment. When Fulvius attended the morning meeting with Augustus, his
'Hail, Caesar' was met with the response, 'Farewell, Fulvius'; he retired and
commited suicide.[57]

Ritual and routine

The story of Vespasian shows that membership of the 'court' was not a
matter of titles, posts or anything objective; you were a friend of the emperor
because you were seen as a friend of the emperor. Your status was dependent
to some extent on what others thought your status was. As Elias (1983: 94)
emphasises, a person belonged to courtly society, no matter what his title or
position, only as long as the others thought him a member. 'Social opinion
is the foundation of existence.' From this comes the fact that our sources
on Roman imperial life are full of stories, rumours, signs of favour, etc.,
because that was what made up courtly life; these were the ways in which
people judged what their own standing and that of others was in society and
in relation to the emperor.

So the court becomes a stage on which the emperor can demonstrate his
favour and continuing approval of his courtiers and receive their expressions
of loyalty, while the courtiers can be seen to be the recipients of the emperor's
good will and to be maintaining their loyal support for the emperor. It is a
characteristic of court societies that they develop routines and rituals. These
become ways of creating and reinforcing predictability and the confidence
of all parties in the world of unenforceable promises which is at the heart of
the relationship between the emperor and the court. These *cotidiana officia*,
daily duties, could be represented by both emperor and courtier as irksome
obligations. However, in reality their regularity and routine nature were a
reassurance and created confidence in all who took part. It is a characteristic
of 'bad' emperors that they often neglected or disrupted these events. So Dio
(78.17.3) complained that Caracalla 'would send us word that he was going
to hold court or deal with some business directly after dawn; but then he

---

[57] Tac.*Ann*.1.5 has a different version associated with Paulus Fabius Maximus.

would keep us waiting until noon and often until evening, and would not even admit us to the vestibule of the palace, so that we had to stand around outside somewhere else. Then usually at some late hour he decided that he would not even exchange kisses with us that day.'

There was another aspect of the routine ceremonial and ritual at court which was a constant source of debate and negotiation between the emperor and the elite. Roman senators expected the emperor to be 'one of us', as Pliny put it,[58] that is, to treat senators as far as possible as social equals. The emperor was to be no more than *le premier gentilhomme*. But on the other hand the dignity of the office sometimes required the emperor to emphasise the distance between himself and members of the elite, and to demand deference. There was always a tension between those two aims – it was another of the dilemmas of office.

Marcus Cornelius Fronto, the orator, tutor and confidant of the emperor Marcus Aurelius, in a letter to the emperor finds a neat and clever way both of complimenting the emperor and also of suggesting that his relationship with the emperor was one founded on true friendship, not simply on any of the conventions. Why, he asks, does Marcus love his servant Fronto so much? It was not as if he had ever held a major position. Indeed, he was not even exceptional in discharging the *cotidiana officia*, daily duties. Far from it. 'For he does not come regularly to your house at dawn; nor does he take part in the daily *salutatio* (greeting) nor does he follow you everywhere as a *comes* (companion); nor is he a constant spectator of your activities.'[59] It is a useful list of the courtly routines of a Roman senator.

It was Augustus who initiated the requirement that, when he was resident in Rome, senators should attend him in a body first thing in the morning. From 12 BC Augustus did not hold the ceremony on days when the senate met, so as to avoid holding up the meeting, and indeed when his health broke down in his last years, he abandoned these public appearances altogether.[60] Why would the emperor impose upon himself and the members of the elite what could be a tiresome obligation on both sides? In reality it was a practical way to solve real problems. To see the members of the senate and the prominent members of the equestrian order together *en masse* prevented the emperor from being pestered constantly by them individually for interviews and meetings and also avoided the inevitable jealousies which could arise when one is seen to be favoured over another. It was a characteristic practice of kings and the imitators of kings 'to make divisions of their throng of

[58] Pliny *Pan.*2.4.   [59] Fronto *ad M. Caesarem* 1.3 (Naber p. 5/6) (Loeb 1 pp. 83f.).
[60] Dio 54.30.1, 56.26.2.

friends' (*discribere populum amicorum*) (Sen.*de Ben*.6.34.2). The strategy played upon the strong sense of social equality among the upper classes. In order to control the numbers, emperors adopted the Hellenistic practice of dividing the visitors into groups (*prima admissio, secunda admissio*), with the whole event controlled by officials.[61] It is extremely unclear on what basis the division was made. Senators and *equites* could both find themselves as part of the *cohors primae admissionis* (see Sen.*de Clem*.1.10), and Winterling (as noted earlier) may be right to see it as simply an arbitrary administrative convenience, rather than a division made with regard to social pre-eminence. Further, it was inevitable that early morning would be chosen for these gatherings. It was in any case the traditional time for the *salutatio*. If the emperor had tried to hold the gathering at any other time, this would have opened the way for people to try to jump the queue, to get to see the emperor early and so on. By holding the gatherings early, both the emperor and courtiers were freed to get on with their lives and work for the rest of the day.

At this morning reception both senators and the emperor were expected to wear formal dress, the toga. Nero caused offence by appearing at the *salutatio* for senators in informal dress. Before he was emperor, Severus Alexander is supposed to have turned up at an imperial dinner in an inappropriate *pallium*, Greek cloak; he was lent one of the emperor's own togas, which was taken as an omen of future greatness![62]

The emperor would greet senators with a kiss. There has been much misunderstanding about the significance of this kiss. It was the normal form of greeting between members of Greek and Roman elites.[63] Arrian (4.11.3) notes that 'on greeting men receive a kiss'. Seneca (*de Ira* 2.24.1) suggests that the kiss was a normal part of a greeting when he imagines a complaint that: 'that man did not give me a civil greeting; he did not return my kiss'.[64] Cicero saw his enemies signifying their support for Clodius by kissing him (Cic.*ad Fam*.1.9.10: *Sest*.111). In his epigrams Martial pictures a world full of kissing. Indeed it was impossible to escape kissers (*basiatores*) (*Ep*.11.98.1): there was the man who insists on kissing everyone even in the cold of winter (*Ep*.7.95); at one point (*Ep*.12.59) he gives a whole list of the undesirables who insist on kissing you on your return from a long stay abroad. The prevalence of kissing among the upper classes was demonstrated by an outbreak among the

---

[61] These officials included assistants (*adiutores*), masters (*magistri*), announcers of names (*nomenclatores*) (*CIL* 3.6107; 14.3457; 6.8931; cf. 6.8698ff).

[62] SHA *Hadrian* 22.2; Dio 63.13; SHA *Severus* 1.7.

[63] Contra Kay (1985: 265) who wrongly asserts that kissing was not a usual form of greeting in the ancient world. On the kiss see Kroll 1931; Friedlander 1921: 56–9 (M. Bang); Kühn 1987.

[64] '*Ille me parum humane salutavit; ille osculo meo non adhaesit.*'

upper classes of *mentagra*, a herpes-like skin infection, which led Tiberius
to ban the exchange of the daily kisses (*cotidiana oscula*) at the *salutatio*
(Pliny *NH* 26.2 and Suet. *Tib.*34.2). The kiss was a gesture towards equality,
a sign of the emperor treating senators as his peers.[65] So 'there was general
delight', claimed Pliny (*Pan.*23.1), addressing the emperor Trajan, 'when you
embraced the members of the senate, as they embraced you when you went
away'. Once again it is the arrogant, 'bad' emperor who does not engage in
this practice.[66] Pliny (*Pan.*24.2) goes on to praise Trajan further: 'You do
not force your citizens to grasp your feet, nor do you simply proffer your
hand to their kiss; your lips keep their old courtesy now you are emperor;
your hand respects its proper place.' To kiss someone on the hand was the
characteristic action of a client begging a favour – so candidates for office
kissed the hands of those whose support they solicited.[67] To kiss someone's
feet was the extreme act of a person begging for mercy, the characteristic of a
defeated enemy or a helpless subordinate.[68] Simply to hold out one's hand to
be kissed thus emphasised the superiority of the ruler, while to allow your feet
to be kissed was the mark of the tyrant. According to Suetonius (*Gaius* 56.2)
the petty attempts of Gaius Caligula to demean Cassius Chaerea included
holding out his hand to be kissed. Later it was said that Maximinus Thrax
acted in an arrogant way at the *salutatio*, 'holding his hand out to be kissed
and allowing his knees and even his feet to be kissed' (SHA *Maxim.*28.7). So
the kiss was an important gesture; but members of the elite expected more
than this. A lack of warmth to accompany the formalities could be taken
as a sign of disfavour. According to Tacitus (*Agr.*40), Agricola on his recall
from Britain was ordered to come to the palace by night, was received just
with the formal kiss by Domitian and then without a word of discussion
was dismissed to join the crowd in attendance.

Emperors also held *salutationes* on some days for the rest of the people
as well. These were the *publicae* or *promiscuae salutationes*.[69] From an early
hour 'a crowd made up of almost all classes' (*multitudo omnium fere ordinum,*

---

[65] Cf. the account by Chares of Mitylene (*FGrH* 125 F 18a, quoted by Plutarch, *Al.*54) on the
introduction of kissing among Alexander and his Companions. At a symposium a friend, after
drinking from a cup given to him by Alexander, kissed Alexander, and all but one of the other
friends did so as well. See Bickerman 1963; Spawforth in this volume.

[66] Dio 59.27.1, 'Gaius Caligula used to kiss very few.'

[67] Seneca *Ep.*118.3; Epictetus *Disc.*4.10.20.

[68] Cic. *ad Att.*1.14.5 on Clodius; *Sest.*145 on his brother Quintus begging Cicero's enemies for
support; *ad Fam.*4.4.3 on C. Marcellus. Seneca noted that when Gaius Caligula stretched out his
slippered foot to be kissed, the victim 'lay as a supplicant before him just as defeated enemies
grovel before their opponents' (*de Ben.*2.12); cf. Dio 59.27.1.

[69] Suet. *Aug.*53.2.

Gell.*NA* 4.1.1) thronged around the area outside the front of the palace – the *vestibulum*.[70] When the announcement came that the emperor was receiving, people divided up into their separate groups for admission.[71] They then proceeded into the palace. Security required that those coming in would be subject to searches, a potentially tricky issue for the emperor and one which was likely to cause offence.[72] The way in which one was received by the emperor was a key indicator of one's standing. For some merely to be present at the *salutatio* was a high honour. Emperors were viewed with approval when they knew your name without prompting from a *nomenclator*. Nero 'greeted all classes instantaneously and from memory' (*omnis ordines subinde ac memoriter salutavit*, Suet.*Ner.*10).

The invitation to dinner with the emperor was a particularly important marker for the elite. The *convivium* raised in an acute way one of the inherent contradictions of the Principate. Was the emperor one of the nobility or above the nobility? As D'Arms (1990) has pointed out, the *convivium* had a long-established principle of reflecting a sense of equality among the guests, as a way of fostering *amicitia*. For example Plutarch in one of the *quaestiones convivales* conveys this idea: 'let men understand that the dinner is a democratic affair and has no outstanding place like an acropolis where the rich man is to recline and lord it over less distinguished folk' (*Mor.*616d–f). The emperor might be expected to go out of his way to put guests at ease. So Pliny (*Pan.*49.4–6) has Trajan taking all his meals in public with his table open to all. He joined in conversation in a relaxed and easy way. The contrast with Domitian is always there. One of the signs of this 'equality' was an element of freedom of speech by all and a willingness of the host to take jokes against themselves in good part: 'at dinner parties a certain freedom is not unseemly in people of humble rank (*humiles*), while *hilaria* is becoming in all' (Quint.*Inst.*6.3.28). To some extent it was possible to plead the effects of drink to avoid any lasting resentment. The niceties of the *convivia* were always a matter of subtle negotiation – and considerable anxiety when a guest overstepped the mark.

Augustus' dinners were always formal; he was good at drawing out even his most reticent guest, and enlivened the meals with music and performance (Suet.*Aug.*74). On the other hand, Dio (67.9) describes the feast given by Domitian for senators and *equites* to commemorate the dead in the Dacian campaign. In a room decked out in black, with place-tags that looked like

---

[70] On the *vestibulum* see Gell.*NA* 16.5.   [71] Gell.*NA* 20.1, 'We were separated up.'
[72] Suet.*Aug.*27.4, *Claud.*35.1; Vespasian tried to create a good impression by abandoning them (Suet.*Vesp.*12).

gravestones, and a menu of dishes offered to the spirits of the dead, and in a silence broken only by Domitian's comments on death, the guests might be forgiven for wondering just whose deaths were at issue. Their terror was only assuaged by the appearance of gifts from the emperor once they had returned home. Misconstrued ceremonial or macabre joke? Historical fact or literary construct? Perhaps both. Let no one doubt that there can be very real terrors in dining with a tyrant (see Simon Sebag-Montefiore (2003: *passim*) on Stalin). Yet different reactions to Domitian were possible. In *Silvae* 4.2 Statius offers a much more favourable account of the *sacra cena* in the palace in Rome, to which he was invited. He is pleased that he got to see the emperor close up and the guests were not required to stand as Domitian circulated round them. Again this is no simple eye-witness account and some might be tempted to dismiss it as flattery by a court poet. However, it was difficult for guests to avoid the feeling that, while they were watching the emperor, they were also on display and the emperor was observing them. It was easy to construe this as malevolence on the part of the emperor.[73]

These stories demonstrate two fundamental points about the study of the court. First, there is no one single correct account of the court; there are many narratives from many points of view, all of which have validity. Allied to this is a second conclusion, which arises from the account of Domitian's doleful dinner. Whatever the intentions of the ruler or of the other participants in court life, it was impossible for anyone, emperor or subject, to impose a single meaning and significance on an event.

The emperor was constantly solicited for favours. As already noted, gift-giving was a key strategy for emperors to win loyalty and support. However, receiving gifts from people was potentially problematic. As Roller (2001: 193ff) shows, emperors were extremely reluctant to be seen to accept major gifts or favours, because it would be thought to have put them under an obligation to the giver. This in turn would be the source of jealousy on the part of other aristocrats and could be seen to undermine the emperor's pre-eminence. Turning down a gift or favour without causing offence was one of the arts of imperial government. When the people of Rome presented Augustus with the subscription they had raised to pay for the rebuilding of his house after a fire, he simply took a small amount, no more than a denarius from each pile. He did not want his house to be a burden to the people; on the other hand his action was an acknowledgement of their kind offer (Suet.*Aug*.57.2). The difficulty of accepting major gifts because of the

---

[73] Pliny *Pan*.49.5 praised Trajan: 'You do not sit menacingly over your guests, watching and marking all they do.'

jealousy it might engender may well be part of the explanation of why the emperor was regularly included in people's wills and why he was prepared to accept such inheritances. These gifts came after death and when the emperor could not show favouritism towards any individual.[74]

This problem of 'equality' is found more generally in the dialogue between emperor and the elite, as Griffin (2003) has stressed. While true equality was impossible and the recognition of the emperor's superiority was unavoidable, the emperor could at least act as though the transactions between him and others were the result of true friendship. So, according to Seneca (*de Ben.*2.13.2), 'the gifts that please are those that are bestowed by one who wears the look of humanity, or at any rate of gentleness and kindness, by one who, though he was my superior when he gave them, did not exalt himself above me, but with all the generosity in his power descended to my own level, and banished all display from his giving'.

Palatium

One of the principal contexts for courtly behaviour was the palace. The same sort of dialogue which was carried on about the nature of the court and courtly behaviour also developed about what was appropriate as a residence for the emperor. We have seen that the houses of the Roman nobility in the Republic were thought of as ways of displaying and demonstrating their status, of re-emphasising the social hierarchy. But they were also in part public spaces, accessible to friends and clients, where the noble also carried on public business at the times when he held a magistracy. There was a lively debate from at least the second century BC among the elite about what was a suitable scale for such buildings. The debate took the form of concerns about the moral effects of luxury, but also about the ways that increasing wealth, combined with the competitiveness of the elite, endangered the elite's sense of being a collective in which all one's peers were in some ways equals. That debate took on a new twist when it became a question of what was appropriate for the residence of the *princeps*.

Julius Caesar solved the problem by basing himself in the Domus Publica on the Sacred Way, the official residence of the *pontifex maximus*. In 36 BC Augustus' solution was to obtain a number of houses, including that of the orator Hortensius and the notably lavish property of Q. Lutatius Catulus,

---

[74] Rogers 1947.

on the south-west corner of the Palatine.[75] This house was partly rebuilt
after a fire in 3 AD. What we have to imagine is a sort of imperial compound of houses, including Augustus', the so-called House of Livia, and
Catulus' house. Here resided not just Augustus, but some at least of his
favourites. In 29 BC he gave the house of Catulus to M. Agrippa, and Suetonius (*Gramm.*17) describes Agrippa's sons, Gaius and Lucius, being tutored
in the atrium of the *Catulinae domus*. It is important to note that from
the start the public 'official' aspect of the residence was emphasised. The
original houses were bought at public expense and the public got together
a subscription to fund the rebuild after the fire, although (as noted above)
Augustus carefully avoided using most of these funds. The whole complex
became state property (Dio 55.12). It contained a temple to Apollo with
two great libraries attached. This became a place for Augustus to receive
embassies. Thus in 13 AD 'Augustus took his seat in the temple of Apollo,
in the Roman Library' to receive ambassadors from Alexandria (*P.Oxy.*2435
verso). Significantly, in Augustus' old age the senate was regularly called to
meet in the library and portico of the temple of Apollo (Suet.*Aug.*129). It is
clear that the practice continued under the Julio-Claudians, as we see from
the Tabula Hebana: 'in the palace in the portico which is near the temple
of Apollo, in which the senate customarily meets' (Thompson 1981). The
destruction in the fire of 64 AD seems to have ended the custom.

Suetonius (*Aug.*72–3) makes much of the apparent limited scale of these
buildings and their modest decoration and furniture. But this is misleading.
Suetonius must be comparing the house with the huge scale of Domitian's
Domus Flavia created at the end of the first century AD. It should rather
be seen as something quite exceptional for its time. It focused attention on
the Palatine (Favro 1996: 203–4) with the gleaming marble of the temple of
Apollo, the tower with Augustus' private study, and the entrance to the whole
complex flanked by laurel trees, surmounted by an oak crown, and with a
display of trophies. Ovid's response to this (*Tr.*3.1.33–4) is noteworthy: 'I
beheld doorposts marked out from others by gleaming arms and a dwelling
worthy of a god (*tectaque digna deo*).' It is worth underlining that once again
this official adornment of entrances is an honour which goes back to the
Republic. From the time of Augustus, as we saw, the imperial residence had
taken over the name of the hill, Palatium.

The presence of Agrippa in a house within the compound is perhaps not
that surprising given his exceptional status. But the palace never developed

---

[75] Dio 49.15.5 and 55.12.4–5, Vell.Pat.2.81, Pliny *NH* 17.2, Suet.*Gramm.*17. See Dumser 2002 s.v.
Domus: Augustus, Steinby 1993–2000 s.v. Domus: Augustus (Palatium) (I. Iacopi).

along the lines of Versailles in seeking to provide apartments for all the court nobility. Maecenas chose to have his residence somewhere within the huge *Horti Maecenati* on the Esquiline. Augustus used to retire there when he was ill. There is a significant number of houses of Augustan date scattered over the Palatine and it is tempting to wonder how many came into the possession of particular favourites of Augustus and his successors. T. Statilius Taurus, consul along with Augustus in 26 BC, had a house on the Palatine (Vell.Pat.2.14.3).

Succeeding emperors proceeded to annex much of the Palatine hill and beyond for their palace residence. The motive for this is less the expanding household and more the desire to impress and to make space for buildings, porticoes and gardens comparable to those found in the great *horti* of sub-urban Rome. In doing so it was possible to cross the line between what was generally acceptable and what was not. So Gaius came in for criticism for his extension which took the palace to the edge of the Forum, 'making the Temple of Castor and Pollux his vestibule' (Suet.*Gaius* 22). Of course most notorious of all was Nero's expansion of the palace to link it up with the *horti* of Maecenas and imperial properties on the Esquiline, first with the so-called *domus transitoria* and then with the elaborate and controversial *domus aurea*, which brought *horti* down into the heart of Rome.

Vespasian ostentatiously rejected the Neronian experiment which had caused such controversy, and on the whole avoided the Palatium as much as possible, preferring to live in the *Horti Sallustiani* (Dio 65.10.4). It was Domitian who renewed the 'century-long quest to find a style of domestic architecture appropriate to the princeps' (Zanker 2002: 107 in the best recent discussion).[76] Several features stand out. The new palace has two built-up and imposing façades – one overlooking the Circus Maximus and the other on the north, facing out onto an impressive open space (the *Area Palatina*) and down a long slope which descended to the Arch of Titus. It dominated the city: hence the appropriate reference to it as an *arx* or citadel (see Klodt 2001: 37–62). People often assembled in the *Area Palatina* to await the *salutatio* (Gell.*NA* 20.1.2). They were faced with an imposing façade which did not have an entrance but had a high socle on which stood a colonnade. It was possible to come out into this colonnade through doors from the major public rooms; but there were no stairs down from this large podium into the *Area*. The emperor might appear in the colonnade looking down on the people in the *Area*. This creates messages of majesty and remoteness, quite different from the accessibility associated, for example,

---

[76] See also Tamm 1963.

with Vespasian – 'the doors of the imperial residences were open all day and no guard was placed at them' (Dio 66.10.5) – or Trajan, whose free-and-easy approach the Younger Pliny (*Pan*.47.5) contrasted unfavourably with the gates and locked doors of Domitian's palace.

The entrance to the palace complex probably lay off to the left of the *Area Palatina* as you faced the palace. Here was likely to have been the *vestibulum* where everyone stood round and chatted, while waiting for the chamberlain to call them in to the *salutatio*. Zanker then plausibly reconstructs a circuitous route through the peristyle of the residential part of the *domus*, into the peristyle of the *Domus Flavia* and then into the main reception halls. As Dickmann (1999) has demonstrated, this sort of tour was common in Pompeian houses and was designed to show them off to visitors. The three biggest rooms of the public part of the palace, the *Aula Regia*, the so-called Basilica and the elaborate *Cenatio Iovis*, were the site not just for receptions but also for the feasts (*convivia*). Zanker suggests these three rooms alone could have accommodated *triclinia* for some 500 guests. It was precisely his *convivia* which were such a notable feature of Domitian's reign (Suet.*Dom*.21). Martial (8.39) notes the unprecedented scale of these rooms:

Previously there was no place that could contain
The banquet tables on the Palatine and the ambrosian feasts.[77]

In Nero's exotic and bejewelled dining rooms in the Golden House, there were ceiling panels which could open to shower flowers upon the guests and piping which sprayed perfume upon them. In such a place it was not clear whether the diners were the audience or the actors. Dining areas in private villas continued to be built to take advantage of the view – that is, the diners inside are able to look outwards while they are dining. But it has been suggested that in Domitian's palace the dining areas look inwards and are constructed like theatres, with the diners acting as the audience and the emperor's *triclinium* functioning as a sort of theatre box, where he can be observed and can observe.[78]

The *Domus Flavia* declined in use over the succeeding centuries. This was in part because emperors from the second century onwards were less frequently in Rome. In addition, emperors from Augustus onwards did not always reside in the imperial palace when they were in Rome; they often stayed in either the urban properties of friends or other imperial properties in the city. They, like the nobility, had their summer retreats in the hills

---

[77] 'Qui Palatinae caperet convivia mensae / Ambrosiasque drapes non erat ante locus'.
[78] Bek 1983: 81ff.

around Rome (see most notably Domitian's Alban villa). They also had properties scattered around Italy for their various tours. More distant tours would take great organisation and planning.

The construction of a suitable palace as the environment for the emperor and his court was subject to the same debate as with all other aspects of court life. All the residences from Augustus onwards functioned in part as public buildings, places where the emperor met with his court and others in spaces designed to impress.

Autocracy and the court

The history of the Principate has often been represented as a gradual descent into absolutism. The development of the court could be seen as part of a process which eventually led to the elaborate bureaucratic and hierarchic court around the remote hieratic emperors of the fourth and fifth centuries AD. However, that would be misleading. In reality Augustus had the power to be as arbitrary an autocrat as any of his successors. From the very beginning, power was centred on the figure of the emperor and there were few, if any, constraints other than those which were self-imposed. So to some extent the character of each emperor's rule depended on the personality of the individual.[79] However, it is not the nature of the emperor's power which changes over time; rather it is the court, the arena in which that power is presented, which develops as a result of the dialogue between ruler and ruled. The character of court society may depend less on the behaviour of the individual than on certain evolving sociological processes. The courtier needs to find new ways of standing out from his contemporaries so as to win the particular favour of the emperor. Hence there is a tendency to make higher and higher bids in the flattery stakes and to propose more and more exotic honours for the ruler. For his part the emperor has to pick his path between the wish to restrain excessive flattery and honours but not to offend the proposer. Even more important was the need to be seen to be fair to all and not to be at the bidding of favourites. As a result the emperor tended more and more to be positioned above the court rather than in the court, and to become a god-like figure invested in glorious costume and surrounded with formal ceremonial. The origins of this process were there from the start with Augustus' right to wear triumphal dress.[80] In such a position of pre-eminence the emperor

---

[79] For an interesting discussion of this see Potter (2004: 60–6).
[80] Crook (1996: 136–7) and the ground-breaking studies of Alföldi (1970).

could be seen as above the daily disputes and bickering of the court. At the same time it was in the interests of both the emperor and the court to formalise procedures and behaviour so as to make it look as though there was a rationale, a fairness in the workings of the court, rather than the arbitrary whim of the emperor. The creation of courtly behaviour provided increasing certainty and clarity in how things got done. So emperors moved from providing individual gifts and rewards for courtiers to the regular payment of salaries for members of the increasing court bureaucracies; posts at court became graded in an acknowledged hierarchy; courtiers' positions within the hierarchy of the court were recognised by the increasingly elaborate assumption of overblown honorific titles. This process can be seen either as the culmination of the development of the court in the early Principate or as a specific response to the conditions of the late empire, as discussed by Rowland Smith in the next chapter. I would argue that the court of the late empire is in many ways very different from that of the early Principate, but both are rational responses to the social logic which leads to the creation of all court societies.

Courtly life was a collaboration, a quest, a dialogue between ruler and ruled. It was full of experimentation – not always accepted or long lasting. The courtier was as important a constructor of courtly society as the ruler – perhaps more so.

5 | The imperial court of the late Roman empire, *c.* AD 300–*c.* AD 450

ROWLAND SMITH

I, [an obelisk], reluctant once, am [now] commanded to obey the Lords
serene . . . [for] everything yields to Theodosius and to his everlasting
offspring; hence I am conquered and mastered and raised up into the
high sky.

> (Inscription on an obelisk-base in the Hippodrome adjoining the
> Great Palace at Constantinople, *c.* AD 390 (*ILS* 821))

O Emperor Augustus [Theodosius], if ever there was any one who was
justifiably in fear and trembling when about to speak in your presence, I
am assuredly he; I both feel it so myself, and perceive that this is how I
must seem to those who share in your council at court.

> Pacatus, *Panegyric of Theodosius*, AD 389 (*Pan.Lat.*II.1)

'We saw in the papers that you had had a long talk with King Theodosius,'
my father ventured. 'Why, yes – the King, who has a wonderful memory
for faces, was kind enough to remember, when he noticed me in the
stalls, that I had had the honour to meet him on several occasions at the
Court . . . An aide-de-camp came down to bid me pay my respects to His
Majesty, whose command I naturally hastened to obey.'

> (M. Proust, *A l'ombre des jeunes filles en fleurs*
> (trans. C. K. Scott Moncrieff))

The imperial court in the late Roman state: 'absolutism', imperial 'decline' and the notion of 'the court society'

Late in the third century, in the wake of several profoundly destabilising
decades of near-constant foreign and civil warfare, the Roman empire's
military and administrative structures were extensively reformed on the
initiative of the emperor Diocletian (AD 284–305). His reforming efforts
reached even to the imperial office: an innovative system of 'tetrarchic'
collegiate rule was developed – a team of four co-reigning emperors, two of
senior rank to oversee the eastern and the western territories respectively,

each with a junior to assist him.[1] That particular configuration was soon undone, chiefly by the ambitions of Constantine. But Constantine was a tetrarch's son, and his own career was rooted in the system: he had spent twelve years at Diocletian's court, and had first tasted power as a junior tetrarch, and many of his own military and administrative reforms would later build on Diocletian's. So, too, in his last years he devised a power-sharing arrangement reminiscent of the Tetrarchy, with his sons placed in regional capitals as junior emperors and Constantine himself residing in a newly founded capital on the Bosporus. That configuration, too, was soon unravelled, but the basic innovation implicit in Diocletian's system – the division of power between co-ruling emperors based in regionally demarcated sectors – would endure; Constantinople became the administrative capital for the empire's eastern sector, and from the mid-fourth century until the institutional demise of the western empire late in the fifth there were usually two emperors co-reigning, one in the east and one in the west.

Modern historians of the empire customarily treat Diocletian's reforms as harbingers of a new phase of imperial government, and in Anglophone scholarship it is conventional to denote the empire from around the end of the third century onwards as 'the late Roman empire'. That said, the modern usage arises less from any verdict on an individual emperor's work than from a more generalised impression of transformation: in many other connections besides its military and administrative organisation – social and economic structures, artistic and religious culture, an 'absolutist' imperial ideology and style – the 'late' empire of the fourth and fifth centuries gives the impression of a world distinctly different from the Principate of the first to early third. Among the deep changes at issue, the most obviously 'transformational' are perhaps the Christianisation of Roman government and society, and the 'barbarising' of the army – the increasing reliance of the authorities on barbarian 'federates' recruited to serve as rank-and-file soldiers and military commanders.[2] To Edward Gibbon, of course, these changes seemed pernicious and enfeebling, a 'triumph of barbarism and religion' that contributed to the fall of the empire; and on these or other grounds many historians since Gibbon's time, notably Michael Rostovtzeff, have represented the late empire as an era of manifest decadence and decline. But in the 1970s Anglophone scholarship took a new and radical turn in the writings of Peter Brown, and that older consensus evaporated: in what sense, if any, the late empire could properly be reckoned a world in decline

[1] Barnes 1982: 196.   [2] MacMullen 1988: 199–204.

became the focus of prolonged debate. Brown himself, revisiting the issue in the mid-1990s, thought the fourth and early fifth centuries could more aptly be styled the 'apogee' of the Roman state, at least in so far as its ability to 'make itself present' to subjects and 'induce particular habits of mind and behaviour' was concerned;[3] and to another expert writing at that time it seemed self-evident that 'no responsible historian would [now] want to address the fall of Rome as either a fact or a paradigm'.[4] To be sure, none would now be willing to apply any model of 'decline and fall' without extensive reservations, but there are currently revisionists as well as radicals in this debate[5] – and there are some facts that are hardly disputable: on a very basic test, its capacity to hold and effectively control territory against external forces, the Roman empire was a less powerful state by the end of the fourth century than it had been under the Antonines in the late second; and by the end of the fifth it had ceased to exist as a state in the west. In that sense, at least, 'decline' in the long run was real enough; and the question whether internal factors as well as external pressures contributed significantly to it remains a real one. The barbarian invasions of the late fourth and early fifth centuries, it is true, were linked to large-scale movements of various peoples beyond the empire's frontiers, and beyond the control of its rulers. But Rostovtzeff, like Gibbon, believed that long-term trends within the empire impaired its capacity to respond to military crisis, and it is implicit in the chapter-title Rostovtzeff chose to head his sketch of the reforms of Diocletian and Constantine – 'The oriental despotism and the problem of the decay of ancient civilization' – that in his view the new style of imperial rule they introduced was itself a significant contributory factor; its authoritarian ideology and centralising tendencies, he thought, further undermined a pattern of urban life and local civic patriotism that was already under strain, and its proliferating bureaucracy encouraged venality and corruption in administration. As Rostovtzeff formulated it, the argument was vulnerable on more than one count, and its underlying premises have often been challenged, but in a modified form it still has its modern supporters.[6] It is undeniable, at least, that the late imperial style of rule emphasised absolutist principles in its ideology and imagery, and that it fostered the growth of a centralised and much enlarged bureaucracy in which offices were often bought and sold; and these two developments are closely bound up with a third – the emergence, from Diocletian's time onwards, of a distinctively 'late imperial' court (we use the term generically here: at most times in our period, we have

---

[3] Brown 1997: 24; cf. Brown 1992: 17.   [4] Bowersock 1996: 29.
[5] E.g. Liebeschuetz 2001: 233.   [6] E.g. MacMullen 1988: 44, 190 and *passim*.

noted, there were at least two emperors co-reigning, and each had his own 'court').

The significance of the court in this connection was barely touched on by Rostovtzeff, but Gibbon had observed it when he sketched the Constantinian political system darkly (and in terms to which Rostovtzeff was clearly indebted) as a 'despotism' in which 'the simplicity of Roman manners was insensibly corrupted by the stately affectation of the courts of Asia': 'every rank was marked with the most scrupulous exactness, and its dignity displayed in a variety of trifling and solemn ceremonies, which it was a study to learn, and a sacrilege to neglect'; 'a severe subordination of rank and office' suffused the system, 'from the titled slaves seated on the steps of the throne to the meanest instruments of arbitrary power'; even the inauguration of consuls 'was [now] performed at the place of the imperial residence'.[7] In Gibbon's view, then, the late imperial court epitomised debasement, and bred corruption in government. On any view, it formed the hub around which the personnel of the expanded imperial bureaucracy lived and worked; ambitious men were drawn to its environs in increasing numbers from cities far and wide across the empire. Not only that: over the fourth century, the court itself came to wear a different face; its hierarchical structures and its ceremonial and art mirrored and articulated the absolutist aspirations of emperors in a pattern of ritualised behaviour that required the participation of a complicit court elite. And these developments clearly had repercussions well beyond the confines of the court: court patronage brokered deals, made careers, helped or baulked the efforts of individual petitioners and civic delegates to gain an audience with the emperor; and the image of power evoked in court ceremonial filtered through to the cities in other ways, more or less direct. When Brown stressed the fourth-century state's ability to 'make itself present' to subjects and to 'induce particular habits of mind and behaviour', he was thinking partly of just such things: the inflated diction of imperial edicts, the grandiose portrait statues of emperors, the elaborate pomp and stylised acclamations that marked a touring emperor's arrival at a city – and the echoes of these practices in the honours cities paid to imperial governors and local benefactors.[8] As for the other underlying factor he had in mind, the wide reach of the state's centralised bureaucratic apparatus, it was plainly in one sense a development that chimed with the absolutist ideology emanating from the court: the expanded bureaucracy of the palace would facilitate a more thorough-going and detailed control of the empire from the centre. But there is also a paradox to observe in this

---

[7] *DF* vol. II, 89–91.   [8] Roueché 1984.

connection: courts, after all, entail court patronage; and a classic Weberian typology treats bureaucracy, at least in its ideal 'rational' form, as a system at odds with the workings of patronage. The palace-based bureaucracy of the late empire was more 'patrimonial' than 'rational', no doubt, but its growth may still have made it harder in practice for emperors to rule as absolute monarchs: there was a greater need to delegate power to subordinates; and as the bureaucracy developed it generated extensive documentary archives, and arguably a secretariat predisposed to conduct its business with textually established rules and precedents strongly in mind – which is to say, conducting it on terms that militated against the arbitrary exercise of autocratic power.[9]

The late Roman court was thus much more than the emperor's home and household and place of relaxation, and more than the place where he deliberated with advisors on particular matters of policy. It was a sociopolitical institution that helped to reshape the bureaucratic institutions of the late empire, and a theatre in which a particular ideology of royal power was visibly enacted and made manifest to an elite within the court and beyond it; and the image of power it constructed arguably impinged on the mentality of subjects in broader political and cultural senses too, for good or ill. On these counts, the court of the late empire is a subject that late Roman historians must take seriously, and not just for its intrinsic interest; its development needs to be studied with an eye to its bearing on the broader debate about 'decline'. The notion that its workings and ramifications might somehow have been detrimental to effective government in the late empire is not, after all, just a modern or Gibbonian notion; it surfaces in ancient texts. In this connection, apophthegms and anecdotes can be particularly interesting, since they will often be reflecting less an individual's judgement than a collective attitude or prejudice. To the question of what it is that makes emperors evil, for instance, the author of the *Augustan History* had a ready answer: 'unscrupulous friends (*amici*), pernicious attendants (*satellites*), surpassingly greedy eunuchs, courtiers (*aulici*) who are either fools or knaves – and [the ruler's] ignorance of public affairs'. And he appealed to an expert witness to bear him out:

The emperor Diocletian, while still a commoner, declared that nothing was harder than to rule well. Four or five men gather and form a plan to deceive the emperor, then tell him what he must approve. The emperor, who is shut up in his palace, cannot know the truth. He is forced to know only what these men tell him; he appoints as judges men who ought not to be appointed, and removes from public

---

[9] Kelly 1994: 161–76.

office men whom he ought to keep in office . . . As Diocletian himself used to say, "An emperor – however virtuous, careful or excellent he may be – usually still gets sold."[10]

One would hardly vouch either for the authenticity of this quote or for the writer's claim to have heard it from his own father, purportedly a contemporary of Diocletian; the author of the *Augustan History* was almost certainly a hoaxer writing very near the end of the fourth century, and writing light entertainment rather than serious history. But if that is so, the whole passage may seem illuminating of the terms in which the workings of the court of the 390s were apt to be perceived and caricatured in the popular opinion of the time. Its vignette of the emperor secluded in his palace, inattentive to events beyond it or misinformed about them by corrupt courtiers, and routinely exposed to the guile of the eunuchs who filled the domestic offices of the court, finds many parallels in other writings of those years: Synesius damned the eastern court of Arcadius as a crowd of petty-minded wastrels swarming around a slothful 'jellyfish' of an emperor; Claudian excoriated its *éminence grise*, a eunuch who had made millions through bribe-taking and intrigue and ended up a consul; and Ammianus recalled the eunuchs of Constantius' court as a scheming brood of vipers – the emperor, he pointedly remarked, 'had considerable influence' with the chief snake.[11] And the impression the hoaxer conveys of the court as an emasculating, introverted world that made for lethargic rulers calls to mind a more precisely contextualised anecdote of the early fifth century, a story preserved in Procopius (*Wars* 3.2.39) about Arcadius' brother, the western emperor Honorius (AD 395–423). Honorius was remembered as a notably feeble sort, a puppet of his guardian and ministers (he had inherited the throne from his father at the age of ten), and in this case the image of courtly decadence is conjoined with a celebrated emblem of imperial 'decline' – the capture of Rome in 410 by a band of Goths. Ravenna was by then the western capital, and it was there, the story went, that Honorius learned of the disaster from one of the court eunuchs, a keeper of the royal poultry: when the eunuch announced to him that 'Rome has perished', Honorius' first thought was that his favourite bird, a cockerel named 'Rome', had died; 'But he has just eaten from my hand!', he exclaimed – and then supposedly sighed with relief when the truth of the matter was explained to him. The story is transparent fiction, and the butt of the joke is an insipid individual rather than an institution; but an institutional malaise is implied, and the humour presupposes an audience inclined to view the court and its trappings as symptoms, at least, of the sickness. That

---

[10] SHA *Aur*.43.1–4.   [11] Syn. *De regno* 14; Claud. *in Eutropium* i–ii; Amm.18.4.3–4.

view may have been quite fatuous, of course, and it plainly does nothing to establish that the workings of the late Roman court, taken in the round, really did tend to be subversive of effective government. But by the same token, if we wish to discuss the court in the round, it would be naive and singularly unhelpful to seek to maintain any absolute distinction between the court's historical 'reality' and the perceptions that contemporaries had of it. We must acknowledge at the outset that 'the late Roman court' is a convenient shorthand expression for a complex historical category: the underlying subject at issue is a distinctively configured field of collective human activity and social experience, and the terms in which late Romans understood and represented it are themselves an aspect of the subject. On that score even fatuous ancient representations of court life, if they spoke to a significant strand of literate opinion at the time, may still be historically significant; 'effective government' in the late empire still required, among other things, the cooperation of the authorities and the urban elites – and hence a certain degree of elite consensus: 'in the fourth century, courtesy was still necessary'.[12]

Gibbon famously likened late Roman government to a 'splendid theatre',[13] but he did not attempt any systematic study of the ritualised behaviour and ceremonial of its court, and nor, for a long time, did modern historians of the late empire. In the 1930s, Andreas Alföldi stressed the visual and sacral aspects of imperial power in two trail-blazing studies that linked coinage and texts to trace the development of imperial ceremonies, insignia and dress styles; but he was not focusing principally on the late empire, nor exclusively on court ceremonial, and until the 1960s late imperial court ritual remained a topic usually left to historians of art or to Byzantinists. It received no serious attention, for instance, in one of the great achievements of modern scholarship on the late empire, A. H. M. Jones' monumental 'social, economic and administrative survey' of 1964; Jones' view of the historical importance of the matter is implicit in his crisp comment on the innovations in court ceremonial introduced under Diocletian: 'such trifles can hardly have made much practical difference'.[14] But already in the early sixties some scholars were discussing the ritualised aspects of court culture on very different presuppositions: there were papers of exceptional originality by Ramsey MacMullen on the court's formalised 'bureaucracy-speak', and on the theatricality and sheer visual potency of late Roman ceremonial; and Gervase Mathew, discussing the fusion of imperial ideology

---

[12] Brown 1992: 7–34 (quoting 25).   [13] *DF* vol. II, 90.
[14] Jones 1966: 29; cf. Jones 1964: 40.

and Christian symbolism in court ritual and art, linked it to the artistic tastes and intellectual interests – the 'Byzantine Confucianism', in his phrase – of the scholars who served in the upper levels of the late Roman bureaucracy.[15] Since then, influential works of the seventies and eighties have made the 'representation' of imperial power through formalised display a mainstream subject for historians of the Roman empire. At one point in *Bread and Circuses* Veyne went so far as to picture the entire City of Rome as mutating in the early Principate into a vast 'court for the emperors', a Versailles-like 'shop-window' in which 'the courtier attitude' shaped the outlook of the population at large, the plebs as much as 'mandarin' senators; that particular image is more provocative than persuasive, but 'the power of images' and of stylised behaviour to 'construct' and 'represent' imperial power from the Augustan age onwards has become virtually an orthodoxy in the wake of Zanker's work on Augustan (and more recently, Flavian) art and architecture.[16] So too, the representational power of the late Roman court's ritualised behaviour and ceremonial has been illuminated through studies of its panegyrics and sculpture;[17] few would now dispute that it helped to shape a society 'addicted to grandiose symbolic gestures' in which 'an acute rank-consciousness permeated . . . self-understanding'.[18]

    If the modern consensus on this point owes a general debt to socio-logical and art-historical approaches of the sort that inform the work of Veyne and Zanker, there is also, of course, a more particular socio-logical influence: Elias' *Die höfische Gesellschaft*. Since its publication in English translation in 1983, Elias' book has become a familiar point of departure in Anglophone 'court studies' of late medieval and early mod-ern Europe; but even before the English version appeared, the model of 'court society' that Elias adumbrated with reference to the Bourbon court of seventeenth- and eighteenth-century France was being com-mended to students of the Roman empire by Keith Hopkins, and it would later be cited as a 'fundamental analysis' in an innovative account of the Julio-Claudian court by Wallace-Hadrill.[19] Others are more scepti-cal, it is true: the aptness of applying Elias' model in the case of the late Roman empire (or indeed, to any pre-modern state) has been disputed[20] – and so, for that matter, has the model's intrinsic historical aptness even in relation to Elias' own chosen test-case, the court of Versailles.[21] The

---

[15] MacMullen 1962 (=1990: 67–77); 1964a (=1990: 78–106); Mathew 1963: 38–61.
[16] Veyne 1990: 383–97 (Eng. trans. of 1976 French original); Zanker 1988, 2002.
[17] Panegyric: MacCormack 1981; sculpture: Smith 1985 and 1997; Kiilerich 1993.
[18] McCormick 1985: 14.   [19] Hopkins 1978b: 181; Wallace-Hadrill 1996: 285.
[20] Schlinkert 1996: 478–81.   [21] Duindam 1994; 2003: 7–11.

conceptual and methodological questions at issue have increasingly engaged the attention of specialists in court studies in recent years, and by 2004 the 'theorizing of the court' was itself the dedicated subject of a colloquium at which Elias' model was discussed as a historical phenomenon.[22] For Roman historians, the work done by Aloys Winterling in the later nineties was already pointing in this direction; besides writing a major study of the development of the Roman imperial court in the first two centuries AD he edited two collections of papers, one on institutional aspects of the late antique court, another on 'ancient courts in context';[23] and in one of his own contributions to the latter (essays on 'ideal types' and 'comparative perspectives') he adapted Weber's typology to formulate a refined 'ideal type' of 'the Court' as a configuration of power.[24]

It was one of Elias' central claims that the 'absolutist' court of the Bourbons essentially functioned as an instrument for the 'domestication' of a feudal warrior-nobility. But even if that held true for Versailles – and it is a claim widely criticised by specialists in that field[25] – it could hardly apply in the case of the late Roman empire. In that case, the traditional senatorial aristocracy could certainly not be classified as even remotely a feudal warrior-elite; indeed, on the supposition that the late Roman court served to 'domesticate' elements of any 'warrior-elite', that elite would be more plausibly associated with the new, non-aristocratic breed of 'soldier-emperors' that had emerged in the mid to late third century (Diocletian himself being a notable instance). There are also certainly some notable aspects of court life omitted in Elias' account; he barely touched, for instance, on the significance of the religion and the clergy of Versailles.[26] But perhaps his critics are inclined to ask too much of his model – and perhaps the rather abstract theoretical refinements and closely focused institutional studies of some 'post-Elias' court specialists do not always convey as clearly as Elias did the terms in which life at court was registered in the experience of contemporaries. Whether his picture of the Bourbon court is empirically or methodologically cogent is a question for historians of Bourbon France or for sociological theorists

---

[22] Duindam 2004.

[23] Winterling 1999 (court in the first two centuries); 1998 (late antique court); 1997b ('court in context').

[24] Winterling (1997b: 25; 2004: 89) proposes a model under six broad headings: the process by which different groups converge to 'constitute' a court; its 'structures of communication'; its roles in the formation of political policy and the representation of the monarch; the principles on which those serving in intimate proximity to the ruler are recruited; the political significance of the court's organisational structures, and of their connections with organised political groupings outside it; and the court's role in the display of social rank in general.

[25] Winterling 1997b: 12–13.   [26] See now McManners 1998: 29–57.

– but whatever its conceptual shortcomings and empirical blind-spots, and however doubtful its applicability to pre-modern social contexts, there are nonetheless many features of Elias' account of the Bourbon 'court society' and its 'sociogenesis' that can hardly fail to strike students of the late Roman court as suggestive, at least. The court that Louis XIV established at Versailles reflected and promoted the ideology of monarchic absolutism in manifold ways; it reconfigured the nobility in relation to the monarch, and fixed its ranking order; it fostered a centralised state bureaucracy functioning in close physical proximity to the court; its spatial configuration and its ceremonial and pageants pictured Louis as a god-like Sun King, and his panegyrists projected the image to a readership beyond the court in the orations they published. So too, the social and cultural values engendered at court rippled out to affect the outlook of a wider social elite (a key feature, surely, of a 'court society' in any strong sense of the term). Transposed in art and literature, they helped to shape the representation of the age in the eyes of contemporaries – and before very long, its representation in a classic work of historiography: when Voltaire wrote his history of 'the spirit of men' in *The Age of Louis XIV* – 'the most enlightened that the world has seen' – he devoted three chapters in it to characteristic 'incidents and anecdotes' in which the doings of the court figure prominently. Writers of Louis' own day could evoke the 'Versailles attitude' in various registers, grandiloquent and playful: in earnest poetic vein, 'the age of Louis the Great' is hailed as a cultural match for that of Augustus; meanwhile, in Perrault's fairy-tales, a resourceful cat can prosper at court to win his master a princess's hand in marriage, and in La Fontaine's *Fables* (a work dedicated to the Dauphin in its first edition) 'sa majesté lionne' reigns unchallengeably in a court of foxes, wolves and dogs, deigning to spare an unwittingly errant rat, or pronouncing his own claws too sacred to punish an unmannerly stag (it is a task for his wolves, he decides).[27] On all these basic counts, we shall see, there are counterparts to be observed in the case of the late Roman court. Even the folk-tales and fables of court life find their ancient parallels: the wit and good looks of a poor girl from Athens can charm an emperor's heart and make her his empress; a pauper's gift of a giant apple sows discord at court and wrecks an imperial marriage; an actress of surpassing beauty takes an empress' brother as her lover, but then sees the light and becomes a holy nun.[28] And whether or not they assent to Elias' particular model of the court,

---

[27] *Fab.*2.11; 7.7; 8.14.
[28] Holum 1982: 112–13 ('Athenais'/Eudocia), 176–7 (apple of discord); Cameron 2000: 182–5 (actress).

it comes tellingly easily to historians of the late empire to draw comparisons with the absolutist ideology and centralised bureaucratic administration of seventeenth- and eighteenth-century France.[29] On the face of it, the late Roman empire has the best claim of any ancient Greek or Roman state to be construed as one in which power was configured and mediated through a court whose scale and complexity can arguably bear comparison with Elias' 'Versailles model', and it is not unreasonable to think of the imperial court of late Roman times as constituting a 'court society' in something like Elias' sense of the term.

In what follows, then, it is not implied that Elias' model is perfect or that it is applicable to the late Roman case in all its features; it is simply that one judges the similarities numerous enough and close enough to illuminate some key features of the late Roman case.[30] Having sketched a basic historical setting, and having outlined how the late Roman court tends to be viewed in modern scholarship (and how the views taken of it, ancient and modern, may impinge on broader issues in the history of the late empire), we pass now to more detailed discussion. This discussion falls under three main headings: first, a brief section on terms of definition and description, and on the range of primary source material that historians of the late Roman court can exploit (pp. 167–71); next, a contextualising discussion of the social and political factors that shaped the development of the late imperial court (in Elias' terms, its 'sociogenesis') (pp. 172–87); then a discussion of some more particularised aspects, a (highly selective) 'anatomy' of the court's physical, institutional and cultural faces (pp. 187–225). A brief closing section will offer some concluding observations in the light of the discussion (pp. 225–32).

'The court': late Roman terms of description and sources of information

'The late Roman court', we noticed earlier, is a generalising term for a complex historical category. In English usage, a royal court can be variously

---

[29] E.g. Brown 1971: 42; 1992: 13, 23; Veyne 1976: 343, 378, 449; MacMullen 1988: 99.

[30] Versailles is not the only case that could have been adduced, of course: we might as easily have cited suggestive parallels, say, from the court world of the 'shining princes' of Heian Japan (see Morris 1964, a brilliant work); but as we have indicated, Elias' work has made Bourbon Versailles a familiar point of reference for historians of the Roman court – and it has a particular resonance for the fact that Louis XIV's own publicists and contemporaries imagined themselves subjects of a second Augustus, and took for granted a historical continuity of sorts between the fifth-century emperors and the kings of France (Jones 2002: 2, 6).

construed: as a material object in a specific location (a distinctive architectural complex within which the ruler resides); as a hierarchically ordered human collectivity (the person of the ruler in company with his household, servants and 'courtiers', wherever located); and as an institutionalised social-political entity within which individuals and factions compete for prestige and power, and through which the ruler and his ministers and advisors make and issue policy-decisions in his name. In late imperial Latin and Greek usage too, we shall see, the terms commonly used to refer to 'the court' embrace all of these bands of meaning: *basileion/basileia* can be Greek for *palatium*, but it often implies more than a royal dwelling, and *aulē* (and its Latin derivative *aula*) often denotes more than a hall; 'those around the *aulē*' means 'court officials'; 'those powerful in the *basileia*' are grandees at court, the sort that Ammianus calls 'holders of the first place *in aula regia*', or 'habitués of the *summa aula*', or simply '*potentes in regia*'.[31] Likewise, the consistory (*consistorium*) was both the place in which elite counsellors gathered in the emperor's presence, and the collective name for those counsellors as a corporate entity. An inner elite among them were styled 'consistory-companions' (*comites consistoriani*) or 'the *comites* within the consistory' (*ILS* 1237); but all members of the consistory were also part of a *comitatus* of court personnel in a broader sense. In 'court-speak', the *comitatus* also included the staffs of the imperial household and the various ministries attached to the emperor's person, and the soldiers of the imperial guard. Like 'the court' in English usage, then, *comitatus* often serves in Latin to denote 'the imperial court' as a whole, when viewed as an institutionalised human collectivity.[32]

Although no author of the time offers a comprehensive description or systematic account of the late imperial court as such, a great deal of information about it can be gathered from the extant historiographic and literary sources; in comparison to what is available for ancient courts in other periods, the evidence is abundant. On top of that, there is a profusion of other types of textual testimony, and the material evidence of art and archaeology.

---

[31] On the range of usage, Schlinkert 1996: 461; Eunapius fr. 67.1 Blockley ('*hoi peri tēn aulēn*'); Lib.*Or*.1.94 ('*dynatoi* in the *basileia*'); Amm.21.15.4; 16.8.11; 26.7.6.

[32] For clarity, we may notice here an ambiguity in the term *comes* in late imperial usage. *Comes* was not just a title held by high-ranking persons at the imperial court; it was also a title attaching to a variety of administrative and military offices in the provinces, and it could be granted, moreover, as a purely honorary title; a man might thus be a *comes* without being a member of the courtly *comitatus*. A *comes* in this looser sense is to be classed rather as a member of the general 'Order of Companions', the *comitiva*, within which he was ranked in one of three 'orders' of status. But in practice, needless to say, there was very often an overlap: many '*comites* of the first order' were officials at the court, and hence also members of the *comitatus*.

Still, there are deficiencies in the evidence, and there are very few aspects of the court and 'court society' of the late empire that one could hope to describe in anything like the detail that historians can aim for in the case of Bourbon Versailles, Elias' chosen paradigm. For example, fourth-century archaeological traces of two of the major palace sites chiefly at issue (Milan and Constantinople) are either nugatory or non-existent, and there are no ancient equivalents of the archives of architectural drawings or the account books detailing the occupancy of apartments within the palace complex that exist for Versailles. As for the formalised daily routine of the emperor and his retinue, it seems likely that a particular ministerial department, the *scrinium dispositionum*, was responsible for organising his timetable,[33] and there are scattered insights to be gleaned from our texts; Ammianus, for instance, remarks of the emperor Jovian that 'he was anxious to imitate Constantius [II], often occupying himself with serious business till after mid-day' – from which one infers that the afternoon was more usually devoted to rest and recreation.[34] In Ammianus, of course, we have an exceptionally valuable witness, a historian writing expansively on the fourth-century empire with personal experience of the workings of its court. So too in the speeches and letters of Julian the Apostate we can glimpse court life as it was seen through an articulate emperor's own eyes. There is also a large body of correspondence extant from persons who had dealings at one time or another with the court, sometimes close up (Ausonius, say, or Ambrose), sometimes from a certain distance (Symmachus or Libanius). Nonetheless, one cannot attempt a description of the daily routine of the court remotely comparable in level of detail to modern historians' accounts of the punctiliously ordered hour-to-hour doings of Louis XIV from *lever* to *coucher* – the twice-daily change of clothes, the garden-walk, the hunt, the meals, the attendance at Mass, the sessions with councillors;[35] no late Roman emperor was a memoirist after the fashion of Louis XIV, and there is no real late Roman counterpart to the voluminous 'insider' memoirs of a Saint-Simon at Versailles or a Lord Hervey (Pope's 'Sporus' and 'amphibious thing') at the court of George II – nor any, either, to the frank letters in which royal servants of Louis serving in administrative posts away from court reported back to their court patrons.[36]

We are better placed so far as court culture, ideology and ceremonial are concerned. Here the discrepancy in the quantity and type of evidence available is less marked and less vexing: an abundance of late imperial panegyric

---

[33] Jones 1964: 578.   [34] Amm.25.10.14, with Matthews 1989: 237.
[35] Elias 1983: 200; Jones 2002: 2–3; McManners 1998: 43.
[36] Brown 1992: 13, citing Beik 1985.

is extant in prose and verse by authors quite the equals of Louis XIV's Bishop Bossuet in their hyperbolic praises of emperors as embodied expressions of divinity,[37] and even texts that do not overtly treat court matters are often revealing in this connection. The abbreviated summaries of Roman history produced by Aurelius Victor and Eutropius, for instance, were works written to win an emperor's attention and favour by authors already ensconced as bureaucrats at the court,[38] and the opening sentences of each convey a lot about the court's cultural ethos: 'In about the 722nd year of the city', Victor begins, 'the custom commenced at Rome of obeying one man alone'; 'In accordance with the wish of your Clemency', Eutropius' preface runs, 'I have gathered a brief narrative . . . so that your Serenity's divine mind may rejoice that it has followed the actions of illustrious men.' So too, even a Christian devotional poem recounting a vision of heaven, it turns out, can inform our understanding of court ideology and ceremonial.[39] The visual evidence of statue portraits and coin-images of emperors – interpreted with the requisite methodological awareness[40] – can enhance the picture (the minting of gold coin, after all, became a monopoly of the court in the course of the fourth century);[41] and for details of ceremonial it is possible also to draw something from the Byzantine 'Book of Ceremonies' compiled by Constantine Porphyrogenitus – a tenth-century text, but one preserving some details from a sixth-century style-book by Petrus Patricius.[42]

As for the administrative structure of the court and its bureaucratic apparatus, there are two sources of outstanding value and importance: the *Notitia Dignitatum* and the Theodosian Code. The *Notitia* as we have it derives from a document compiled for a high-ranking official (the *primicerius notariorum*) connected to the consistory at the court of Milan in the early fifth century, and it essentially provides what its full title implies – 'A Register of All Ranks and Administrative Posts, both Civilian and Military' in the late empire. Some of the manuscripts transmitting it, moreover, include many coloured illustrations of the 'heraldic' badges (the shield devices and insignia) of the posts at issue, making it a rich source for ceremonial as well.[43] The Theodosian Code collects the laws and edicts (over 2,500 items) issued by the emperors from Constantine to Theodosius II. The Code was published in 438 in sixteen books, Books One and Six of which collect

---

[37] MacCormack 1981; Kantorowicz 1963; cf. Jones 2002: 3–4.
[38] Bird 1993: xiii; 1994: viii–ix.   [39] Bremmer 1988.   [40] Smith 1997.
[41] Jones 1964: 437.
[42] Av. Cameron 1987: 109–26; McCormick 1985: 4, for traces of earlier, fifth-century 'procès verbaux'.
[43] Kelly 1998: 163–5; Berger 1981 (insignia).

all edicts relating to state-offices and to the ranking of imperial bureaucrats. Formally, it was compiled at Theodosius' order, but what is known about the process of compilation is itself a testimony to the potent influence of the inner elite at his court, and appointment to the body overseeing the task was itself a mark of high honour – and a route to yet higher promotion.[44] Moreover, since the edicts were drafted by a leading court official, the *quaestor sacri palatii* (an office created by Constantine)[45] and were then pronounced at meetings of the consistory, and since a date and place are specified for each edict's delivery, the Code also serves as our basic guide to the whereabouts of the emperors and their court retinues at particular points in time over a century and more (AD 313–438) – on which score, it shows beyond doubt that for most of the fourth century the court was an itinerant body. The *Notitia* and the Code, then, provide a plethora of evidence about the institutional face of the court; but the form in which they provide it also raises problems of interpretation. It is often observed of the Code in general that where a particular matter recurs again and again in its laws, the behaviour they demand is probably more a pious aspiration than any accurate reflection of what was actually happening;[46] likewise, the Code will to some extent distort a court reality messier than the impression it may seem to project of a stable, hierarchical order overseen and sustained by imperial fiat: beneath its compilers' systematised section-headings, the diachronically ordered lists of laws in the Code disclose the court and its bureaucratic structures in a complex process of development throughout the fourth century. It was only in the 370s, for instance, that a single comprehensive ranking system universally applicable to the upper levels of all military and civilian administrative offices became formalised in law, and what A. H. M. Jones observed of the order of precedence of office-holders in this connection could fairly serve as a more general motto for the late imperial court's administrative face: 'it was immensely complicated and became progressively more so'.[47]

No attempt can be made here to engage at length with the details of the court's evolution as an administrative entity: we shall attempt only to indicate the influences affecting the development of the late Roman court in its main lines (pp. 172–87), and then a selective description of its distinctive formal features in terms that can convey something of its underlying social-political importance (pp. 187–225).

[44] Schlinkert 2002: 283.   [45] Harries 1988: 148.   [46] Jones 1964: viii; MacMullen 1990: 67.
[47] Heather 1998a: 188–9; Jones 1964: 534.

Elite reconfiguration and the 'sociogenesis' of late Roman 'court society'

A discussion that aims to contextualise the late Roman court with an eye to Elias' account of the court of Versailles can aptly open with a comparison adduced by a leading Francophone sociologist-historian of imperial Rome. To Paul Veyne, Constantine seemed in one respect a figure closer to Napoleon than to a Louis of the *ancien régime*: over half a century, between AD 260 and AD 310,

> [a] new ruling caste [had] emerged, not from a political or social revolution [as in France] but from a transformation of institutions and the army . . . From every standpoint (including its literary culture), the [elite] political personnel of Constantine's time was as different from that of the early empire as the political personnel of nineteenth century France was from that of pre-Revolutionary times. So ended the Hellenistic and Roman period of ancient history. Constantine meant to heap favours on this new caste (like Napoleon creating barons and counts and making them wealthy). But [he] wished also to be reconciled with the Senate in the strict sense . . . (like Napoleon trying to reconcile the nobility of the *ancien régime*).
>
> (Veyne 1990: 449 n. 210)

Historians of the Roman empire (and of revolutionary France too, perhaps) may think this a formulation in need of qualification on various counts, but few would dispute the basic premise that, notwithstanding any countervailing continuities, the composition of the fourth-century Roman imperial elite was markedly unlike that of the Julio-Claudian or Antonine elite. It is only on this premise that it makes real sense to differentiate the 'late Roman' court as a subject of historical discussion, for 'court' and 'elite' go closely together: Veyne's remarks imply a radical reconfiguration of the court elite, and construe it as an emblem – and maybe also an engine – of the broader shift from 'high' to 'late' empire.

Active initiatives on Constantine's part were certainly central to this reconfiguration, but they need to be set against the Tetrarchic background from which the Constantinian dynasty emerged. Diocletian, too, we have stressed, was a proactive reformer, and his military and administrative innovations – not to mention the absolutist ideology of divine kingship promoted under the Tetrarchs – clearly set the stage for what followed. This point has particular force in connection with court ceremonial; it is to Diocletian, we shall see, that the ancient sources tend to ascribe the introduction of a key ceremonial feature of the late imperial court, the so-called 'adoration of the purple'. But in his case in turn there are continuities as well as innovations to reckon with. Tetrarchic 'absolutism' only amplified on a strand that had been implicit in Roman imperial ideology from its Augustan beginnings,[48] and Diocletian was certainly not the first emperor to lay overt claim to status as a god-emperor elected to rule by divinity, with all that that implies for the formal intercourse between emperor and elite, and for the role of ceremonial as an enactment of absolutist ideology. As formal imperial titles, for instance, *dominus noster* and *deus et dominus* – titles that prompted moderns to coin the term 'the Dominate' to refer to the empire under the Tetrarchs – are quite frequently attested in pre-Tetrarchic third-century usage; particularly significant, perhaps, is the precedent of the emperor Aurelian in the 270s, who is advertised in his coinage as *deus et dominus natus*, 'born god and master' (Alföldi 1970: 211), and reckoned (by a late source, admittedly) to have quelled a mutiny with the declaration that the soldiers erred if they believed they governed the emperor's fate, 'for God alone could grant him his position and decide the length of his reign'.[49] The same is the case with sundry details of titulature and visual features in coin-images and portrait statues that are attested for Diocletian and/or Constantine, and which are taken in combination to mark a distinctively 'absolutist' late Roman style of rule. Constantine, it should be granted, not Aurelian (the claims of late literary sources notwithstanding) was the first Roman emperor to wear the jewelled royal diadem;[50] but for many other titles and symbolic appurtenances there were clear precedents. The orb held by the emperor as an emblem of power over the world, for instance; or his claim to possess a divine *comes* (an especially piquant item for us, with its implication that the emperor has recourse to a heavenly as well as an earthly *comitatus*); or the routinised application of the epithet *sacrum* to things pertaining to the emperor and his doings, until in Constantinian 'bureaucratese' it has effectively come to mean simply 'imperial' (*sacrae constitutiones* for imperial legislative acts, *sacrum palatium* of the imperial palace, *sacra largitio* of the imperial treasury, *sacrum cubiculum* of the imperial bedchamber, and so on); even, perhaps, the ritual 'adoration of the purple', or elements of it (see below, pp. 175–6) – each of these features finds pre-Tetrarchic counterparts in the mid to late third century.[51] When Millar characterised that period as 'even on our inadequate evidence, one of the crucial periods in European history'[52] he was not thinking principally of the court, but if we

---

[48] Veyne 1990: 292–306; Crook 1996: 113–23; Garnsey and Humfress 2001: 24.
[49] Petrus Patricius, fr. 10.6 (=*FGH* IV.197).   [50] Alföldi 1970: 267; Smith 1997: 177.
[51] Alföldi 1970: 117–20 (orb); 1970: 216 (divine *comes*; cf. Nock, 1972: 653–75); Alföldi 1970: 32–3 (routinised application of *sacrum*); 1970: 53–9, with Stern 1954: 184–9 ('adoration').
[52] Millar 1967: 248.

take an Eliasque view of the significance of court ritual his judgement has a special edge. In the symbolism of its ceremonial and titulature, at least, the late Roman court clearly owes something substantial to third-century innovations in imperial style and ideology: if a distinctively late imperial court style can be said to have emerged under Diocletian and Constantine, then, it was constructed partly by a combining and reconfiguring of pre-existing elements into a pattern that to some extent became systematised in their reigns.[53]

To identify third-century precedents for features of ideology and ritual that show up in the fourth-century court does little in itself, however, to explain why or how the ideology and ceremonial of that court took on the shape it did; it really only shifts that question back in time. There will almost always be continuities of a kind to observe, and on that basis one could trawl further back again for 'precedents' of some sort till one ended up, say, with the *deus et dominus* Domitian and his *Domus Flavia*.[54] To give explanatory force to the particular third-century precedents we have noticed, one needs to look beyond them to their broader third-century historical context, and to consider what background conditions and developments could have caused an overtly absolutist imperial style, one that Tacitus or Suetonius would have judged monstrous or mad, to come to appear quite normal and proper features of court practice to a fourth-century eye. The question is potentially a very large one: here it must suffice to indicate certain key developments and to comment briefly on their likely significance. We touch in turn on the emergence of 'soldier-emperors' in the third century; on possible 'oriental' and Hellenistic influences on court style; on the political marginalisation of the traditional senatorial elite; and on the rise of a non-aristocratic professional bureaucratic elite.

'Crisis' and 'recovery' were long the watchwords for historians of the third-century empire. Over the last generation, the notion that a generalised 'crisis' afflicted the empire overall in this period has been challenged on many counts, but in the decades around the mid-century there was indisputably a military crisis, and it is clearly more than a coincidence that imperial ideology subsequently takes an overtly 'absolutist' turn in its emphasis on the image of the emperor as soldier and guarantor of victory and its correspondingly diminished concern to maintain the style of the *civilis princeps*

---

[53] Only 'to some extent', one ought to stress: in Eliasque terms, the 'sociogenesis' of late Roman court society was a long-drawn-out affair that continued beyond Constantine's reign, and perhaps only crystallised with the emergence of Constantinople and Ravenna as permanent imperial capitals and court residences in the late fourth and early fifth centuries.

[54] Zanker 2002. See Paterson in this volume.

as a senator-emperor closely identified with the traditional aristocratic elite (see Paterson in this volume). We can note as particularly significant on this score the progressive decoupling of emperors from the social milieu of the Roman senatorial aristocracy, and finally from the city of Rome itself; early in Diocletian's reign, Rome was to cease to serve as an imperial residence.[55] From around the mid-third century, as is well known, many of the Roman emperors were career-soldiers hailing from the Balkans who had risen to power through the ranks and will of the Danubian legions – emperors without family roots in the Roman senatorial milieu, and with less reason than their earlier counterparts had had to publicise themselves in conformity with the old ideology of the *civilis princeps* ruling by senatorial consensus.[56] The intensified emphasis in their publicity on the symbolism of military authority and divine charisma was surely partly driven by their need to sustain the supra-personal mystique of the imperial office in symbolic terms that spoke effectively to their key target-audience – the armies – and fostered a sense of awe and loyalty. The practical difficulty that 'soldier-emperors' faced on this score is implicit in the proliferation and quick turnover of emperors and pretenders in this period; they tended to rule a short time, and to die at the hands of disaffected troops or in civil warfare against rival generals. This would clearly seem a highly significant background factor for our purposes: the symbolism of military authority and divine charisma suffused the ceremonial and titulature of the Tetrarchic and Constantinian courts, and both Diocletian and Constantine's own father, Constantius – and for that matter the other two original Tetrarchs also – were men from just the stable at issue: all were Balkan-born career-soldiers of low social status and obscure stock who had won promotion through talent or luck.[57]

In some of its particular features, late Roman court ceremonial was conceivably influenced by non-Roman cultural practices. A major constituent of the military crisis of the third century was the rise of a new power in the east laying claim to the heritage of the Achaemenid empire, the Sasanians, and in third-century imperial ideology Sasanid Persia became 'the enemy' *par excellence*, a prime focus of attention for Roman emperors in both warfare and diplomacy (see Wiesehöfer in this volume). It has often been suspected (it is implicit in Rostovtzeff's phrase 'the Oriental Despotism') that the symbolic elevation of late Roman emperors as socially remote, depersonalised beings displaying themselves to subjects in motionless, imperturbable posture may owe more than a little to an 'oriental' royal style encountered by the Romans in this connection: Ammianus, after all, identified distinctive features of

---

[55] Potter 2004: 281.   [56] Wallace-Hadrill 1982.   [57] Barnes 1982: 30–8.

the court ceremonial and of the stylised costume and deportment of the emperor – the ritual adoration of his purple robe of office, and his wearing of jewelled clothing and footwear – as 'Persian customs', and attributed their introduction among the Romans to a Diocletianic innovation.[58] One might even look for a stimulus in particular diplomatic and military episodes; in 387 (if the panegyrists are credited), Diocletian went to Syria to make a treaty with the Sasanian king which involved the latter prostrating himself at Diocletian's feet in a ritual *proskynesis*, and in a campaign of 298 his junior colleague Galerius captured the camp and household and much of the court of King Narses – 'his wives, sisters and children, a vast number of the Persian nobility and a huge amount of Persian treasure' – and led them back in triumph to Diocletian.[59] Admittedly, some moderns doubt the relevance of the 'Persian model',[60] and Alföldi judged the hypothesis of direct external influence from Sasanid (as opposed to old Achaemenid) Persia redundant: he traced the origins of the *adoratio purpurae* back to a first-century blending of a Roman tradition (the *supplicatio*) and Hellenistic royal ceremonial, and argued on numismatic evidence that the ritual had already become firmly established in the Roman imperial court at least twenty-five years before Diocletian's accession.[61] But Alföldi was probably misleading on that last count, and in any event it is important to stress that, so far as the political and social workings of the fourth-century court are concerned, the issue is to do not simply with factual realities but with fourth-century perceptions. Whether or not 'Persian customs' were in fact a significant influence on late Roman imperial ceremonial and stylised deportment, it is telling in itself that fourth-century sources talk as if they were; they look back on the reign of Diocletian as the point of entry of a new 'despotic' imperial style that they choose to associate with foreign, Persian, practices.[62]

Hellenistic court style was no doubt also important as a residual influence, as Alföldi supposed. The royal diadem that makes its first appearance on a Roman emperor's head in coin-images of Constantine was modelled on the Hellenistic diadem;[63] and from Augustus onwards, of course, ceremonial ruler-cult rooted in a Hellenistic model was always an element in the self-representation of Roman emperors – an element that might be evoked overtly or by association, emphatically or 'modestly', in different contexts. If the ideology of *civilitas* had prompted 'good' emperors in the early empire to

[58] Amm.15.5.18; cf. Victor 39.2, Eutrop. 9.26.
[59] *Pan.Lat.*10.10.6, with Potter 2004: 292 n. 151; Eutrop. 9.25.
[60] Nixon and Rogers 1994: 51.
[61] Alföldi 1970: 6–25, 45–73; cf. Kolb 2001: 39–40; but NB the response to Alföldi in Stern 1954.
[62] Matthews 1989: 244–5.   [63] Smith 1997: 177.

affect modesty on this score, third-century soldier-emperors had less cause to play shy in their dealings with the senatorial elite, and features of ceremonial once chiefly associated with provincial emperor-worship may easily have seeped into court ritual. A particular Hellenistic cultural icon arguably spoke loudly in this connection. The image of Alexander the Great had figured in the repertoire of imperial self-publicity ever since Augustus gazed on Alexander's mummy and chose to use his portrait head as his official seal,[64] but the re-emergence of Persia as the enemy *par excellence* may have encouraged third-century emperors and their publicists to take a sharper interest in the figure of Alexander. Even before the rise of the Sasanian dynasty, the emperor Caracalla (211–217) was seeking to project himself as a ruler in the mould of Alexander; and by the 230s the formal titulature of an African *municipium* could flatteringly associate the reigning emperor Alexander Severus, currently campaigning against the Sasanians, with his great namesake.[65] In the anonymous text extant as *Alexander's Itinerary* we have evidence of a lively interest in Alexander at the court of Constantius II in the mid-fourth century: composed *c.* 340, the *Itinerary* was a work of court literature dedicated to Constantius at a time when he too was fighting a Persian war; it measured his achievements against Alexander's, and a good case can be made for ascribing authorship of both the *Itinerary* and a near-contemporaneous translation into Latin of the *Alexander Romance* to a highly placed figure at court – Flavius Polemius, a consul of 338.[66] Imperial publicists could likewise pick up on features of Alexander's own court style – or on what was taken for such, on the strength of stories in the popular tradition: Julian, for instance, wrote panegyrics to be delivered at court in Constantius' presence in which, like the author of the *Itinerary*, he flattered the emperor by comparing him to Alexander, notably for his generosity to *philoi* at court.[67] For the philosophically minded, of course, Alexander was hardly an impeccable model, and in the texts of moralists his desire to be worshipped as a god had often figured as a topos for excessive pride. Nonetheless, the image of Alexander could still have helped to disarm lingering chauvinist suspicions that the ritual 'adoration of the purple' was an utterly alien 'oriental' practice unbecoming at the court of a Roman emperor. If Diocletian, for instance, was indeed the emperor under whom the ritual 'adoration of the purple' was formalised, one wonders whether he would have wished to be viewed (or to view himself) as importing a Persian custom

---

[64] Suetonius, *DA* 18; 50.
[65] Potter 2004: 142–4 (Caracalla); Gascou 1981: 231–40 on Giufi (cf. Dio 80.18.3).
[66] Lane Fox 1997: 239–52.   [67] Jul.*Or*.1.43c.

outright; it would seem unlikely, to judge by his excoriation of 'the detestable customs and depraved laws of the Persians' in his celebrated *Edict against the Manichees*. Alexander could offer a mediating precedent; the *adoratio* plainly has a close connection with *proskynesis* – a Persian custom originally, but famously one that the Macedonian Alexander had taken up, and hence, in a sense, had 'domesticated' (see Spawforth in this volume). Alexander's court style, in any event, had more than one dimension that could be evoked in imperial publicity; over against the conqueror who adopted Persian dress and demanded *proskynesis* as the son of Zeus-Ammon, there was a homelier Macedonian side – the tough soldier-son of Philip who hunted and dined at ease with a band of intimate *philoi*. This aspect may perhaps have been in Julian's mind when he set about purging the hypertrophied court of his predecessor Constantius II. Julian was (on balance) an admirer of Alexander,[68] not least because he had proverbially judged a ruler's true wealth to lie in his possession of true *philoi* (Jul.*Or*.2.86b), and as a junior emperor in the 350s Julian had evoked the Alexander-image in his own publicity and correspondence; in his *Self-Consolation on the Departure of Sallustius* Julian likened his own need for an honest herald to Alexander's, and implicitly cast the friend departing from his western court as a loyal Hephaestion, and on one view a later coin portrait of Julian was modelled on a well-known coin-image of Alexander.[69]

On the ideological plane, aggrandising features of court style could easily be accommodated in the rhetoric of court panegyric and propaganda by recourse to Hellenistic philosophic theories of kingship, as they later were in the fourth century by Themistius and Synesius, and (with an overtly Christian tilt) by Eusebius in his *Tricennial Oration*.[70] So too, more generally, Greek intellectual currents of the period could impinge on educated minds at court – the pagan henotheist strain that developed in third-century (neo-)Platonist 'solar' theology, for instance, with its emphasis on a transcendent unifying Godhead, depersonalised and far distant, working its effects through a hierarchy of subordinate *daemones*. Quite what the lines of relationship were between such philosophic ideas and the increasingly absolutist strain in imperial ideology and publicity is a matter we must leave aside – but it is irresistible to observe that Plotinus himself enjoyed close contact with the court of Gallienus, and that one of his star pupils, Cassius Longinus, fetched up in Palmyra as a rhetor at the court of Odaenathus, and

---

[68] Smith 1995: 12–13.
[69] Alföldi 1962: 403 (coin-image); Jul.*Or* 8.250d–251c, with Smith 1995: 33 (Sallustius' departure).
[70] Euseb.*Tric.*, esp 5.4–7; Baynes 1955: 168.

wrote a speech about the prince which was still being read in the late fourth century.[71]

We pass from questions of the court's ideology and style to a more basic matter: the progressive marginalisation of the traditional senatorial class in army and administration in the course of the third century, and its implications for the social composition of the imperial court. In the early empire, the senatorial order had furnished the emperor with his generals and provincial governors and with the bulk of the *amici* and *comites* from among whom he selected his advisory counsellors at court. The senatorial ethos of public service had been studiedly non-professional; senators were typically 'all-rounders' who held both civilian and military office in the course of careers punctuated by long periods of residence at Rome as *privati* and habitués of the Palatine court. By the second century the expansion of equestrian offices in the imperial administration had increased the pool of equestrian *amici* and *comites* from whom court counsellors could be drawn, but the dominance of the senatorial class in the mixture had remained uncontested until the reign of Commodus (180–192).[72] The military and economic pressures of the third century finally dissolved this pattern, further enhancing the role of elite equestrians in the administrative and military branches, and making them a powerful presence at court: by the 270s, equestrian legates had come to replace senators as legionary commanders and governors of praetorian provinces.[73] The effective redundancy of the old senatorial elite was underlined by the reforms of the Tetrarchic age. Under Diocletian, the provincial administration was reconstructed and the command structure of the army was further modified:[74] the traditional provincial territories were subdivided into smaller units, effectively doubling the total number of provinces to around a hundred, and these new units were subordinated within a new hierarchical structure; sets of adjacent provinces were assigned to one of a dozen 'dioceses', with governors assigned at both levels, 'vicars' for the dioceses, *praesides* in provinces, each with a substantial office of support staff – three hundred for a vicar, one hundred for a *praeses*.[75] In the fourth century, probably soon after Constantine's death, a new administrative layer would be established: the dioceses themselves were divided into three (and later into four) units, each assigned to a praetorian prefect.[76] At the same time, provincial governors were stripped of their former military functions, which were now transferred to a new order of provincial military officials

---

[71] Rist 1967: 13; Potter 2004: 261. [72] Eck 2000: 197–203. [73] Potter 2004: 229–32, 258.
[74] Jones 1964: 42–9. [75] Jones 1964: 592 (on fourth-century figures).
[76] Jones 1964: 270.

(*duces*). The net result was a vast increase in the total number of offices to be filled in the military and provincial administration, the great bulk of which were simply no longer open to senators; military command was a professional preserve, and almost all of the new provinces were to be administered by equestrian governors. And there were repercussions, too, for the imperial bureaucracy. As the number of military and provincial posts increased, so did the number of bureaucrats needed to service them (and in the tetrarchic arrangement, furthermore, there were four emperors, each with his own *comitatus*). In the earlier third century there had been around 200 salaried senior civil servants at most, equestrians working with the clerical assistance of around 2,000 slaves and freedmen of the imperial household; estimates of the total size of the bureaucracy in the fourth century, by contrast, put it at around 30,000–35,000, of whom perhaps as many as 6,000 were holders of prestigious 'upper-level' posts.[77] The proportionate increase is immense, and an obvious question arises: how were the professional personnel of this greatly enlarged bureaucracy to be integrated and status-ranked in the social hierarchy of the late empire?

Against this background, the exuberant development of the fourth-century imperial court and its attendant bureaucracy – the sheer increase in the number of personnel, the elaboration and systematising of ceremonial and protocols, the complexity of its hierarchy of offices – can plausibly be viewed as central both to the political and social integration of a new professional elite and to the forging of a rapprochement of sorts between the soldier-emperors and the traditional ideology of civilian society.[78] 'Every form of rule', Elias maintained, 'is the precipitate of a social conflict: [it consolidates] the distribution of power according to its outcome, [and] the moment of consolidation . . . has a determining influence on its specific form.'[79] In the case of the late empire, the long reign of Constantine is a key period of consolidation, and for our purposes it would be hard to overstate the importance of three Constantinian developments in particular.

First, Diocletian's effective separation of the military and civilian career ladders in the imperial service was completed and institutionalised under Constantine.[80] Generals were from now on almost exclusively men of purely military background appointed from the junior officer ranks – and, increasingly, of Germanic ethnic extraction. The attention of the educated urban classes, and of at least some of the elite senatorial class, now fixed on the imperial court, and on office-holding at one level or another in the departments

---

[77] MacMullen 1988: 144, 264; Heather 1998a: 189.   [78] Matthews 1975: 47–54.
[79] Elias 1983: 146.   [80] Jones 1964: 101.

of its bureaucratic apparatus, as prime means of advancement; a successful career in the bureaucracy could gain a non-senator senatorial status, not to mention wealth. Nor could those already possessed of senatorial status and wealth in abundance afford to ignore the court if they entertained political ambitions; proximity to the emperor offered influence and powers of patronage, and appointment to the ranks of the *comites* of the consistory and to the high offices at the pinnacle of the bureaucracy.[81] The jargon and trappings of the bureaucracy, it is telling, continued to evoke the aura of the military units in which the senatorial and equestrian elites had formerly served as officers and generals: departmental posts were formally styled *militiae*, military offices, and those who occupied them were all technically soldiers; their pay was received (or at least calculated) in kind, as 'rations' and 'fodder' (*annonae* and *capitum*); officials wore 'uniform' (*vestis*) – a military cloak (*chlamys*) and belt (*cingulum*) – and sported embroidered patches (*segmenta*) on their tunics as badges of office; on entry to their posts, they had their names added to the strength of a fictive military regiment.[82] In practice, though, the distinction between real military service (*militia armata*) and a civilian office in the bureaucracy (*militia officialis*) was clear and sharp. To gain entry to the latter, one used whatever means one could; a decent level of education was assumed, and legal expertise could help especially. But so could patronal influence, and so could cash: purchase of offices is very well attested for this period, and indeed became normalised.[83] This is as one would expect: in Weberian terms, we have observed, the late Roman bureaucracy remained a 'patrimonial' bureaucracy – a system still closely linked to the emperor's household and court in which patronage and favouritism could still trump criteria of seniority or 'merit'. Court service patently served as a key avenue of social mobility; ambitious men were willing to pay not just for an immediate appointment to office at court, but even to have their names, or those of their children, entered as supernumeraries on waiting lists for posts years before they became vacant.[84]

Second, Constantine created a new 'Order of Imperial Companions' – a *comitiva* whose members were hierarchically ranked internally as *comites* of the First or Second or Third Order.[85] The title *comes* was by no means new in itself – it had long been used to designate the *amici* who accompanied the emperor on his travels[86] – but the formalised subdivision into three grades was a major innovation, and the rank was from now on officially conferred

---

[81] Jones 1964: 557.　　[82] MacMullen 1990: 95–100; Kelly 1998: 168; Jones 1964: 566.
[83] Ste Croix 1954: 38; Veyne 1981: 339.　　[84] Jones 1964: 570; Heather 1998a: 196.
[85] Jones 1964: 104–5; Scharf 1994.　　[86] Eck 2000: 206–7.

by codicil. Moreover, as we have noted earlier, in the fourth century the title of *comes* came to be awarded often as an honorary grant to men who were not actually members of the emperor's *comitatus*, and who might not be holding an official post at all. Constantine's creation of this newly formalised category of imperial *comites* can be viewed *inter alia* as a means of reconciling and integrating the old senatorial aristocracy and the new breed of professional administrator: the title could be bestowed on both senators and high-ranking equestrian officials in imperial service; as a new, 'third' order of nobility that overlapped with the established senatorial and equestrian orders, it became a status-category to which members of both those orders (and, for that matter, men who were members of neither) could aspire.[87] It also advertised the centrality of the court, of course, and the practical importance of access to its 'high authorities' (Amm.28.6.9), either directly or through a court patron. Inasmuch as the rank of *comes* was likely to be granted for what the emperor viewed as loyal and useful service, it illuminates a basic choice facing Rome's traditional senatorial aristocracy in the fourth century:[88] either to keep one's direct contact with the court to a minimum and to rest content with a life of *otium* and local dignity in a historical 'show-piece' of a city that was rarely even visited by the emperor, and fast becoming a political backwater; or else to accept that high birth now counted for less than it once had, and to make for the court and seek high office and advancement in imperial service. It was a choice to which Symmachus frequently alluded in his letters. Symmachus himself was temperamentally inclined to the former path; he was awarded the honorary title of *comes*, admittedly, when he visited the court of Valentinian I at Trier on the senate's behalf, to present the emperor with a gift of gold to celebrate the fifth anniversary of his reign, but he remained only a '*comes* of third rank', and never sought or held an office in the imperial bureaucracy. His near-contemporary Petronius Probus, by contrast, the head of the great house of the Anicii, followed the other path: 'more at home amid the intrigues of court than the salons of Rome', he became 'the greatest aristocrat and courtier of his time', winning the praetorian prefecture four times over – and immense riches in the process.[89]

Third and last, Constantine set in motion a process that over the course of the fourth century would utterly transform the senatorial order itself, both in the numerical strength and the social composition of its membership,

[87] Jones 1964: 106.   [88] See Matthews 1975: 9–31.
[89] Cameron 1985: 164; Matthews 1975: 17, 187.

and in its basic relationship to the imperial court and bureaucracy.[90] Various Constantinian measures contributed to produce this transformation. The most significant, in the long term, was the practice of awarding senatorial status as of right to numerous categories of equestrian office-holders on appointment – to all provincial *praesides*, all diocesan 'vicars' and all praetorian prefects, for instance – or when they retired; likewise, it also came to be awarded routinely to retiring military officers down to, and including, the rank of tribune. Then there was the opening up again to hereditary senators of some of the administrative posts that Diocletian had reserved exclusively for equestrians. And on top of that there was the creation of a new imperial senate for Constantine's newly founded capital in the east. Around the mid-century, the senate of Constantinople was raised to parity of dignity with Rome's, and senators resident in the eastern provinces were transferred from the Roman to the Constantinopolitan senatorial roll: whereas the entire senatorial order under Diocletian still numbered around 600, as it had in Augustus' day, by the 380s there were about 2,000 Constantinopolitan senators, and probably as many again at Rome.[91] Senatorial status, moreover, remained hereditary, so growth would continue exponentially as time passed. This massive expansion was comparable to what had already occurred earlier in the case of the (non-hereditary) equestrian order, whose numbers had been increased many-fold by the appointment of commoners to a plethora of Diocletianic posts that conferred equestrian status on the holder, and by retrospective grants of honorary equestrian status to reward loyal service.[92] The scale of increase in the case of the senatorial order, and the transformation of the relationship holding between it and the imperial bureaucracy, can be appeciated if we collate figures from the mid-third century and the start and end of the fourth; around AD 250 there were probably about 200 top-ranking bureaucrats, all equestrian; under Diocletian, we have just noted, there were perhaps 600 senators overall, again effectively excluded from the offices of the bureaucracy; by around AD 400, by contrast, there were nearly 6,000 high-ranking posts in the imperial bureaucracy conferring senatorial status on the holder, either on appointment or on retirement.[93]

Overall, then, both of the traditional aristocratic orders, senatorial and equestrian, became grossly enlarged in the course of the fourth century. The predictable result was status inflation. In the case of equestrians, only enrolment in the inner elite category of *perfectissimi* now conferred any real

[90] For what follows, see Heather 1998a: 184–204; Potter 2004: 386–91.
[91] Heather 1998a: 187.   [92] Jones 1964: 526–9.   [93] Heather 1998a: 190.

prestige; and as the holding of senatorial status became more widespread, the lustre even of the equestrian 'perfectissimate' declined. So too with the senatorial order itself: as possession of senatorial status *per se* became more common, its prestige diminished, and a formalised hierarchy developed within the order – in ascending order, the senatorial ranks of *clarissimus*, *spectabilis* and *illustris*; over time, effective membership of the senate was to be confined to the top-ranking band of senatorial *illustres*, and the prestige and privileges associated with the lower two bands were reduced. The broad effect of this internal banding was 'to transform the aristocracy from one of birth to one of office'; [94] senatorial status as such was still hereditary, but a hereditary senator, even if he was the son of an *illustris*, only inherited the rank of a *clarissimus*; in order to obtain the rank of a *spectabilis* or an *illustris* for himself he needed either to win appointment to an office in the imperial bureaucracy that conferred it automatically, or else to be awarded the rank by the emperor's special grant. Either way, an entrée at court, or the help of a well-placed patron there, was normally a *sine qua non*. In the case of the new imperial senate at Constantinople, the lesson was particularly clear: its rapid growth from the mid-fourth century onwards discloses it as increasingly an epiphenomenon of the imperial court and central bureaucracy. Unlike its Roman counterpart, the new senate in the east was linked to the court from the first, and the links became closer as Constantinople developed into a permanent imperial residence and administrative capital: the emperor's high ministers, top generals and elite *comites* ranked as *illustri* in Constantinople's senate; subordinate court officials ranked as *spectabiles* or *clarissimi*, either while still in post or by grant of these statuses on retirement. So too, in some circumstances, appointment to the new senate could ease the way to preferment at court. When Constantius II wished to enlarge the senate of Constantinople in the 350s, he looked especially for recruits from the old propertied classes of the eastern cities;[95] part of the attraction of membership for men of this background was the immunity from local curial burdens that it conferred; but once enrolled as 'backbench' *clarissimi*, they were well placed if they wished – and many were – to tap into the network of court patronage and seek posts in the palatine ministries or as provincial administrators. Like Constantine's new 'Order of Companions', then, the transformed senatorial order of the fourth century undercut the older status-categories, drawing its membership from a much broader band within the propertied classes of the empire, and stimulating the development

[94] Jones 1964: 529.   [95] Heather 1998a: 187–8.

of a new, court-dependent, 'aristocracy of service'.[96] If the fourth-century court was permeated by an acute rank-consciousness, it was also a powerful vehicle for social mobility. The poet Ausonius offers a striking example of the way it could transform an individual's political and social horizons: a Gaul of respectable but quite modest family background, Ausonius had prospered quietly for decades as a well-to-do professor of rhetoric in his native Bordeaux before his reputation earned him the post of tutor to the future emperor Gratian at the court of Valentinian; once established there, he could strike up friendships with the likes of Symmachus, and he went on to become a *comes* as 'Quaestor of the Sacred Palace', 'the arbiter of petitions and creator of laws', and finally a praetorian prefect and a consul.[97] The case of Ausonius is in some respects a special one, and luck played its part in his meteoric rise, but it exemplifies a broader trend: 'the real story of the fourth century', it has recently been asserted, lies in 'the rise of the [new] senatorial bureaucrat and the adaptation of the old aristocracy to new conditions'; moreover, since the court-centred bureaucracy drew many of its personnel from a class of men who would otherwise have tended to pursue local careers in their home cities, the transformation of the senatorial order 'represented a political revolution not only at the imperial centre . . . but also in the localities'.[98]

Inasmuch as a sound education was normally a prerequisite for a good career in the imperial bureaucracy, social mobility had its limits: the bulk of the office-holders who won entry into the senatorial order through service at court would still come from the class that could afford to pay for a liberal education for its sons – around ten years' worth of professors' fees (Ausonius' family had managed that – with difficulty). All the same, if Libanius' testimony is credited, service in the palace secretariat had on occasion launched men of much lower birth than Ausonius into spectacularly successful careers in the 'aristocracy of service': Flavius Philippus, who rose to hold two praetorian prefectures and the consulate under Constantius II, and to be publicly commended by that emperor as 'Our parent and friend . . . [a great man] celebrated on the lips of all civic communities and of diverse nations',[99] was reputedly the son of a sausage-maker; so too, Datianus, whose father had been a cloakroom-attendant at the public baths, ended up a top-ranking *comes* of Constantius, with patrician status and a consulship to his name.[100] These are extreme cases and perhaps arise out of a particular mid-century

---

[96] Heather 1998a: 191.
[97] Symm.*Ep.*1.23; Hopkins 1961; Matthews 1975: 51–5, 69–72; cf. MacMullen 1964b.
[98] Heather 1998a: 209, 197.   [99] Swift and Oliver 1962: 247–8.
[100] Lib.*Or.*42.23–5; Jones 1964: 129; Matthews 1975: 41.

political context; the impact of social mobility on the inner aristocracy at court arguably peaked around that time, and was decreasing again by the late fourth and fifth centuries.[101] But they can still serve as an emblem of the broad change in the social composition of the imperial court elite that prompted Veyne, in the provocative passage we cited at the start of this section, to speak of the reign of Constantine as 'the end of the Hellenistic and Roman period of ancient history'.

In discussing the transformative impact of Constantine's measures on the fourth-century court, we have said nothing of his Christianity. The omission may seem an odd one: Constantine, after all, did engage in high-profile Christian devotional observances at the palace (a point on which we shall have more to say later), and Eusebius claims that he 'offer[ed] up regular prayers with all the members of his court', ordering the observance of the Sabbath day;[102] and Christian bishops, for their part, were clearly well aware of the practical need to cultivate contacts and maintain agents at court as a channel of access to the ruler – and quick to exploit the possibilities in the wake of Constantine's conversion. 'Bishops at court' are a familiar presence from the beginning of the reign,[103] and the court is the backdrop to some of the most celebrated episodes that bear on Constantine's engagement with the clergy: the opening session of the Council of Nicaea was convened in the judgement hall of the imperial palace, with the emperor presiding, bejewelled, diademed and clad in purple, and after the business of the Council was done the bishops were entertained at a palace-dinner so magnificent that Eusebius was put in mind of the paradisal feasts of Christ and his apostles; so too, Constantine's much-discussed claim that he himself was a 'general bishop' outside the Church was made at an imperial dinner party.[104] Nonetheless, our omission of the topic from the discussion has its logic, at least as far as the fourth century is concerned: notwithstanding the fact that every fourth-century emperor from Constantine onwards except for Julian professed the Christian religion, there is no real sign that Christian ideology or practice exerted any significant formative influence on the imperial court's ceremonial or administrative structures. At Louis XIV's Versailles there were around 200 ecclesiastical posts, chief among them that of the *grand aumônier*, 'almost as ancient as the monarchy itself', an office which conferred on the holder by virtue of appointment the rank of commander in

---

[101] Heather 1998a: 196; Jones 1964: 550–1.   [102] Euseb. *VC* 4.17.

[103] Hunt 1998: 238–40; Drake 2000, chs. 6–8 *passim*; cf. Kolb 2001: 70–2.

[104] Nicaea: Euseb. *VC* 3.10, 3.15, with Barnes 1981: 315, 219; Const. as '*koinos episkopos*': Euseb. *VC* 4.24, with Straub 1967: 37–56.

the order of the Saint-Esprit, the grandest of all France's chivalric orders.[105] There was no late Roman equivalent: no prestigious religious office was created at court to be held by eminent churchmen, and emperors did not yet need priests to crown them. Insofar as there was a high priest at court, the 'sacred' emperor himself fulfilled the role; it is well known that until the 380s the Christian emperors continued to take the traditional title of *pontifex maximus*[106] – and for a good century after that, deceased emperors were still formally styled *divi*. As for the elite at court, the proportion of individual Christians among them will clearly have been growing through-out the period; but construed as a collective group, the new governing elite 'owed little or nothing to Christianity' in its configuration and its ceremonious practices and culture.[107] The court elite, that is to say, still cohered as a class around a body of traditions and rituals which had developed directly from a non-Christian imperial past – and the continuing power of those traditions to affect the social and cultural outlook of Christian as well as pagan subjects is witnessed not least by the very lines along which Christian art and architecture and liturgy developed in our period: 'in the stratum of the court', it has been judged, 'the architectural vocabulary remained anchored firmly in the classical tradition, [and] emperors, courtiers, court bishops and court architects remained the mainstays of the classical heritage of the Christian empire far into the fifth century'.[108]

Descriptive particulars: the late Roman court and its workings

We pass now from discussion of the context within which the late imperial court took shape, and the configuration and social composition of the fourth-century court elite, to more particular aspects of the court and its workings: first, the physical setting of court life (pp. 187–96); then the organisation and behaviour of its personnel (pp. 196–209); then its role as a theatre for formalised self-display and royal ceremonial (pp. 209–25).

The court as a physical entity: late imperial 'palaces' and residences

'The royal residence', a writer of the early third century observed, 'is called *Palatium* ['palace'] not because it was ever decided that this should be so, but

---

[105] McManners 1998: 39.   [106] Cameron 1968.   [107] Brown 1998: 651.
[108] Krautheimer 1986: 68–9 (quoted); cf. Grabar 1967 (iconography); Shepherd 1967 (liturgy); Brown 1995; Salzman 1990. Admittedly, the older scholarly consensus on this point has been challenged recently – but hardly decisively (see Brown 1995, reviewing Mathews 1993).

because the emperor lives on the Palatium [i.e. the Palatine Hill at Rome] and has his headquarters there. His house also gained somewhat in prestige from the hill itself, for Romulus had previously dwelt there; for this reason, if the emperor resides anywhere else, his stopping-place receives the name of *Palatium*.'[109] Under the Tetrarchs, we have noticed earlier, Rome ceased to serve as an imperial residence, and if one excepts the few years when the usurping son of a tetrarch, Maxentius (AD 306–312), based himself there, and Constantine's three-month sojourn after his victory over Maxentius at the Milvian Bridge, this remained the case throughout most of our period (Constantine only twice came to Rome thereafter, on brief visits[110]). In Dio's sense of 'stopping-places', though, *palatia* (in Greek, *basileion/basileia*) were scattered far and wide across the empire; thus Eusebius (*VC*.1.22.2) could speak of Constantine's father dying in a *basileia* at York in 306 (a building in, or close by, the legionary fortress, one assumes); and Julian on his march out east from Antioch on his Persian expedition of 363 could write in a letter of his stopping over at Batnae in a modest *basileia* made of wood and clay.[111] But by the early fourth century, linguistic usage was shifting; rather than simply denoting an emperor's headquarters, wherever he happened to be, *palatium* normally implied an actual imperial building, whether or not it was currently occupied by the emperor. The shift indirectly discloses the emergence of a distinctively late Roman court, for the word that came to replace *palatium/basileia* to denote the imperial headquarters in an institutional sense is *comitatus*, a term indicative of the migratory and militarised character of the court. Its counterpart in Greek, *stratopedon* (literally, a 'military camp'), continues in usage well after the founding of Constantinople as an imperial capital: thus Constantine, ordering councillors from Tyre to Constantinople, can summon them 'to the *stratopedon* of our Clemency'.[112]

Palatium/basileia, meanwhile, comes to be applied particularly to imperial residences in half a dozen or so cities of special importance: Trier in the Rhineland; in Italy, Milan especially (the first 'capital' to be spoken of as a rival to Rome[113]); Serdica, Sirmium and Thessalonica in the Balkans; Nicomedia – and later, of course, Constantinople – on the Bosporus; Antioch in Syria. The geographical disposition again marks out military considerations as a driving factor, and the broad background to this development clearly lies with the Diocletianic creation of the arrangement under which several

---

[109] Dio 53.16.5; see Millar 1977: 30; also Paterson in this volume.
[110] Barnes 1982: 72, 77.   [111] Jul.*Ep*.58 (98 Bidez) 401a.
[112] Millar 1977: 42–3, citing Athanasius, *Apol.Sec*.86.
[113] *Pan.Lat*.III.11(AD 290/1).

emperors ruled simultaneously in allocated regional sectors of the empire, each tetrarch residing with his own *comitatus* in camps or cities in his allotted region.[114] Most of these cities continued to function as regional imperial residences or 'capitals' long after the Tetrarchic age; fourth-century emperors remained itinerant rulers by military necessity, engaging with barbarians in the Rhineland and the Danube regions and with Sasanians in the east, and, as we noted earlier, there was usually more than one emperor ruling at any given time in our period, each with his own regional responsibilities, 'palaces' and *comitatus*. It was only in the late fourth and early fifth centuries that certain cities emerged clearly as permanent imperial residences and administrative capitals for the eastern and western sectors of empire: in the east, the 'New Rome', Constantinople; in the west, Milan (and then, from 402 onwards, Ravenna in its stead). The ceremonial and social and administrative structures of the court could hardly have been unaffected by this development. It is surely significant, for instance, that the Byzantine tradition of composing treatises and style-books on court ceremonial begins in the fifth century.[115] The stable landscape of the Great Palace and its surrounding architecture at Constantinople would encourage a formalisation of ritual practice; when fifth-century emperors returned there from a journey away, court officials gathered at specified locations to welcome them back amidst chanted acclamations; particular routes were established for imperial processions from the Great Palace to the Great Church (the first St Sophia) and to the state granaries; the Hippodrome adjoining the Palace and the Hebdomon, a military complex in the European suburbs, became prime stages for imperial self-display (at the Hippodrome, the ceremonial *pompa circensis* recalled the ceremonial inauguration of Constantine's 'New Rome' on 11 May 330; at the Kampos, a parade-ground in the Hebdomon, the emperor accompanied by his retinue of courtiers mounted a statue-girded platform 5 metres high to be acclaimed by his troops on his accession). Even the departures of emperors to the suburban *palatia* and to the nearby rural estates to which they withdrew to relax became occasions for processions (according to a catalogue prepared *c.* 430, there were already by then four other imperial *palatia* at Constantinople besides the Great Palace, and several smaller imperial 'mansions' (*domus*)).[116] It is all the more vexing, then, that there are virtually no extant archaeological traces of the spatial layout of the fourth-century palaces at Constantinople or Milan, or of the

---

[114] Barnes 1982: 47–87, listing known tetrarchic residences and stopping-places.
[115] McCormick 1985: 4.
[116] McCormick 2000: 137, 157–9; Seeck 1962: 229–43; Noethlichs 1998: 22–6.

Figure 5.1 The 'palace' of Diocletian at Split (artist's reconstruction)

early fifth-century palace at Ravenna.[117] Only at Ravenna (and only on one recent view) are there sparse material traces hinting at a complex adapted from a military base within a perimeter wall, and at an enlargement of the palace buildings under Valentinian III (AD 425–455).[118]

To draw any picture of the influences and purposes at play in the architectural configuration of these complexes that goes much beyond hints in literary testimonies, we have to proceed by analogy from other palace sites. The best-preserved complex of likely relevance (admittedly, it was built in a non-urbanised setting as a retirement residence for a ruler who had abdicated, rather than as the palace of a still-active ruler) is the seaside 'Palace of Diocletian' at Split (Figs. 5.1 and 5.2).[119] The model of a military fort (*castrum*) and its commanding officer's administrative and residential quarters (*praetorium*) is clearly influential in this case: the complex occupied a rectangular area enclosed by a circuit of walls with protecting turrets, and divided by axial colonnaded streets running east–west and north–south from three monumental gates on the north, south and west sides. The northern half of the enclosure contained service and military buildings; in the southward half there were two large rectangular precincts, one housing the emperor's own mausoleum, the other a temple, and beyond them, in the southernmost sector, secluded and furthest distant from the gates, the residential palace-wing itself. The central area of this wing, accessible via a circular vestibule, contained three large rectangular halls which presumably served as public rooms. Of these, one of the two flanking halls is apsed and seems likely to have served as a basilica (audience-hall); the other was perhaps a *triclinium* (dining-hall); beyond these, extending to the western and eastern extremities of the wing, lay the domestic rooms and bathing suites; and running along the entire southern edge of the complex there was a terraced promenade looking directly out to sea – a feature prefiguring the outlook from Constantine's Palace at Constantinople.[120] Details of design at Split, particularly on the principal (northern) monumental gate, have often been construed to suggest that eastern (Syrian) as well as Roman architectural influences were at play, perhaps echoing the style of palaces built earlier for Diocletian in the east: there was one such at Antioch (a structure known only from

---

[117] The palace at Milan, first developed as the residence of Diocletian's colleague Maximian, is only known from texts; at Constantinople the overall site of Constantine's Great Palace is locatable, but later building has completely obscured the picture for the fourth century. Krautheimer 1983: 69–71 (Milan), 49 (Constantinople).

[118] McCormick 2000: 136–7, citing Deichmann, 1989.

[119] Ward-Perkins 1981: 454ff; Wilkes 1986; cf. Duval 1997: 143–7 (doubting its value as a model).

[120] Dagron 1974: 93.

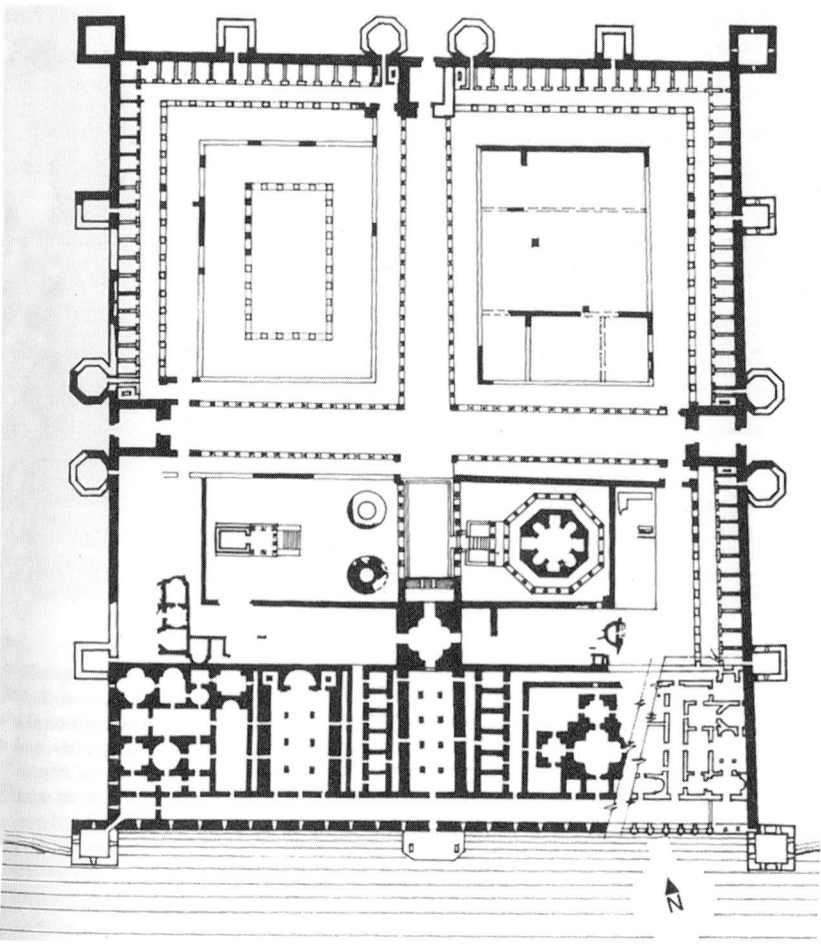

Figure 5.2 The 'palace' of Diocletian at Split (plan)

a description in Libanius), and another at Nicomedia which had become established as his principal residence before his abdication in 305.[121]

From Diocletian's time until the inauguration of Constantinople in 330, Nicomedia remained the prime 'capital' of the eastern empire. In this case, too, the palace is known only from texts – but they offer vivid glimpses of the physical setting of court life there. An entry in the *Suda* discloses the emperor Licinius (AD 308–324) relaxing beside a fountain in a courtyard garden in the palace, attended by a retinue of courtiers and bidding one of them to cut down a bunch of grapes.[122] A passage in Lactantius, who had

---

[121] Ward Perkins 1981: 458; Millar 1977: 50–1; Duval 1997: 140–1.

[122] *Suda*, s.v. 'Auxentius'; for the Christian twist to this story, see Millar 1977: 52.

lived at Nicomedia in Diocletian's reign, indicates the impact of the new palace complex on the urban environment around it, and the ideology that underpinned its development: 'Here there were basilicas, here a circus, a mint, an arms factory, a house for his wife, and one for his daughter . . . such was [Diocletian's] incessant mania for making Nicomedia the equal of Rome.'[123] As a Christian, Lactantius was a hostile witness in this case, of course; more often, the tone of such remarks is laudatory. For instance, a panegyric of 310 delivered in praise of Constantine at Trier dwells on the emperor's generosity to the city: 'I see a Circus Maximus to rival, I believe, that in Rome, I see basilicas and a Forum, royal buildings (*regia opera*), and a seat of justice – I see these being raised to such a height that they promise to be worthy neighbours of the sky and stars.'[124] Here, at least, we have a surviving structure to set beside the text, an exceptionally well-preserved apsed basilica of the early fourth century, built adjacent to the palace to serve as an *aula regia*, an imperial audience-hall. The building's design reveals an accomplished architect creating a theatre for the visual expression of absolutist ideology; its proportions and internal optical devices are ingeniously contrived to draw the eye to the apse, in which the ruler sat enthroned against a background of richly coloured mosaic.[125]

Specialists remain divided as to whether any single underlying architectural model generally determined palace structure in the late imperial period.[126] On one view, there was a Hellenistic architectural model at play, picked up on and mediated through the Romanised military layout of a mid-third-century palace built for Philip the Arab at Syrian Philippopolis, and later at Split. That view is hard to sustain, and whether the Diocletianic site at Split can be treated as a detailed template for others for which little or no material evidence exists is disputable: it is hardly clear, for instance, that the Great Palace at Constantinople, constructed over an expanse of around 100 hectares, walled-off and terraced like Domitian's *Domus Flavia*, ever replicated the tight, near-symmetrical *castrum* organisation of Domitian's 'palace' at Split. That said, the material traces and panegyrists' praises of tetrarchic 'capitals' such as Trier, or Thessalonica, or Sirmium, show the late imperial 'palace' as usually a unit standing in an intimate relationship to another architectural element so as to form a broader spatial complex encompassing a circus/hippodrome,[127] and whether or not the Palace at Constantinople was laid out in conformity with a specific architectural

[123] Lact.*De morte pers.*7.9.   [124] *Pan.Lat.*VI.22.5.   [125] Ward-Perkins 1981: 444–5.
[126] Dagron 1974: 93; Duval 1997: 127–53 (a sceptical critique).
[127] Millar 1977: 47; Ward-Perkins 1981: 442, 449–50; Duval 1997: 139.

model, there was surely a broader sense in which the imperial residential area on the Palatine at Rome – a complex bounded on one side by the Circus Maximus, and overlooking the Forum and Senate-House on the other – was a shaping influence. Constantine's particular choice of site for the Great Palace seems to have been influenced by the location of a pre-existing hippodrome at Constantinople – which is to say that one of the best-known features of the complex, the arrangement giving the emperor and his retinue direct access from the Palace to the imperial box (*kathisma*) in the Hippodrome, a prime locus for imperial self-display lying immediately adjacent to the western edge of the Palace, replicated the pattern at Rome.[128] So, too, the Great Palace was from the first conceived of as a focal element in a larger monumental centre; just as the Palatine complex stood close by the Temple of Palatine Apollo and looked out onto the Forum and Senate-House and Jupiter Capitolinus' temple, so the view from the Great Palace's monumental entrance, the 'Brazen Gate' (*Chalke*), looked out to what had formerly been Byzantium's civic centre in the high empire, the *Tetrastoön* – a space now reconfigured as the *Augusteion*, a vast porticoed square creating an arena for imperial processions; at the square's eastern edge was a senate-house for the newly constituted imperial senate of Constantinople, and beyond that, on the slope rising towards the old acropolis of the city, the church of St Irene (and later, from 360 onwards, St Sophia).[129] The parallels suggest that in the layout of his new eastern capital Constantine wished to appropriate and evoke the charismatic imperial aura of the Palatine residential complex and its surrounding public space and architecture.

In the absence of material traces, the internal configuration of the fourth-century palace area at Constantinople eludes us. Texts indicate some of its major component parts – but very little about how they were spatially related.[130] The overall layout was perhaps less regular than the analogy with the compact symmetrical suites of Diocletian's 'Palace' would suggest; arguably it resembled rather the sprawl of an aristocratic country-villa complex. In any event, we hear of a monumental entrance, the *Chalke*; a large court, the 'Tribunal' (or *Delphax*), with smaller meeting chambers attached; the *Magnaura*, an apsed basilican reception hall; two consistoriums, the 'Summer' and the 'Small Consistorium';[131] a great dining-chamber, the

---

[128] Krautheimer 1983: 49; Dagron 1974: 320–47; cf. Zanker 2002: 109 on the *Domus Flavia*.
[129] Dagron 1974: 98–9, 138–40.   [130] McCormick 2000: 140; Bardill 1999.
[131] As we have indicated earlier, '*consistorium*' was a term that could refer not just to a body of advisors but also to the place in which they assembled – in architectural terms, a structure akin to a basilica, a meeting-chamber with an elevated recess from which the enthroned emperor issued his judgements. On the relation of the two consistoriums, see Guilland 1969: 56–8.

'Triclinium of the Nineteen Couches', capable of seating over 200 guests; the imperial residential suite, the *Daphne*, from which a spiral staircase gave access to the imperial box in the Hippodrome (above); kitchens and quarters for the domestic staff; garden terraces and courtyards; several chapels; the barracks and stables and armoury of the imperial guard; an imperial mint; and the offices of the various other departments of the imperial bureaucracy.[132]

In time, other *palatia* were built around the Great Palace as mansions for great courtiers. Immediately to the west of the Hippodrome, palaces were built in the first half of the fifth century for two high-ranking eunuch *praepositi* (grand chamberlains), Lausus and Antiochus. The archaeological remains of Antiochus' palace are securely identified, and its dimensions do something to suggest by comparison the massive scale of the chief rooms of the Great Palace: a stairway led up to a semi-circular entrance portico nearly 50 metres in diameter, beyond which stood a hexagonal reception-chamber, each side of which was over 10 metres wide; the identification of Lausus' palace from material evidence is more problematic, but it too was evidently very large; it housed a choice collection of sculptural master-pieces acquired by the Chamberlain, among them Pheidias' statue of Olympian Zeus, a piece 12 metres high.[133] And as we have noticed earlier, other imperial palaces and villas developed in the suburbs and outside the city.[134] In the west and the Balkans, too, named country villas are attested by Ammianus as occasional imperial residences in the vicinity of regional capitals or fortresses.[135] The archaeological evidence in these cases points to substantial, semi-fortified complexes, and to call such places imperial 'retreats' perhaps carries misleading connotations. 'Contionacum' near Trier, say, has been plausibly identified with the remains of an extensive villa complex at

[132] Kelly 1994: 162–3. These offices must have occupied many rooms; by the sixth century, for instance, the contents of the archive of the Praetorian Prefect of the East alone seem to have filled over twenty storage-rooms located under the Hippodrome.

[133] Krautheimer 1986: 71; McCormick 2000: 139; for the (disputed) dates of construction, see Greatrex and Bardill 1996: 193–7; and for the location and artworks of Lausus' palace, Bardill 1997: 67–9.

[134] E.g. Theodosius II's sisters were fond of 'Rufinianae', a palace on the Asian shore, and emperors had country properties at which they could relax: a letter of Julian's describes his gift to one Evagrius (arguably a rhetor attached to Julian's court) of a small villa and estate on the Bithynian coast bequeathed by his grandmother – in Julian's memory, 'a most delightful summer resort' affording a view of Constantinople in the distance across the Bosporus. Callinicus, *V Hypatii* 37.3; Julian, *Ep.*25(4 Bidez).

[135] 'Pistrensis', for instance, 20 miles or so distant from Sirmium, or 'Murocincta' ('the wall-encircled villa') near Carnuntum, or 'Contionacum' near Trier. Amm.29.6.7; 30.10.4; Matthews 1989: 401.

Konz that included an apsed audience-hall, and it figures in the Theodosian Code as a place from which Valentinian I issued laws in 371.[136] These details nicely illustrate a basic point already remarked on earlier: until quite late in the fourth century, emperors were by and large still rulers on the move; even in the fifth, emperors based at Constantinople might move in some seasons to another nearby city (Thracian Eudoxiopolis, for instance, or Diocletian's old capital at Nicomedia) and in the west Rome began to figure again as a temporary imperial residence for the emperors based at Ravenna.[137] And wherever he went, an emperor on his travels was accompanied by an entourage of servants, soldiers, *comites* and bureaucratic functionaries. We pass now to consider 'the court' in this aspect, as an ordered collectivity of persons.

The court as a human collectivity: the emperor's *comitatus*

In the formal language of the Theodosian Code, the court personnel are collectively the *sacer comitatus* or the *domus sacra* or *domus aeternalis*; Ammianus usually calls them simply 'the *comitatus*' or 'the *comitatus* of the Augustus'.[138] A variety of expressions were used by Ammianus and others to refer to its leading members: 'those powerful in/holders of first place in the emperor's hall (*regia aula*)', or more simply *palatinae dignitates*, '[holders of] palace honours'. In Greek, the expressions used by writers like Libanius and Eunapius and Zosimus show a comparable range, speaking of the personnel collectively as the 'royal household' (*basilikē oiketia*) or as 'those around the *aulē*', and of the leading members as 'the *dynatoi* in the palace (*basileia*)', or 'those in the *hetairia* around the emperor' (that is, his *comites*).[139] The tendency of such locutions to continue to evoke a material object, a hall or courtyard, is noteworthy – but so is the fact that they are often manifestly being used to designate the court as a human collectivity or a political institution, without reference to any particular topographical location at a given time.

The *comitatus* of a fourth-century emperor probably numbered around 6,000 persons – on the move, a massive group requiring a great deal of the *mensores* (the palatine officials who supervised arrangements for the billeting and supply of the court on its journeys): we must envisage roads packed for miles with columns of soldiers, carriages carrying the imperial household and its *comites* and high officials, waggon trains loaded with

[136] *Cod.Theod.*4.6.4; 9.3.5; a drawing in Weitzmann 1979: 116 reconstructs the site.
[137] Jones 1964: 366.   [138] Schlinkert 1996: 460–1; Neothlichs 1998: 15.
[139] Schlinkert 1996: 460–1 for refs., adding Libanius *Or.*11.194 (on *comites*).

clerks' file boxes, coined money and gold bullion – for the imperial treasury travelled with the ruler, and by the late fourth century the minting of gold had itself become exclusively a matter for the *comitatus*.[140] Constantine himself acknowledged the strains that the migratory life imposed on his bureaucrats: 'Nor are the *palatini* [clerks] strangers to the toils of the camp, [since] they accompany Our standards and are always present at Our official acts, and as they devote themselves to their clerical duties they are exposed to lengthy journeys and difficult marches' (*Cod.Theod.*6.36.1). No extensive account of the bureaucratic departments within which these clerks served can be undertaken here, but even a summary and highly simplified description of the divisions of the *comitatus* will suffice to convey both the scale of the emperor's personal retinue and the striking degree to which the business of imperial government had come to centre on a departmentalised palace bureaucracy under the control of an inner elite of courtiers and ministers appointed by the emperor.

For convenience, we can divide the *comitatus* into four basic constituent parts. First, soldiers. The infantry and cavalry regiments of the palace guard, the *scholae palatinae* (at Constantinople, there were originally seven such regiments) accounted for roughly half of the *comitatus* – about 3,000 crack troops (in the fourth century, at least), predominantly of Germanic origin, drawn from the emperor's field army; and a band of forty picked men from these regiments formed the white-uniformed *candidati*, the emperor's elite personal bodyguard.[141] By the sixth century, the *scholae* had become largely decorative units and the regimental posts were up for sale; a new corps, the *excubitores*, had taken over their practical military functions. The duties of the *candidati* had likewise by then become mainly ceremonial; but in the fourth they still functioned as a true bodyguard, and would accompany the emperor on his campaigns.[142] There was also an elite corps of officer-cadets attached to the court, the *domestici et protectores*: some were soldiers of proven worth promoted from the ranks, others ambitious younger men who had obtained their commissions by influence or purchase – sons of military officials, sons of German nobles, civilians in search of a sinecure.[143] The corps of cadets – and military service at court in general – was accordingly a potent force for social mobility; the father of the emperor Valentinian, for instance, had been a Pannonian peasant-soldier whose strength and skill as a wrestler had earned him promotion from the ranks as a *protector*, from

[140] Jones 1964: 367, 437.   [141] Jones 1964: 613, 658.
[142] Frank 1969: 127–42; Whitby 1987: 464, with Amm. 25.3.6 (*candidati* with Julian in Persia).
[143] Jones 1964: 612, 638–9.

which post he then rose further, ending up a military *comes*; and Valentinian himself, at the time of his accession, had recently been given command of a *schola* of the imperial guard (Ammianus 30.7.2–4; 26.1.5).

Second, the emperor's personal household establishment, the *sacrum domesticum*, classified into three broad divisions: the *cubicularii* (eunuch chamberlains), the *castrensiani* (domestic personnel such as cooks, pages and hairdressers) and thirty *silentarii*, a corps of court-ushers who attended the emperor at meetings of the consistory.

Third, the 'sacred' consistory itself – a 'privy council' made up of high-ranking officials and imperial *comites*, and served by a secretariat of *notarii* under the headship of a chief secretary, the *primicerius notariorum*.[144] The consistory had its origin in the informal *consilium principis* familiar to historians of the earlier empire, but its very name hints at the changes wrought by the 'absolutist' strain in late imperial ideology: its members remained standing (*consistentes*) in the emperor's presence throughout its meetings, and a good part of its business was formal or ceremonial; it functioned not simply as an advisory cabinet, but as a council of state and a court of justice: it was at sessions of the consistory that civic delegations and foreign envoys were received, 'dignities' and titles of high office conferred, and imperial largesses bestowed. In principle, moreover, formal sessions of the full consistory were one-way affairs, events technically termed *silentia* at which the membership was supposed to listen quietly to the ruler's announcements, with the *silentarii* in attendance brandishing golden wands to ensure silence. The reality, as several passages in Ammianus indicate, by no means always conformed to this solemn image; in the fourth century, at least, meetings could still be the occasion of uninhibited debate about policy matters.[145] But it seems clear that key decisions were often taken by a smaller circle of intimate *comites* of the consistory meeting less formally, and then presented to a full consistory-meeting as *faits accomplis*; and in the fifth century the consistory turned into an essentially ceremonial body.

Fourth and last (here we gather a large and heterogeneous bureaucratic category under one broad heading) there were the officials and functionaries of the various departmental ministries and their sub-offices (*scrinia*), military and civilian. If we exclude the *notarii* of the consistory, already mentioned, the central bureaucratic staff can be divided into four principal palatine 'ministries' (*officia*):[146]

---

[144] For what follows, see Jones 1964: 333–41.   [145] Matthews 1989: 268.

[146] For detailed discussion of the bureaucratic structures, see Jones 1964: 562–86; Noethlichs 1991: 1111–58 (=*RAC*, s.v. 'Hofbeamter'); Noethlichs 1998: 27–39.

1 the staffs of the three *sacra scrinia*, the imperial secretariats of the *magistri memoriae, epistularum* and *libellorum* respectively, who drafted responses to individual and communal petitions, prepared legal cases and issued certificates of enlistment to members of the imperial service;

2 the *largitionales*, the staff of the *sacrae largitiones*, the ministry of imperial finance, which processed tax revenues, regulated the minting of coin and was responsible (among much else) for the provision of the clothing of courtiers and bureaucrats;

3 the *privatiani*, the staff of the *res privata*, administering the collection of rents from all imperial property and land;

4 the 'regiment' (*schola*) of the *agentes in rebus*, a corps whose members began their careers as imperial couriers and then progressed to posts as imperial inspectors and agents of various sorts, some of whom remained based at the court.

A rough indication of the size of the central bureaucracy as it existed *c.* AD 400 can be got by calculating a notional total from the number of men recorded in the Theodosian Code as serving in these various ministries at various points in the late fourth or fifth centuries in (usually) the eastern sector of the empire: 520 *notarii* (AD 381); 130 clerks in the *sacra scrinia* (AD 470); 224 *largitionales* (AD 399) (with over 600 more entered on the waiting lists as supernumeraries); 500 *privatiani* (AD 399); 1,174 *agentes in rebus* (AD 430) (not all of them, of course, present at court). The total figure for the east alone is thus well in excess of 2,500.[147] And on top of the bureaucratic divisions so far mentioned, one must allow for the presence of the central staff of whichever praetorian prefect was attached to a given *comitatus* – in the case of Constantinople, the 'Prefect of the East', in the case of Milan, or Ravenna, the 'Prefect of Italy'.[148]

To convey a flavour of the *modus operandi* of the *comitatus*, we can pick out here only a few of the key posts for comment. The members of the consistory constituted an elite group. Most were appointed to it as *comites* by the emperor's personal grant, many after service as a governor of a province or diocese, some simply as valued imperial favourites at court (the low-born Datianus, for instance, noticed earlier as a high-ranking *comes* of Constantius II, had never held any office in the bureaucracy). The four top civilian ministers at court, however, were *ex officio* members: the 'Master of Offices' (a post created by Constantine), who had overall charge of the three *sacra scrinia*, the corps of the imperial couriers, and (later) the regiments of the

---

[147] Heather 1998a: 189 draws up a table from figures in Jones 1964: 572–86.
[148] Jones 1964: 370–1.

palace guard; the 'Quaestor of the Sacred Palace' (another Constantinian innovation), who served as the emperor's chief legal officer and representative at court and proclaimed his edicts to the consistory (he was usually a prominent lawyer or rhetorician: we have noted Ausonius as a case in point); and the heads of the two financial ministries, the *comes largitionum* and the *comes rei privatae*, who between them controlled the tax revenues, the administration of imperial estates, mines and mints, and the payment of salaries. As well as these four, collectively styled the *comites consistoriani*, the Praetorian Prefect in attendance at court (the supreme civilian minister of state overseeing the administration of the provinces and dioceses in his allotted region of empire) was also a member *ex officio*;[149] and so likewise were several high military officials: the commander of the officer-cadets (*comes domesticorum*); the commanders of the regiments of the palace guard; and two 'Masters of Soldiers in Attendance' – frequently of non-Roman (usually Germanic) extraction – who commanded divisions of the mobile field army in the vicinity of the court. The consistory's membership – in the fourth century, at least – is thus emblematic of the broader reconfiguration of the court elite as an 'aristocracy of service' that we have discussed earlier: some men of traditional Roman senatorial background could turn up in it, either among the ex-proconsular governors or ex-*vicarii*, or simply, like the grand Nummius Albinus,[150] as esteemed advisors; but the heads of the four great Palatine ministries in this period were always 'new men', and a good few of them had risen through service as *notarii*: either emperors did not care to place the traditional aristocracy in these four high posts at court, or else the old senatorial families viewed them as involving a form of personal service to the emperor that they shunned as undignified.[151] So too, the high military posts that conferred membership *ex officio* were now no longer available to the old senatorial families, and while Roman aristocrats still show up often as Praetorian Prefects of Italy, the Prefects in the East were usually parvenus (a conspicuous example, Flavius Philippus, allegedly the son of a sausage-seller, has been noted earlier). In the consistory, then, a smattering of traditional aristocrats kept company with ambitious ex-*notarii*, Frankish or Gothic or Burgundian generals, and *comites* of widely divergent social background.

Among the corps of *notarii* who served as the consistory's secretariat, the longest-serving member, the 'First Senior Notary' (*primicerius notariorum*), emerged at court as an important official in his own right; by 381, if not earlier, *primicerii* were formally ranked on a par with proconsuls –

---

[149] Gutsfeld 2004: 85–7.   [150] *cos.* AD 345; *ILS* 1238.   [151] Jones 1964: 134.

and were hence members of the senatorial order.[152] The *primicerius* had responsibility for the preparation of the codicils issued to all senior officials to mark their appointment, and of comprehensive lists of all holders of high-ranking offices (*dignitates*); it was thus a *primicerius* for whom one of our key sources, the *Notitia Dignitatum*, was compiled. The corps of *notarii* that he headed was perhaps originally staffed by men of low social standing, but it soon came to form a prestigious company at court, and in the course of the fourth century competition for appointment to it became intense. By the mid-century, emperors were already entrusting *notarii* with important tasks and missions as special agents, couriers and ambassadors, and some of them were subsequently raised to the highest ranks and offices at court. As the corps' prestige grew, its social composition changed; posts once thought suitable only for uncultured clerks with short-hand skills, or unappealing because of the long years of service involved, came to attract well-educated sons of the urban propertied classes – and by the fifth century, even some members of the old Roman aristocracy.[153] And as the corps became fashionable, the overall number of *notarii* grew: in AD 381, we noticed earlier, there were apparently 520 in the East alone. The number actually in service at court at any given time is another matter, and very hard to judge: the figure of 520 will include not only men serving as imperial agents in the provinces, but also a good number of persons who had obtained the rank as a sinecure by influence or payment. But whatever the number, the corps of the *notarii* holds a special interest for us, and, likewise, the secretariats of the four main palatine ministries supervised by the *comites consistoriani* – the Master of Offices, the Quaestor of the Palace, and the two financial *comites*. They were a point at which the privileged milieu of the court and its bureaucracy clearly intersected with the wider world of the non-aristocratic but respectable propertied urban classes, and through which the image and values of the emergent 'court society' of the fourth century could impinge directly on the consciousness and aspirations of those classes. More than that, it could be argued that the social ethos of the 'typical' upwardly mobile, non-aristocratic, notary – educated, technically capable, status-oriented, conscious of his own worth and rank but with an insider's consciousness also of the distance that lay between him and the lofty heights of the inner elite at court, the *celsae potestates*[154] – informs some of the key source material for our period. The fourth-century historical 'epitomators' Victor and Eutropius, we have noted earlier, were both bureaucrats in the secretariats of either the consistory or the *sacra scrinia*, and Ammianus

[152] Jones 1964: 573–4.   [153] Amm.29.1.1; Jones 1964: 127–8, 572–4.   [154] Amm.28.6.9.

himself, if his career had taken another turn than it did, might quite easily have become a notary in the bureaucracy; he had begun his career as an officer-cadet at court, and the cadet corps was a well-established route to a post as a notary. As for the *Notitia* and the Theodosian Code (along with Ammianus, the fundamental texts for any reconstruction of this period), both were documents produced by the court-based bureaucracy, and thoroughly imbued by its values and outlook: they were drawn up for the *primicerius notariorum* and the Quaestor of the Sacred Palace respectively – which is to say, of course, drawn up by the notaries in their offices.

Within the section of the *comitatus* serving in the emperor's domestic household, the dominant functionary was (or soon became) the *praepositus sacri cubiculi*, the 'Grand Chamberlain', who had overall charge of the *cubicularii*, the staff of palace eunuchs who acted as personal servants to the emperors (and to empresses: in time, indeed, the empress came to possess a designated *praepositus* of her own). The *praepositus* was himself a eunuch, selected by the emperor and serving at his pleasure rather than for a fixed period; *praepositi* thus tended to outlast many of the high officials at court, whose tenure of a particular office would normally be limited to a year or so. Under the *praepositus* were other eunuch high officials, among them the 'Superintendent of the Bedchamber' (*primicerius sacri cubiculi*), the 'Count of the Sacred Wardrobe' (*comes sacrae vestis*) and the 'Steward (*castrensis*) of the Palace', in charge of the non-eunuch staff of the imperial household.[155] The presence of eunuchs as domestic servants in the imperial household was nothing new *per se* (they were already there in Julio-Claudian times),[156] but the high visibility of the eunuch staff at court in the fourth and fifth centuries, and the high functions and titles assigned to them, constitute one of the most obviously distinctive features of the late Roman court as compared to (say) that of the Antonine age. It is not just that the eunuchs now routinely served at the royal table, prepared beds and royal clothing, and locked the emperor safely in his bedroom at night: they were frequently assigned as tutors to the royal children (Julian, for instance, remembered his own eunuch tutor notably fondly);[157] and by the mid-fifth century, at least, the posts of captain of the emperor's personal bodyguard (the *spatharius*) and keeper of the privy purse (the *sacellarius*) both went to eunuchs.[158] Above all, one is struck by the political influence, the formal honours and the sheer wealth accruing to the eunuchs who served as *praepositi*. Living in

---

[155] But n.b. Costa 1972: 358–87, arguing that in the early fourth century the *castrensis* was superior to the *praepositus*, and not originally himself a eunuch.
[156] Suet.*Claud*.28.   [157] *Misop*.352a–d; Smith 1995: 24–5.
[158] Jones 1964: 567–70; Delmaire 1995: 165–72; cf. Guilland 1955: 65; Noethlichs 1998: 37–8.

close physical proximity to the ruler and effectively controlling access to him in a private setting, the *praepositus* could often determine the success or failure of an approach made by a delegate or petitioner; Ambrose, for instance, ascribed his failure to secure his objective on a diplomatic visit to the court of the usurper Maximus in the 380s partly to the fact that the *praepositus* Gallicanus would not grant him a private audience with the emperor, but only a reception in the consistory.[159] By the late fourth century, the post of *praepositus* had come to confer on its holder the highest senatorial rank of *illustris* automatically on retirement, and in one notorious case (Eutropius, in AD 399) a *praepositus* even won the ultimate accolade of a consulship – and thereby immortality of a sort in a classic work of court literature, as the butt of a vitriolic invective by Claudian (even the most grotesque freak of nature, the poet declared, paled in comparison to a consular eunuch).[160] According to one observer (admittedly, a highly disaffected one, and probably not to be trusted on the point), some men were so determined to win Eutropius' patronage that they had themselves castrated, 'los[ing] their wits and their testicles'.[161] That is hard to believe, but the post of *praepositus* certainly became a byword for fabulous wealth corruptly acquired through the sale of offices and bribe-taking: in 432, for instance, when Bishop Cyril of Alexandria wished to gain the support of Theodosius II against the Nestorians, he sent 200 pounds of gold to the emperor's *praepositus*, and another 50 to the empress's, to ease the way for his representative at court.[162] By that time, we have noticed, *praepositi* at Constantinople could afford to build sumptuous palaces on their own account, and to fill them with extensive collections of classical sculpture.

It is important to emphasise that on the face of things the exercising of such influence and power at court by eunuchs was an extraordinary development. In Roman eyes, eunuchs in general were a thoroughly contemptible species; Roman law banned castration on Roman soil as a monstrosity, and in society at large eunuchs were usually encountered as domestic attendants of aristocratic women, or (when young) as catamites for masters with exotic sexual tastes. The imperial eunuchs at court, then, were slaves or ex-slaves, and typically barbarians to boot, slaves imported as castrated children from Persia, Armenia or the Caucasus.[163] In the eyes of fourth-century writers, the acquisition of political influence and power at court by such persons was an outrage: they ascribe it to the eunuchs' artful flattery of weak emperors and

[159] Ambrose, *Ep.*24; Scholten 1998: 54.   [160] Claudian *in Eutrop.*1.22; Cameron 1970: 126–37.
[161] Eunapius Fr. 65.7 Blockley.   [162] Brown 1992: 17; Holum 1982: 180.
[163] Matthews 1989: 274–7. Not *all* came as children: at least one *praepositus* had first arrived as an adult emissary from the Persian court; for the context, Greatrex and Bardill 1996: 173.

to their inordinate greed as a type, and the *praepositi* and their underlings are accordingly damned by the likes of Ammianus and Claudian as guileful, malevolent freaks – so many 'lizards and toads', bare-bottomed 'apes' in eastern silks, sallow-skinned 'snakes' with squeaky, boyish voices, a tribe of 'bats' who, once outside the protective ambit of the court, hide themselves away in dark places to avoid public odium.[164] These prejudicial images of deceitful minions hood-winking impressionable rulers were to shape Gibbon's view of 'eunuch power' as a monstrous oriental import that degraded and enfeebled the Roman state: 'If we examine the general history of Persia, India and China, we shall find that the power of the eunuchs has uniformly marked the decline and fall of every dynasty.'[165] There are certainly interesting parallels to be drawn in this connection with the role of court-eunuchs in eastern settings – in Han China, say, as discussed by van Ess in this volume – but the propensity of the ancient writers and of Gibbon to account for the prominence of eunuchs in the late Roman court as a situation arising from the 'oriental' guile of a succession of individual *praepositi* and the vanity or weakness of individual emperors does not constitute an adequate account of a state of affairs that lasted centuries; the role of the eunuchs at court needs to be viewed and explained as a normalised, 'systemic' phenomenon in which provision was made, say, for a trainee corps of adolescent eunuchs.[166]

'Eunuchology' currently flourishes as a specialised sub-field in the study of antiquity, and of associated later periods too: there are fine explorations of the 'construction' of a third gender in the figure of the eunuch at Byzantium and its traces in eunuchophiliac Christian texts.[167] The institutionalised status of the late Roman court eunuchs has been closely studied in recent years,[168] but the key account remains a brilliant paper by Keith Hopkins first published in the sixties.[169] Hopkins saw the key to the explanation of the influence of the *praepositi* not in the weakness of individual emperors, but in a deep structural tension inherent in an absolutist monarchic system – the tension between the emperor and the political and military aristocracy, however configured. 'Absolute' or not, no emperor could ever in practice rule the empire (or his portion of it, when two were co-reigning) by himself; he needed to delegate power to others as generals and administrators, and

---

[164] Basil, *Ep.*115; Claudian *in Eutrop.*1.303; Amm.16.6.17; 19.7.7; 18.4.4.

[165] *DF* vol. II, 177.

[166] Matthews 1989: 276, inferred from Amm.18.4.4.

[167] Ringrose 2003 (third gender); Mullett in Tougher 2002 (eunuchophilia); Marmon 1990.

[168] Schlinkert 1994; Scholten 1995; 1998: 51–74.

[169] Hopkins 1963 (=1978: 172–96); qualification of his stress on eunuchs as 'outsiders' in Tougher 2002.

the corollary was the recognition and maintenance of an elite grouping of some sort. But while the delegation of power was unavoidable, the power accruing to the elite helpers selected always constituted a potential threat to the monarch, and emperors sought to limit it by various means – partly by conciliating the elite to keep it loyal, partly by maintaining a balance of power within its constituent parts. In the early empire, the threat had lain mainly with the traditional senatorial aristocracy from whom the emperors chiefly drew their executive helpers, and emperors had checked it partly by adopting a conciliatory ideology of *civilitas* that represented senators as the emperor's social peers, partly by restricting the length of senators' tenures of military and civic offices and by fostering a counterbalancing element of non-senators, *equites*, deployed as praetorian prefects and as functionaries in administrative roles that senators regarded as menial. By our period, the position was much changed: the image of the emperor as a divine, or god-like, power had consigned the ideology of *civilitas* to the sidelines, and the social composition of the senatorial order had been transformed, the old senatorial aristocracy having been quite eclipsed by the rise of the equestrians; by the later fourth century, we observed earlier, the two old orders had effectively coalesced in a reconfigured and much enlarged senatorial order in which new senators were constantly being created by virtue of office-holding in the emperor's service; senatorial status was now itself a reward for loyalty. But the basic problem facing emperors still remained; to control the armies and raise the taxes from the provinces effectively, they still had to delegate power; and the elite class thus created, however it was configured, still potentially threatened the centralising power of the monarch: it was still apt to aspire to the privileged social and economic status of a traditional landed aristocracy, and Hopkins pointed in this connection to a worrying 'centrifugal' tendency in the west, with the emergence of proto-feudal estate owners (*potentiores*) resistant to taxation and to the levying of military recruits from their work-forces.[170] And in some ways the problem was accentuated by the absolutist ideology which elevated rulers as 'sacred' beings far removed from even their most elite subjects. Whereas the style of the *civilis princeps* had facilitated social interaction between the ruler and his privileged elite, the absolutist ethos emphasised the social distance between them. In practice, though, a channel of contact with the elite was still essential for both parties; emperors needed to know (and to be seen to know) what influential subjects were thinking in order to control them; they needed to play powerful individuals off against one another with a sense of their likely reactions, rewarding the

[170] Hopkins 1978: 188.

loyal and punishing or accommodating the disaffected – and to be seen to be doing so. Conversely, the members of the elite required a channel of contact with the emperor to mark out and maintain their privileged status in the eyes of others.

In some historical periods (see Brosius and Spawforth in this volume), the rendering of personal service to the ruler by nobles at court could help to meet these needs and fostered a degree of social intimacy; at Versailles, say, domestic posts in the ruler's household such as the *premiers gentilhommes de la chambre* or the *grand maître de la garde-robe*, were honorific charges awarded to dukes.[171] In the case of the late Roman court, there was no 'domestication' of the nobility in the literal fashion that Elias claimed for Versailles; the prevailing aristocratic ethos precluded it. Some other means of bridging the divide was required by the 'sacred' emperor, and in Hopkins' view it was principally the corps of eunuchs serving in the imperial house-hold who came to function as the key intermediary channel, 'a lubricant preventing too much friction between the emperor and the other forces of the state that threatened his superiority'.[172] At court, the eunuchs' ease of movement around the palace kept the emperor well informed of goings-on, and they provided (for a price) access to the emperor's person – but access meted out in such a way that it could not be taken for granted, would not deprive the imperial office of its aura of power and grandeur in the minds of petitioners, and would not require the emperor to award honours and financial benefits more liberally than he wished. Deployed away from court as envoys on special missions, they could keep a check on, and if need be take pre-emptive action against, military commanders, governors and leading bishops. Although no ancient source explicitly says that emperors consciously raised the eunuchs up as a means of controlling the elite, it is hard to think they were blind to their potential value on that score. At quite what point in the fourth century the eunuchs' corporate role at court was decisively enhanced is also unclear, but the *praepositi* were well ensconced by the mid century. The key innovation at issue was surely the consistent allocation to eunuchs of a traditional post in the imperial household – the chamberlain's – and it is tempting to follow Hopkins in associating this change with the elaboration of court ritual that began with Diocletian, and to suggest that the implication in the ancient sources that an oriental model was at play may be well founded; we had occasion to notice earlier that in 298 the junior tetrarch Galerius captured and led back to Diocletian the harem and household and many of the courtiers of the Sasanian king – and

---

[171] Elias 1983: 162; Antoine 1989: 214–15; Jones 2002: 16.   [172] Hopkins 1978: 180.

the eunuchs who attended the king's wives and children were presumably also taken along with them.

Eunuchs were not the only category of court functionary that could be deployed to control the elite, of course, but on various counts they were particularly well suited for this purpose from the emperor's point of view. Since they were wholly dependent for their influence and power on the favour of the emperor who had picked them as his servants, their own self-interest would tend to keep them loyal to him. And in the nature of the case, with eunuchs there were no inherited family allegiances or ambitions harboured for sons to undercut that personal loyalty. Their barbarian and servile origins, the impossibility of their fathering upwardly mobile sons, and the widespread odium attaching to their name and physical appearance all meant that eunuchs could not hope to be other than socially marginalised persons; unlike, say, the recruits to the corps of the palace *notarii* whose social composition we discussed earlier, the imperial eunuchs could never be assimilated into the ranks of the new aristocracy. An emperor might be prepared to permit a valued *praepositus* to acquire riches and badges of dignity on a scale that might have raised his suspicions in an aristocrat's case, but no matter how much wealth a eunuch amassed, or how high the ranks and titles the emperor awarded him, he would always be an upstart and outsider in the eyes of the aristocracy. Even the opprobrium attaching to eunuchs generally could work to the ruler's advantage; by delegating the implementation of unpopular measures to the agency of eunuchs he could deflect criticism and unpopularity from himself, and if need be he could at one and the same time mollify the elite and emphasise his autocratic power by throwing an unpopular *praepositus* to the wolves, and then redistribute his wealth to favoured *comites*. Arcadius chose to do that in the case of Eutropius in 399, only months after creating him a consul; and the exemplary lesson that contemporaries could draw from Eutropius' dramatic fall is vividly witnessed in the homily that the bishop of Constantinople delivered in its wake: 'Where now, [Eutropius], are the brilliant trappings of your consulship? . . . Where is the applause which once greeted you in the city, where the acclamations in the Hippodrome, the flatteries of spectators? Gone, all gone . . . mere dreams.'[173] The position of even the greatest of the *praepositi* was thus always intrinsically far more precarious than that of a superficially comparable figure in the courts of sixteenth-century Europe, the *privado* or 'minister-favourite'; the influence of court grandees such as Olivares or Richelieu may have depended heavily on the monarch's favour

---

[173] Holum 1982: 62–3; Buck 1988: 28–30; J. Chrysostom *Hom. in Eutrop.*1.

and provoked elite resentment, but the favourites' social origins were emi-
nently respectable, and often impeccably aristocratic.[174]

On several counts, then, the role served by the imperial eunuchs at court
seems nicely calculated to 'lubricate' the interactions of the ruler and the
elite. A more radical tactic was potentially available to the ruler, of course:
to cut back the exuberant growth of the court personnel that secluded him
from easy social contact with subjects and revert to a simpler pattern of
behaviour that resurrected elements of the older, more accessible style of
the *civilis princeps*. Julian arguably had a 'reactionary' purpose of that sort
in mind when he purged his predecessor's palace staff at Constantinople,
expelling 'hordes' of barbers, cooks, butlers and waiters, eunuch *cubicularii*
'more numerous than flies in the spring', and most of the 'villainous' and
overbearing *notarii* and the *agentes in rebus* serving as imperial agents and
couriers.[175] In their stead, he summoned back 'upright men' of culture to
be his companions at court, and the appeal of this accessible imperial style
in the eyes of elite subjects is plain from the compliments paid to Julian
by court panegyrists: 'As Emperor, he maintains in the same affection all
whom he accepted in friendship as a private citizen . . . no one is debarred
from access to him, the doors of the palace are closed to none.'[176] But it
is plain, too, that the tactic was riskily double-edged: the well-to-do classes
in the fourth century might still value the old imperial virtue of *civilitas*,
but emperors were nonetheless expected to project an aura of grandeur
and power, and unguarded shows of affability could easily deflate it. Julian
himself did not escape criticism on this score, even from his admirers; he
demeaned the dignity of the imperial office, Ammianus judged, when he
'leapt from his judgement seat' in the senate house, 'forgetful of who he was',
and ran out to greet a philosopher-friend with a reverent kiss, as if they were
social equals.[177] Significantly, Julian's 'reactionary' experiment – if such it
was – was not repeated by later emperors. They were aware, of course,
that a semblance of *civilitas* was appreciated by elite subjects, and they still
engaged on occasions in judiciously modulated displays of openness and
bonhomie which panegyrists were pleased to register as marks of imperial
virtue: thus Pacatus can affirm that Theodosius had not merely 'summoned
"Friendship" (*amicitia*) to the palace, but [had] arrayed [it] in purple and
installed [it] on the throne', and Claudian can recall how, on a state visit paid
to Rome in 389, Theodosius had 'played the citizen's part . . . suffering himself

[174] Elliott and Brockliss 1999: 1–7, 297–9.
[175] Libanius *Or.*18.130–5; Amm.22.4.10; Dvornik 1955: 71–81; Smith 1995: 44–6, 170.
[176] Mamertinus [*Pan.Lat.*III], 25.5–26.4.   [177] Amm.22. 7.1–4; cf. Socrates *HE* 3.1.

to exchange jests with the people ... and to visit the houses of senators and the doors of private subjects, setting aside the haughtiness of rank'.[178] But before this bonhomie there had been a spectacular ceremonial procession (an *adventus*, of which we say more below), and the images of royal 'friendliness' in these texts were topoi that came easily to the lips of speakers who had read Pliny's *Panegyric* of Trajan or Dio of Prusa's orations *On Kingship*. The fourth-century panegyrists' variations on them, moreover, are artfully nuanced to emphasise the distance between the ruler and his subjects;[179] in his inestimable goodness, Theodosius takes Friendship to his bosom by lifting it up to his high throne, and in his awesome power he permits himself to descend fleetingly to the houses of senators like some kindly *deus praesens*, a sight to be adored and wondered at. As the 'reluctant' obelisk erected by his order in the Hippodrome at Constantinople was compelled to acknowlege, 'everything yields to Theodosius and to his everlasting offspring' (*ILS* 821); and when he died, the poets avowed, Theodosius would reascend to his proper home in the Heavens: the Bear and Orion would vie 'to welcome the new star, each wondering ... which constellation he thought worthy of his presence'.[180] Late Roman emperors, that is to say, were celebrated above all else as embodiments of an irresistible and potentially terrifying sacred power: Christian emperors after Constantine did not overtly claim to be gods in the manner of Diocletian, who had identified himself with Jupiter, but it is well known that in a modified form the adoration of the image of the emperor in ruler-cult persisted well into the fifth century.[181] We pass now to the projection of this image of embodied sacredness in the pomp and ceremony of the court.

The 'sacred' emperor's self-display: court ceremonial and protocol

A memorable passage in Gibbon likens the system of late Roman government to an intricate stage-play: 'by a philosophic observer, [it] might have been mistaken for a splendid theatre, filled with players of every character and degree, who repeated the language, and imitated the passions, of their original model'; and it has been nicely observed that the tendency to represent

---

[178] Pacatus [*Pan.Lat.*II], 16.2; Claudian *VI Cons.Hon.*590–62.

[179] Konstan 1997: 124–30 (topoi); Kelly 1998: 148–9 (distance); but n.b. the qualifications as to the 'inaccessibility' of the emperor in Garnsey and Humfress 2001: 311–13, citing Valentinian's evocation of old *primus inter pares* style in a law of 371 (Cod.Theod.8.5.32).

[180] Claudian *II Cons.Hon.*171–3.

[181] Cult: Bowersock 2000: 53–6; Brent 1999; Salzman 1990: 130–46, 178–81; on *office* of emperor as divine, Kolb 2001: 63–72.

the late Roman emperors as star-actors in a courtly masque minutely stage-managed to advertise their resplendent power through gesture and costume goes back to Ammianus.[182] An abundance of textual and visual material could be adduced to illuminate the late Roman court in its ceremonious face.[183] Here we can only pick out for comment some especially character-istic forms of ritualised display: imperial processions and acclamations; the ritual 'adoration of the purple'; the ceremonies at which appointees to office in the emperor's service were formally invested at court with their codicils and symbolic appurtenances of office; and (briefly) religious observances, royal banqueting and hunting.

In AD 357, Constantius II and his mobile court paid a rare state visit to Rome. Ammianus, writing thirty years afterwards as one who had himself witnessed Theodosius' state visit of 389, describes his passage into the city as follows:

He came on [along the *Via Flaminia*], preceded by standards on both sides, sitting alone in a golden chariot, shining with all kinds of brilliant precious stones which seemed to spread a flickering light all round. The chief officers who went before him also were surrounded by dragons embroidered on various kinds of tissue, fastened to the jewelled points of spears, the mouths of the dragons open to catch the wind, which made them hiss as if inflamed with anger . . . After these marched a double row of soldiers glittering with brilliant light, clad in radiant breastplates . . . and the cavalrymen in cuirasses whom they call *clibinarii* ['Oven-men'], iron-masked and breast-plated, girdled with iron belts – you might take them not to be men, but rather statues polished by Praxiteles . . . The emperor as he proceeded was saluted as 'Augustus!' by voices of good omen, the mountains and shores re-echoing the shouts of the people, amid which noise he preserved the same immovable countenance that he was accustomed to display in his provinces. For though he was a man of short stature, yet he bowed down when entering through the city's high gates, looking straight ahead, as if he had his neck in a vice; he turned his eyes neither to right nor left, as if he were a graven image of a man; nor did he sway when jolted by the wheel of his chariot, nor was he ever seen to spit or wipe or rub his face or nose, or to move his hands about. And though this calmness was an affectation, yet these and other portions of his inner life were indicative of a most extraordinary patience – a patience granted, as it was given to be appreciated, to him alone [of men]. (Amm.16.10.8–10)

This set-piece description of the *adventus* (ceremony of arrival) of an emperor is justly famous as an illustration of the transmission of im-perial ideology in visual form through gesture and display; in stressing the

[182]   *DF* vol. II; Matthews 1989: 247.
[183]   For late imperial visual imagery in art, Brilliant 1963: 163–211; Weitzmann 1979.

imperturbability of the emperor in his absolute power, the spectacle implicitly depersonalises the individual ruler and projects an emblem of eternal power and victoriousness; as Ammianus notes, it was meant to evoke a triumphal procession.[184] The same ideological turn can be discerned in the new style that comes to the fore in imperial statue portraiture in the fourth century; unless an accompanying dedicatory inscription is extant, late imperial portrait-statues are notoriously difficult to identify (the so-called 'Barletta' statue, for instance, has been identified by different scholars with half a dozen emperors), because the sculptors have little interest in reproducing any individual emperor's facial features; what they aim to portray is not an individual ruler's likeness but an idealised type – not *an* emperor but *the* emperor, stylised as a 'pantocratic superman'.[185] There is an evident evocation of this brand of imperial portraiture in Ammianus' account of the *adventus* of 357; Constantius is transmuted into an unmoving statue – a condition to which emperors were explicitly advised to aspire by an intellectual protégé of Constantius who delivered a speech in his presence at Rome on this very occasion. This was Themistius, leading senator (and later prefect) of Constantinople, advocate of the theory of the emperor as 'Divine Law Incarnate', court-philosopher and propagandist to a succession of fourth-century rulers, tutor to an emperor's son – a 'born survivor' whose adroitness in negotiating the hazards of dramatic regime-change makes him a fitting ancient match for Talleyrand.[186] What is being displayed for glorification in the ritual *adventus*, then, is not so much an individual emperor as a depersonalised, absolute power inhabiting the body of an emperor, an 'eternal presence' deriving from the heavens.[187] In Ammianus' passage there is one point only at which Constantius breaks his self-willed rule of regal immobility, and it is tellingly symbolic; although he is physically a man of short stature, the power embodied in the emperor has rendered him a god-like giant who must duck his head to pass under the high-arched monumental gates of Rome. Around his carriage and bodyguard, by contrast, a crowd of onlookers were jostling and shouting excitedly – but even on that score there was an established etiquette for the occasion in the cries saluting the Augustus. Chanted acclamations of the emperor figured in many settings – at the *adventus*, in the Hippodrome at the epiphany of the ruler before his

---

[184] Matthews 1989: 231–4; MacCormack 1981: 17–89, esp. 41–2; Amm.16.10.2.

[185] Brilliant 1963: 163; Smith 1985: 219–20; 1997: 194–201.

[186] MacMullen 1990: 85–6, 303 n. 18 (emperor as *eikon*), cf. Themistius *Or*.5.64b (Law Incarnate); MacCormack 1981: 40 (Them.*Or*.3 delivered at Rome); on Themistius' charmed career as an imperial propagandist, 'the Talleyrand of his day', Heather 1998b: 125–49.

[187] MacCormack 1981: 55.

people, and quite often in the senate. Although the custom was well established before our period, it predictably now takes on a more baroque appearance.[188] The most celebrated example occurred at a meeting of the Roman senate on 25 December 438, on the occasion of the promulgation of the Theodosian Code: after a reading of the edict ordering its compilation, the senators chanted a sequence of forty-three ritual acclamations, each one much repeated: 'Augustuses of Augustuses, greatest of Augustuses' (chanted eight times); 'God gave you to us, God gave you to us' (twenty-eight times); and on, and on – the whole sequence, it is reckoned, would have taken a good hour to complete.[189]

Ammianus' account of the *adventus* focuses on the magnetic presence of the emperor, but the spectacle in the ceremony it describes was not just Constantius II, but also a body of several thousand people, the itinerant court *en masse*, marching into Rome in ranking order in a choreographed procession that must have taken hours to pass under the high gates. We should think of the event Ammianus described as a visual projection not only of the sacred power invested in the individual monarch, but of the principles that ordered the hierarchy of the whole 'court society' over which he presided. Ammianus, for instance, does not mention the empress Eusebia in his account of Constantius' *adventus*, but he later discloses that both she and his sister Helena had accompanied him on his journey from Milan to Rome, and we know from Julian that upon her arrival at Rome she was formally received by the senate, and that she presided at a distribution of largesse to representatives of the plebs.[190] It is hardly conceivable that the managers of imperial ceremonial had neglected to train her, too, in the etiquette of gesture and deportment called for by the occasion, and the same holds true for the ranks of *comites* and their staffs; they themselves, and the shrewder among the spectators, would both take good note of where they figured in the line as it processed.

As long as emperors were itinerant, the *adventus* was associated particularly with the arrival of the emperor in a provincial city (for most of whose inhabitants, it would most likely be the only time they encountered the emperor in the flesh), but as Constantinople developed as a permanent residence the ceremonial associated with the *adventus* also became 'internalised' in the imperial processions regularly staged in the capital city. We have noticed earlier the processions to the Great Church and the granaries,

[188] Alföldi 1970: 82–8; Roueché 1984: 181–99; MacMullen 1990: 81.
[189] Matthews 1989: 248.   [190] Amm.16.10.18; Jul.*Or*.3.129b.

but there was another that holds a special interest for its symbolic resonance. Constantine had marked the inauguration of the city in 330 with a grand procession: the emperor and his courtiers gathered in the Forum at the foot of a porphyry column to witness the placing on its top of a golden statue of Constantine crowned radiantly as Apollo-Sol. From there they had processed to the imperial box of the Hippodrome adjoining the Palace to acclaim a uniquely privileged charioteer: a golden image of Constantine borne in a golden chariot completed a circuit round the race-track, accompanied by troops of the imperial guard in full regalia; in his right hand the golden emperor held another golden image, the *Tychē* of his City.[191] For centuries afterwards, the ceremony of the *pompa circensis* was re-enacted on the anniversary of its first performance, the emperor of the day in the imperial box honouring at once the founder of his capital and the eternal power of imperial office in company with his people. And from 390 on, moreover, the imperial entourage gathered for the occasion looked out across the track onto a near-reflection of itself, sculpted in relief on the base of the giant obelisk that Theodosius erected in the *spina* of the Hippodrome that year. The panel facing them showed the emperor, flanked by his 'everlasting offspring' Arcadius and Honorius, standing on a platform below the *kathisma* with a victory wreath in his hand, surrounded by high officials and rows of guards; beneath them, assembled spectators watch musicians and dancers (and underneath the panel itself stands the commemorative inscription we quoted from to open this chapter) (Fig. 5.3). The exact symbolic associations are debated (on one view, the Hippodrome is symbolic of the cosmos, and the obelisk at its centre represents the sun), but their basic thrust is hardly in doubt: the panel celebrates the eternal victory and triumph of the emperor, the embodiment of imperial majesty. The Hippodrome adjoining the Great Palace thus emerged as the locus *par excellence* of the divine power attaching to the ruler, the point at which royalty's aura was most densely concentrated; by the late fifth century, it is telling, it was coming to supplant the military Kampos of the western suburbs as the setting for the ceremonial accession of the emperor; the emperor was now acclaimed not by the soldiers, but by his people gathered at the symbolic centre of the world.[192]

At the *pompa circensis*, as the golden images of Constantine and his city's *Tychē* were paraded around the Hippodrome, the reigning emperor came forward from the imperial box and prostrated himself before it as it passed.

---

[191] Dagron 1974: 37–41, 307–9; Kantorowitz 1963: 149–62 (solar imagery in Byzantine court ritual).
[192] Kiilerich 1993: 37, 48–9; Geyssen 1998; Dagron 1974: 314–16.

Figure 5.3 Theodosius I and his court in the Hippodrome in Constantinople, from the base of the Obelisk of Theodosius

On one very special symbolic occasion, then, the emperor performed an act of obeisance comparable to those that his subjects routinely performed for him. In the ceremony of the 'adoration of the purple', the subject approached and prostrated himself before the emperor's dais in the consistory and was offered the gold-embroidered hem of the ruler's purple robe to raise to his lips and kiss – a 'fetishising' of the purple, so to speak, as a material expression of depersonalised imperial power. The Theodosian Code discloses that the possession of a purple robe or the acquisition of purple dye by any unauthorised person was an act of treason punishable by execution, and an episode relating to 'Diocletian's Palace' at Split suggests that this law was taken seriously. Ammianus tells how, in 356, an innocent man was arraigned on a charge of treason after his estranged wife claimed that he had stolen the purple coverlet draped over Diocletian's tomb in his Mausoleum;[193] half a century after his death, then, Diocletian still wore the purple. The garment's potency as a visible manifestation of the 'everlasting divine [power] by which the Roman State will ever stand unshaken' is strikingly conveyed

---

[193] Amm.16.8.4.

in Ammianus' account of the ceremonial investiture of Gratian as emperor at the hands of his father: Valentian 'adorned his son with a crown and the robes of the supreme *fortuna*' and displayed him before the ranks of the army present; 'Behold', he said, 'the imperial robe [now placed on you] by the wish of myself and my soldiers . . . Gird yourself now, then, as a colleague of your father.'[194]

The earliest explicit reference to the 'adoration of the purple' occurs in a law dated to 354 in the Theodosian Code (8.7.4), in which it is implicitly treated as already a well-established practice. It was quite likely a Diocletianic innovation:[195] we have noticed earlier that the *adoratio* was at least thought by Ammianus and other fourth-century writers to owe something to Persian practice, and to go back to Diocletian. For our purposes it is less important to fix an exact date for its introduction at court than to stress the degree to which it became routinised in the fourth century as a key feature of court ritual which – to judge from Ammianus and the Theodosian Code – was not viewed as 'un-Roman' in the sense that it entailed any dishonourable or slavish self-abasement on the part of the adorer: rather, they imply that it was regarded as an honour and privilege and mark of favour for the adorer as well as the adored. In this connection, it has an evident counterpart in the older custom of the morning *salutatio* of the emperor in earlier centuries (see Paterson in this volume); at meetings of the consistory, the members kissed the purple in an established order of rank.[196] Men appointed to an imperial office routinely performed the ritual at their formal investiture, and Ammianus, who had been enrolled as an officer-cadet in Constantius' court, must himself have kissed the purple. He does not speak of his own case in his history, but as an officer in the service of the general Ursicinus he witnessed and later described a particular *adoratio* in 355 which for our purposes is highly instructive. Ursicinus had been under a cloud – suspected of complicity in a revolt, and slandered at court. When news that the rebel leader had declared himself emperor reached the court one evening (significantly, the would-be usurper had donned a makeshift purple robe made up of strips of silk from a military standard[197]), Constantius had to decide immediately whether Ursicinus was innocent and should be rehabilitated in the eyes of the court, or condemned by association. Ammianus records the outcome: 'He summoned an emergency meeting of the Consistory', and 'all the nobles hastened to the palace . . . Ursicinus was sent for by the *praepositus*, which

---

[194] Amm.27.6.1; 27.6.11–12.   [195] Avery 1940; Stern 1954.
[196] Winterling 1998: ch. 7 *passim* (*salutatio*); Avery 1940: 69 (kissing in order of rank).
[197] Amm.15.5.17.

is the most honourable kind of summons, and as soon as he entered the consistory-chamber he was offered the purple much more graciously than on any previous occasion.'[198] For Ursicinus, then, the invitation to perform the *adoratio* was a demonstration before the assembled 'lofty powers' at court that the emperor held him in high regard as a loyal and trustworthy general – and Ammianus is content to report the episode in that spirit. The passage also implies that the *adoratio* was performed fairly routinely at court, and there is a well-known case from Egypt to show that persons much less grand than Ursicinus had their chances to kiss the purple – and that for them, too, it was a badge of esteem that could be used to 'pull rank' to practical advantage. In 340, a petition reached Constantius' palace from one Flavius Abinnaeus, an army officer in Egypt who had been passed over for promotion by his local commander in favour of another candidate. The rival had used local patronal influence, but Abinnaeus had a better card to play: some years earlier, service on a military escort had taken him to the court of Constantinople, and by chance into the presence of the emperor himself – on which occasion, 'Your Divinity ordered me to adore the venerable purple.' Now, years later, he petitioned the emperor to intervene in order to secure him promotion to the post in dispute: 'for it is clear that [the letters by which my rival procured the post] were advanced by patronal influence (*suffragium*), whereas I was advanced by your sacred decision [to have me kiss the purple] . . . may Your Clemency therefore vouchsafe that I be the man appointed'.[199] This petition is known to have succeeded – an eloquent witness to the mystique evoked by the *adoratio* in an officers' mess thousands of miles distant from Constantinople; and at a more elevated level, it has an analogy in an imperial law of 387 enhancing the ranking order of the emperor's officer-cadet corps at court by granting a privilege that the ruler deemed undeniable 'to those who are thought worthy to touch our Purple'.[200]

At the formal investiture of a palace official or provincial administrator, the appointee performed the *adoratio* and received a commemorative notice of his appointment in the form of a scroll or bound book inscribed with an acclamation to the recipient wishing him success in the name of the emperor. If the post awarded was a high-ranking one, the appointee usually also received an ivory diptych – a hinged pair of gold-edged ivory leaves, decorated on the outer sides with carved reliefs of the emperor, and with his codicils of office enclosed. The ceremoniousness of the moment

---

[198] Amm.15.5.18, with Matthews 1989: 244–5.
[199] Abinnaeus Archive, *Pap.Abinn.*1.11–14; Jones 1964: 637.
[200] *Cod.Theod.*6.24.4; Matthews 1989: 247.

Figure 5.4 The 'Missorium of Theodosius' (AD 388)

of investiture is well conveyed in a magnificent work of late fourth-century art, the 'Missorium of Theodosius' – a large silver plate representing an investiture of a high official, and presented to him as a commemorative gift (Fig. 5.4). Three emperors – Theodosius I, flanked by two juniors, Arcadius and Valentinian II – sit enthroned under arched lintels, attended by imperial guards, and dressed in finery: belted tunics with ornamental borders, imperial cloaks fastened at the shoulder with jewelled fibulae, and jewelled sandals. Each of them wears a diadem made up of two bands of pearls with a large jewel at the crest, and each is nimbed. The two flanking emperors hold symbolic orbs, while Theodosius himself, sitting upright and looking impassively out towards the viewer, extends his right hand to slip a codicil of appointment into a fold in the cloak of a kneeling official (clearly a very high-ranking subject, perhaps a Praetorian Prefect); below the tableau, meanwhile, a reclining female figure holds a cornucopia. The imagery elevates

Figure 5.5 Leaf of an ivory diptych commemorating the entry of a Vicarius of Rome into his term of office (about AD 400?)

the emperors as quasi-divine universal rulers, the source of all riches and honours, glorying in the fecundity of the 'everlasting' Theodosian house.[201] High office, now, was a gift plucked out from an imperial horn of plenty, and graciously bestowed by the sacred hand extended downwards by the enthroned emperor. On this count, the representation of Theodosius on the Missorium conforms to a standard iconographic type; it has an evident parallel in a visual image preserved in Filocalus' 'Codex-Calendar of 354' of Constantius II dispensing largesse: bejewelled and nimbed, the ruler sits on a raised dais within a curtained *aedicula*, with coins pouring down from his outstretched right hand – and a line of silver lanxes (ceremonial plates) stacked up behind his throne to be distributed to elite subjects.[202]

The carved ivory diptychs of appointment are objects well known to historians of late antique art (Fig. 5.5). They were highly prized as markers of status, and the recipients kept them afterwards on display in their offices, on tables covered in blue cloth. In the case of high posts in the civil administrative service, a set of candlesticks and a large ceremonial inkstand were also awarded, and likewise displayed in the post-holder's office.[203] So too, it pleased an appointee to a provincial governorship to be represented with his codicil of appointment in his hand in a commemorative statue.[204] For us, the particular interest of these appurtenances lies in the style of communication they imply. In the earlier empire, the style of the *civilis princeps* had encouraged emperors to communicate with high officials with a degree of openness and informality; in the fourth century, that pretence of social 'equality' is replaced by a highly stylised pattern of communication in which gesture, gift-giving and chanted acclamations combine to emphasise the asymmetry of the relationship between imperial majesty and even the highest-ranking imperial subjects. The obvious textual analogue to this visual grammar of dominance and submission lies in the contorted periphrases adopted in the letters of petition addressed to emperors by the likes of Flavius Abinnaeus, and in the emperors' own *de haut en bas* pronouncements in the Theodosian Code, as drafted by the secretariats of the palace ministries for promulgation through the consistory. Petitioners have recourse to the 'optative of courtesy', asking favours of 'Your Clemency', 'if it should please Your goodness'; emperors announce their laws or wishes in the royal plural through the mouth of the Quaestor in the consistory, referring to themselves as 'Our

[201] Kiilerich 1993: 19–23.   [202] Weitzmann 1979: 79 (no. 67); Matthews 1989: 232.
[203] Matthews 1989: 255.   [204] Smith 2002.

Serenity', 'Our Clemency', 'Our Wisdom', 'Our Eternity', 'Our Tranquillity', 'Our Imperial Divinity'.[205]

Processions, acclamations and the formal ceremonial of the consistory were not the only occasions for imperial self-display at court, of course; the emperor, and often members of his family, were on show in a variety of other settings too. Two secular communal activities – banqueting and hunting – will serve as our prime examples here, but religious observances performed in the presence of courtiers within the palace demand a word: they could plainly serve to underpin the sacred emperor's claim to a unique degree of affinity with divinity, and in this connection the devotional behaviour of rulers keen to promote a sectional religious interest could take on particular exemplary significance. The most obvious cases in point are Constantine and Julian. Constantine, Eusebius insists, had 'modelled his palace into a church of God and afforded an exemplar of piety to those gathered within it', offering up regular prayers with all the members of his court; he ordered Sundays to be observed there, 'instruct[ing] his bodyguard in the practice of piety'; each day 'at a stated hour' he would retire to a private chapel 'in solitary converse with his God'; at Eastertide, 'in imitation of the Saviour's gracious acts, he lavished abundant bounties'; and his preparations for the Persian campaign he was planning in his last years included the making of 'a tent of great splendour in the shape of a church' to serve as a mobile chapel for the emperor and his entourage during the campaign.[206] Julian did virtually the same, but in a pagan register, performing a daily morning-sacrifice 'under the trees in the palace garden' before a crowd of attendants, dedicating a shrine to Helios (or Mithras?) 'in the middle of the [Great] Palace' at which he presided at initiations, compelling the palace guard to sacrifice in his presence on their pay-days.[207]

The repercussions at court of Constantine's 'conversion' were not confined to the court's devotional activities: we noticed earlier that it brought a new breed of guest, the Christian bishop, to the palace dining-rooms. Banqueting is a familiar topic for historians of courts (as the other chapters in this volume attest). It can be construed both as a mode of conspicuous expenditure that can emphasise the ruler's power and as a communal activity that can foster a sense of social cohesiveness among the privileged group invited to dine in the ruler's company. Within that group, a *comes'* place in the dining-hall could serve as a visible demonstration of his place

[205] *Cod.Theod.*15.1.26; 15.1.30–31; 16.4.1–4; MacMullen 1990: 67–77, esp. 71–3; Matthews 1989: 255.
[206] Euseb. *VC* 417–18, 22, 56.   [207] Lib.*Orr.*1.121;18.127; Sozomen 5.17.

in the ranking order at court, depending on how closely he was placed to the emperor's own couch, but any invitation to dine at court with the emperor was a mark of high honour and potentially a path to preferment. Themistius, for instance, was quick to let friends know when Constantius invited him to dinner – and in his case the invitations to the palace went hand in hand with his rapid rise to eminence as a Constantinopolitan senator in 355. Themistius' friends in their turn could hope that crumbs from the emperor's table would fall their way. Libanius' reply on hearing of the invitation speaks volumes on this score: 'Your presence at [the emperor's] table', he wrote, 'denotes a greater intimacy – so that, inasmuch as your professions arise from a concern for your friends, anyone you mention is better off.'[208] Libanius had particular cause around this time to wish to be spoken of favourably in Constantius' presence – and to appreciate what a place at the emperor's table could accomplish. In 354 he had resettled at his native city, Antioch. Antioch was at that time the seat of the junior emperor Gallus, and a local rival of Libanius had sullied his name at Gallus' court by bribing a young man 'whose good looks had earned him many a dinner' there to accuse Libanius of using black magic against both Gallus and Constantius: an absurd charge, Libanius insisted – 'but still, it was believed that the emperor thought me disloyal, and would show it when he appeared in public by not sparing me a glance'.[209]

As for 'conspicuous consumption', there was a balance to be struck: the luxurious gourmand was a moralising topos – 'Where now are your drinking-parties and suppers . . . the manifold dainties prepared by your cooks?', it was mockingly asked of the fallen eunuch Eutropius[210] – and self-control (*continentia*) was traditionally an imperial virtue. For Ammianus, an emperor's attitude to the pleasures of the table offered a telling test-of-thumb: he praises Julian for sharing the simple fare of his soldiers while in Gaul, and Valentinian for choosing to dine elegantly rather than extravagantly; by contrast, Jovian's excessive love of food and wine had impaired his 'imperial dignity', and his *castrensis* (the official in charge of the services at table) is scornfully styled 'the minister of bellies and throats'.[211] Imperial panegyrists were accordingly inclined to play down the luxury of the imperial table, indulging in conventional topoi that surely minimise the true level of expenditure involved. Pacatus, say, praises the fare on offer at Theodosius' palace-feasts as wholesomely modest by comparison with the excesses of Neronian times – but a hostile source insists on

---

[208] Lib.*Ep*.52 Norman (= 66.2 Forster).   [209] Lib.*Or*.1.98–9.
[210] J. Chrysostom *Hom.in Eutrop*.1.1.   [211] Amm.16.5.3; 30.9.4; 25.10.15; 26.8.5.

their unprecedented luxury.[212] The hostile source is probably here the better guide, even if it exaggerates: on Ammianus' and Libanius' testimony, at any rate, the Great Palace at Constantinople was already awash with cooks and waiters in Constantius' day, and the existence there of the grand 'Triclinium of the Nineteen Couches' suggests provision for state banquets on a scale that easily matched the feasts at Domitian's *Domus Flavia*.[213] A precisely contextualised story in Eunapius, moreover, reports a particularly grand banquet provided by none other than Theodosius – a feast for a company of Gothic 'federates' and their leader, the 'Master of Soldiers' Fravitta, which had notoriously ended in drunken mayhem.[214]

Lastly, we touch on the hunt as a setting for imperial self-display. Hunting was deemed a fitting relaxation for emperors, and their prowess in the field was a standard theme in court poetry; even Theodosius II, reputedly an effete and bookish character who rarely left the palace, was praised for 'draw[ing] the bow like [Homer's] Teucer', and he certainly did hunt: he died from an injury incurred when he fell from his horse while hunting.[215] To treat 'the hunt' abstractly as a stage for the display of imperial virtue and power is perhaps to discuss the issue in an over-schematised way; emperors needed to relax, after all, and hunting was well established as the favoured pastime not only of kings but of aristocrats in general. Hunting scenes proliferate in the art produced for the late imperial elite – in the mosaics and tapestry-curtains of their villas, on the glassware and silver plates they dined off, on their sarcophaguses, on their very clothes: in Ammianus, the tunics of Roman aristocrats shimmer 'with the shapes of many animals', and to a fourth-century Christian homilist's eye the vanity of the rich was manifest in their love of garments emblazoned with 'lions and leopards, bears, bulls and dogs, forests and rocks and hunters'.[216] Still, the hunting done in the parks of the emperors' rural retreats was a form of communal activity that made for a bond between a ruler and the courtiers who rode with him (cf. Spawforth in this volume, on Alexander). The symbolism of the staged hunting-shows in the capital at which the emperor presided over the dispatch of lions and wild beasts conveyed much the same lesson as the 'once reluctant' obelisk erected in the Hippodrome, now 'conquered and mastered' and hoisted skywards against its will: 'all things [must] yield to Theodosius and his everlasting

---

[212] *Pan.Lat* III.14; Zosimus 4.33.1.

[213] Lib.*Or*.18.130; cf. Amm.22.4.10; Zanker 2002 (*Domus Flavia*); for the persistence of the high imperial 'triclinium' couch-arrangement at late imperial state banquets, Dunbabin 1991.

[214] Eunapius *Fr*.59 (Blockley).

[215] Holum 1982: 101, 208; Cameron 1982: 228–9 (quoting from Cyrus' panegyric of *c.* 435).

[216] Amm.14.6.9; Asterius *Hom*.1, *PG*. 40:165 (quoted from Maguire 1999: 242).

offspring', the 'serene lords' of the world (*ILS* 821). On both these counts, analogies with the role of the Royal Hunt in other antique settings come easily to mind. The Persian tradition of the royal lion-hunt went back to the Achaemenids (see Brosius and Wiesehöfer in this volume): its representation on Sasanian reliefs and fabrics was certainly later a stylistic influence on the Byzantine iconography of the hunt,[217] and it perhaps contributed something to the association of emperors in Late Roman art with the figure of the 'Great Huntsman', whose spearing of a lion symbolised the triumph of imperial *Virtus* over all obstacles and enemies.[218] In any event, the symbolism of the hunt could certainly evoke the image of the emperor as an instrument of the Eternal Victory that ensured the defeat of Rome's enemies: hunting had strong military associations – sometimes, indeed, large-scale hunts seem to have been organised with a practical military purpose in mind, as training-exercises in manoeuvring for the imperial cavalry[219] – and on this score the troops that Julian led out against the Persians in 363 enjoyed a symbolic victory, at least, when they encountered a hunting-park of the Persian king stocked with lions and bears: 'our cavalry forced the gates of the enclosure and killed them all with hunting-spears and arrows'.[220] In Ammianus' eyes, accordingly, the ruler's skill in the hunting field was another test of his character – but here again, the creation of a favourable impression was a matter of deportment as much as expertise: whereas Constantius' horsemanship and skills with the spear and the bow combined with a dignified presence to do him credit, Gratian's passion for shooting wild beasts in the imperial enclosures bespoke an over-eagerness to impress his companions (*proximi*) and struck Ammianus as excessive.[221] In Gratian's case, at any rate, there were private beast-shows staged for the court in the palace-complex at Milan as well as public shows in the amphitheatre: a Christian source recalls an occasion when Bishop Ambrose went to the palace to bring an urgent matter to Gratian's attention and only gained a hearing by joining the hunters in a purpose-built enclosure in the palace grounds.[222]

As distinct from the staged slaughter of fierce beasts in the arena, there was the mounted hunting of wild game in the vicinity of imperial estates – an energetic pastime less trammelled by the strictures of court ceremonial and protocol, and perhaps valued all the more as a setting that still allowed for spontaneous human contact between the ruler and a select band of courtiers. But even here, behaviour could be stylised, and for some the prospect may

---

[217] Grabar 1936: 60–1; Patlagean 1992: 257–63.
[218] Brilliant 1963: 183–8, esp. 184 (medallion-image of Constantine II).
[219] Rance 2000: 254–7.   [220] Amm.24.5.2, with Smith 1999: 97.
[221] Amm.21.16.7; 31.10.19.   [222] Sozomen 7.25.

have carried echoes of Alexander the Great relaxing with his intimate *philoi*. We noticed earlier that in the third and fourth centuries interest in the figure of Alexander as a paradigmatic warrior-king seems to have intensified as the Sasanians emerged as an energetic power in Persia, and this sharpened interest is reflected in images of Alexander fighting and hunting on horseback in late imperial art: a giant fourth-century cameo seems to associate him with a contemporary emperor (Constantius II perhaps?) in the guise of a diademed cavalier galloping in triumph over the bodies of slain barbarians; and like the emperors Alexander could be associated too with the talismanic figure of the 'Huntsman' who secures the triumph of good over evil in the world.[223] But on decorated table-ware the mounted Alexander is also depicted hunting stags and boars in a more informal mode, under a legend wishing him long life with his family and friends;[224] Julian, for one, admired this homelier, Macedonian side to the 'Alexander-style', and perhaps had it in mind when he added a post-script in his own hand to a letter summoning a trusted friend to his court in Gaul in his days as Constantius' junior emperor: 'There is good quarry of deer [here]', he remarked.[225] For some emperors, then, the hunt may have indeed appealed as a means of 'bonding' with one's *comites*. That said, the 'friendliness' of emperors could never be taken for granted, in this or any other sphere: their power was 'god-like', and like gods they could grow angry. Indeed, exemplary anger in some measure was always integral to their projection of power. Around the very time he summoned 'upright men' to be his friends at court, the 'friendly' Julian ordered several prominent courtiers of Constantius to be burned alive, and in Valentinian's case the sudden bouts of rage were notorious and sometimes lethal to those in his entourage (and finally to himself: Valentinian was struck down by an apoplectic fit at a meeting of the consistory, infuriated by the speech of a delegation of German tribesmen who had come to sue for peace).[226] In Ammianus' view, 'a semblance' of imperial 'clemency' was the most that Valentinian could manage, and his behaviour on the hunting field and at the beast-shows revealed as well as anything the choleric nature underneath the mask: an attendant who spoiled his day's hunting by releasing a hound too soon was summarily beaten to death, and his household functionaries had reason to fear two notably uncivil courtiers privileged to live close beside his bedchamber – 'Morsel' and 'Innocence', a pair of pet bears, both ferocious man-killers. They were presumably set loose for exemplary purposes in the palace's hunting pits, and 'Innocence', at least, was finally rewarded

---

[223] Weitzman 1979: 91, 83.   [224] Weitzman 1979: 89.   [225] Jul.*Ep*.6 (9 Bidez).
[226] Amm.22.3.11 (Julian); 30.6.3 (Valentinian).

by the emperor with the freedom of the forests for years of murderous 'service'.[227]

Concluding remarks

We have aimed to indicate how the late Roman imperial court came to take on its distinctive shape, and to describe its workings in terms that convey something of the court's social-political importance. It was not central to our purpose to debate the merits or shortcomings of any particular model of 'court society' on this score, and the question whether Elias' 'Versailles model' is apt or 'true' in its correspondence to Roman (or for that matter Bourbon) historical realities is not, for our purposes, a crucial one: the 'court society' is a historical paradigm, not a historical fact, and inasmuch as paradigms make universalising claims they will always be vulnerable to criticism in specific historical cases. We adduced the case of Versailles, rather, as a starting-point that could offer suggestive counterparts to the late Roman case in certain telling features. On that count, our discussion has surely established that the social-political milieu in which late Roman emperors lived and worked can safely be reckoned a complex 'court society' in something like the sense that Elias proposed for Versailles; the late imperial court can certainly be said to have 'configured' and mediated monarchic power in a particular form through its reconfiguration of the court elite, its palace-centred bureaucratic apparatus, its 'absolutist' ceremonial, and its transmission of 'courtly' social and cultural values to a wider elite in the empire at large through literature and art.

   We have emphasised as a background factor the ideological and structural changes associated with the emergence in the third century of emperors from within a non-aristocratic military elite of career-soldiers, rulers with social origins in the provincial (often Balkan) peasantry; the traditional image of the virtuous emperor as a citizen-princeps ruling in close cooperation with a peer-group of Roman senatorial aristocrats did not utterly fade away, but it was sidelined as imperial ideology took an overtly authoritarian, 'absolutist', turn which celebrated emperors as gods or vessels of divine power; and the great bulk of the military and administrative offices of the empire came to be filled by non-senators. The structural and ceremonial distinctiveness of the late imperial court and its expanded bureaucracy betokens a rapprochement of sorts between the ethos of the new 'professional' governing

---

[227] Amm.30.8.2; 29.3.3; 29.3.9; see Matthews 1989: 260.

class and an older aristocratic social ethos – a progressive accommodation of the new elite within the traditional structures of Roman 'civil' society in a new 'aristocracy of service' which greatly expanded the membership – and quite transformed the social composition – of the senatorial order. Court ceremonial articulated and normalised these ideological and structural adjustments. Ceremonies such as the *adventus* and the 'adoration of the purple' emphasised the sacred emperor's remoteness from the common run of humanity, but at the same time they enabled a reconfigured and considerably enlarged governing elite – the emperor's *comites* especially – to interact with the ruler in a setting which fostered a collective sense of social identity and established an internal ranking order. There was no serious effort made (except, on one view, in Julian's case) to revert to the older style of rule that had fostered an illusion of social equality between ruler and elite, but the image of the *civilis princeps* could still be evoked to conjure a semblance of openness; Constantius, we have seen, could publicly commend a high official as a 'parent and friend', and when Valentinian I reaffirmed the right of Roman senators to travel to the court at the state's expense by means of the imperial carriage-service, 'because We very often desire to see [them] on account of the merits of our confraternity (*collegium*)', he echoed the style of the 'citizen-king'.[228] Even in the later fourth century, there was still a sense in which the workings of the 'court society' could help, if need be, to legitimise and 'domesticate' particular emperors in the eyes of the elite. On one recent view, for instance, the court-panegyrists' intricate praises in the 380s of the 'serene lord' Theodosius I as the founder of an everlasting dynasty, a paragon of imperial virtue who had only reluctantly accepted the crown at the behest of the then-senior emperor Gratian, masks the rise of a military usurper.[229] Or there is Gratian's father Valentinian, who hailed from the same humble Pannonian stock as many of the 'soldier-emperors' of the third century (his own father, we noticed earlier, was a talented peasant soldier who had risen to become a *protector* in the *comitatus*, and finally a military governor). In Ammianus' judgement, Valentinian's violent rages (not to mention his pet bears) disclosed a temperament that was 'patently ferocious'.[230] But Ammianus also judged that he 'strove as best he could to restrain his fierce urges' to counter his reputation for harshness, and at least 'affected a friendly style' at times, and his obituary-notice of Valentinian portrays a cultivated side to the man: he wrote and spoke with eloquence and fluency, painted and sculpted gracefully, dined elegantly – and radiated 'royal

[228] *Cod.Theod.*8.5.32, with Garnsey and Humfress 2001: 31.
[229] Sivan 1996.   [230] Amm.27.7.4.

majesty' in his appearance and deportment.[231] And as we noticed earlier, he selected a notably cultivated teacher for Gratian, in the shape of the poet Ausonius. These are not qualities one readily associates with third-century soldier-emperors, and the difference is surely due in part to Valentinian's exposure to a court society in which 'influences of environment and education counted for as much as those of heredity and regional origin';[232] his father the *protector* had clearly had the young Valentinian reasonably well tutored, and the Pannonian supporters who prospered at Valentinian's court were not illiterate troopers: they were mainly educated professionals, lawyers and clerks with a background in the court bureaucracy.[233]

These are particular cases, and it would certainly be over-schematic to ascribe to the late Roman court in general a 'domesticating' or 'civilising' function of the sort that Elias sought to establish in his 'Versailles model'. To contemporary observers such as Ammianus, the court looked more like a 'snake-pit' in which individuals and cliques – high officials, bureaucratic functionaries, eunuchs, empresses – were constantly intriguing for influence or riches or power, and the leading courtiers lived precarious lives: seemingly unshakeable grandees like the eunuch Eutropius, or Honorius' guardian and generalissimo Stilicho, could suddenly fall from favour and be summarily exiled or beheaded; innocent men could be gruesomely tortured on trumped-up charges of seditious magic, condemned at show-trials and strangled or burned alive; informers and spies hovered in the palace's corridors and dining rooms, reporting back to sinister imperial agents with mafioso-like nicknames: under Constantius II, the prosecutor 'Paul the Chain' would link up a sequence of charges with ingenious malice, and the network of informers controlled by Mercurius the 'Count (*comes*) of Dreams' seemed to give him access almost to one's private thoughts.[234] Constantius, in Ammianus' view, was a morosely suspicious individual all too ready to believe himself surrounded by conspirators and to act on that belief,[235] and the personalities of individual emperors will certainly have affected the complexion of the imperial court at given times; some were forceful and energetic, some were insipid and lazy, some only children when they took the purple. But even the capacity of a strong-willed emperor to impose his personality on the court was necessarily limited. The delegation of power to functionaries in the enlarged court bureaucracy, we noticed earlier, was likely to generate textually established precedents and

---

[231] Amm.27.7.4; 30.8.2; 30.9.4–6.   [232] Matthews 1975: 48.   [233] Matthews 1975: 44–5.

[234] Amm.29.1.5–2.20 (show-trials and terror under Valens, AD 370–1); 15.3.4–5 (Paul and Mercurius).

[235] Amm.21.16.9.

routines that reduced the scope for arbitrary autocratic interventions, and while court ceremonial might ascribe an aura of omnipotence the monarch, in reality the 'remote' emperor at the apex of the court hierarchy was necessarily dependent on his agents and advisors for his knowledge of how things stood within his *comitatus*: what they chose to tell him must often have been coloured by their own interests, and emperors who failed to check the truth of their reports were liable to be hoodwinked.[236] To safeguard his position, then, the monarch too had to engage shrewdly as a player at the court, calculating his interests and options with an eye to the impression his actions would make on the minds of courtiers. The smooth running of the court, for instance, required regular procedures to be observed – but an emperor who allowed them to run wholly undisturbed risked conveying the impression that power lay effectively with the secretariats of the palace bureaucracy; selective interventions would always be needed to emphasise that, if he wished, the ruler could disrupt and override the regularities. Features of late imperial court practice that on the face of things seem arbitrary or irrational or corruptive of effective government – the trumping of the regular, seniority-based arrangements for promotion in the imperial service by acts of royal favour, the sudden and apparently arbitrary withdrawals of support from individual grandees, the overlapping of bureaucratic functions within different sections of the palace secretariat and the resulting interdepartmental jealousies – need to be appraised in that light: from the monarch's viewpoint, they could help to prevent power devolving to an unsettling degree upon particular ministers or sectional interests within the court. A 'rational' bureaucracy, that is to say, would have served the ruler's own interest less well than the 'patrimonial' arrangement that in fact obtained. Whether the way the palace bureaucracy worked had significantly deleterious consequences for imperial government in the round is another question. 'Corruption' in the form of 'tips' (*sportulae*) and the sale of offices was undoubtedly rife, both at a high level and in the poorly paid lower echelons, for whose staff bribe-taking offered an obvious means of supplementing their salaries, but whether the cost of running the bureaucracy and the private initiatives in which its functionaries indulged did significant damage in the end to the government's capacity to fund military recruitment effectively in the face of barbarian invasion is much less clear, and remains a controversial matter: A. H. M. Jones, at any rate, judged on balance that the bureaucracy, despite its manifest flaws, played an important part in the

---

[236] Amm.29.1.20 (of Valens); cf. the story about Diocletian in SHA *Aur*.43.1–4 (quoted earlier, pp. 161–2).

preservation of the empire – and if his verdict has since been doubted, it has not been conclusively disproved.[237]

Like the Bourbon kings of pre-Revolutionary France, the late Roman emperors espoused an 'absolutist' ideology. But in practice, we have seen, no aspiring *roi absolu* could rule an empire without delegating some power to others, and those who obtained a share of it would always potentially pose a threat to the monarch's personal supremacy and security. The problem that the emperors had constantly to juggle with in their dealings with the elite is a problem inherent in monarchy, a dilemma nicely conveyed to an eighteenth-century readership in Swift's classic satire on the absolutist pretensions of the European monarchs of his day: ensconced with his airborne court on his floating island, the king of Laputa 'would be the most absolute prince in the universe, if he could but prevail on a ministry to join with him; but these, having their estates below on the continent, and considering that the office of a favourite hath a very uncertain tenure, would never consent to the enslaving [of] their country'. The late Roman empire, too, had its clergymen who mocked the vanity of courtly pomp (and also its landed aristocrats who disliked paying tax), but on balance the court was an institution that served the interests of both the ruler and the elite quite well. 'At the political centre of any complexly organized society', it has been said, 'there is both a governing elite and a set of symbolic forms expressing the fact that it is in truth governing.'[238] In the late Roman empire, the elite in question was centred in the imperial court, and the symbolic forms expressing its capacity to govern were expressed through a 'court society' (in a fashion analogous to the Later Han arrangements analysed by van Ess in this volume). The ceremonious delegation of high offices through the emperor's 'sacred' person in the court consistory, and the grandiose symbolism of imperial self-display in general, will certainly have helped to sustain in the minds of influential subjects a presupposition basic to the survival of any dynastic monarchy – the sense that power was ultimately invested in a family that was somehow destined to rule. The emergence in the late fourth and early fifth centuries of child-emperors who by definition 'reigned but did not rule' is testimony to the strength of that sentiment: Honorius was ten when he took the purple, Theodosius II seven, Valentinian III only six. It is highly significant that, in such circumstances, it was not the elite officials of the consistory who in practice ruled collectively in the emperor's name, but usually an empress –

---

[237] Jones 1964: 601–6, 1056–64; cf. Garnsey and Humfress 2001: 47–9; for a darker view, MacMullen 1988: 171–97 (impact on military resources), MacMullen 1990: 68 (vocabulary of corruption).

[238] Geertz 1983: 124.

either the mother or an older sister of the emperor – or else a general who sought to secure his position by a marriage link with the imperial family, as Stilicho did. Even in the fourth century, empresses could wield considerable political influence within the imperial household (Julian had good reason to be grateful to Constantius' wife Eusebia for her support in the 350s),[239] but in the fifth their prominence and political importance at court is especially notable: they acquired their own households and designated *praepositi*, and managed their own revenues; they had coins issued in their own names; they dispensed largesse; they exercised patronage; their statues were placed in public places alongside images of emperors, and adored in their company.[240] The enhanced role of the fifth-century 'Theodosian empresses' would appear to derive from a lively conviction on the part of Theodosius I that the absolutist claims of imperial ideology must be underpinned by basic blood-ties of dynastic kinship: the majority of the fifth-century empresses were themselves daughters of emperors, women brought up in the court society from birth, and most of them took the title *Augusta* on the occasion of their marrying an emperor, or bearing him a child. In most cases, moreover, they lived longer than the men-folk of their generation. The prominence of the empresses at court thus affirmed a dynastic continuity and transmitted a dynastic tradition. Strictly speaking, their formal standing as *Augustae* was still a boon bestowed by the emperors, but in practice the influence of a determined empress could by now determine particular imperial policies. It was Theodosius II's empress-sister Pulcheria, not the emperor himself, who planned and devised a 'crusade' against Persia in 421 to win her languid brother credit as a 'master of victory', and after his death in 450 Pulcheria reigned alone for a month – and then effectively decided the succession herself, by marrying a serviceable military tribune and personally investing him with the imperial robe and crown. The bride was fifty years old and sworn to holy virginity, so the marriage remained unconsummated – but that merely renders it all the more telling as a witness to the symbolic role that the royal women of the court had come to play as vessels of 'sacred power'.[241]

In 431, Pulcheria's actions had probably also been decisive in securing the condemnation of the 'heretic' Constantinopolitan patriarch Nestorius against the wishes of her brother's own counsellors and eunuchs. That was certainly the belief of Orthodox Christians: after her own death, Pulcheria was revered as a saint in the company of the Virgin *Theotokos*, the Mother of

[239] Aujolat 1983.   [240] Holum 1982; St Clair 1996: 158–62; McCormick 2000: 146–7.
[241] Holum 1977; 1982: 208.

God.[242] Her brother, too, notwithstanding their disagreement over Nestorius, was renowned for his piety, and their cases could plainly be exploited to shed light on the evolving relationship of the court and the ecclesiastical authorities in the late empire. In the course of our discussion we have occasionally touched on particulars that bear on this matter: Eusebius' dressing-up of the ideology of monarchic absolutism in Christian theological terms in his *Tricennial Oration* (a panegyric of Constantine delivered at court in the emperor's presence in the palace at Constantinople in 336); Bishop Cyril's payment of a massive bribe in his efforts to win over Theodosius II's *praepositus*; Bishop Ambrose entering a hunting enclosure in the gardens of the palace at Milan to seek out Gratian; Constantine's daily prayers in a dedicated chapel in the palace; the presence of bishops as guests at his dinner-table, and of bishops sent as observers to his court from major sees. Apart from that, we have left the church aside: our discussion has leaned particularly towards the itinerant court of the fourth century, for which the evidence is particularly plentiful and suggestive, and we judged earlier that in the fourth century, at least, Christianity did not exert a significant shaping influence on the structures and ceremonial of the court. But the late imperial court was not a static entity, and although we have not aimed to describe the fifth-century courts of Constantinople and Ravenna separately or in detail, we have still tried to convey something of the way the court came to function in the earlier fifth century, too, at a time when these cities were emerging as 'permanent' capitals in the eastern and western zones of the empire. Our selection of *c.* AD 450 as an end-date was not meant to suggest any sudden mid-century demise or radical transformation of the 'court society' in either of these cities; there was nothing of the sort. Nonetheless, '*c.* 450' seems a reasonable closing point on several grounds, one of which touches again on the question of Christianity. The deaths of two long-reigning emperors in east and west, Theodosius II (408–450) and Valentinian III (425–455), mark the end of a dynasty that had lasted seventy years, and in the west the institutional framework of imperial rule on which a complex 'court society' depended was patently unravelling well before the deposition of the 'last Roman emperor' in 476; for the previous twenty years, barbarian generals had been blatantly ruling in the west in all but name. At Constantinople, of course, a 'court society' would continue to flourish for centuries under the Byzantine emperors – but under a guiding ideology in which the ruler's sacral aura came to rest closely on his affiliation with the Christian church and his standing as an 'imitator' of Christ; and in the

[242] Holum 1982: 163–5; 226–7.

eastern Roman empire there were developments in the mid and late fifth century that seem to presage the change to come: in 450, when Theodosius II's successor was solemnly invested with crown and purple robe, the ceremonial was performed by an empress who had dedicated herself to holy virginity as a bride of Christ, and before the century was out, the patriarch of Constantinople was crowning late Roman emperors.[243] In the long run, then, Christianisation, which changed so much else in the Roman empire, would indeed come to change the face of the imperial court.

[243] Kantorowicz 1963; Cameron 1976: 163, 178; Dagron, 1996, chs. 4–5 passim (on evocation in Byzantine ideology of OT model of priest-king); Holum 1982: 208.

6 | The imperial court in Han China

HANS VAN ESS

Introduction

A book on the imperial court of ancient China's Han dynasty has yet to be written. Most specialists working in the early China field see the court as one specific part of central administration and descriptions subsume it under this category.[1] Thus, the court is seen as the central institution which some offices belonged to, whereas the heads and senior members of other offices and ministries went there from time to time in order to discuss matters which were important for the empire. As well as being constituted by the imperial household, the Han court was also the place where high officials were convened from time to time, especially when court audiences took place at which, at least in theory, people could speak up freely. Although Michael Loewe has described the Han concept of sovereignty, he did not stress the importance of the court as an institution.[2] Of course, there are historiographical descriptions of political intrigues going on at specific times.[3] Hans Bielenstein has characterised the history of the Later Han period in terms of power struggles between two or three large factions, each consisting of a clan, which in turn represented several families interrelated by marriage. These factions alternately dominated the court, making it work for the interests of the clan, which had its power-base far away from the capital. The question which this chapter wishes to address is whether the court as such, and beyond the struggles of personal interest, did actually play an important role in stabilising the Chinese empire.

The court of the Han as an institution was closely related to the palace, erected shortly after the dynasty rose to power. Hence the Han court, at least most of the time, was not an itinerant one. Most emperors did not travel, but instead held audience every morning in their palace. In fact, 'ch'ao', the word which our dictionaries translate as 'court', means nothing else than 'morning-audience'. Pronounced 'chao', the same character used for writing the word 'ch'ao' means 'morning'.

---

[1] See e.g. Bielenstein 1980. An abridged version of Bielenstein's argument can be found as Bielenstein 1986a; see also Bielenstein 1979. Compare also Loewe 1986b.

[2] Loewe 1986a.   [3] See for example Loewe 1974 and de Crespigny 1975.

As in other cultures, it seems useful to introduce for Han China the distinction between an inner and an outer court. The inner court, the enlarged household of the ruler, was for a long time not the real centre of power. Only during the last decades of the Han did this change. In contrast to the practice at the court of an absolutist ruler, power was generated through the interaction of the inner court and its permanent members with the changing members of the outer court, who were not necessarily present every day. Most of the officials who came to an audience belonged to the outer court.

Thus, the court of the Han in the first place was a fixed locality within the palace where officials and the nobility had to come from time to time in order to report on their duties and on other matters relevant for government. Besides the emperor himself, permanent members of the court included his women and a great number of eunuchs. In addition, there were male palace-attendants and other gentlemen-of-the-palace. These were positions usually given to young men who had first to pass a test assessing their suitability for a career in government. In fact, they often owed their position to the standing of their fathers. These were only temporary members, who sooner or later were promoted to other positions, often in the provinces, far away from the capital, where they had to prove their talent once again. Eventually, a successful official would come back and serve as minister or bureau-head in one of the ministries, which would bring him into contact with the court again. Among these ministries, some were responsible for court affairs. But their heads, too, belonged to the civil bureaucracy and usually held their positions for a limited time, only to receive other positions at the end of their term of office. Nevertheless, this system ensured that to be at court was seen as the crowning of a successful career by every member of the bureaucracy.[4]

The Han court in a historical perspective

The period of more than 400 years dominated by the rule of the Han dynasty saw many changes. These meant that the imperial court of Kao-tsu, the founder of the Han, did not resemble that of the last emperors of the Later Han. Therefore, a short historical overview is needed, before we can turn to the court itself.

---

[4] Winterling (1999: 35) points to the doubts recently raised, especially by French historians, as to whether we can really talk about a 'court' as far as imperial Rome is concerned. They reject the concept on the grounds that the Eliasque type of the courtier, residing in the ruler's palace, is not found in the Rome of the early Caesars (see Paterson and Smith in this volume). The same criticism could, of course, apply to Han China as well. Nevertheless, as Winterling has pointed out, there is sufficient justification for using the word 'court' for the ancient monarchies. It is his definition which this chapter follows.

Ssu-ma Ch'ien, the major historian for the period, describes the rise of the Han to power as unprecedented. Prior to the Han, for as long as there had been rulers and subjects, it had taken decades or sometimes even centuries for a ruling dynasty to be toppled by a rival family.[5] According to the historian, since the era of the Yellow Emperor all the families ruling China had belonged to one and the same clan-system. There was a dynastic cycle: a dynasty normally began with a founding father, who excelled by means of the virtuous behaviour inherited from his father and grandfather. The first rulers of a dynasty normally could build on what the founder had accomplished, thus establishing a splendid house which would bring peace everywhere. Subjects would come to court on their own initiative, convinced that nobody under Heaven disposed of as much virtue and power as the ruler. In the course of time, however, this virtue declined and the ruling house degenerated. Often a dynasty would experience a so-called 'middle-resurrection', until finally a virtuous founder established a new dynasty, supported by most of the leading families under Heaven.

This paradigm could be observed with the Chou dynasty, which took power from the Shang sometime in the middle of the last century of the second millennium BC. Their rule gradually declined until the dynasty almost became extinct in the ninth century BC. It was restored to power by two virtuous rulers, before a gradual decline recommenced in the eighth century. Powerful states began to arise in all parts of the world. Although modern scholarship tends to see in these states independent units with no real ties binding them to the nominal sovereign, the ancient historiographers say that these states were nominal vassals of the Chou; their ancestors had been invested by the founder of the Chou, but their power now overshadowed the court of the Chou king. Nevertheless, so long did the virtue of the Chou's founding father last that several hundred years lapsed before a new dynasty, the Ch'in, could finally unify the whole world under its own rule. As a result, according to Ssu-ma Ch'ien's tale, in 221 BC the Ch'in ruler assumed the role of an emperor (ti), a title which implied divine power. The Chou rulers had been only 'kings' (wang), but in the centuries prior to their final demise so many other rulers had also called themselves 'king' that it seemed logical to find a new title for a ruler whose power was unchallenged.

The First August Emperor of the Ch'in (Ch'in Shih Huang-ti)[6] thought that he had learned the lesson of history. In order to prevent a new period of bloodshed he decided that henceforth there should be no more feudal

---

[5] Preface to Table no. 4, 'The Table of [Events] During the Time of the Change from Ch'in to Ch'u, [arranged] by Months', *SC* 16/759.

[6] Ch'in Shih Huang-ti thought that his dynasty would last for 10,000 generations. Therefore his posthumous name was simply 'First-Generation Ruler of Ch'in'.

lords. He renounced the investing of members of his own family with territory, declaring that in future everyone under Heaven would be governed by functionaries owing their position to their knowledge of law and order, not to hereditary privilege. China became a bureaucratic state, with the consequence that there was no hereditary nobility at the court of the Ch'in. Yet, although the First Emperor thought that this reform would preserve rule over the world within his own family for 10,000 generations, after only a dozen years fighting broke out again. The rivals for the throne came from the small 'lanes and alleys'[7] – that is, they were mere commoners, a phenomenon previously unseen in Chinese history. This lack of a noble pedigree influenced their behaviour.

Liu Pang, later canonised as Han Kao-tsu, defeated his competitors as well as the peers who had helped him after a bloody struggle for power, doing so through a mixture of a peasant's slyness and the ability to listen to people who were more intelligent than himself. Allegedly he then did away with the cruel laws of the Ch'in. However, what else he should do with his newly acquired power was not immediately clear to him. On the one hand he was unable single-handedly to rule a territory the size of China, which even then was huge, and, on the other, his family was not numerous. His solution was to split up the eastern part of China into eleven large kingdoms. With the exception of Ch'ang-sha on the southern periphery, these kingdoms were ruled by his relatives, since most of the old nobility had been killed off in the wars leading up to the firm establishment of Han rule. These relatives received the title of 'kings', and as soon as they had been invested they had to leave the capital of Ch'ang-an for their kingdoms. Their relations with the central court in western China, where the bureaucratic structure of the Ch'in had survived, were strained. The kings rarely came to court, and when they did, there were debates as to whether they should be allowed to enjoy familial intimacy with the emperors, or be treated and comport themselves as real subjects. Several wars during the second century between these kings and the emperors finally led to a structure in which the former were reduced to little more than titular rulers with hardly any actual power. Until the end of the Han period the kings were required to live in their own capital cities in the provinces. Usually, they were not allowed to play a role at the imperial court. Rather, their own courts were miniatures of the imperial court. Therefore we do not need to treat them as part of the court here. They came as visitors to the imperial palace from time to time, at most annually.

[7] *SC* 16/759.

After Emperor Kao's death, for several years his widow, Empress Lü, ruled on behalf of several under-age emperors, but without making institutional changes relevant to our topic. Empress Lü was ousted from power by senior members of the Liu family who feared that she might establish a dynasty of her own. The reign of her successor, Emperor Wen, is usually seen as an uneventful time of imperial recovery after a long period of unrest. This period of recovery was only briefly interrupted by the revolt of several kingdoms against the central authority in 154 BC, under Emperor Wen's successor. Their defeat marked the end of provincial lords able to challenge the ruler at Ch'ang-an. Emperor Wu acceded to the throne in 141 BC and brought the power of the Han to its peak. He expanded imperial territory far into central Asia and southern China, a region inhabited by non-Chinese people. His successor, Emperor Chao (87–74 BC), however, reigned as a minor and died without an heir shortly after reaching manhood. This same problem would recur frequently later on, resulting in a series of succession crises. At the same time, the second half of the first century BC saw a thorough Confucianisation of many aspects of life, including the prevailing attitudes at court and in the imperial living quarters. In AD 9 this Confucianisation culminated in the usurpation of Wang Mang, who fourteen years later was killed by forces loyal to the Han. Kuang-wu, the founder of the Later Han dynasty, shifted the capital from the city of Ch'ang-an in western China to Lo-yang in the east. New palaces and ritual structures had to be built there, and existing palaces enlarged. Life at court, however, was modelled on the example of the Former Han. This worked well until the reign of the third ruler of the Later Han, Emperor Chang (75–88 AD). The ensuing period of more than a hundred years is generally seen as a time of decline. Government was no longer in the hands of the emperors – usually minors – and their officials, but fell into those of eunuchs and the families of imperial wives. This was probably the period when the Han court changed most dramatically.

The palaces and the establishment of the court

As the Liu family of the Han, as well as their helpers, had lowly origins,[8] Liu Pang had no idea of what being emperor involved. Ssu-ma Ch'ien and Pan Ku tell us that it took some time until the emperor understood why it

---

[8] Apparently the Liu started to claim to be descendants of the mythical Emperor Yao (traditional dates 2356–2255 BC) only during the first century BC. The first hint of this claim is to be found in the biography of Sui Hung in *Han-shu* 1962, 75/3154. Ssu-ma Ch'ien in his *Shih-chi* draws attention to the lowly origin of the Liu several times.

was necessary to invest in the creation of a capital and a seat of power larger than his immediate needs required.

At first he saw this investment as an unnecessary luxury, and one of his closest followers had to explain its purpose to him:

In the second month [of his seventh year, i.e. 200 BC, the emperor] went to Ch'ang-an. Hsiao Ho was building the Wei-yang Palace, and was erecting the Eastern Portal, the Northern Portal, the Front Hall, the Arsenal, and the Great Granary. The Emperor saw their greatness and elegance and was very angry. He said to [Hsiao] Ho, 'The world is full of tumultuous cries; I have toiled and suffered for many years; my success or failure cannot yet be known – why are you building these palaces and halls beyond measure?' [Hsiao] Ho replied, 'The world is not just yet subjugated – for that reason we should take this opportunity to complete the palaces and halls. Moreover the Son of Heaven has the four seas [and all within them] for his household. Without great and elegant [buildings], you will not [be able to display] your authority and majesty. We should not moreover let it be that later generations should find anything to be despised.' The Emperor was delighted, removed from Yüeh-yang, and established his capital at Ch'ang-an. He established the office of the Superintendency over the Imperial House to arrange the precedence among his nine [classes of] relatives.[9]

This anecdote describes the creation of the physical structures of the Han court at Ch'ang-an. It is clear that an important motive for building the palaces was the need to express the splendour of the dynasty. For this purpose, palaces had to be constructed. Textual sources as well as excavations show that the Han erected two major and several minor palaces at Ch'ang-an. The two main palaces were the Palace of Prolonged Joy (Ch'ang-lo kung), where the empress dowager lived, and the Eternal Palace (Wei-yang kung), where the emperor himself resided along with his harem. Although little of these palaces survives, excavations have shown that the total area of the Palace of Prolonged Joy was about 6 square kilometres, which was one-sixth of the total area of the city. Interestingly, the Eternal Palace, with an area of 5 square kilometres, was slightly smaller than the palace of the empress-dowager. Both palaces lay in the southern part of the city, the Eternal Palace in the west and the Palace of Prolonged Joy in the east. In addition there were two smaller palaces and two markets within the city walls.[10] Unfortunately, we do not know where the officials and the nobility lived, but we must assume that, like the commoners, they had their residences outside the walls, although they may have had houses or rooms for temporary residence within the palace, too. With the exception of the

[9] *Han-shu* 1962, 1B/64, trans. Dubs 1944, 118ff. Compare also San-fu huang-t'u chiao-cheng, Hsi-an, 1980, p. 35.
[10] Wang Zhongshu 1982: 5.

armoury, which had to be within easy reach of the palaces in an emergency, it also seems that government offices were sited some distance from the palaces.[11]

We are slightly better informed about Lo-yang, the capital of the Later Han. Lo-yang also had two palaces, namely the Southern and the Northern Palace. There was no clear functional division between these two palaces. Rather it seems that the emperors moved freely between them. The Southern Palace covered an area of 1,300 metres from north to south and 1,000 metres from east to west. Most of the time it seems to have been the imperial residence, although some rulers preferred the Northern Palace. The palaces were interconnected by covered passageways. Textual sources tell us that the palaces mainly served a dual function. They housed the living quarters of the emperor, his family and the harem. These were the 'forbidden apartments' to which, at least in theory, nobody besides the emperor, the closest members of his family and the eunuchs had access. Secondly, there was a public space consisting of several audience halls, the most important being the Main Audience Hall or Front Hall. Other audience halls seem to have been used for less formal occasions. An important part of the Southern Palace housed schools for the sons of the elite and imperial libraries. There were at least two libraries in the Southern Palace and one in the Northern Palace. In addition, there were several palace offices.[12]

Within the city walls and south-east of the Southern Palace, so that their officials were within easy reach of the emperor, were located the ministries of the three highest administrative bodies of the state. The residential districts of the high officials and aristocrats were also located within the city walls, as were the Grand Store-house and (as seen earlier) the Armoury and several markets. Commoners had to live outside the walled city.[13] Unfortunately, Lo-yang was burnt down at the end of the Later Han and, as the sources make clear, its destruction was complete.

Soon after his final victory, the founder of the Han was faced with the problem of unruly peers arguing over their respective merits in what can only have been a provisional palace, where they got drunk, abusing each other and furiously hacking the pillars of the building with their swords. Only then did the emperor understand the need to introduce a proper court ceremonial which established a fixed etiquette for his followers.[14] This ceremonial prescribed the position and comportment of participants at the

---

[11] But compare Giele 2006: 76–81. On p. 77 Giele states that some records suggest that some of the offices of the executive council members and ministers of the Former Han may have been situated within the palace precincts.

[12] Most of the evidence has been assembled by Bielenstein (1976: 22–33).

[13] Wang Zhongshu 1982: 32–5.   [14] *SC* 99/2722.

emperor's annual New Year audience for the nobility and the higher echelons of the bureaucracy. It is clear that the primary aim behind the establishment of this court ceremonial was to achieve order.

This same episode of the squabbling entourage prompted the creation of the Han nobility and the birth of the outer court as a centre of the state.[15] In a ceremony of enfeoffment which, by the end of the Han, would take the form of handing out a small bag filled with mud from a central altar of earth,[16] Liu Pang gave all of his followers fiefs and the rank of a 'hou', a title usually translated as 'marquess'.[17] The practice of ennobling meritorious subjects continued throughout the Han period, although during later reigns territory was not necessarily involved when a man was ennobled. In many cases the person concerned received a title alluding to his merit and a stipend, consisting of the taxes of a certain number of households. In addition, Emperor Wu introduced the principle of real division of the land. This allowed kings to divide up their territories among their sons who, with the exception of the eldest, also received the title of marquess. Until Wu's reign primogeniture had held sway, with the eldest son inheriting his father's title and territory. Although our sources claim the opposite, the new measure was not passed out of pity for the impoverished offspring of the Liu family. Rather it has to be seen as part of the successful attempts by the dynasty to reduce the size of the kingdoms.

Under Kao-tsu and during the following two reigns of his son Emperor Hui (194–187 BC) and widow Empress Lü (187–180 BC), the marquesses – unlike the kings – were allowed to stay in the capital. The main positions in the bureaucracy inherited by the Han from their Ch'in predecessors were divided among them. Most of the second level of the administration, the so-called nine ministers, was also filled with former military supporters of Liu Pang. They comprised the Grand Master of Ceremonies, the Superintendent of the Imperial Household, the Commandant of the Guards, the Grand Coachman, the Commandant of Justice, the Grand Herald, the Director of the Imperial Clan, the Grand Minister of Agriculture and the Privy

---

[15] Cf. Butz and Dannenberg 2004: 11–12: 'The court appears now as a centre of power which served the aim of attaching those persons to the prince whose support he necessarily needed for his self-preservation.'

[16] *Hou Han-shu* 1965, chih 9/3202f, com. 8. The passage has been translated by Müller (1979: 310–19).

[17] The question as to whether the system of the early Han should be described as 'feudal' is, of course, disputed. In the light of the source mentioned in the previous footnote, my own view is that we should be allowed, for the sake of simplicity, to speak in terms of 'fiefs' and 'enfeoffing' as far as this period is concerned. Compare the detailed guidelines for enfeoffing of a feudal lord in Po Hu T'ung, trans. Tjan Tjoe-som 1949 and 1952, pt VII, 410–12.

Treasurer.[18] All these ministers belonged to the outer court: that is to say, they were working in localities which (if the archaeological data provided by Wang Zhongshu can be trusted) were clearly separated from the palace itself, although from time to time they had to come to the emperor's audiences to discuss important measures. These officials, then, on the face of it were not 'courtiers' as in the Versailles-based analysis of Norbert Elias. Their primary function was bureaucratic.

Among the nine ministries some deserve special mention. The Superintendent of the Imperial Household was responsible for security within the public parts of the palace compounds and for protecting the emperor when he left the palace. The private apartments were protected by the eunuchs.[19] Under the superintendent's authority fell the palace-attendants and other palace gentlemen who were armed and served as imperial bodyguards. In addition to this protective function, the superintendent and his staff had to provide the emperor with advice and criticism. Finally, the superintendent was also in charge of overseeing seventy internuncios or receptionists. On behalf of the emperor these people undertook various activities, such as offering condolences on the death of less important officials. All in all, within the palace precincts there were probably between several hundred and over a thousand officials under the superintendent's authority.

Some of his duties overlapped with those of the Commandant of the Guards, whose office under the Former Han was also located within the palace precincts. The guards controlled the palace entrances and apparently patrolled within the palace too. Under the Later Han, this ministry lay outside the palace and was staffed with about 3,000 guards.

Aloys Winterling points out that typically the medieval European courts were organised around four departments, namely the treasury, the provision of food and of drink, and the stables.[20] Although we cannot find exactly the same structure in Han China, all four aspects were important there as well. The function of the Grand Coachman was to supervise the imperial stables and at the same time the horses for the army. There were several stables and coachhouses in the capital and at least one or two in the palace itself, and we can assume once again that large numbers were employed there. The office of the Privy Treasurer was particularly important. He was the only minister serving the emperor alone, supervising all those who – mostly as eunuchs – waited on the emperor inside the palace.[21] In addition to the emperor's private purse, he also oversaw payments for his food, drink, clothing, etc.

---

[18] I am following the translations of Bielenstein (1980).
[19] Bielenstein 1980: 23.   [20] Winterling 2004: 83.   [21] Bielenstein 1980: 47.

The management of these court activities must have been a complex task, not least because their cost was funded by the emperor from his own purse, separate from the government treasury.[22]

It is not possible and – since the work done by Bielenstein (1980) – certainly not necessary to enumerate and describe all the offices at the Han court. The important point is that under the Former Han there were two major divisions, one between the nobility and the commoners, the other between the military and civilians. As was said above, during the reigns of the first three Han sovereigns (the third being the only Han empress who actually ruled[23]), nobles were allowed to stay at court. The fourth emperor, Wen (180–157 BC), who like Emperor Hui was a son of the founder of the dynasty, tried to oust the faction formed by his father's military supporters by ordering the marquesses to leave the capital for their fiefs, which were often far away. Even so, the nobility created by the founder of the dynasty continued to play an important role until the accession of Emperor Wu in 141 BC. Full marquesses were expected to reside in their fiefs, and we know of cases where the heir to a marquessate renounced his title so as to play a role in government. Yet, exceptionally, some enfeoffed nobles were permitted to live in the capital.

The reign of Emperor Wu as a watershed in the development of the Han court

Emperor Wu introduced the custom of ennobling the highest member of the bureaucracy, the chancellor, as a marquess. At this time the many descendants of the former military supporters of Kao-tsu by far outnumbered the marquesses enfeoffed under his successors,[24] and still dominated life at court. Succeeding as a mere sixteen-year-old, Emperor Wu sought to infuse

---

[22] The Privy Treasurer was responsible for the management of the emperor's purse during the Former Han, whereas under the Later Han the Grand Minister of Agriculture performed this function. Bielenstein 1980: 46 and 55.

[23] The case of Empress Lü is complex. As the chief wife of the founder of the dynasty she was very powerful. In name, two child-emperors followed Emperor Hui on the throne. Yet, Ssu-ma Ch'ien and Pan Ku devoted an imperial annals section to Empress Lü in her own name, obviously because the two minors either were not taken seriously or were seen as illegitimate. This matter is not easy to decide, since Lü is one of only two empresses in Chinese history who managed actually to rule (the other one being Wu Tzu-t'ien of the T'ang). Both women have been described as cruel and ruthless.

[24] *SC* 18 lists 143 men who were ennobled by Kao-tsu, whereas *SC* 19 has only three men ennobled by Emperor Hui, 31 by Empress Lü (most of whom where deposed upon her death and the subsequent ousting of her faction), 29 by Emperor Wen and 30 by Emperor Ching.

new blood into his bureaucracy. Probably he was trying to free himself from the forces in power over the last sixty years, who did not want a strong-willed emperor. The court not only offered the ruler a means of controlling and structuring the families of people who were his nominal subjects, but also controlled the emperor himself.[25] One important constraint on the emperor came in the form of young officials serving as palace-attendants and thereby temporarily forming part of the inner court; their main duty was to remonstrate. Some may have done so independently, but many were closely connected to the households of senior members of the outer court, that is, marquesses and high officials. They not only protected the emperor, but also guided him.

For a strong emperor who wanted to free himself of such restraints it was crucial to recruit fresh blood into the nobility and the bureaucracy. Emperor Wu sought to achieve this aim by two means. First, he introduced an examination system requiring many (but by no means all) candidates for office either to master one of six disciplines attached to the Confucian canon, or to become experts in the legal code. Taking almost a century to become firmly established, this system at first was regarded with disdain by our major historiographical source for the period, since it promoted petty scholars lacking the broad experience needed to govern even a province or a provincial district, let alone a state. They were tools in the hands of the emperor, who could manipulate them for his own ends.[26] Although in theory the ruler always occupied the pinnacle of the hierarchy, many saw the court as the centre for the brokerage of power. On this view the emperor was not all-powerful, but, as the nominal head of the system, had to be driven in the desired direction.

Secondly, under Wu the bureaucracy as well as the nobility was transformed by the fact that some people were now admitted to the court through their personal relationship with the emperor. This development will be explored in more detail in the next section.

When Emperor Wu came to the throne, the empire enjoyed peace and had recovered its natural prosperity after a period of decline. This was an ideal situation for a young ruler with many ambitions. He wanted to expand the frontiers of his empire in all directions. Since this enterprise involved a long

---

[25] As Bielenstein (1980: 143) put it, the Han emperors were no autocrats.

[26] There is as yet no scholarly consensus on the position of Ssu-ma Ch'ien. The interpretation given above is the one I am going to argue for in a forthcoming book which compares the two major sources for this period, namely *Shih-chi* and *Han-shu* (see Appendix). However, many scholars tend to the opinion that Ssu-ma Ch'ien was actually a Confucian and that he agreed with many of Emperor Wu's measures. See, e.g., Hardy 2000.

period of war, it obviously ran counter to the interests of the old nobility, whose taxes had to fund imperial ambitions. A series of depositions of feudal lords began. In many cases the heirs of the founding nobility were simply accused of some crime, and then either beheaded or allowed to buy themselves off, becoming commoners or serving in the army. The fiefs reverted to the state. By the end of Wu's reign almost none of the old nobility survived. They were replaced by military officers on the basis of merit. As the wars continued, however, many of these new nobles were deposed as well. Therefore, there was great instability in the composition of the outer court. Nobody could be sure that he would retain his position from one day to the next. Whereas some commoners rose to important positions rapidly, their fall from grace could be even quicker.

Many scholars entering the bureaucracy and thus becoming members of the outer court under Emperor Wu came from the eastern empire. They challenged the position of the old elite in the capital, Ch'ang-an, which lay in western China. Among the social obligations of the old elite, its members were expected to assert their influence and status by entertaining huge crowds of so-called guests and retainers. As with Elias' portrayal of the nobility of medieval Europe, they were under pressure to spend money on their entourages and build up courts of their own. Under Wu there was a marked change: the emperor viewed with suspicion any subject who displayed too much wealth and power.[27] Thus, the social role of the nobility changed radically. They no longer dared to entertain lavishly.

Of course, the historians draw this picture for one period only; if a true picture, it certainly did not last. Although the examination system was nominally based on merit, once firmly established and accepted throughout the empire it became a convenient means for a small group of rich families to secure their local power. It is highly unlikely that the Han Chinese examination system encouraged a high degree of social mobility. The sons of important families received an education in a certain set of texts, thereby proving that they were fit to occupy the most important positions in the state. Although a few poorer men may have risen into the ruling class by this route, education was much too expensive to be available for all. This becomes very clear when we look at the history of the Later Han. In this period, mastery of a canonical discipline had become the chief means of admission into the bureaucracy. But upward mobility remained virtually impossible for individuals without the protection of one of the dominant

---

[27] *SC* 111/2946, *HS* 55/2493. On the phenomenon of the reduced social role of the new elite cf. also Fu Lo-ch'eng 1977: 23. I have argued for this in more detail (van Ess 2004).

two or three factions, which together comprised no more than ten or twelve big clans.

However, as a result of the reforms and changes under Emperor Wu, some forty or fifty years after his death the rhetoric of power had become markedly different. Whereas the old elite at court had entertained lavishly, often creating small courts of their own, in later times such conspicuous consumption became much less common. We often find influential persons claiming a poor background, although we know that they were not poor at all.[28] These claims are contradicted by descriptions of the wealth and affluence of the influential families found in many sources.[29] Confucian rhetoric demanded modesty from the elite, although social reality was certainly very different from the ideal; as a result, interpretation of our sources can be problematic. Furthermore, after Wu's reign noble rank no longer guaranteed influence at court. Rank usually followed power, rather than conferring it.

Role and function of the emperor at court

As mentioned already, the word 'emperor', used posthumously of a ruler, implied a divine nature. The same is suggested by the title 'Son of Heaven', by which formulation subjects often referred to the living emperor. The emperor was not supposed to mingle freely with the common people, although there are many popular stories about emperors doing so. Normally the emperor was seen outside the court only on solemn occasions of a ritual and religious, or a ceremonial, nature. The two main types of sacrifices reflected the fact that the emperor at one and the same time ruled over the whole empire and was the head of the imperial family. First, there were the sacrifices of the state cult, offered on behalf of the empire, and second, those for the imperial ancestors. The ancestors were buried in funerary mounds outside the capital; the sacrifices for the state-cult took place at religious centres inherited by the Han from the Ch'in dynasty. These sites lay some 100 kilometres to the north and west of the capital – further than the tombs, but still within the region of the capital.[30]

Apart from sacrificing, the emperor's main duty was to hold audiences, which allowed his officials to present governmental and legal business. Han

---

[28] Bielenstein 1979: 88. Here we see a big difference from the grandiose self-representation which, according to Norbert Elias, ruined sections of the European nobility in the seventeenth and eighteenth centuries.

[29] For a convenient overview of these questions of wealth, see Ch'ü T'ung-tsu 1972: 181–5. Compare also Yü Ying-shih 1967.

[30] Cf. Loewe 1992.

intellectuals were strongly of the opinion that the emperor should inter-
fere as little as possible in public affairs. Assessing the rule of Empress Lü,
Ssu-ma Ch'ien alludes to the concept of Lao-tzu: the emperor rules the
empire without acting and without leaving his house. The people never see
him, yet the empire is well governed.[31] The same is true for military affairs.
Although the emperor discussed these with his generals, military theorists
of the time believed that as a non-specialist with no military training the
sovereign ought to leave all decisions in the field to the general-in-chief. As
soon as he left his palace and entered the camp, he was no longer the supreme
commander but had to bow to specialist knowledge.[32] Yet, despite the fact
that officials worked out everything, the emperor nevertheless retained a
very important function: his was the last word. Every political decision,
no matter who drew it up, had to be issued in the form of an edict from
the emperor himself. In other words, if the high officials exerted executive
power, the emperor fulfilled the legislative role in governance.

Because of his many functions, the life of the emperor was highly ritualised. The chapter of the *Li-chi* called 'Jade Ribbons' (Yü-ts'ao) describes
the different robes worn by the emperor on different occasions during the
year. At the routine morning audiences he had to wear a leather cap.[33] He
changed his robes for breakfast and for lunch. A scribe sitting to his left
recorded the emperor's acts when he was seated, whereas a scribe sitting to
his right did this when he was up and about. Many other texts prescribe the
morning audience as obligatory for the emperor. *Tso-chuan*, a historical text
from the turn of the fourth and third centuries BC, says: 'The gentleman has
four times: In the morning he listens to matters of government, at daytime
he makes visits and inquiries, in the evening he improves the ordinances
and at night he reposes.'[34]

Shuo-yüan, a collection of anecdotes compiled under the Former Han,
several times praises rulers who rose early in the morning to hold audience.[35]

---

[31] The quotation comes from *SC* 9/412. Lao-tzu chapter 47: 'During the time of the Hsiao Hui
Huang-ti (The August Emperor Hui the Filial) and Kao-hou, the black-haired [common]
people were able to part from the suffering of the Warring States, and lords and vassals all
intended to rest in non-action. For this reason, Hui-ti let fall his robes and folded his hands,
Kao-hou as a female ruler announced [she would issue] the imperial decrees and managed to
govern without going out of her chambers, and the world was peaceful' (trans. Nienhauser
1994–2002, II: 137). At the end of the treatise on the rites, as well as in the biography of his
father and his autobiography forming the last chapter of the *Shih-chi*, Ssu-ma-Ch'ien stresses
the idea that the emperor should not leave his palace (*SC* 23/1173 and 130/3292).
[32] See for example *SC* 57/2074, 102/2757–9.
[33] *SSC* 1473C–1474A, Couvreur, Li Ki, 678.
[34] *Tso-chuan*, Duke Chao, first year. See Legge 1861–72, V: 580.
[35] Chapter 1, 'The Way of the Ruler'.

The didactic nature of these anecdotes may raise doubts as to whether all emperors really complied with their ceremonial and official obligations. The common-place admonitions of Confucian officials include warning an emperor against neglecting his duties, which often could be said to presage even the fall of the dynasty. Officials were obliged to remonstrate with their rulers,[36] and often did so if we believe our historical sources. Hence an audience was not necessarily a pleasant experience for the emperor, although these occasions could also be dangerous for ministers who transgressed certain unwritten but nevertheless well-defined boundaries. Because of these risks, few chancellors under the Former Han died a natural death.

In theory, the emperor held a court audience for his officials every morning at day-break, before breakfast. On these occasions he received officials who had already handed in memorials; these had been checked in the interim by the responsible authorities, who had deemed them worthy of discussion. Usually several high ministers were present at these court debates. Some proposals were passed on for deliberation by a larger circle, comprising not just the higher echelons of the bureaucracy but also specialists, such as experts in canonical scriptures, much in demand in matters of ritual. Sometimes a minister requested a private audience, which in exceptional cases was granted. The other discussants would be ushered out, and the minister could speak openly. Once a high official managed to convince the emperor that an opponent had been beheaded, even though the emperor had just seen this person in the previous audience.[37] Court officials were supposed to be present daily, but every fifth day was a so-called bathing-day, when they could go home and look after family affairs.

Under the Later Han, when most emperors were children, court audiences were often held by the empresses, who listened to officials from behind a curtain. Once a year the kings and marquesses were obliged to attend an audience and bring presents. On such occasions a drinking party was organised, and the dynasty celebrated itself and put the splendour of the imperial house on display. However, when Emperor Wu needed money for his wars, he ordered each marquess to present a golden sacrificial vessel, made to an exacting standard, at the annual audience. Many of those who came could not afford this and were deposed accordingly.[38] Thus, the emperor did not always use conspicuous consumption to reveal the power of the dynasty: instead, at times he used his position to collect the resources which he needed.

---

[36] Tjan Tjoe-som 1952: 463.   [37] *SC* 101/2742 and *HS* 49/2273 and 2300f.
[38] *SC* 30/1439.

Foreign guests were received in a ceremonial audience too. Whether these 'barbarians' should be given precedence in seating arrangements over the Han nobility was a hotly debated matter.[39] Not only this question but many others relating to court ceremonial were subject to constant change and heated discussions. A compromise on many of these issues was agreed under Emperor Chang, the third ruler of the Later Han, following a long discussion in the so-called Hall of the White Tiger. Pan Ku is said to have been the compiler of the decisions surviving under the name of 'Comprehensive Discussions in the White Tiger Hall' (*Po-hu t'ung-i*). Although this is one of our best sources for the actual treatment of ritual questions under the Han, probably it was the solution only of a given historical moment.

If we accept the evidence of such works as the *Po-hu t'ung-i* or several chapters of the *Li-chi*, we have to conclude that the minutiae of the life of the Han emperors were no less prescribed than those of Louis XIV as evoked by Elias (following Saint-Simon). It was not just their daily routine which seems to have followed fixed rules. In addition, their duties also included roles in ceremonies attached to several festivals during the year. The beginning of the chapter 'Monthly Ordinances' (Yüeh-ling) of the *Li-chi*, only one of several comparable texts attached to the calendar, serves as a good example of how ancient normative texts prescribe imperial behaviour:

In the first month of spring ... the Son of Heaven occupies the apartment on the left of the Ch'ing-yang (Fane); rides in the carriage with the phoenix (bells), drawn by the azure-dragon (horses), and carrying the green flag; wears the green robes, and the (pieces of) green jade (on his cap and at his girdle pendant). He eats wheat and mutton. The vessels which he uses are slightly carved, (to resemble) the shooting forth (of plants).

In this month there takes place the inauguration of spring. Three days before this ceremony, the Grand Recorder informs the Son of Heaven, saying, 'On such and such a day is the inauguration of the spring. The energies of the season are fully seen in wood.'[40] On this the Son of Heaven devotes himself to self-purification, and on the day he leads in person the three ducal ministers, his nine high ministers, the feudal princes (who are at court), and his Great officers to meet the spring in the eastern suburb ...

In this month the Son of Heaven on the first day prays to the Powers on high for a good year: and afterwards, the day of the first conjunction of the sun and moon having been chosen, with the handle and share of the plough in the carriage, placed between the man-at-arms who is its third occupant and the driver, he conducts

---

[39] Discussed, e.g., by Chia I. See *HS* 48/2240.

[40] In the Chinese system of Five Elements (Wood, Fire, Earth, Metal and Water), wood is the element of spring since it is associated with the green colour of the young shoots.

his three ducal ministers, his nine high ministers, the feudal princes and his Great officers, all with their own hands to plough the field of the Powers [on high]. The Son of Heaven turns up three furrows, each of the ducal ministers five, and the other ministers and feudal princes nine. When they return, he takes in his hand a cup in the great chamber, all the others being in attendance on him and the Great officers, and says, 'Drink this cup of comfort after your toil.'[41]

Similar regulations follow for every single month of the year. At fixed intervals the emperor has to change his robes from green (or blue) to red, the colour of summer, and yellow, the colour of the centre and midsummer, in turn switching to white in autumn and black in winter. Of course, it is unlikely that the Han rulers followed all these prescriptions.[42]

Another task of the emperor, the tour of inspection, was handled in different ways over the four centuries of Han rule. Whereas the founder of the dynasty came to know the empire from his wide-ranging wars, his successors did not travel very much. Emperor Wen grew up in a frontier province adjoining the territory of the Hsiung-nu and returned several times to the scene of his childhood. But his son, Emperor Ching, stayed in the vicinity of the capital throughout his life, as did Emperor Wu during the first thirty years of his reign. In the years following 110 BC, however, Wu often travelled for the sake of a ritual at Mount T'ai in eastern Shan-tung. We should certainly take seriously the emperor's religious motivation on these occasions, which formed part of a larger search for immortality. But we should not forget that these journeys also provided an opportunity to get to know the empire much more thoroughly than his predecessors. Yet the historian criticises Wu's travels for the damage which they did. He claims that two provincial governors committed suicide because they were unprepared for the imperial visit and had not been able to procure the huge amount of provisions needed to feed the imperial entourage.[43] No later emperor travelled as much as Emperor Wu, despite the fact that *Po-hu t'ung-i* justifies imperial tours of inspection and prescribes them at least every five years.[44] Once again this formula may reflect an attempt to reconcile the advocates of a strong imperial presence in the provinces and those in favour of the emperor staying in the capital. The latter faction was to retain the upper hand under the Later Han and during

---

[41] *Li-chi*, Yüeh-ling, trans. Legge 1885: 249–55, slightly altered.

[42] We know that a ritual structure cited in the work just quoted, the so-called 'Hall of Light' (Ming-t'ang) where governmental orders were proclaimed, was not built in the capital until the end of the Former Han, although some Confucian scholars had tried to convince Emperor Wu of its necessity much earlier, around 140 BC. A hall of this type evidently existed throughout the Later Han at the new capital of Lo-yang.

[43] *SC* 30/1438.   [44] *Po-hu t'ung* nos. 128–30, especially 130, Tjan Tjoe-som 1952: 497.

much of imperial China's subsequent history. Keeping the emperor in his palace saved money and gave the bureaucratic class the opportunity to exert power unhindered. More importantly for understanding the significance of the court as an institution, when the emperor stayed at home, access to him was limited to inner and outer court members. Other channels were closed.

The emperor at leisure

The abundance of material on ritual should not mislead us into thinking that the emperor had no life of his own. The sources provide a vivid picture of leisure at court, especially for Former Han times. The two major ancient histories of the Former Han period, *The Records of the Historian* (*Shih-chi*) and *The Book of Han* (*Han-shu*), tell us that Emperor Wen used to attend private parties at the home of his favourite Teng T'ung[45] and that he once climbed a mountain together with his favourite concubine, savouring the view and pointing out her home-town.[46] However, in this connection we always find scholar-officials who remonstrate with the emperor and tell him that he should stick to the etiquette requiring the concubine to remain a step lower than the empress, despite the emperor's love for her. Emperor Wu is well known for having left the palace incognito, and from later times there is a whole genre of literature telling how he went to eating houses and mingled unrecognised with the common people. When he was young, just after his accession, one of his greatest pleasures was hunting. On these outings he would roam far and wide with the best riders and archers, both from the palace and from whichever region he was visiting:

Some time before this, in the third year of the chien-yüan era [138 BC], the emperor first began going out on incognito expeditions . . . The emperor was accompanied by the gentlemen in constant attendance and armed riders, along with the sons of good families from Lung-hsi and Pei-ti who had been assigned to await his command and who were skilled at horsemanship and archery. They were instructed to rendezvous at the gate of a particular palace . . . The group would set out in the evening, at the tenth notch of the water-clock, announcing themselves as the party of the marquess of P'ing-yang,[47] and by dawn would reach the foot of the Southern Mountains. There, they would pursue and shoot at deer, boar, fox, and rabbit, and wrestle bare-handed with black and tawny bears, galloping wildly through the fields of rice and

[45] *SC* 96/2683.   [46] *SC* 102/2753.   [47] This was the fief of Emperor Wu's sister.

grain while the common people all shouted and screamed curses at them. Once the people got together and reported the matter to the magistrate of Hu-tu, who went and asked for an interview with the marquess of P'ing-yang. The horsemen were about to set upon the magistrate with their whips, but the magistrate in a rage instructed his clerks to shout at the hunters and command them to halt. Several of the horsemen were accordingly detained, and it was only after they had shown him the carriages and other equipment and revealed the true nature of the expedition that they were at last able to obtain release . . . The emperor went on a number of such trips, but he was still somewhat intimidated by his grandmother, the empress dowager, and did not dare to venture very far away.[48]

Later, Wu is said to have become aware of the trouble which his hunts caused the common people and to have established the Shang-lin park, where imperial hunting parties could take place without disruption to rural life. Pavilions and pleasure seats were erected in the countryside, staffed with servants, maidens and even concubines. Wild animals were introduced into the park, along with exotic fruits from central Asia. However, although ritual texts depict hunting as a necessary exercise since it served as a military training,[49] literati often criticised emperors for their hunting expeditions, claimed as dangerous and expensive.[50] Once again we see here the tendency to reduce the emperor to his role as a performer of sacrifices and the focus for discussions about policy. The emperor was needed to provide a centre, but he did not have to take an active part in decision-making. A centre had to be there, hollow though it may have been.

Other pleasures were considered less harmful. We know of the existence of jesters at court, although once again the written sources stress that one of their functions was to remonstrate with the ruler, albeit in a humorous way. Slabs from Han tombs carry reliefs on which jesters are clearly visible, suggesting that we should not take our sources too seriously in this context. It seems very likely that jesters were employed as professional entertainers for the frequent court banquets.

Music should not be overlooked either. Ritual texts stress the importance of music in several matters, including such different contexts as the ceremonies in the temple of the ancestors and educating the people. Archaeological finds, including complete sets of bells and chime-stones, suggest that music was also an important part of entertainments at court. Emperor Wu fell in love with dancing girls at least twice; the same befell

---

[48] *HS* 65/2847, trans. Watson 1974: 83–4.

[49] This was very much the case with the nomadic people who occupied China in later times, and it is a feature recognisable in other cultures, e.g. ancient Greece.

[50] *SC* 101/2740 against racing, *SC* 117, Ssu-ma Hsiang-ju change from hunting to literature.

Emperor Ch'eng. Lady Fu, one of Wu's palace ladies, came from a family of musicians and singers. Her elder brother had been castrated after breaking the law. When she came into the palace, he too was summoned, becoming an imperial favourite. He was given the task of introducing new music in place of the old style, now considered out-of-date and dull.[51] For court entertainments Wu also established a Bureau of Music. However, this was abolished a century later because its melodies were considered licentious.[52]

All in all, the early emperors seem to have been much freer in their daily life than the later ones. Literature was the only imperial pleasure which remained unchallenged until the end of the Han, replacing hunting and music in the later reigns, to judge from the sources.[53] Under emperors Ching and Wu we know of several kings who tried to become Maecenas-like patrons of poets and philosophers. They invited these people to their courts either for simple pleasure or because they wanted to comply with the old Chinese ideal of the sage king who governs by means of virtue and who exerts a civilising influence on his people. These efforts were not always welcome to the central government or the emperor himself because they were seen in some cases as signs of intolerable ambition.

An early example of such a patron-king was the king of Huai-nan, the compiler of the first summa of Taoist thought. Accused of an attempted rebellion, he was forced to commit suicide. Somewhat later, another example concerns a king who asked the imperial government to obtain for him a copy of Ssu-ma Ch'ien's *Records of the Historian*. The request was refused on the grounds that this text contained too many strategies and tactics from the time before the empire's unification – a clear sign that historical literature was deemed to be simultaneously both precious and subversive.[54] And when the Later Han disintegrated at the end of the second century AD, local warlords arose who competed to attract the best literary talents as a kind of brains-trust. It should not be forgotten that the recitation of poems was a form of entertainment for rich kings and the emperor himself. But poetry – at least the serious kind – was always seen as a means of indirect criticism and remonstrance. There were long discussions about the poetic tension between wishing to criticise and wishing to write beautiful lines of artful poetry. Criticism is what was asked for in theory, but in practice the aspect of entertainment was becoming more and more important.[55]

[51] 125/3195.   [52] Bielenstein 1980: 52; Loewe 1974: 193–210.
[53] In this respect, the Han court again resembled the medieval European court. Butz and Dannenberg 2004: 25.
[54] *HS* 80/3324f.   [55] Yang Hsiung.

The role of the harem

One factor which guaranteed a family the acquisition of influence and power at court was the successful introduction of one or more daughters into the imperial harem. The role of the harem in Han times can hardly be overestimated. During the Later Han it was probably the most important court institution because – as will be explained – it formed the 'hinge' between inner and outer court. However, once again we need to realise that the institution underwent major changes over time. Normative texts from China's early times on stress the function of a king's chief wife as the first lady of the palace.[56] They celebrate the virtue of a young woman who is selected to become the ruler's chief wife. The chapter on marriages in *Records of the Rites* (*Li-chi*) says that of old the Son of Heaven had one main wife (hou), three ladies (fu-jen), nine imperial concubines (pin), twenty-seven chamber wifes (shih-fu) and eighty-one 'women to sleep with' (yü-fu).[57] The ruler was regarded as the father of the empire and his chief wife as its mother. Therefore, her position was extremely sought-after. The family and connections of a woman who became empress could expect to enjoy wealth and favour. The passage from the *Records of the Rites* probably has to be seen as an attempt to systematise a much more complicated reality prevailing at the Han court – where indeed there was, however, a bureaucratised harem system. At the beginning of the Han there were six ranks of palace ladies below the empress. Emperor Wu added four additional ranks, and Emperor Yüan (48–33 BC) a fifth. At the end of the Former Han the number of harem women is said to have totalled about 3,000.[58] Many of these women from time to time were released and married off, especially after an emperor's death.[59]

Kao-tsu is well known for his sexual adventures. Fearing for the influence and the very survival of her own clan, his chief wife, Empress Lü, threatened to kill every concubine whom the emperor favoured. This was one reason why it was difficult to find a suitable candidate for the throne after her own death. Fortunately, a concubine whom Liu Pang had once favoured had left the harem to follow her son to a dangerous border region where he had become king when still a minor. Another woman had originally been a concubine of a king whose territory the emperor once visited. Offered to the emperor on this occasion, she fell pregnant and bore a son. But shortly

[56] E.g. the first poem in the canonical Book of Odes: Legge 1861–1872, IV: 1–4.
[57] *SSC* 1681C.
[58] Bielenstein 1980: 73f.   [59] See, e.g., *HS* 4/123.

afterwards she was thrown into prison when the king in question fell out of favour. This behaviour by the founder of the dynasty later made his son by this poor concubine the source of serious problems.[60]

The father of Emperor Wu changed his chief wife three times. The historian Ssu-ma Ch'ien gives us all the details about the intrigues leading to the deposition of the crown prince, who was replaced by the son of the third empress. The imperial women, and probably also their families, forged alliances in order to succeed in this extraordinarily important matter. Emperor Wu himself had inherited the sexual proclivities of his great-grandfather Kao-tsu. He preferred commoner girls over ones from good families. Ssu-ma Ch'ien and Pan Ku report the following about the manner in which the second empress of Emperor Wu gained admission to the palace:

Empress Wei's name was Tzu-fu. She was of very humble birth.[61] Her family bore the name of Wei and came from the village of the marquess of P'ing-yang, the husband of Princess P'ing-yang. Tzu-fu was a singing girl in the household of Princess P'ing-yang. After Emperor Wu ascended the throne several years passed and he was still without a son. Princess P'ing-yang, his elder sister, had sought out ten or more girls of good family whom she dressed in fine clothes and kept in her house, and when Emperor Wu was returning from a sacrifice at Pa-shang and stopped to pay a visit with her the princess showed him the beautiful young ladies she had gathered together to serve in her house. The emperor, however, was not impressed by any of them. After wine had been served the singing girls came forward to perform. Looking them over, the emperor found only Wei Tzu-fu to his liking. In the course of the day, when he rose and left the hall to change his clothes, Tzu-fu went along to wait on him and assist him with his robes, and in the passageway he bestowed his favour on her. The emperor returned to his seat, looking exceedingly pleased, and presented the princess with a thousand catties of gold. The princess accordingly offered him Tzu-fu, and it was arranged that she should be sent to live in the palace.

When Tzu-fu was about to climb into the carriage Princess P'ing-yang patted her on the back and said, 'Go! Eat well and take care of yourself. If you should become honoured, do not forget me!'

Tzu-fu remained in the palace over a year, but was never in that time favoured by the emperor. The emperor in the meantime had decided to select those ladies in waiting who were performing no useful function and dismiss them and send them home and, when Wei Tzu-fu was granted an audience with him, she wept and begged to be sent away with the group. But the emperor felt sorry for her and favoured her once more. In time she became pregnant and the honour and privilege which

---

[60] He was obliged to commit suicide after an attempted rebellion (*SC* 118/3083–94, Watson 1961, II: 359–87).

[61] Probably a pun. The surname Wei is a homophone of 'wei', which means 'small', 'lowly'.

she enjoyed increased daily. Her older brother Wei Ch'ang-chün and her younger brother Wei Ch'ing were summoned and made palace attendants. After this Tzu-fu enjoyed extraordinary favour with the emperor. She bore him three daughters and a son.[62]

Because the empress was childless she was later deposed and replaced by Wei Tzu-fu. Interestingly in this narrative, even the Princess of P'ing-yang, a sister of Emperor Wu, seems to have been very eager to find a suitable wife for her brother. She certainly did not do so out of altruism. The idea was rather that, if successful, she would be able to influence decision-making at court. But the fact that Wu promoted a woman of low origins to the rank of empress can also be explained by precisely the same reasoning. By selecting a wife without prominent kin he could find allies who would share his own ideas rather than pursue their own interests. The brother of Wei Tzu-fu soon became generalissimo of the Han armies even though – as Ssu-ma Ch'ien intimates – he had neither sufficient military experience nor an education justifying his promotion. Together with the brother, a whole clique was raised up. Again, the historian seems to imply that one aim of the wars in central Asia which began only a few months after Wei Tzu-fu became empress was to give the new elite a chance to shine, so that Emperor Wu could then enfeoff them. However, one can also see the whole story the other way round: the old elite would probably not have followed Emperor Wu in his military adventures. Interestingly, twenty years later, long after Empress Wei had fallen out of favour, the pattern repeated itself. Wu again took a strong liking for a singing-girl, and again her brother was chosen as general-in-chief of a campaign in central Asia. To rely on people recruited by the emperor in person was a means of bypassing the regular court, whose members might have challenged imperial policy.[63]

Emperor Wu is an exception both in terms of the length of his reign and in his autocratic style of rule. Late in his reign, he deposed his empress once again. Her son, the crown prince, had to commit suicide after a failed rebellion against his father in 91 BC. In order to see what the regular pattern of power at court looked like, we have to look at the following reigns in detail as well. When Emperor Chao ascended the throne in 87 BC he was still a seven-year-old minor. His reign was dominated by Huo Kuang, a

---

[62] *SC* 49/1978f, trans. Watson 1961, I; also *HS* 97A/3949.

[63] Compare the remarks by Winterling (1998: 11): 'Die Bevorzugung von Personen niedriger Herkunft in der engsten kaiserlichen Umgebung läßt auf eine latente Bedrohung der Kaiser durch Personen hohen aristokratischen Prestiges schließen.' (The preferential treatment of persons of a lowly background in the closest vicinity of the emperor suggests that the emperors were potentially threatened by persons who enjoyed a high aristocratic prestige.)

regent whose father had once had an affair with a sister of Empress Wei. Huo Ch'ü-ping, the second most important general of the Hsiung-nu campaigns, was born as a result of this affair, which in turn brought his half-brother, Huo Kuang, into the palace. However, as a half-brother Huo Kuang was not directly related to the Wei family, a fact which probably had saved his life in 91 BC. Huo Kuang arranged a marriage between the daughter of one of his close allies and Emperor Chao, but managed to get rid of the family in question when it became too independent. The girl was merely five years old when she was officially made empress in 83 BC. Emperor Chao died only three years after receiving the cap of manhood in 77 BC, a ceremony which in theory allowed him to rule on his own. His empress was thirteen or fourteen at that time and the two had failed to produce an heir. This fact allowed Huo Kuang to manipulate the succession and to continue to rule for some years until his own death.

After a cabal led by Huo Kuang successfully prevented one son of Emperor Wu from ascending the throne on the grounds of alleged misconduct in a ritual matter, a great-grandson of Wu-ti became emperor at the age of seventeen. He had previously lived among the common people and was probably selected by the regent because he had no prior ties to the imperial clan. But the new emperor was not grateful. Only three years later, he ousted the Huo clan from power. He was the last emperor of the Former Han to rule without the support of an empress' powerful family. The reign of his son, Emperor Yüan (49–33 BC), was dominated by the clan of his wife, Empress Wang. Emperor Ch'eng (33–7 BC) is portrayed as a weak ruler. Like Emperor Wu, he is known to history for stripping power from his empress, member of one of the great clans, deposing her, and installing a new empress, the famous Chao Fei-yen.[64] The *Han-shu* tells us that when Chao Fei-yen was born, her parents – apparently too poor to raise her – exposed her for three days, taking her back only because she turned out to be still alive. She was trained as a singing-girl and a dancer, eventually performing before the emperor, who took a great liking for her. It is said that when Emperor Ch'eng planned to install Chao Fei-yen as his new empress, he had first to enfeoff her father so as to allay the doubts of the empress-dowager, who considered the family too lowly.[65]

The reign of Emperor Ch'eng is usually seen as the beginning of the decline of the Former Han. For traditional Chinese historiography the story of Chao Fei-yen has always been a lesson in the devastating impact on a ruling house

[64] Chao the Flying Swallow, a name which was given her because of her graceful appearance.
[65] *HS* 97B/3984; for Chao Fei-yen see *HS* 97B/3988f.

when an emperor's love strayed from his chief wife. In later times this story was subject to hundreds of poems and other literary reworkings. In Ming times the Chao Fei-yen material even formed the basis for a pornographic novel.[66] But the impression remains that in reality the story is the historiographer's attempt to gloss over the fact that the powerful Wang clan tried to forestall a challenge to its position from the family of Emperor Ch'eng's new empress. The negative tone to the story of Chao Fei-yen as told in the *Han-shu* stems partly from the fact that the emperor's erotic adventures failed to produce an heir, thereby further strengthening the Wang clan. But it also reflects the fact that a female member of the clan of the historian himself had unsuccessfully aspired to the position of empress.

The dominance of the Wang clan was only briefly interrupted when Emperor Ai (7–1 BC) came to the throne. Although he tried to promote the clans of his own relations, he too failed to produce an heir. For this misfortune the historian blamed the fact that his reign was dominated by a male favourite who slept in the emperor's bed and received all kinds of benefits as a result of this intimacy. Imperial protection of male favourites was seriously frowned upon by all traditional Chinese historians,[67] mainly because this particular avenue of access to the emperor was denied to ordinary members of the bureaucracy, to which the historians themselves usually belonged. The heterosexual relations of the emperor also provided opportunities to bypass the usual career pattern (see above), but these were deemed unavoidable in the interests of dynastic reproduction. But same-sex liaisons were seen as an unnecessary luxury detrimental to all parties. First they offended the career bureaucracy, at least in theory based on merit. Secondly, they challenged the raison d'être for the presence of the great clans at court, which was closely bound up with the provision of an imperial heir.[68]

---

[66] *Chao-yang ch'ü-shih*, trans. into German by Engler (1980).

[67] There is a chapter with biographies of male favourites in *Shih-chi* and *Han-shu*. *Hou Han-shu* lacks such a chapter, replacing it with one on eunuchs, for whom see below.

[68] *Shih-chi* relates the story of Teng T'ung, the male favourite of Emperor Wen, who 'did not have any other talents . . . than caring for his body in order to bewitch the sovereign'. Once, when Emperor Wen suffered from an ulcer, Teng T'ung sucked it. When the emperor asked him who loved him most, he answered that no one in the empire loved the emperor more than the crown-prince. The emperor called the crown-prince in and ordered him to suck his ulcer, which he duly did, but with an expression of disgust on his face. Thereafter the crown-prince hated the favourite and removed him as soon as his father had died (*SC* 125/3192f). The career bureaucracy did its best to discourage the emperor from promoting Teng T'ung to too high a position (*SC* 96/2683). However, it is not clear what exactly imperial relations with a male favourite involved. For example, it is said about Li Yen-nien that he slept in the emperor's bed (literally: 'he slept and got up together with the sovereign'), although we know that he was a eunuch (*SC* 125/3195).

An eight-year-old emperor linked to the Wang clan succeeded Emperor Ai, but died only five years later without an heir. In AD 6 Wang Mang, the leading male member of the Wang clan, put another child on the throne, this time a one-year-old. The child was deposed only three years later by Wang Mang himself, who reigned as a usurper until AD 23.

The Han dynasty was restored by a distant member of the founder's family, who shifted the capital to Lo-yang, a city in eastern China, much closer to his origins in what today is northern Hu-pei, in southern-central China. Three factions dominated court politics during the next two centuries. One was an alliance between several families of rich landowners from the fertile plain of southern-central China. The other two factions, based in northern China, had trading interests in central Asia. Pan Ku himself, the author of the *Han-shu*, belonged to one of these.

Hans Bielenstein has described how during the Later Han the pendulum swung back and forth between expansionism, driven by the northern factions, and peace advocated by the landowners from Ho-nan and Hu-pei. A swing of the pendulum was always accompanied by the enthronement of a new empress from one of these three competing factions.[69] Whereas the founder of the Later Han, his son and his grandson were all adults capable of ruling in their own right, from around AD 75–100 the families of the empresses steadily gained in power. The rulers were children, and almost all died before reaching twenty. *The Book of the Later Han (Hou Han-shu)* by Fan Yeh (AD 398–446; see Appendix) several times implies, and at least once openly suggests, that some of these child-emperors were poisoned. If they had children, their chief wives were not the mothers. Therefore, on several occasions sons were removed from less well-placed members of the harem and claimed as children of the empress. In such cases the real mothers were usually killed and their family, if allowed to live, would be banished to places sufficiently removed from the capital for the crime to stay hushed up.

Often the empresses were older than the emperors. Nevertheless, they were manipulated by the leading male members of their families, who became regents, a position usually accompanied by the title of 'generalissimo' (ta chiang-chün). Empresses who tried to assert their will were sometimes deposed. The members of a particular clan most involved in government were routinely annihilated when the pendulum swung in favour of another clan.[70] Usually this happened when the regent or the empress-dowager died.

---

[69] See Bielenstein 1986b.

[70] For the empresses of the Later Han see Bielenstein's condensed account in Bielenstein 1986b; also de Crespigny 1975.

The resulting vacuum was then filled by the family of the new empress. While some of the regents are described as honest men, others are said to have been addicted to all kinds of licentious behaviour – chess, dog- and horse-races, cock-fighting, football, gambling, women and alcohol. According to our sources, government increasingly fell into the hands of big men who were not 'virtuous'.

After all this historical detail, the conceptual question to be asked is why the position of emperor remained so important. As the great clans were so powerful and the throne so weak, one might think that the dominant clan of the moment would not have needed the court. Was there a religious belief in the sanctity of the emperor which overrode all political and sociological reasons for a central institution at the heart of the empire? Respect for the institution of the court is clearly demonstrated by the desperate attempts of the great clans to dominate it. Were individual clans too afraid of the risks involved to dare to leave the court and attempt to create a new imperial centre elsewhere? These questions are addressed again in the conclusion.

The eunuchs

Strong rulers used the harem to promote new members of the elite as allies against the old elite. When the ruler was weak, as was the case for most of the Later Han period, he was dominated by the great clans. Domination of weak child-emperors by important families was the rule, strong rulers the exception. Power at court was divided among the regent and his family, the career bureaucracy and the throne itself, usually consisting of the emperor and his empress. As described above, in theory this could sometimes mean that all three groups belonged to a single faction. But in practice the system was much more complicated. Although one clan could try to infiltrate as many of its own members into the scholar-bureaucracy as it could, it never managed completely to dislodge the other clans. If a ruler died and a child-emperor succeeded, the empress-dowager often supported pre-existing policies, and it was not easy for the regent to go against her will.

In difficult matters court conferences had to be held and compromises found, often through the mediation of scholars expert in the canonical texts and able to draw on them to construct convincing arguments. In the middle of the second century AD, scholars at an imperial academy in the capital, feeling that they were increasingly bypassed by the ruling clans, became a strong voice of opposition at the heart of the empire. According to the *Hou Han-shu* the number of students grew to more than 30,000 at this time, and they influenced the language and rhetoric of the court. The students were opposed both to the regents, whose might hindered them from using their newly acquired knowledge to start a career at court, and to another group which grew very powerful during the second century AD: the eunuchs.

From the most ancient times Chinese rulers relied on eunuchs for many duties in the Inner Palace. The *Hou Han-shu* is the first standard history of China to contain a chapter specially devoted to biographies of select eunuchs. In his preface to this chapter Fan Yeh writes:

The *I-ching* says: 'Heaven has hung up images [namely the stars] and the sage takes his model from this [in his government on earth].'[71] There are four Eunuch-stars which are situated next to the position of the Emperor. Therefore, when the [author] of the *Rites of the Chou* established the offices, he also filled this number. 'The doorkeeper watches over the prohibitions of the middle doors [which separate the inner from the outer].' 'The court eunuch is responsible for compliance with the warnings regarding the women's palace.' Furthermore it says that 'There are five men in the inner chamber of the king.'[72] The *Monthly Ordinances* say: 'In mid-winter he orders the prefect-eunuch to inspect the doors and to take care of the bed-rooms.'[73] In the *Lesser Elegantiae* of the *Odes*, too, there is a piece by a [eunuch called] Hsiang Po who criticizes the slanderers.[74]

This shows that eunuchs have since olden times been present at the court of the king. Was this not due to the fact that their body was not endowed with the complete physical abilities and that their feelings and will were therefore concentrated and good so that they could have contact with the palace ladies and were easy to put to labour and to nourish?[75]

In an example of analogical thinking, the idea at the beginning of this passage is that the structure of the firmament is duplicated on earth. Every star corresponds to a position on earth. The pole star is the star of the ruler and is surrounded by stars which represent court officials. Therefore, the position of the ruler during court audiences was always in the northern part of the audience hall, whereas his guests were in the southern part. On the western side, facing east, stood the military officers, and on the eastern

---

[71] *I-ching*, Hsi-tz'u A/11 (Harvard Yen-ching concordance), Richard Wilhelm, trans. *I Ging*, 296.

[72] The *Chou-li* is one of three canonical texts concerning the all-important subject of the Rites. Its traditional composer was said to be the duke of Chou, one of the founders of the Chou dynasty almost a thousand years before the rise of the Han. However, modern scholarship agrees that, although the text may contain very early elements, it is probably a third-century BC systematisation of the hierarchy of the Chou. For the passages quoted here see *Chou-li*, *SSC* 686C–687A and 644C.

[73] *SSC* 1382C.   [74] Legge 1861–1872, III, The Book of Odes, no. 200, 346–9.

[75] *HHS* 78/2507.

side, facing west, the civilian officers.[76] What is important for us is that in this passage the eunuchs are considered not as a discrete group but as part of the throne. If we look at the court as a centre of power composed of different interest groups, we probably have to adopt the idea that emperors and eunuchs usually fought for the same interests against those of the clans and the career bureaucracy.

The historian clearly says that eunuchs were good for guarding the harem but should not be given higher positions. As in later times, scholar-officials in Han China looked down on eunuchs as on male favourites. Castration was the most serious punishment after the death penalty.[77] Although some poor families apparently castrated their sons so that they could live in the palace, eunuchs were certainly seen as inferior creatures. It seems that eunuchs did not play an important role in politics or at court for most of the Former Han period. Interestingly, in the *Han-shu*, which deals exclusively with this period, the biographies of eunuchs are found in the chapter devoted to the emperors' male favourites and do not have their own chapter.

This reflects the fact that although under the Former Han there were, exceptionally, eunuchs influential in court politics, it was only during the second century AD that they came to constitute a political faction in their own right. Of course, this was due to the declining role of the emperor and his empresses. Before the power of omnipotent regents, the only people these poor imperial children could turn to for help were their eunuchs. The young emperors did have teachers, who were usually well-known scholars. The office of the teacher of the heir-apparent – and later often the emperor himself – was nominally one of the highest in the hierarchy, but it did not imply actual power. By contrast, the eunuchs did have access to the levers of power. They were the only attendants who could provide the young emperors with real support.

During the second half of the second century AD tensions arose between the great families and the eunuchs. Following a dispute over the succession to Emperor Huan (AD 146–168), these tensions culminated in a show-down between the forces of Tou Wu, the regent, and the eunuchs. The eunuchs won, and as a result were able to dominate the entire reign of Emperor Ling (AD 168–189). A career in the court bureaucracy became impossible for anyone without the support of the eunuchs. A butcher's daughter became empress – this was obviously a manoeuvre to exclude the

---

[76] The system goes back to Shu-sun T'ung who is said to have created the court ceremonial for Han Kao-tsu. See his biography in *SC* 99/2723. Compare also *T'ung-chih* of Cheng Ch'iao, 44/589A.

[77] As already noted, Ssu-ma Ch'ien was castrated. However, according to *Han-shu* he was given a high-ranking eunuch office afterwards (*HS* 62/2725).

big clans. However, this did not save the eunuchs. When Emperor Ling died, the dynasty had almost come to its end, and the turmoil of rebellions and uprisings produced independent military leaders. One of them marched to the capital and massacred the eunuchs. As a result they vanished from the political scene, only to be replaced by military leaders.[78]

The eunuchs became powerful just as the old system of power-brokerage at court was breaking down. When the great families had lost their ability to dominate the emperor, eunuchs filled the vacuum and became the representatives of the court. Their rise was the last stand of the Han court. When they fell, the inner court ceased to exist and consequently the outer court, namely the elite bureaucracy, lost its influence as well.

Conclusion

As seen above, the initial raison d'être of the court of the Han was to establish order after the rise to power of a new elite of former nobodies. The court ceremonial was probably invented by members of the old elite, the survivors of a long period of war, to domesticate a group of rough military leaders. Rituals and ceremonies served this goal of achieving order. The court was certainly a ritualised space where a mistake in ceremonial matters could easily cost a courtier his position. It soon became the centre of culture and refinement as well. But the sociological model of the court as a distributor of favours and as a cultural showcase does not suffice to explain its longevity.

It also seems that belief in the divine nature of the emperor grew with the longevity of the dynasty. This shows that, despite the emperor's role as a kind of high priest in religious matters, we should not think of Han China as a theocracy. The court did not exist simply because the emperor was god-like and therefore had to be served by the elite.

In exploring this question, it is more helpful to look at the institutional aspect. The court was the institution where people struggled for power. 'Intrigue' is an important term in accounts of the court in ancient Chinese historiography. Apparently there was a big difference between the Former and the Later Han. As far as our historians are concerned at least, court life during much of the Former Han period was dominated by humble people from a rustic background. But at the end of the Former Han and during the Later Han, an oligarchy of rich families emerged which controlled access

---

[78] This has been conveniently summarised by Burchard Mansvelt-Beck in Twitchett and Loewe 1986: 317–45. On the role of the eunuchs under the Later Han in general see Jugel 1976.

to the high bureaucracy. This oligarchy would keep its position of power for many centuries to come.[79] Nevertheless, the institution of the court remained the same and was accepted.

If we want to understand why a court was needed and why it survived for over four centuries, it is instructive to look at the Later Han period, when the court continued to exist for a long time even without strong emperors. This shows that the court cannot be seen merely as an instrument for the display of power by an autocratic ruler. As was shown above, the emperor, and with him the throne as an institution, constituted the head of the legislative body. It seems that there was some kind of pre-modern division of powers. The emperor and with him the permanent inner court had legislative power, either with a great clan, represented by an empress, or with eunuchs as the real decision-makers. The outer court on the other hand, consisting mainly of the bureaucratic elite, served an executive function. This means that the emperor functioned as a counterbalance against the bureaucracy. Legal authority belonged to both sides: whereas the minister of justice had to lead investigations and function as chief prosecutor even against members of the imperial clan, the emperor had to approve his decisions in all important cases, after they had been submitted to the throne in the form of a memorial.

Precisely because of this balancing function, for a long time a consensus existed that a court was the best possible mechanism for ordering the world. Because the inner court was the heart of this mechanism, there was the desire to control it. As long as no one was powerful enough to challenge a weak dynasty which still retained the support of other clans, and as long as these clans in turn were not strong enough even if they were to act in concert, the throne remained the centre of the empire. Its domination by great families for more than half of the whole Han period is probably – again – to be explained in institutional terms. The big families monopolised executive power because their members dominated the bureaucracy. However, if a family introduced a daughter into the harem and by this means gained direct access to the emperor, it added legislative power and the final word in juridical matters to its executive functions. The last point may also explain why regents were often executed after an empress-dowager's death: the throne was being used to approve immediate measures against a faction whose power had become much greater than that of the other factions. To leave it in place threatened the system of checks and balances.

Norbert Elias has explained the phenomenon of court culture in sociological terms. There are indeed some features of his model which fit the Chinese

[79] Johnson 1977.

case. Normative texts from the early Chinese past as well as descriptive texts about the Later Han contain, for example, very detailed prescriptions for distinguishing ranks, recalling the complicated hierarchies of the absolutist European courts. Similarities with Europe are also to be found in the fact that the daily life of the Han emperors was structured by a great many rules. Yet, overall Elias' model does not really work in the Chinese case. The inner court with its two main political factors, the harem and the eunuchs, has no equivalent in late medieval Europe, and the outer court is clearly different because its protagonists were members of a career bureaucracy. Certainly, the role of the court as a refined centre of culture and literature was extremely important in both parts of the world, serving the same purpose of presenting the court as the high centre of the state. But in Han China Confucian influence prevented the ideal courtier from displaying his affluence. Therefore, at least in theory, one of the main elements in the Eliasque model of the court – the aristocratic compulsion to assert status through conspicuous consumption – was missing from the Chinese case. For this reason, the constitutional model suggested above offers the best explanation for why the Han needed a court.

Appendix: the sources

Our understanding of the history of the Han dynasty (207 BC–AD 220) is mainly shaped by three sources. The first is the *Records of the Scribe* (*Shih-chi*) or, as it was earlier known, the *Documents of the Lord Grand Scribe* (*T'ai-shih kung shu*). This work attempted to record the history of China from its very beginnings under the mythical Yellow Emperor (traditional dates 2697–2597 BC) until the time of the authors. It was begun by Ssu-ma T'an (died 110 BC) and almost finished by his son, Ssu-ma Ch'ien (*c.* 145 BC–*c.* 86 BC).[80] However, the bulk of the *Shih-chi* deals with the history of the Ch'in (221–207 BC) and the first century of the Han. Ssu-ma T'an and Ssu-ma Ch'ien both served as 'Lord Grand Scribe' (T'ai-shih kung) at the court of the sixth Han emperor, Han Wu-ti (reigned 140–87 BC). The main task of this official was to watch over and calculate the imperial calendar, to observe the movements of the stars and to interpret them. Historiography was only a secondary duty, derived from his role as

---

[80] A few passages had clearly been added after the death of Ssu-ma Ch'ien. But by and large the book can be said to be the work of the two Ssu-ma.

an astronomer. Moreover, when reading the *Shih-chi* it must always be kept in mind that Ssu-ma Ch'ien was opposed to many imperial policies. In fact, he finished his work after suffering castration for defending a general who had surrendered to the Hsiung-nu, a nomadic people living on the northern frontier and China's main external threat. Therefore, the *Shih-chi* is certainly not an official history of the Han. Indeed, it is plausible that its version of events is coloured by Ssu-ma Ch'ien's personal experiences. It is dangerous, then, to take the *Shih-chi* at face value. This chapter has emphasised many changes which took place under Emperor Wu. But the reader should be aware that Wu's reign may receive more attention here than it deserves – reflecting the weight which Ssu-ma Ch'ien himself accorded it.

The account of the Han empire in the *Shih-chi* has strongly influenced our second source, namely the *Book of the Han* (*Han-shu*), another joint venture by a father and his son, namely Pan Piao (AD 3–54) and Pan Ku (AD 32–92). We are told that when Pan Ku began the continuation of his deceased father's work, he was imprisoned on a charge of unauthorised tampering with dynastic history. Fortunately for us, his younger brother Pan Ch'ao, later an important general in central Asia, managed to convince the emperor that Pan Ku was a loyal subject. Even so, Emperor Ming (AD 57–75) of the Later Han only allowed Pan Ku to finish his father's work after he had proved his loyalty. He did this by writing the annals of the founding emperor of the Later Han, Kuang-wu (reigned AD 25–57), and of several other persons, including at least one rival for Kuang-wu's throne. The *magnum opus* to which he then returned began with the rise of Liu Pang, posthumously named Kao-tsu ('Founding Ancestor', reigned 206 or 202–195 BC), and went beyond the fall of the Former Han in AD 9 to the so-called 'usurpation' of Wang Mang (AD 9–23).[81] The *Han-shu* is usually said to be a more orthodox source than the *Shih-chi*. Yet it too has its own agenda, namely to support the interests of the Pan family in central Asia and the politics of expansion associated with Emperor Wu of the Former Han. Pan Ku was executed in AD 92, when a peace faction at court sought to end the frontier wars. This fact is relevant for Pan Ku's treatment of certain prominent Han courtiers.

Thirdly there is the *Book of the Later Han* (*Hou Han-shu*). This, our major source for the period AD 25–220, was written much later, albeit based on earlier sources. Its author, Fan Yeh (AD 398–446), also died a violent death. With this work too there are grounds for suspecting bias. As little work has

---

[81] See his biography in *HHS* 40A, 1333f.

been done so far on the authenticity of the *Hou Han-shu*,[82] its huge historical scope means that for the time being we have to rely on it. A second history of the Later Han, the *Hou Han-chi* of Yüan Hung (AD 328–376), has largely escaped the notice of modern scholars, probably because it was excluded from the semi-official canon of standard histories drawn up much later by traditional Chinese historians.

[82] But note Bielenstein 1954. The author concludes that the complex process of source-composition which underlies the compilation of the *Hou Han-shu* guaranteed a high degree of objectivity. I am much less optimistic about this.

7 | Court and palace in ancient Egypt: the Amarna period and later Eighteenth Dynasty

KATE SPENCE

> I shall make Akhetaten for the Aten, my father, in this place . . . Nor shall
> the Great King's wife say to me 'Look, there is a nice place for Akhetaten
> in another place', nor shall I listen to her. Nor shall any official in my
> presence – whether officials 'of favour' or officials 'of the outside', or the
> chamberlains, or any people who are in the entire land – say to me: 'Look
> there is a nice place for Akhetaten in another place', nor shall I listen to
> them.
>
> Oath of Akhenaten (Murnane and van Siclen 1993: 40)

Around 1347 BC, King Akhenaten stated under oath his intention of founding a new city as his residence and cult centre for the visible sun-disk or Aten,
whom he had recently promoted to the position of sole god, excluding the
majority of the traditional Egyptian pantheon.[1] Details of the foundation
and reaffirmation ceremonies were carved onto boundary stelae cut into the
cliffs around the site and these are amongst the most important historical
documents for the period (Murnane and van Siclen 1993). The above statement emphasises the king's resolve to stand by his chosen site for the city. In
passing, he makes an unusual acknowledgement of the potential influence
of royal women and courtiers.

Official royal texts in Egypt rarely mention individuals other than the
king. Royal projects such as building temples, fighting wars and performing
ritual were recorded as historical events but were usually presented as if
kings acted in isolation. The major exception occurs in a genre of literature
known as *Königsnovelle* (Hermann 1938; Spalinger 1982: 101–19; Loprieno
1996), to which this part of Akhenaten's boundary text is related. In some of
these texts, the king decides a plan of action in the company of his advisors.
The officials offer sound advice which the king usually ignores, choosing
instead a course of action which often sounds over-ambitious, foolhardy
or downright dangerous. The officials agree with his decision because he is

---

[1] The author wishes to acknowledge valuable comments on an early draft of this chapter made by
participants at the workshop in Newcastle University; Professor Barry Kemp read a later draft
and made some perceptive points which have been incorporated into the text. Any errors remain
the responsibility of the author.

king. The activity then takes place and is reported to be a success. The reason for the inclusion of these rather unusual narratives in royal records was to emphasise the divine insight of the king who was inspired and guided by the gods. It was also presumably thought to show him as a strong leader, over-riding the conventional earthly wisdom of his advisors in a manner that was clearly to be considered positive by the intended audience.

In practice, these texts also provide a rare reflection of life at court and the process of decision-making. The king was an individual with great power whose decisions, however idiosyncratic, affected the lives of his household, the elite and the whole populace of Egypt; but he was also surrounded by a group of people who sought to advise and influence him. He was as reliant on them for information and for the promulgation of his authority as they were on him for their position and prestige; these courtiers formed both his social milieu and the highest officials of his government. Underlying ancient Egypt's pervasive official image of absolute royal authority, divine approval and social stability were fluid, symbiotic relationships between kings and the courtiers who promoted this ideal.

The sources

In sharp contrast to most of the other periods discussed in this volume (but see Wiesehöfer on Sasanian Iran), we have no contemporary descriptive accounts of life at the ancient Egyptian court prior to the Hellenistic period. Instead, information must be gleaned from royal inscriptions, literary and administrative texts, private tomb autobiographies and representations, and archaeology. There is much scope for study, but the record is fragmentary and largely devoid of detailed evidence for the important personal dimension of social interaction and intrigue that emerges from studies of better-documented examples as a fundamental aspect of court society (Elias 1983: 70–1; Duindam 2003: 248–9). Despite the paucity of textual sources there can be no doubt that a court existed: in private inscriptions, members of the elite list titles acquired during their career and, alongside those relating to roles in administration, are courtly ranking titles such as 'sole companion [of the king]' and 'royal acquaintance'. Titles such as 'palace administrator' and 'overseer of the audience chamber' attest to the importance of the palace as an institution and the existence of a courtly society within it, while titles such as 'cupbearer' and 'fan-bearer on the right hand of the king', held by individuals of high status, show that some aspects of personal service for the king were provided by courtiers and were considered great honours. There is hierarchy implied in the various courtly titles as well as in administrative ones: for example, in addition to the title 'companion', the office of 'head of the companions of the king' is known (*LÄ* II: 1237).[2] There is also clear evidence for the importance of etiquette and ritual at court (*LÄ* II: 1229, 1237; Coulon 2002).

Evidence for the court can be drawn from a number of types of textual source. Royal documents such as the *Königsnovelle* texts have already been mentioned. These tend to focus on the king and to be fairly formulaic; thus their value for illuminating the court is limited. Well-preserved lists of titles and autobiographical inscriptions on objects, statuary and tomb walls have formed the basis of a number of important prosopographical studies which have shed light on the structure of the administration and career paths through it, as well as positions and roles at court (e.g. Helck 1954; Baer 1960; Kanawati 1977; Strudwick 1985; for the New Kingdom: Helck 1958; Bryan 1991: 242–331; Kitchen 1982: 125–53; Murnane 1998). Autobiographical texts found in private tombs often focus on a particularly close relationship between an individual and the king (usually described in terms of unusual duties or assignments entrusted to the official, honours conferred and the reasons for favouritism) but they often avoid referring to peers at court as this might detract from the presentation of this relationship as personal and exclusive (unless the king is said to distinguish the individual above his contemporaries). The king was rarely represented alongside humans in art as this was not considered decorous, and scenes of life at court are found infrequently before the Amarna period. The primary exceptions to this are Early Dynastic representations of the king with members of his court (such as the scene from the Narmer Palette shown in Fig. 7.1) and images of courtiers with the king displayed on the walls of pyramid temples of the Old Kingdom.[3]

A few administrative documents survive which provide evidence for studying the court. The most important of these is Papyrus Boulaq 18 which provides an account of palace income and expenditure for a period of twelve days in the late Middle Kingdom (Quirke 1990). The question of the broader applicability of conclusions drawn from this document is problematical: it derives from the Thirteenth Dynasty when the power and authority of the king were somewhat limited and it relates to a palace at Thebes that was not the principal residence of the king. The short period covered also renders

---

[2] The God's Father Ay held both titles in the reign of Akhenaten.

[3] See, for example, scenes from the pyramid temple of King Sahure (Borchardt 1913: pls. 17, 19, 32–4).

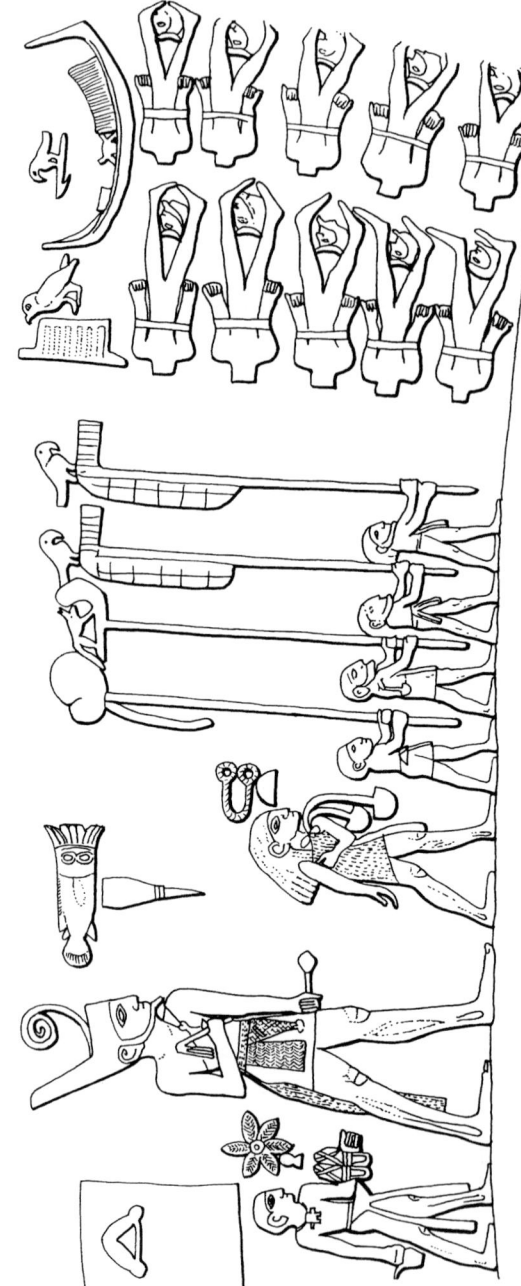

Figure 7.1 The king inspects the decapitated bodies of enemies in the company of senior courtiers and standard-bearers. From the Narmer Palette.

it hard to assess broader trends, but it remains our only document detailing the constitution of the royal household (albeit in a presumably limited form, as it was constituted on a royal visit) and is extremely informative. This document will be discussed in more detail later in the chapter.

Middle Kingdom stories provide our most vibrant illustrations of the Egyptian court. The story of Sinuhe describes the flight and self-imposed exile of a courtier who fears he may be implicated in the assassination of King Amenemhet I. The latter part of the story describes Sinuhe's return to Egypt and includes an audience at court and Sinuhe's rehabilitation there, which, although probably fictional, must have been credible to its audience given the popularity of the text. Some of the stories, such as those in Papyrus Westcar (Lichtheim 1973: 215–22), present rulers of the Old Kingdom in a less than favourable light which is clearly intended to contrast with the exemplary behaviour of the Middle Kingdom kings in whose courts they were composed. These stories do not describe the court – they were written for an audience already familiar with its structure and nature – but the incidental details of the texts are nonetheless valuable even though the stories themselves must again be treated as largely fictional.

There is a strong tendency for discussions of courts to be based on textual evidence, and there are good reasons for this: texts describe the relationships, intrigue and behaviour on which much of the discussion is focused. However, the Egyptian textual sources are not only limited and biased – invariably deriving from the elite or court itself – but were also subject to a strict sense of decorum (Baines 1990). It seems likely that the extent to which decorum has rendered the sources unrepresentative tends to be underestimated: a few examples will suffice to illustrate the problem. First, interaction between the king and his officials and courtiers is rarely described (or represented in art) whereas in reality this must have formed the focus of life at court. Second, from the Fifth Dynasty royal sons are virtually invisible in the sources (with the exception of the sons of Ramesses II) but they are present and prepared for kingship when the throne is vacated: it thus seems unlikely that they had no experience of court life before coming to the throne. Third, although we know that kings of the New Kingdom were decidedly militaristic in outlook, the evidence for military influence at court is relatively limited. These are obvious examples; there must be many more, invisible to the modern reader.

For much of Egyptian history the court was the focus for the production of the luxury artefacts (including the statuary, paintings and relief carving labelled today as 'art'). The form and style of these artefacts spread outwards from the residence city, influencing production throughout the country and further afield, although regional styles are also apparent, particularly before the New Kingdom. Architecture can also reveal much about social interaction, status and position at court. For most periods there is significant evidence in the form of tomb chapels, but preservation of the domestic architecture of royal settlements is limited outside the New Kingdom.

This chapter focuses on the Amarna period and its aftermath, equivalent to the latter part of the Eighteenth Dynasty (Akhenaten–Horemheb, c. 1352–1295 BC, with some discussion of the reign of Amenhotep III, c. 1390–1352 BC, which preceded that of Akhenaten). The late Eighteenth Dynasty yields a particularly broad range of relevant material, allowing discussion to move beyond the limited historical sources and highlighting the importance of the archaeological record. In addition to royal and elite inscriptions, there is an important corpus of diplomatic correspondence between Egypt and Near Eastern rulers surviving from this period – the Amarna Letters (Liverani 1990; Moran 1992; Cohen and Westbrook 2000) – while the private tombs at Amarna are decorated with an unprecedented set of representations of Egyptian royal and courtly activity (Davies 1903 to 1908b). Horemheb seems to have felt it necessary to justify his position in the post-Amarna era and issued royal texts and decrees, which are particularly revealing with regard to life at court (Murnane 1995: 230–3, 235–40). The archaeological remains of the city of Amarna provide concrete evidence for palatial and ritual settings, as well as institutions and the houses of courtiers and other members of society (Kemp 1989: 261–317); such archaeological evidence is limited and fragmentary for other periods of Egyptian history. Even for this period, however, the evidence remains thin as far as charting the nuances of court politics and the shifting factions of courtiers is concerned, although historians of the Eighteenth Dynasty have long been prone to speculation, particularly with regard to the Amarna period (Montserrat 2000: 12–54).

The historical context

Egypt was ruled by around thirty dynasties of kings, from c. 3000 BC when the country was first unified until the Roman conquest in 30 BC. Before the first millennium BC most of these rulers were of Egyptian descent;[4] all were resident in Egypt (as far as is known). Egyptian history is conventionally divided into periods of centralised control under divine kings punctuated by

---

[4] The major exception being the Hyksos rulers of the Second Intermediate period (c. 1650–1550 BC) who resided at Avaris in the eastern Delta and were of Asiatic (probably Syrian or Palestinian) descent (Bourriau 2000: 186–95).

'intermediate periods' in which the country was divided under competing rulers.[5] The Egyptians themselves placed great importance on the concept of unity, expressed prominently in the iconography of kingship through images of the unification of the two halves of Egypt (Kemp 1989: 27–9) and in the titles of the king (*LÄ* III: 641–59; Baines 1995: 125–8). Those historical kings who had reunified Egypt after a period of 'disorder' (i.e. an intermediate period) were held in particular reverence (Redford 1986: 35). The majority of the evidence for the royal court derives from periods of unity, as it was only when control was centralised that the palace could draw on the resources of the whole country and divert this wealth into the production of the art, architecture and literature which form the bulk of the available source material for studying Egyptian culture.

Consideration of the historical setting raises a number of issues of relevance to the treatment of sources. First, the limited evidence renders it necessary to draw on material from many periods; such an approach is encouraged by the superficially conservative nature of the Egyptian sources. However, alongside a degree of continuity there are changes in administration and in the composition of the court over time, even when one allows for the patchy nature of the evidence (Leprohon (1995) provides a useful summary). The Old Kingdom (until its latter years) produced extensive court cemeteries in the Sakkara region, containing the burials of courtiers, administrators and members of the king's household, attesting to a high degree of centralisation and showing the extent to which wealth was concentrated around the king (Roth 1993). From the Middle Kingdom we find significant wealth displayed in provincial cemeteries, and the relationship and power-balance between centre and provinces is clearly complex: provincial officials bore titles granted to them by the king and played an important part in the administration, but some of these provincial leaders built up their own households into small court-like configurations with their own title-holders and officials.[6] The New Kingdom court shows a significant degree of centralisation but there seems to be more emphasis on the military than

---

[5] Manley (1996) provides a short overview of Egyptian history. Shaw (2000) gives a more detailed, multi-authored treatment. The period under discussion here (up to the end of the New Kingdom) is usually divided into the Early Dynastic period (Dynasties 1–2, *c.* 3000–2686 BC), the Old Kingdom (Dynasties 3–8, *c.* 2686–2125 BC), the First Intermediate period (Dynasties 9–early 11, *c.* 2160–2055 BC), the Middle Kingdom (Dynasties 11–14, *c.* 2055–1650 BC), the Second Intermediate period (Dynasties 15–17, *c.* 1650–1550 BC) and the New Kingdom (Dynasties 18–20, *c.* 1550–1069 BC). The dates follow Shaw (2000: 479–83). There remains disagreement as to when the divisions between some of these periods should fall.

[6] The process of decentralisation can be traced back to the late Old Kingdom. See Franke (1991) for a nuanced discussion of the role of provincial rulers and their relationship with the court.

formerly. Kings of the Eighteenth Dynasty used their armies to build up an empire which brought significant wealth to king and court. The court appears, at least superficially, to have been less introspective than its earlier counterparts as a result of military campaigning abroad and diplomatic activity. Our evidence for the various periods is not equivalent, however, and it remains likely that such broad generalisations are crude.

Second, this chapter focuses on the Amarna period on account of the broad nature of the available evidence, but this is probably the most controversial episode in Egyptian history.[7] Akhenaten's decision to abandon the traditional Egyptian pantheon and attendant religious practices in favour of worship of the visible sun-disk was accompanied by changes in the style and content of art and literature and also in architecture. Opinions differ as to the extent of his changes and also the underlying motivation for them: to some they derive from religious zeal while to others they represent a desire to curb the rising power of the priesthood of the state god Amun-Re. Although precursors of his religious changes can be identified in preceding reigns, there can be no doubt that they had a significant impact on life at court, particularly given Akhenaten's decision to uproot the royal household and move to a newly constructed residence in Middle Egypt. However, although the atmosphere at court may have been particularly bitter and difficult during the early years of his reign and many of the actors may have changed, the institution of the court seems to have survived relatively intact: the king could not have effected and maintained the changes he made without his courtiers.

Although the Amarna period represents a particularly extreme example, it also illustrates the fact that, in addition to the broader historical trends that can be isolated, there are likely to have been significant differences between reigns. The constitution of the court and the nature of life there would have been strongly influenced by the personality of each individual king, and there is no guarantee that a conclusion drawn from isolated material dating to any reign is broadly applicable. Murnane's detailed study of the government of Egypt during the reign of Amenhotep III mentions some of the differences between the reigns of Amenhotep III and Akhenaten that can be established on the basis of prosopographical and broader textual study (Murnane 1998).

---

[7] Van Dijk (2000: 272–94) gives a recent and brief outline of the period. More substantial treatments are found in Aldred (1988) and Redford (1984), the latter focusing particularly on the early years of Akhenaten's reign and his activities at Karnak. Baines (1998) gives a nuanced interpretation of Akhenaten's changes within their historical context. See Montserrat (2000: esp. 12–54) for a discussion of modern interest in Akhenaten's reign and its rendering in historical studies, literature and art.

Third, evidence tends to derive from periods when writing was widely used and power was centralised, but these parameters are not equivalent to those marking the existence of the royal court. Although archaeological material can be difficult to interpret, it can provide valuable information on periods that textual sources do not cover and material on aspects of the court ignored or unclear in the texts. The importance of archaeological source material is highlighted in the following discussion on the origin of the Egyptian court and in the treatment of Amarna palaces later in the chapter.

The origins of the Egyptian court

The origins of the Egyptian court are difficult to pin down but must lie in the predynastic period. In the fourth millennium BC increasing social complexity can be traced in the material record of southern Egypt. A group of competing 'proto-states' emerged under the leadership of local chiefs (Kemp 1989: 31–5; Bard 1994; Baines 1995; Wilkinson 2000). These groups produced artefacts which gradually became widespread throughout the whole country, cultural unification thereby preceding political unification which probably occurred shortly before 3000 BC under leaders deriving from the Thinite region, known primarily from their tombs at Abydos. It was around this period of unification that writing first appeared in Egypt, providing the first examples of the names and titles of kings and officials (Baines 1995).

Dating to this period, perhaps even depicting the decisive battle of the political process of unification, is a richly decorated siltstone palette dedicated by King Narmer and left as a votive offering in a temple at Hierakonpolis. The palette's decoration strongly suggests that the Egyptian court was well established before the country was unified (Fig. 7.1). The king wears crowns, false beards and a kilt with an apron and a tail, and carries regalia, all of distinctive designs characteristic of the dress and regalia of later Egyptian divine kings. Hierarchy of scale is used to show relative importance, with the king's figure dominating the fields in which he is represented. Behind the king walks an individual depicted about half the size of the king who carries the king's sandals and a vessel; early hieroglyphs describe him only as a 'servant of the ruler' (Smith 1992: 244). Yet he is clearly an important official: he wears a cylinder seal around his neck, perhaps suggesting a role in administration. In the scene shown in Figure 7.1 (the upper field on the front of the palette), the king walks with his sandal-bearer behind him from a rectangular object (probably a building) towards two rows of headless corpses. Preceding him are four quarter-size figures bearing divine standards and a half-size figure with long hair or wig, unusual costume and accessories, and a title that may be related to that later used to designate the vizier or 'chief minister' (Wilkinson 1999: 137) although others identify him as a priest (Baines 1995: 120) or 'shaman' (Helck 1986: 12–13). In the border at the top of the object the king's name is written within a rectangular frame with niches, thought to represent the early palace. We thus find characteristic examples of the architecture, costume, titles, ranking, subordination of high officials, divinisation of the king and ceremonial activities of later court life expressed in a nuanced way on this one artefact, and also on other royal objects of the period (Gundlach 1998: 62–84).

It should come as no surprise that the court predates the historical period. The existence of absolute power is not confined to literate societies and, where very significant political power is represented in an individual, the possibility of advancement through personal favour rather than individual merit or popular support encourages congregation around that individual. Attempts to gain influence give rise to cycles of behaviour involving flattery and intrigue, characteristic of court societies.[8] As a group emerges around a leader, ceremonial activity emerges or is imposed which serves further to differentiate the leader from his courtiers and to perpetuate this symbiotic relationship. The problem with the early Egyptian evidence is that court society is characterised primarily through figurations of individuals and particular modes of behaviour and these are very difficult to trace in ancient societies in the absence of historical sources. Duindam (2003: 318) argues that the term 'court' should not be used 'as a bland equivalent of group dynamics around leaders', but defining the precise moment at which these group dynamics become a court proper is extremely difficult, particularly when the evidence is archaeological.

Cemeteries and objects deriving from tombs form the bulk of our evidence for early periods in Egypt, and archaeological studies have identified a number of factors of relevance to the development of the state (Wilkinson 2000) that may also be of interest for charting the emergence of the court. At a number of sites in the late predynastic period there is evidence that some elite individuals were buried in cemeteries isolated from the burial places of the majority of the local population, suggesting an attempt to differentiate rulers, and in some cases other members of the elite, from their subjects. The concentration of imported and manufactured prestige goods in the graves of these individuals suggests significant control of trade and production but also shows the desire to express power and wealth through display of

---

[8] But by no means unique to them (Duindam 2003: 318).

expensive luxury goods. The artistic motifs Bard (1994: 111) described as 'state symbolism' also occur in a few elite tombs from the Naqada III period (from *c.* 3200 BC) immediately preceding unification, although Wilkinson (2000: 380–1) suggests that such symbolism is found even earlier in the Naqada I period (before *c.* 3500 BC). The richness of burials at other sites was gradually eclipsed by that of the tombs at Abydos, suggesting that the authority of the rulers buried here was increasing at the expense of others, and that those not connected directly to the rulers at Abydos had more limited access to wealth and prestige goods. A. M. Roth suggests that the phyle system into which staff of temples, royal mortuary cults and the palace were organised during the Old Kingdom derives from local groups or families ('clans') prominent during the pre-literate period. She proposes that this kinship-based system was then modified into the organisational system required by the centralised government and bureaucracy (Roth 1991: esp. 205–16). The existence of such kinship groups was presumably essential to the early development and stability of the royal circle, but the breaking of explicit links between kinship lines (hereditary nobility) and the king in favour of non-hereditary official positions expressed through titles was essential to the way the court developed in Egypt.

The origins of the Egyptian court thus clearly pre-date the historical period and lie in the processes of social stratification and in the nucleation of individuals around a ruler perceived to be absolute.[9] Following unification, the Egyptian king wielded enormous personal power but was faced with governing and exploiting a large territory. Egyptian bureaucracy and administration are thought to have developed in the Early Dynastic period as king and court rapidly adjusted to governing the country from the royal residence (Wilkinson 1999: 109–49). Over the first three dynasties there was a proliferation of administrative titles as the bureaucracy took shape (Trigger et al. 1983: 66). Large and well-equipped tombs of officials of the First Dynasty are found at Sakkara, adjacent to the new royal centre at Memphis. These, like the funerary enclosures of contemporary kings at Abydos, were decorated with elaborate buttressing in a style known to Egyptologists as 'palace façade'. This is thought to link the tombs visually with the royal palace, constituting an indicator of association with the king and of distinction from the general population, and thus a court style (Kemp 1989: 55; Wilkinson 1999: 225).

Interestingly, this 'palace façade' niching seems be an example of the conscious borrowing of ideas and imagery from the Near East, showing

---

[9] 'Courts are the most general arrangement of power in pre-modern society' (Duindam 2003: 302).

that, despite the early and indigenous origins of kingship and the court, ideas were borrowed to aid the expression of power and the differentiation of king and court (Smith 1992; cf. Brosius in this volume on Achaemenid-Persian borrowings). The Narmer Palette again indicates that this borrowing is early: the rosette-shaped hieroglyph used to refer to the king in the caption above the sandal-bearer (Fig. 7.1) has its origins in the Near East (Smith 1992: 241–4). Borrowing is also clear in the cylinder seal worn by the king's servant, in the 'palace façade' motif within which the king's name is written and in the design of the long-necked serpopards which form the central motif on the front of the palette (Smith 1992: 235–8). The court setting and the need to administer the palace and extensive territories also seem to have been the impetus for the development of writing, first attested in Egypt in the labelling of commodities (Postgate et al. 1995); here again some influence from the Near East is possible, although the hieroglyphic signs and writing system that emerged in Egypt are very different from those in use in Mesopotamia.

The court thus emerges alongside kingship as part of an ongoing and slow process of social stratification. In a period of more rapid change sometime before unification, the court took significant steps to differentiate itself further from the rest of society, presumably as part of a process of self-legitimisation. This involved distinguishing the king (as the figurehead and focus of both court and country) from his followers through association with the gods, providing distinct regalia and a separate cemetery. The court itself profited through its association with the king. In the First Dynasty the king was buried surrounded by members of his household (Wilkinson 1999: 235–7) although the practice of retainer sacrifice did not last long in Egypt. Alongside this, attempts were also made to distinguish courtiers from the majority of the population; early evidence includes the use of titles and elaborate tombs and burial arrangements.

King and court

It is the absolute nature of a ruler's position which distinguishes his associates and establishment as a court. In the ancient world this position was often, although not always, associated with very considerable power and authority. The behaviour and interaction of individuals at court belong to a broader spectrum of behaviour around leaders, but it is the unchallenged authority of the position of ruler (rather than the individual incumbent) that leads to the concentration of resources, the ritualisation of the ruler's sphere and the invocation of divine legitimisation so characteristic of court life.

Egyptian sources of relevance to the court are dominated by the figure of the king whose complex nature encapsulated both human and divine attributes (Posener 1960; Redford 1995; Silverman 1995; Gundlach 1998). The Egyptian king wielded very significant power and, although his commands were executed by others in his name, there can be little doubt as to the extent of his personal power or of public perception of the origin of that authority (Lorton 1991: 306). The king was also closely associated with the gods and played an essential role in the welfare of Egypt by mediating between its people and the gods. Time was recorded back through lists of ancestral kings to the reigns of spirits and before them the gods (Redford 1986: xix–xx), providing divine precedent and ancestry for the ruling king. Theoretically it was the king who performed all temple ritual for the gods, although most of the time priests stood in for him. Although many commentators have argued that the extent of the king's divinity (as it was perceived by his subjects) waned over time, Quirke (1999: 63–4) has pointed out that the paucity of surviving records makes any accurate assessment of change over time virtually impossible. It is, however, clear that while the king was considered a divine being in his own right, he (or she) was also believed to be human and capable of error and weakness (Posener 1960).[10]

The divinity of the king differentiated him (and at some periods also members of his immediate family) from the courtiers and household that served him. This differentiation seems likely to have been particularly useful when ruling families changed as, once established, it provided clear distinction between the king and the group from whom he emerged as leader.[11] On a day-to-day basis this difference was presumably marked through ritualised behaviour around the king and through royal regalia, dress and setting. Rituals of kingship often followed ancient precedent, although traditional formulation often masks considerable innovation. The court itself must have provided a significant degree of continuity over long periods of time, enforcing smooth transitions of power between one monarch and the next and working to legitimise and empower the kingship on which the courtiers depended for their own position and authority.

---

[10] Although the literary texts which provide most of the evidence for this at least in part serve propagandistic purposes. For example, the Middle Kingdom stories which emphasise the amoral characters of a number of Old Kingdom kings were probably intended to emphasise positive aspects of the characters and interests of the contemporary kings in whose courts they were composed. Silverman (1995: esp. 50) comments on the relationship between secondary literature and the primary evidence on which the various interpretations are based.

[11] Tuthmosis III and Horemheb both claim to have been chosen to rule through oracles of the gods.

The structure of the Egyptian court

The existence of a royal court in Egypt is accepted throughout the discipline, and the courtly context of much of the material studied by Egyptologists is widely acknowledged. 'Court' and 'courtiers' are referred to frequently in secondary literature but the court as an institution has rarely formed an explicit focus of study (although see, for example, Quirke 1990; Lorton 1991; Coulon 2002; Gundlach 2004; Raedler 2004; forthcoming). Egyptological dictionaries seem not to contain entries on the court or courtiers, although the seven-volume *Lexikon der Ägyptologie* has short entries under 'Höflichkeit und Etikette' (*LÄ* II: 1229), 'Höfrang' (*LÄ* II: 1237) and 'Hofzeremoniell' (*LÄ* II: 1237–8). However, there is a vast body of literature on related subjects that are of relevance to the topic;[12] these include historical and prosopographical studies, and analyses of the art and literature produced within a court setting.

On close inspection, the Egyptian court proves a surprisingly elusive topic for research. The major problems seem to lie in defining the court and its membership and in establishing exactly how it was understood by the Egyptians themselves. Our textual sources are limited and inexplicit and our understanding of related lexicography is at present insufficient.[13] The closest equivalent to our terms 'court' and 'courtiers' is found in the Egyptian term *shenyt* which derives from the verb *sheni* 'to encircle' and in English translations is most commonly rendered as 'entourage' although in German we find 'Hofstaat' or 'Hofleute' (Erman and Grapow 1930: 511–12; Faulkner 1962: 267–8). It is a collective term, most usually written with a human determinative, that seems to refer to a small group of high-status individuals close to the king rather than the whole royal household or even all of the officials present at the palace at any time.[14] The *semeru* 'companions' or 'friends' seem to have been an even more limited group of high-status officials. There is also a title *rekh nesu*, 'royal acquaintance'. However, as the opening statement of Akhenaten shows, those around the king with potential influence were frequently referred to simply as *seru*, 'officials' or 'functionaries', making it difficult to distinguish between those serving the

---

[12] The bibliography presented here is far from exhaustive and where possible cites accessible sources in English.

[13] For example, there are at least five terms for the royal palace which have been the subject of several studies (e.g. Goelet 1985, 1986) but the significance of each is still debated. Lorton (1991) has a limited discussion with references.

[14] '. . . the members of the king's entourage are at their exact places and the Thirty [the royal council] are at their customary positions' (Murnane 1995: 240).

king directly and other functionaries (see Quirke 1990: 43); the highest administrators often seem to have been designated 'royal scribes', but also bore titles designating a particular area of administration (Helck 1958: 277–8). This blurring of categories perhaps links all in authority to king and palace but makes it hard to define the court, particularly as the use of the more specific terms seems to be rather fluid, at least in the Middle Kingdom (Quirke 1990: 51–7). Quirke (1990: 65) also notes that the composition of the inner palace personnel at this period seems very variable, being made up of those high-ranking officials who happened to be present.

Akhenaten's classification of those who might have influence over him is extremely interesting but unfortunately appears to be unique (Murnane and van Siclen 1993: 60). The list comprises: the queen and 'any official in my presence – whether (they are) officials "of favour" or officials "of the outside", or the chamberlains, or any people who are in the entire land' (Murnane and van Siclen 1993: 40). Ranked above the chamberlains, who are unquestionably palace officials, are two classes of official: 'favoured' and 'outsiders'. Does this mark the distinction between the 'companions' or 'entourage' allowed access to the inner palace and those serving in the outer parts of the palace? Are those serving in high administrative offices outside the palace the 'outsiders' or do they fall with their minions under the category 'any people who are in the entire land'? This latter term is unlikely to mean absolutely any Egyptian, given the royal context and the fact that the phrase is one of a listed subset of officials.

In his study of the courts at Vienna and Versailles, Duindam (2003) stresses the importance of considering the wider household of the king rather than just high-status courtiers. There can be no doubting the high status of royal women in Egypt, but personal attendants without significant administrative titles may also have had exceptional access to the king and therefore have had the potential to wield considerable influence. Unfortunately the evidence for royal households in New Kingdom Egypt is considerably sparser than that for courtiers, although in the Old Kingdom fine tombs were provided for favoured palace staff such as guards, musicians and low-ranking officials, attesting to their favour with the king (Roth 1995: 40–3; Kanawati 2003: 14–24).[15] A number of terms for those working at the palace are found, including a problematical title, *khenty-she*, recently translated as either 'palace attendant' (Roth 1995: 40–3) or 'guard' (Kanawati 2003: 14–19), and another, *aq*, translated 'ordinary entrant' (Quirke 1990: 36–7); Lorton argues that

---

[15] It may be significant that in the Old Kingdom the court seems to have been dominated by the royal family and perhaps to have been more entrenched than at later periods.

the term *per-nesu* or 'king's house' encompasses those who worked in it (i.e. the household) as well as a physical place (Lorton 1991: 304). Servants are shown working in palaces at Amarna but, unsurprisingly, are not listed by Akhenaten as possible influences in his boundary stelae.

It is worth noting that, although the Egyptian court was dominated at most periods by prominent wealthy families, there is no hereditary nobility in a strict sense. Appointments were made by the king, and those from humble backgrounds are known to have achieved high office occasionally, at least in the New Kingdom (see below). It may be, therefore, that particularly favoured attendants (if they existed) could be promoted to palace or administrative offices, thus rendering the distinction between courtiers and very influential members of the 'household' less stark than it may have been in medieval or early modern European courts. Also, as some official positions involving apparently menial personal service for the king (such as 'cup-bearers' who looked after the king's comfort) were known to provide privileged access, they were highly sought after (cf. Brosius and Spawforth in this volume): many cup-bearers had close links to other insiders such as royal nurses or tutors, or had been brought up in the palace themselves. Many seem to have gone on to high office (Murnane 1998: 216). It thus seems likely that many of the king's personal attendants were drawn from the families of the officials associated with the inner palace, reducing the potential influence of outsiders.

Papyrus Boulaq 18 provides an account of palace income and expenditure for a period of twelve days in the late Middle Kingdom (Quirke 1990). The date of the document (Thirteenth Dynasty), the fact that it does not refer to the principal residence, and the short period it covers render it hard to assess the broader applicability of some of the conclusions drawn from it, but it remains our only document detailing the constitution of the royal household (albeit in a presumably limited form as it was constituted on a royal visit). At least some of the royal family were present: a royal wife is mentioned along with a son, three daughters and a sister of the king. Although the king is not mentioned in the text, Quirke (1990:120) argues that he was present during at least part of the period under discussion. Officials are presented in hierarchical 'ranking blocks' within the lists (Quirke 1990: 73). There are nurses, magicians, musicians, a cosmetician and a hairdresser listed and also menial serving staff and guards. Interestingly, the families of some officials also seem to have been present (Quirke 1990: 90–4), but there are a number of conspicuous absences of high administrative officials: Quirke points out that neither the treasurer nor any priests were present (Quirke 1990: 51, 81).

On the basis of this document, Quirke establishes that the personnel of the palace was administratively divided into three groups. Some, such as the royal family, families of officials, nurses and musicians were associated with the inner palace (*kap*) (Quirke 1990: 36–8, 87–97), while the outer palace (*khenty*) was a sector which Quirke suggests dealt with state affairs and was headed by the vizier (Quirke 1990: 36–8, 72–86). Finally a class of 'ordinary entrants' or menial serving staff is documented (Quirke 1990: 36–7). Also prominent in the text is an audience area of the palace where banquets were held.

The Egyptians thus seem to have focused on an inner circle around the king, made up of small groups of favoured officials with their families, and other advisors.[16] The numbers involved appear to be relatively small. All of these individuals seem to have held specific courtly titles and, given their role in the council chamber, were presumably involved in decision-making although many may have been absent from the palace on official duties at any one time. The outer palace also served as an important administrative centre with its own officials, who presumably had links with inner palace officials although they were usually classed separately. Links between the palace and the provinces and other institutions were presumably maintained through senior officials who held titles showing close ties to the king and court alongside those indicating roles in institutions or the provinces. As a result of this there is considerable blurring between the designation of courtiers and administrative officials (cf. van Ess in this volume on the – in some ways comparable – structure of the Han Chinese court).

Offical documentary sources tend to fall into two groups: royal texts associated with activities of the king, in which he is represented as an absolute power ruling and acting in isolation, and texts associated with administration and officialdom which suggest that the country was governed by a hierarchical administration under one or more viziers but make little reference to the king, apparently for reasons of decorum (Quirke 1990: 120; 1999). The court is the link between these two representations of power and authority, as is clear from the courtly context and titles of those with high administrative positions, and repeated statements that these individuals carried out the king's wishes. However, the mechanisms of decision-making and the balance and exercise of power are extremely difficult to isolate (Quirke 1990: 50–7; Lorton 1991).

---

[16] Note also the list of officials meeting King Amenhotep III at the gate of the palace for his jubilee celebrations in year 30: 'the officials, the king's friends, the chamberlain, the men of the gateway, the king's acquaintances, the crew of the bark, the castellans, and the king's dignitaries' (Murnane 1998: 217).

The courtier

The majority of high officials in Egypt seem to have derived from established elite society (Murnane 1998: 212). Powerful, wealthy families are attested in burials and inscriptions from provincial centres as well as the royal residences. Some of these families were bound to the ruler through marriage alliances, and family members frequently held important administrative titles; however, such titles were not hereditary (although at some periods they were monopolised by single families as is the case with the provincial rulers (nomarchs) of the late Old Kingdom to early Middle Kingdom). Technically therefore, there is no 'hereditary nobility' in Egypt. However, when Tutankhamun restored the Amun cult a few years after Akhenaten's death, he dedicated a stela in which it is stated that 'he installed lay priests and higher clergy from among the children of the officials of their cities, each one being the "son-of-a-man" whose name was known' (Murnane 1995: 213). The desire to bequeath one's office (and the wealth, rank and privileges accruing to it) to one's eldest son is a common theme in Egyptian texts and there are examples of minor official positions being sold, suggesting that possession was, at some periods, considered to be a hereditary right (e.g. Parkinson 1991: 110–11).

Appointments of the highest functionaries (i.e. those who would have visited the palace and played a role at court) were made by the king. Although relatives were occasionally appointed to vacated posts, this was unusual during the mid to late Eighteenth Dynasty and the king's favour would have been essential to ensuring such continuity (Murnane 1998: 213–14).[17] All official posts brought material reward, often in the form of proceeds from land set aside to support the post but also sometimes in payments from the treasury. Proximity to the king brought with it the opportunity for a courtier to distinguish himself, and favour was richly rewarded and expressed materially. Kings could award promotions (which brought with them wealth) or supply material gifts such as elaborate tombs and burial equipment, jewellery, luxury goods or even captives of war; these gifts are sometimes detailed in the private tombs of the recipients. Such rewards have significant communicative value and were actively sought by courtiers: the majority of the decorated private tombs at Amarna contain a scene showing the king rewarding the tomb owner; these scenes and their architectural setting will be discussed in more detail below.

---

[17] At certain periods offices were more closely tied to single families; several examples are found among the priesthood in the Nineteenth Dynasty (Kitchen 1982: 46–7, 170–1).

Those from more humble backgrounds were not precluded from rising through the ranks and gaining status at court, however, as there is occasional evidence for those from obscure backgrounds rising to positions of considerable power. Several examples derive from Amarna itself. The 'fanbearer on the King's right hand', May, was granted a large and impressive tomb at Amarna by Akhenaten (Davies 1908a: 1–5, pls. I–V). He held significant offices, including 'the king's scribe, scribe of recruits, steward of "Pacifying Aten", steward of Waenre in Heliopolis, overseer of the cattle of the House of Re in Heliopolis, [overseer of] all [the works projects] of the king, the general of the Lord of the Two Lands' (Murnane 1995: 145). He also held ranking titles such as 'sole companion' (Davies 1908a: 4–5). Despite his wealth and status during the reign of Akhenaten, May writes: 'I was a poor man on both my father's and my mother's side – but the ruler built me up, he caused me to develop, he fed me by means of his Ka[18] when I was without property . . . he caused me to mingle with officials and courtiers when I was the least of underlings' (Murnane 1995: 145). The treasurer Suty also states that his background was humble (Murnane 1995: 186), while the general Ramose claims to be an 'official of the ruler's making' (Murnane 1995: 183).

The case of Senenmut, a prominent official and courtier during the co-regency of Hatshepsut (a female king) and Tuthmosis III, is a particularly revealing example dating to the earlier Eighteenth Dynasty. Senenmut's father had held a very lowly title and had originally been interred in a pit burial wrapped only in a shroud, until his body was exhumed and reburied in a more elaborate tomb at Thebes by Senenmut when he became wealthy and influential (Dorman 1988: 165–9).[19] Senenmut was accorded extraordinary privileges during Hatshepsut's reign: his image was inscribed behind the doors on many of the door jambs in her mortuary temple, and the burial chamber of his lower tomb lay beneath the forecourt of the temple, although the entrance was outside it. He had two tombs at Thebes and large numbers of statues portraying him have survived, suggesting very significant wealth. Senenmut seems to have fallen from favour during the sole reign of Tuthmosis III and damage to his Theban tombs and his images in Hatshepsut's temple suggests that he had made significant enemies (Dorman 1988).

This case is revealing for a number of reasons. It demonstrates that significant changes in social status were possible in Egypt but are likely to have owed much to the personal intervention of the king: 'You have a powerful

---

[18] The *ka* can here be roughly translated as 'divine essence'.
[19] When the body was excavated, soil from the original burial was found adhering to the shroud.

office, given you by the king.'[20] Whether such promotions resulted from talent, loyalty or simply royal favour cannot be established with certainty; autobiographical texts usually claim all as factors. There is no doubt, however, that privileges accrued through service at court could raise an official to a position of wealth and prestige equivalent or superior to that of an established member of elite society, as the examples of May and Senenmut show. Interestingly, the case of Senenmut may also demonstrate limitations to the king's power when it came to appointments and promotions as, despite the extraordinary privileges accorded to him, he never achieved the highest-ranking positions within government: his wealth, authority and status must have derived instead from his position at court and his relationship to the king. This in turn suggests that our understanding of Egyptian government, which is almost entirely based on prosopographical studies of the administrative hierarchy, may not always be an accurate reflection of influence and decision-making processes.

Here the role of favourites amongst royal women and members of the household must also have been significant, although this is often difficult to trace in the archaeological record. It is interesting to note here that Akhenaten's cup-bearer Parennefer, who is given no administrative or ranking titles in his Amarna tomb inscriptions, was nonetheless accorded a fine decorated tomb complete with a royal reward scene (Davies 1908b: 1–6, pls. II–X). As an official in charge of the personal comfort of the ruler a cup-bearer is likely to have had particularly privileged access to the king (Murnane 1998: 216). Interestingly, the same Parennefer is known from a tomb at Thebes and appears to have held a priestly title at Karnak before the move to Amarna (Redford 1984: 60). His influence thus perhaps reached beyond his rank.

The individuals making up the royal court and their backgrounds varied considerably from reign to reign and even within a single reign, as the subtle balance of power shifted. Kings promoted or retained people whom they trusted. Some kings maintained the services of those who had served under their predecessors and some promoted 'new men' such as Senenmut or May who were entirely reliant on the king for their wealth and prestige. Sometimes those brought up and educated with or under the king achieved high office (Bryan 1991: 261–3), although the title 'child of the inner palace' is not found in any of the private tombs at Amarna. Sometimes particular families were well represented amongst high officials, suggesting considerable

---

[20] Lichtheim 1976: 171. From a New Kingdom text exhorting the reader to become a scribe. Although the text is undoubtedly biased, the importance of literacy in advancing social status through employment in administration seems to be supported by prosopographical evidence.

influence, and royal relatives such as the God's Father Ay, who later became king, might also be prominent at court.[21]

The composition of Akhenaten's court is interesting as it shows remarkably little continuity with that of his predecessor (Murnane 1998: 214). His father's vizier, Ramose, survived into Akhenaten's reign and is represented in his tomb being rewarded by both rulers, but in separate depictions in the different artistic styles of the two reigns. His nephew, Ipy, was steward of Memphis, in charge of the treasury, granary and workshops attached to the royal domain, but then went on to become steward and 'overseer of the inner palace of pharaoh in Akhetaten' (Murnane 1998: 213–14). A man named Aper-el (thought to be a name of Semitic origin) served as vizier under Amenhotep III and is also described as a 'child of the inner palace' (Zivie 1990: 151–2, 156–7). He bore the title 'First servant of the Aten' which is attested only under Akhenaten, so it seems likely that he also survived the transition. His son Huy, who was buried in the same tomb, bore military titles, and seems to have served under Akhenaten until at least year 10 (Zivie 1990: 159–66). We therefore have evidence for a few prominent individuals and families who seem to have survived the transition of power, but other old retainers are difficult to identify.

Following the move to Amarna, courtiers are known primarily from their inscribed tombs (Davies 1903 to 1908b), although the houses of some prominent individuals such as the vizier Nakht can be identified in the city itself (Peet and Woolley 1923: 5–9, pls. III–V).[22] The majority of these individuals served the king, although two are closely associated with royal women: Huya held the offices of steward, treasurer and overseer of the harem under Akhenaten's mother, Queen Tiye (Davies 1905b: 1–25, pls. I–XXV; Murnane 1995: 130–41), while Meryre II has titles associating him with Nefertiti as well as the king (Davies 1905a: 33–45, pls. XXVIII–XLVII; Murnane 1995: 162–5). Almost all of the individuals represented in the tombs have titles and epithets which link them closely with the king, although there are a few exceptions such as the Chief of Police, Mahu (Davies 1906: 12–18, pls. XIV–XXIX, XL–XLII; Murnane 1995: 147–51) and the standard-bearer Suty (Davies 1906: 25, pls. XXXVIII–XXXIX; Murnane 1995: 185–6). Those with priestly titles such as Meryre I (Davies 1903; Murnane 1995:

---

[21] Ay was probably a close relative of Queen Tiye. His wife had also been Nefertiti's wet-nurse (Redford 1984: 150–1; van Dijk 2000: 292). For his tomb at Amarna see Davies (1908b: 16–24, pls. XXII–XXXIV, XXXVI–XLIV).

[22] A brief introduction to some of the Amarna courtiers is given by Redford (1984: 149–53). Up-to-date translations of the texts from the tombs and other sources are provided by Murnane (1995: 107–204).

151–62) and Panehesy (Davies 1905a: 9–32, pls. II–XXVII; Murnane 1995: 169–77) are particularly prominent, but royal scribes and military officials are also present. The decoration of all the tombs is focused on the king and his family and the majority claim that the king favoured them. A few have titles which suggest that their activities were not entirely focused within a single institution: Pentu seems to hold office both in the palace (as a royal scribe and the king's physician) and in one of the Aten temples (Davies 1906: 1–6; Murnane 1995: 179–82), while May holds courtly titles such as 'fanbearer on the King's right hand', priestly titles associated with the temple of Re at Heliopolis and also military titles such as 'general' and 'scribe of recruits' (Davies 1908a: 1–5, pls. I–V; Murnane 1995: 143–7).

Many kings of the early to mid Eighteenth Dynasty had been powerful military leaders, and soldiers had sometimes ranked highly at court (Bryan 1991: 279–93; 1998: 37–8).[23] Although Akhenaten's reign is usually presented as a time of peace and diplomacy, the military seems to have been more prominent at court during this period than is initially apparent. Messages to the Egyptian king among the Amarna Letters suggest the importance of the army with greetings such as 'For my brother and his household, for his horses and his chariots, for his magnates and his country may all go very well' (Moran 1992: 13). In the tomb of the chamberlain Tutu, the official is shown addressing those assembled before the palace: 'Pharaoh . . . [has ordered (?)] the commanders of hosts, masters of the horse, commanders [of the army] and [every commander of] troops . . . every servant of Aten belonging to the Aten . . . all [. . .]s belonging to the House of Aten [and all] people . . .' (Murnane 1995: 194). The various army officials are therefore given precedence over priests and others. There are a substantial number of military officials amongst the courtiers at Amarna: Ay is described as 'the king's true scribe, his beloved, the God's Father, Ay. The troop leader and master of the horse, the God's Father, Ay' (Murnane 1995: 107). Others such as the general Ramose, the chief of police Mahu, the chief bowman and master of the horse Nekhuempaaten, and the general Paatenemheb all had tombs at Amarna (Murnane 1995: 183–4; 147–51; 168). Although Horemheb is known to have been an important general, his military title tends to be listed after a string of courtly titles during the reign of Tutankhamun: 'the hereditary prince, the fan-bearer at the king's right hand, the generalissimo Horemheb, justified' (Murnane 1995: 229).

There were significant numbers of foreigners at the royal court in the Eighteenth Dynasty. Although there is no evidence to suggest that any of

---

[23] For the military during the New Kingdom see in particular Spalinger (1982) and Gnirs (1996).

the nobles represented by the tombs at Amarna were foreign, visiting dignitaries are well attested in the Amarna Letters and might spend a considerable period of time at court. Egyptian kings sometimes married the daughters of foreign rulers and it is clear from the Amarna Letters that these might arrive with very large entourages and escorts (Moran 1992: 21, 81). Amenhotep III is known to have had at least two Mitannian and two Babylonian wives and one from Arzawa (Schulman 1979: 183–4). They may still have been present in one of the royal harems during Akhenaten's reign, and Akhenaten himself is known to have had at least two foreign wives (Schulman 1979: 185). It has even been suggested that Kiya, a secondary wife of Akhenaten who may have been the mother of Tutankhamun, should be identified with the Mitannian princess Gilukhepa who had arrived in Amenhotep III's harem some thirty years earlier (Redford 1984: 150). Bilingual scribes must have translated the diplomatic documents that passed between Egypt and her neighbours in the Near East and some of the Amarna Letters are actually lists of foreign words with their Egyptian equivalents (Moran 1992: xv–xvi). It was also common practice in the New Kingdom for children of foreign rulers to be taken as surety and brought up and educated at the palace. These are among the 'children of the inner palace', some but not all of whom went on to serve in official capacities in the Eighteenth Dynasty, although they are not prominent during Akhenaten's reign. Several foreigners achieved high office within the government and foreign service of Amenhotep III (Murnane 1998: 202).

Female members of the royal family seem to have been exceptionally prominent during the reign of Akhenaten. The king is frequently shown with Nefertiti, his 'great king's wife', and with their daughters of whom the eldest three are often depicted. Akhenaten's mother, Tiye, was prominent in the city with her own household (for her chief steward, Huya, see Murnane 1995: 130–41) and 'sunshade' temple (Kemp 1995: 459–61). His secondary wife, Kiya, had a brief period of exposure around the time that Nefertiti disappears from the record, but Kiya's images, names and titles were later replaced by those of Meritaten, Akhenaten's eldest daughter who held the position of 'great king's wife' in the later years of the reign. There are likely to have been other royal women and children, but they may not all have lived at Amarna itself. There were 'harem' palaces elsewhere in Egypt at sites such as Medinet Gurob (Kemp 1978) and less central members of the royal family may have lived fairly permanently in these establishments. Other women also played a role at court, with the title 'royal ornament' bestowed on some wives of officials. Tiyi, wife of the God's Father Ay, bore the title 'king's ornament' and is also described as the 'one whom the King's Chief

Wife favoured' (Murnane 1995: 107); she had also been the wet-nurse of Nefertiti and is described as 'the great nurse who nourished the goddess' (Murnane 1995: 109). Quirke (1990: 90–4) shows that the families of high officials formed part of the community of the inner palace in the late Middle Kingdom; this seems likely to hold also for the New Kingdom although the nature of that interaction within the residence city is uncertain.

The dual role of the court as the centre of government and the social circle of the king is interesting. The presence of higher-ranking officials at court presumably allowed the king to keep an eye on them and ensured that his functionaries remained focused on his own person and the social competition of life at court rather than on establishing entrenched power-bases within institutions. The fact that some courtiers held titles associated with more than one branch of the administration (see above) must have assisted here. The dual role of individuals as courtiers and as governmental officers results in considerable blurring of the divisions between the palace and other institutions, perhaps useful for maintaining an aura of ultimate authority (Quirke 1990: 51–7).

The opportunity for interaction with the king would be essential if a courtier were to gain royal favour. Most kings of the Eighteenth Dynasty travelled extensively, moving within the country for religious ceremonies and other royal activities, and many also ventured outside Egypt on military expeditions although there is little evidence that Akhenaten himself travelled abroad (but see Murnane 1995: 101–3). Some courtiers and members of the royal household moved around the country with the king (as is apparent from the Middle Kingdom Papyrus Boulaq 18) but others presumably remained at the principal residences undertaking administrative duties. Many officials also served away from the royal palace for significant lengths of time, undertaking duties at Memphis or in provincial government, leading mining expeditions or armies, overseeing building work and conducting diplomatic missions; the Amarna Letters suggest that envoys might be detained at foreign courts for many years (e.g. Moran 1992: 7, 13). Successful discharge of a mission could, however, result in royal favour and reward on the individual's return to the palace. Raedler (forthcoming) suggests that courtly titles expressing physical closeness to the king symbolically maintained proximity when officials were absent from court.

The Eighteenth Dynasty court was therefore cosmopolitan and inclusive of people from a variety of social backgrounds. Courtiers were not idle. While some were employed in the personal service of the king and in running the palace, others governed the country and ran the various institutions such as the temples, treasury and army. Some officials would have been permanently present at court, while others were absent for long periods of time on official or private business. Although some members of established families may have had sources of personal wealth and prestige in their home towns, the emphasis in mortuary architecture on the king and the relationship of the deceased to him strongly suggests that personal interaction with the king, and thus presence at court, was an essential component in gaining wealth and social prestige.

Court politics

Access to the palace and the king seems to have been strictly controlled, with security enforced by palace guards and their overseers. In addition, a number of officials such as the 'overseer of the audience chamber' and the 'chamberlains' controlled and regulated access to, and activities within, different parts of the palace. The inner parts of the palace had their own staff, and Ipy, 'steward of Memphis', also served as 'overseer of the inner palace of pharaoh in Akhetaten' (Murnane 1998: 214). Stewards administered the king's property and various supervisors oversaw the supplies kept in the palace magazines (Murnane 1998: 212–17). The majority of officials who worked in the outer parts of the palace seem not to have been allowed access to the inner parts of the palace.[24]

The Middle Kingdom 'Story of Sinuhe' gives a brief account of a visit to the palace and a royal audience. Sinuhe was a courtier who had fled Egypt fearing he would be implicated in the aftermath of the assassination of King Amenemhet I. After many years in the Near East he returned to Egypt, having received a royal pardon. The following extract describes Sinuhe's entry to the palace: 'Ten men came and ten men went to usher me into the palace. My forehead touched the ground between the sphinxes, and the royal children stood in the gateway to meet me. The courtiers who usher through the forecourt set me on the way to the audience-hall. I found his majesty on the great throne in a kiosk of gold. Stretched out on my belly, I did not know myself before him' (Lichtheim 1973: 231).

The evidence suggests that prostration ('kissing the ground' in Egyptian terminology) before the king was common practice. Amarna Letters sent by vassal states refer in their opening lines to falling at the feet of the king: 'Rib-Hadda says to the king, his lord, the Sun of [all countries]: I fall at

---

[24] For the administration of the palace in the Eighteenth Dynasty see, in particular, Lorton (1991) and Murnane (1998: 212–17).

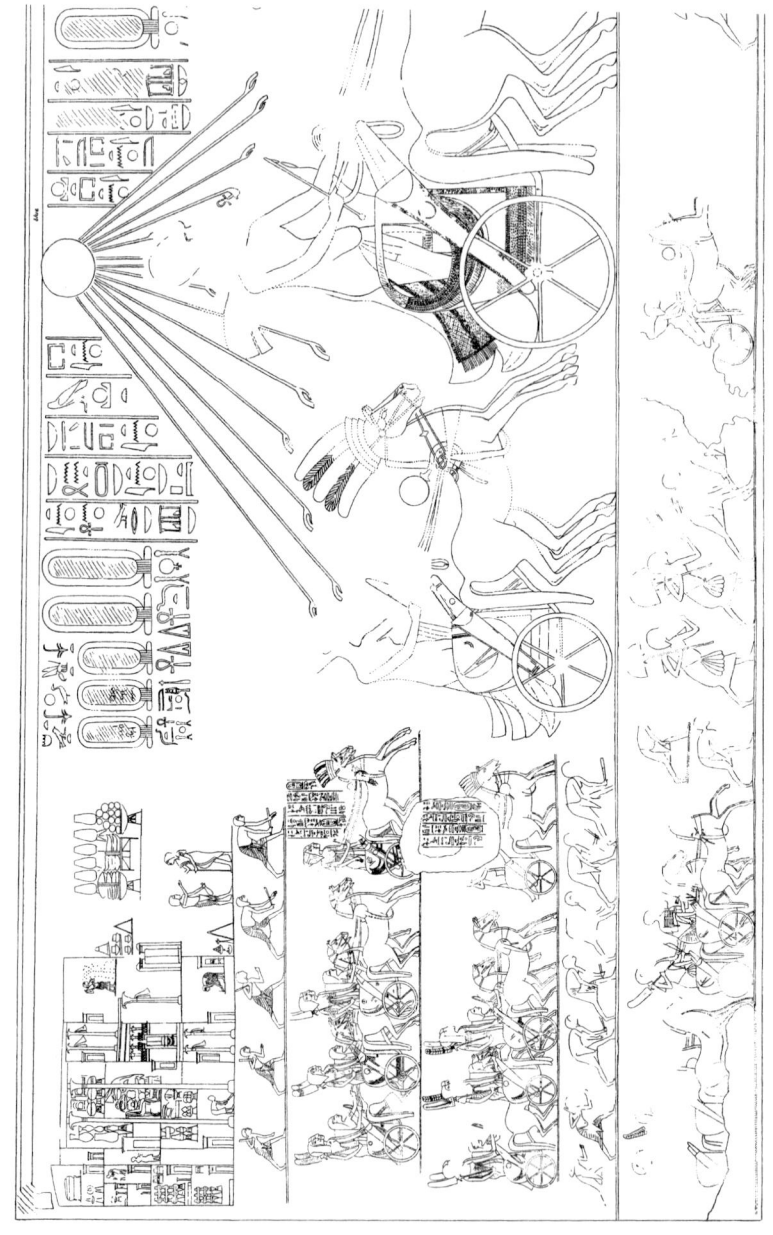

Figure 7.2 The royal family ride in their chariots from palace to temple. The palace, with a closed Window of Appearance, is shown in the upper left corner of the depiction. From the tomb of Meryra at el-Amarna (Davies 1903: pl. X).

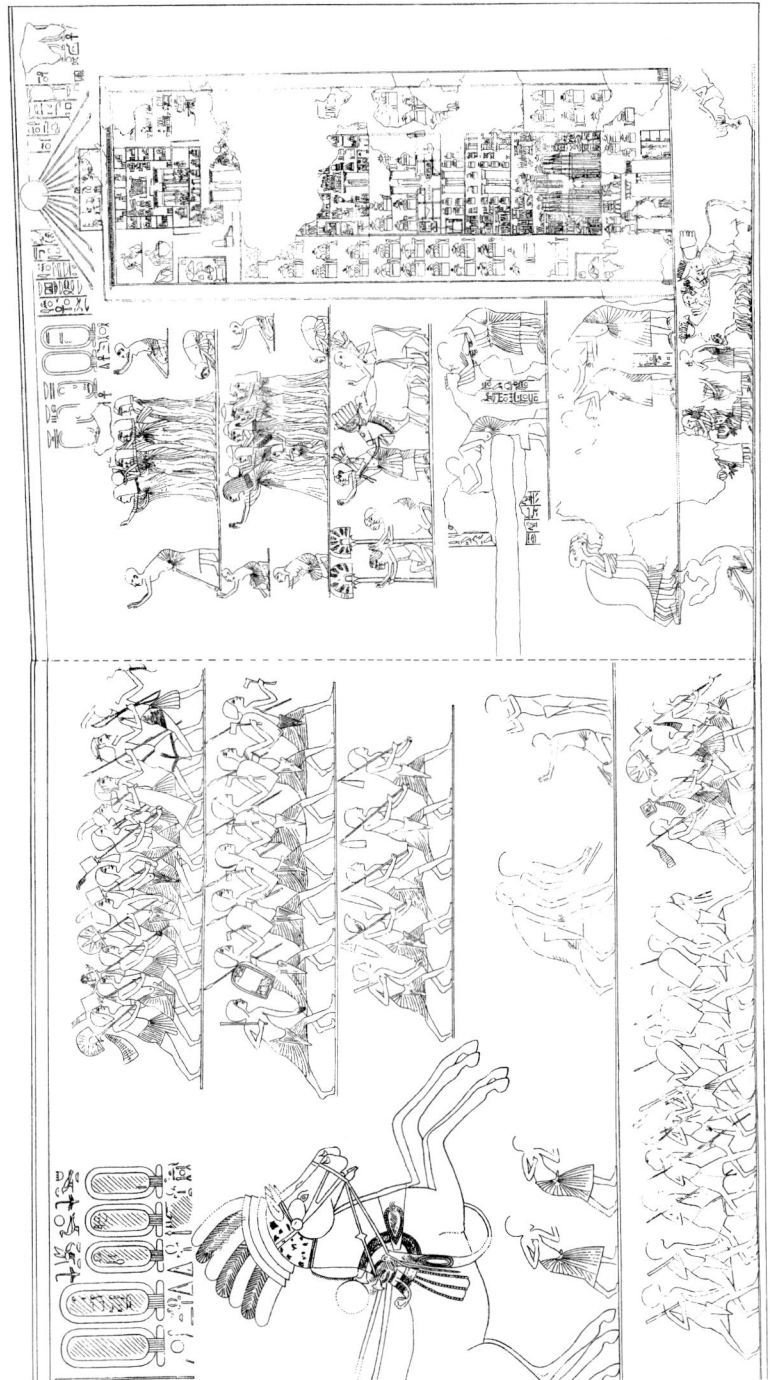

Figure 7.2 (cont.)

the feet of my lord, [my] S[un] 7 times and 7 times' (Moran 1992: 166). Amarna period reliefs from Karnak show the king emerging from the palace in his jubilee costume with the chamberlains lying prostrate before him (Redford 1984: 119, fig. 7.12). Prostration was also appropriate before gods, and even Akhenaten himself is shown prostrate before the Aten with his family on a balustrade block (Aldred 1988: 275, fig. 25).

In a stela dating to the early Middle Kingdom an official describes himself as 'one who keeps the commoners distant from him [the king]' (Fischer 1960: 261). Ordinary people had virtually no access to the king and had to approach figures of authority by petitioning at their gates and through intermediaries. This is well illustrated by another Middle Kingdom story, the 'Eloquent Peasant' (Lichtheim 1973: 169–84). In this, a travelling trader has his goods confiscated by a corrupt official. The trader petitions the high steward Rensi who is in charge of the region in which the crime has taken place, waylaying him as he emerges from his house and requesting that a servant be sent so that he can make the complaint known. The trader's petitions are so eloquent that they are written down and presented to the king, who is pleased by them. Ultimately Rensi confiscates the corrupt official's goods and gives them to the trader. The 'peasant' in question thus comes to the notice of the king without ever having entered his presence – via a courtier and his servant as intermediaries.

Although ordinary people would not be able to approach the king, they might catch sight of him as he journeyed between his palaces and the temples. The journey of the king between these structures, often accompanied by his queen and sometimes by the royal daughters, is a common theme of depictions in courtiers' tombs at Amarna (Fig. 7.2). The king most often travels in a golden chariot. Sometimes the queen rides with him; on other occasions she follows in her own chariot. The royal daughters and some high officials also ride in chariots, while soldiers run along beside the group and onlookers bow down and raise their arms in adoration of the king. Occasionally the king and queen are carried in sedan-chairs, similarly richly decorated (Davies 1905b: pl. XIII). Royal barges serve a similar purpose on longer riverine journeys: the barges are shown moored outside a palace in the tomb of May (Davies 1908a: pl. V).

In his study of the courts of Vienna and Versailles, Duindam points to significant differences in the nature of court life at the two royal centres, contrasting the closed style of the Habsburg court which was small and housed few courtiers with the openness of the French court at Versailles where thousands were housed and lived and shared entertainments with the royal family (Duindam 2003: 308–9). It is the closed style of the Habsburg court which seems to correlate more closely with what we know of the ancient Egyptian court. Sites such as Amarna and Malkata, which will be discussed in more detail below, show only limited provision of accommodation within the palace compounds, and the number of high officials associated with the inner palace is likely to have been limited (on this aspect of ancient courts see also the chapters by Paterson and van Ess in this volume).

The closed style of the German courts is associated with creating distance between the royal family and courtiers, whereas accessibility is created by the open style (Baillie 1967). The existence of significant differentiation between king and courtiers fits well with what we know of the Egyptian court and its role in promoting the divine aspects of the king's nature. Even in the Amarna period, the vast majority of our evidence for court life relates to its official aspects: diplomatic activities; major royal ceremonies such as the *sed*-festival (jubilee) and the Reception of Foreign Tribute in year 12 of Akhenaten's reign; official visits to the temple; and reward ceremonies. Some unusual wall paintings from the palaces themselves show the royal family relaxing and eating (e.g. Arnold 1996: figs. 49 and 108), and a few private tomb depictions show similar images of the royal family. A depiction from the tomb of Huya, steward to the king's mother, Queen Tiye, shows the royal family eating, with the tomb owner waiting on them (Fig. 7.3). In commissioning such a scene Huya is presumably depicting for all to see his privileged access to the divine family.

Power, influence and intrigue

There is little documentary evidence from Egypt for the day-to-day intrigues which studies such as those of Elias (1983) and Duindam (2003) suggest formed such a prominent part of court life. We have documentary evidence for only the most serious court conspiracies: usually those culminating in the actual or attempted assassination of a ruler. A fascinating, although perhaps rather speculative study by Naguib Kanawati (2003) collates textual evidence for conspiracies from the Fifth Dynasty and analyses deliberate damage to tombs, which Kanawati suggests was carried out in association with the punishment of a group of palace officials for involvement in the assassination of King Teti. References found in the Old Kingdom autobiography of Weni at Abydos relate to another such incident in the reign of Pepi I and the courtier's role in investigating the plot (Lichtheim 1973: 19).

In Akhenaten's boundary stelae we find oblique and fragmentary references to dissent, apparently culminating in year 5 of his reign and thus

Figure 7.3 Huya in attendance on the royal family. The three principal figures are Akhenaten's mother, Tiye (*left*), Akhenaten (*centre*) and Nefertiti (*right*). The figure raising a stick-like object is identified in the caption as Huya himself. From the tomb of Huya at el-Amarna (Davies 1905b: pl. VI).

probably coinciding with the decision to move to Amarna. The dissent is described as being worse than anything which had occurred in the reigns of his immediate predecessors (Murnane and van Siclen 1993: 41–2). Discontent and political struggles at court are thought likely to have led to the significant change in personnel which is apparent early in Akhenaten's reign and the fact that a number of 'new men' are attested in high office in his reign. Beyond this we have no direct textual references to the events associated with the move to Amarna and the changes affecting religious practices at the time.

The danger of being implicated in a court conspiracy is vividly illustrated in the Middle Kingdom story of Sinuhe (Lichtheim 1973: 222–35). At the beginning of the text Sinuhe is described as a servant of the royal harem in the service of the wife of the crown-prince. Despite the apparent implications of his title, he was actually serving with the army under the leadership of the crown-prince when the reigning king, Amenemhet I, was assassinated, although only allusions are made to this event in the text.[25] Sinuhe found

---

[25] The assassination is described in more detail in the 'Instruction of King Amenemhet I' (Lichtheim 1973: 135–9; Parkinson 1991: 48–52). According to this text the king was killed by his own guards as he slept after supper. This text warns the future king against trusting a

himself in the wrong place at the wrong time and overheard a conversation between one of the other royal sons and a messenger. Terrified, he fled: 'I did not plan to go to the residence. I believed there would be turmoil and I did not expect to survive it' (Lichtheim 1973: 224). He travelled to the Near East and found favour and success in the service of foreign kings. We are never told what it was that Sinuhe had overheard; his flight perhaps seems unlikely to a modern audience, given his claims of innocence. However, the popularity of the text suggests that the idea of an innocent bystander being implicated in a plot was an entirely understandable premise for flight to its ancient readers.

Sinuhe returns to Egypt in old age, after a lifetime spent promoting Egypt's interests abroad, tempted back by a letter from the king and the promise of a good burial. He is given the title of 'companion' and is counted among the 'entourage'. Meals are delivered to him four times a day from the palace and he receives gifts and a fully equipped burial place. Interestingly, he is given 'a house and garden that had belonged to a courtier' (Lichtheim 1973: 233), which suggests that goods belonging to officials might be confiscated and reallocated by the king, a practice corroborated by other evidence.[26]

Sinuhe's early association with the harem is interesting as this seems to have been the most prominent source of intrigue and conspiracy, for rather obvious reasons (cf. van Ess in this volume). Egyptian kings often had many wives of varying rank. Ideally the eldest son by the 'great royal wife' succeeded his father, but wives and their associates seem to have schemed to get their own sons into positions of favour and ultimately onto the throne. The best-documented case of a harem conspiracy occurred in the reign of Ramesses III (*c.* 1153 BC) and involved eleven harem officials, a number of other functionaries and six wives of officials (de Buck 1937; Kemp 1989: 222; Vernus 2003: 108–20). The records even document an attempt to pervert the course of justice by arranging for the investigating officials to be seduced by beautiful women (Vernus 2003: 119–20).

The threat posed by potential heirs (usually brothers or sons) as the foci for court conspiracies must have been clearly apparent to reigning kings. From the early Fifth Dynasty onwards, royal sons become difficult to identify in the record, and it seems that they were no longer given important official posts as

---

brother, friend or intimate: 'It was one who ate my provisions that made insurrection; one to whom I had given my arms was creating plots with them; one clad in my linen was looking at me as if needy; one anointed with my myrrh was passing water' (Parkinson 1991: 50).

[26] The king thus uses both rewards and punishments in his treatment of courtiers. See also the Middle Kingdom 'Story of the Eloquent Peasant' in which a corrupt official's goods are confiscated and bestowed on his victim (Lichtheim 1973: 169–84, esp. 182).

they had been in the Fourth Dynasty (Strudwick 1985: 337–46). Presumably this measure was intended to prevent them from building up power-bases at court. From this date, evidence for king's sons and brothers is very patchy until the Ramesside period, although there is occasional evidence for military training or positions in the priesthood (Dodson 1990). Royal nurses and tutors are known and some sons may have been brought up in provincial palaces or perhaps even within the houses of trusted officials or relatives rather than at the centre of court life. By contrast, wives and daughters are more prominent and are sometimes represented in the company of the king.

The situation changed when a son was either designated as heir or appointed to a co-regency with his father.[27] Co-regencies were particularly popular in the Middle Kingdom but are also known from the New Kingdom (Murnane 1977). As a practical way of ensuring a smooth transfer of power the policy seems to have been successful, although the practice may seem to us difficult to reconcile with Egyptian ideology which stressed the existence of a single divine king. Akhenaten had an older brother, Thutmose, who was designated as crown-prince but died before his father (Dodson 1990); while we know a little about this Thutmose, we know almost nothing about Akhenaten himself before he ascended the throne. It is possible that there was a short co-regency with his father Amenhotep III, although this topic remains controversial (van Dijk 2000: 274–5). Evidence that Akhenaten was concerned about the succession towards the end of his reign is provided by clear evidence that he appointed a co-regent, named Smenkhkare (van Dijk 2000: 279–81), although the identity and even the gender of this ruler remain hotly debated topics.

Power might also become concentrated in the hands of individuals, particularly if they acted as regent for a young king (as is the case with Horemheb during the reign of Tutankhamun, although it was Ay who initially succeeded Tutankhamun when he died) or as vizier (Ramesses I was Horemheb's vizier and was appointed prince regent by him). In his coronation inscription Horemheb describes his relationship with the young king and his role in

---

[27] A scene in Hatshepsut's mortuary temple at Deir el-Bahari shows her investiture as royal heir by her father, Tuthmosis I. In the scene, Tuthmosis I sits in a pavilion with Hatshepsut standing before him as he presents her to his high officials and courtiers (Naville 1898: 5–7, pls. LX–LXII). Although this representation is usually interpreted as an invention of Hatshepsut's (post-rationalising her position as king) the basic premise of the scene must have been credible. It should also be pointed out that an alternative explanation of the scene – that Hatshepsut was indeed chosen as heir but was prevented by factions at court from taking the throne on the death of her father – seems to me equally likely. The fact that Tuthmosis III later states that he was chosen as king by an oracle of the god Amun suggests that his appointment was unusual and probably stage-managed to legitimise his position.

governing the country at that time in such a way that his consolidation of power is clearly apparent:

> When he [Horemheb] was called upon in the presence of the sovereign – the palace having fallen into a rage – he opened his mouth and answered the king and made him happy with what came out of his mouth. Unique and effective was he . . .
>
> So he was administering the Two Lands for a period of many years. [The dues of the Two Lands and the deliveries of Upper and Lower Egypt were] reported [to him], and the councils [came] to him, bowing at the gate of the king's house. The chiefs of the Nine Bows, south as well as north, appealed to him, their arms outspread at his approach, as they did reverence to his face as to a god. (Murnane 1995: 231)

However, kings could and did change the structure of official posts or create new offices to manipulate the power balance. For example, at some point in the early to mid Eighteenth Dynasty the office of vizier was split into two, one governing the north and one the south of Egypt (Murnane 1998: 201).[28] That the king was able to upset the existing power balance at court and within government is also clear from the fact that – regardless of his motives – Akhenaten managed to disband the powerful and institution-alised priesthood of Amun, and presumably also that of Ptah at Memphis. A comparison between Akhenaten's changes and the power of Horemheb during the reign of Tutankhamun only a few years after Akhenaten's death shows clearly that the power balance between king and courtiers was fluid and prone to rapid and major shifts.

Akhenaten's changes highlight the ability of the king to manipulate his situation and succession to a certain extent. However, changes made in the reign of one king might rapidly become entrenched and could have far-reaching implications. For the early Eighteenth Dynasty, this is particularly apparent in the promotion of royal women culminating in the accession of Hatshepsut. Ideally the Egyptian throne passed from father to eldest son by the principal wife, following the divine model in which the god Horus succeeded his father Osiris. Problems were particularly likely to occur if the king produced no sons at all, or no sons by his 'great royal wife'. This situation seems to have arisen with surprising frequency in the early Eighteenth Dynasty. The problem was solved by marriage to the wife or daughter of the previous divine king and, despite several changes in the male lineage, the rulers of this period were grouped together in a single 'dynasty'. In terms of the succession, this placed emphasis on the transmission of divinity through the mother and the female blood-line, with some of the

---

[28] For discussion of administrative reforms in the Old Kingdom see in particular Kanawati (1980).

more important queens given the title 'God's Wife of Amun' (Bryan 2000: 226–30). Princes by minor wives who became king also married half-sisters by more senior wives.[29] This seems to have been widely accepted as a method of legitimising political power and could elevate a prominent official and courtier to the position of divine king.[30]

Some of these women also wielded considerable political power, in addition to the influence that their proximity to the king may have offered (Bryan 2000: 228); one of the Amarna Letters actually suggests that Akhenaten consult his mother, Tiye, about a matter concerning international diplomacy (Moran 1992: 91). The power to appoint the holder of the office of 'second prophet of Amun' lay in the hands of the king's wife from the beginning of the Eighteenth Dynasty (Bryan 2000: 229). Ahmose Nefertari, Hatshepsut and possibly also Ahhotep ruled as regents. The practice of appointing women (almost always mothers) to rule as regents for their sons dates back at least as far as the Early Dynastic period, and is thought to have been considered a good way of ensuring that the country was governed well in the best interests of the child-king. However, during the early years of Tuthmosis III's reign, Hatshepsut was elevated from regent to king. She was represented wearing the crowns and regalia of a king as a full co-regent with her step-son. There has been much speculation on the nature of her relationship with Tuthmosis III, but whatever the motivation behind her assumption of the throne (in reality an ideological acknowledgement of her existing political power – but a surprising one) there can be no doubt that she must have found support for her actions within the court. Following this reign, royal women are considerably less prominent for several generations, perhaps a deliberate attempt to prevent them amassing political power (Bryan 1998: 40). However, in the Amarna period, royal women again become prominent, with Nefertiti appearing alongside Akhenaten with extraordinary frequency (van Dijk 2000: 276). Both Nefertiti and Tiye had their own establishments at Amarna with their own officials and households, perhaps constituting offshoots or subsidiaries of the main royal court.

Women also figure prominently in the international diplomatic correspondence with other Great Powers. Letters convey greetings between queens

---

[29] This is known to have happened in the case of Tuthmosis II. Tutankhamun and Smenkhkare may also have married half-sisters (although questions about the parentage of these two kings allow some room for doubt). Tuthmosis III was probably intended to marry his half-sister Neferure (Hatshepsut's daughter).

[30] As may have happened in the case of Tuthmosis I. However, Barry Kemp points out (personal communication) that we know little about Tuthmosis I's background. The 'non-royal' individuals who came to the throne during this dynasty could actually have been close relatives of previous kings who did not advertise these relationships for reasons of decorum.

as well as kings, and marriage was used as a way of cementing alliances between these states (Schulman 1979; Meier 2000). Foreign brides arrived in style, with considerable entourages, and must have brought alien customs to the Egyptian court. No Egyptian princesses were sent abroad to marry foreign kings in reciprocal arrangements during this period, a fact that has been interpreted as showing that the Egyptians felt themselves superior to the other powers with whom they corresponded (Schulman 1979: 179–80). The extreme reluctance of Egyptian kings to send their daughters abroad actually seems more likely to relate to the fact that royal daughters featured so prominently in the process of political legitimisation, raising the possibility that these foreign kings or their children might be viewed as legitimate heirs in the case of the Egyptian king's death.[31] Such an interpretation corresponds well with the implications of an Amarna period queen's extraordinary request to the Hittite king: 'My husband died. I do not have a son . . . If you would give me one of your sons, he would become my husband . . . We are seeking a son of our Lord for the kingship in Egypt' (quoted in Schulman 1979: 177 n. 1). This letter was most probably sent by Ankhsenamun, third daughter of Akhenaten and wife of Tutankhamun (Schulman 1978; Giles 1997: 311–21). The son in question was dispatched but seems to have been intercepted and murdered before he reached Egypt. Ankhsenamun disappears from the record and Ay, a relatively elderly royal relative who bore the title 'god's father' and seems to have been influential during the reigns of both Akhenaten and Tutankhamun, took over the throne of Egypt. Although evidence is slim outside the meagre evidence for conspiracies, it seems clear that courtiers must have played an important role in managing smooth successions and that they also formed the main players within factions when the succession was disputed.

These extreme cases must represent the tip of the iceberg. There must have been a continual underlying stratum of faction and petty intrigue, flattery and back-stabbing, set against the perhaps volatile temper of an extremely powerful ruler who could destroy a courtier. Horemheb's pride in his ability to calm the pharaoh (see above) reflects more than the personal relationship of ruler and advisor: it speaks of power achieved through the ability to diffuse a situation that must have been dangerous for many courtiers. One of the most common genres of Egyptian literature at all periods is the instruction text (Lichtheim 1996; Coulon 2002). These preach restraint,

---

[31] The only known husbands of royal princesses at this period are reigning kings, as a result of which many relationships within the royal family were incestuous. Akhenaten probably 'married' at least three of his daughters, with his eldest, Meritaten, serving as 'great royal wife' in the latter part of his reign.

humility, fairness and respect for elders and superiors as the way to achieve success, happiness and a good burial (the ultimate aim of all Egyptians). The reason for the popularity of these texts becomes clear if they are interpreted as a guide to weathering the difficulties of court life: avoiding pitfalls and achieving success within a very hierarchical society. Recommendations not to engage in 'a mischievous errand, nor be friends with him who does it' (Lichtheim 1976: 150) prove particularly valuable advice within the dangerous world of court society and intrigue.

The residence city and the architectural settings of court life

The royal court was a social configuration reliant on the presence or proximity of the king. The dwelling place of the king formed the setting for court life, and spatial aspects of the palace were fundamental to configuring and expressing status within the court and to structuring the relationships between king and courtiers. The architecture was also of immense importance in projecting the king's authority and situating him physically in relation to other beings. Thus palaces are often located in close proximity to temples or even incorporated into them, expressing unequivocally the close relationship between king and god (O'Connor 1989; 1995; Spence forthcoming). Palaces were surrounded by high walls, excluding the majority of the population and promulgating an air of secrecy around activities within, as was also the case for temples.[32] The sheer scale of preserved palaces in relation to all buildings other than temples also emphasises their importance. Egyptian kings had a number of palaces around Egypt and, interestingly, these differ considerably in architectural layout.[33] Kings also moved around the country in boats and stayed in tents when on campaigns abroad; Akhenaten himself records that he stayed in a 'pavilion of matting' on an early visit to the site of his new city at Amarna (Murnane and van Siclen 1993: 100, 105). Elements of the court must have travelled with the king and must have been configured in these temporary settings as well as in the larger palaces.

The king's principal place of residence at any period was also the centre of administration and government, and was referred to simply as 'the Residence'. This seems to have comprised at the very least a dwelling place and official palace of the king, plus temples, institutional headquarters, ancillary

---

[32] For the semantic relationship between the notions of secrecy and seclusion in Egypt see Hoffmeier (1985: 171–98).

[33] For a summary of the most important evidence for New Kingdom palaces with bibliography see Lacovara (1997: 24–41, figs. 19–38, 43); O'Connor (1989, 1995); the latter focuses on interpreting the symbolic signficance of palace architecture.

structures and residential areas. Rolf Gundlach points to the important role played by the main state temple and royal necropolis in relation to the Residence, although it is so common to find that these were situated far from the Residence (Gundlach 2004: 229) that they can hardly have been considered a unity. Although the roots of the Eighteenth Dynasty were at Thebes – the location of a number of royal palaces, the state temple at Karnak and the royal necropolis now known as the Valley of the Kings – increasing emphasis had been placed on Memphis during the course of the Eighteenth Dynasty: royal palaces were sited there, while the elite cemetery at Sakkara attests to the important administrative activities in the region.

Textual information from the early Eighteenth Dynasty places the main royal palace at Thebes adjacent to the temple of Karnak, close to the pylon of the main entrance (O'Connor 1995: 272–4); no archaeological traces of the palace have yet been found. Amenhotep III built a major palace complex at Malkata on the west bank at Thebes for the celebration of his *sed*-festivals or jubilees, held in the last decade of his reign (Kemp 1989: 213–17). He also built a small, more isolated palace structure nearby at the site of Kom el-'Abd (Kemp 1977),[34] while the main residential palace was still situated on the east bank near Karnak (O'Connor 1989: 79). There were several New Kingdom palaces at Memphis, including one dating to the reign of Tuthmosis I, and we have textual evidence for 'mooring-places of Pharaoh', small structures in which the king could stay during his journeys around the country; estates might be attached to these to provide provisions for the royal retinue when they stayed in the palace (Kemp 1989: 218). Provincial palaces are also known from textual sources, and archaeologically from remains such as those at Medinet el-Ghurob (Kemp 1978). From the later New Kingdom, palaces were attached to the mortuary temples of kings, although the role of these structures is a matter of debate.

Akhenaten's royal residence at el-Amarna is the only example of a residence city for which we have very substantial archaeological remains, although a study by Peter Lacovara (1997) has highlighted similarities with the surviving features of other royal palatial centres such as Deir el-Ballas and Thebes. Four major palace structures can be identified at el-Amarna (Fig. 7.4), in addition to smaller royal pavilions within temples and at other ceremonial sites.[35] The major palaces seem to occur in pairs, with a relatively small ceremonial palace (the North Palace) situated near the large, poorly

[34] Although Kemp interprets the archaeological remains of the palace as a platform, the plan visible in the casemate construction of the foundations rather suggests that it was a complete building with a bedroom and columned halls.

[35] Kemp (1989: 261–317) provides an excellent introduction to the archaeology of the site.

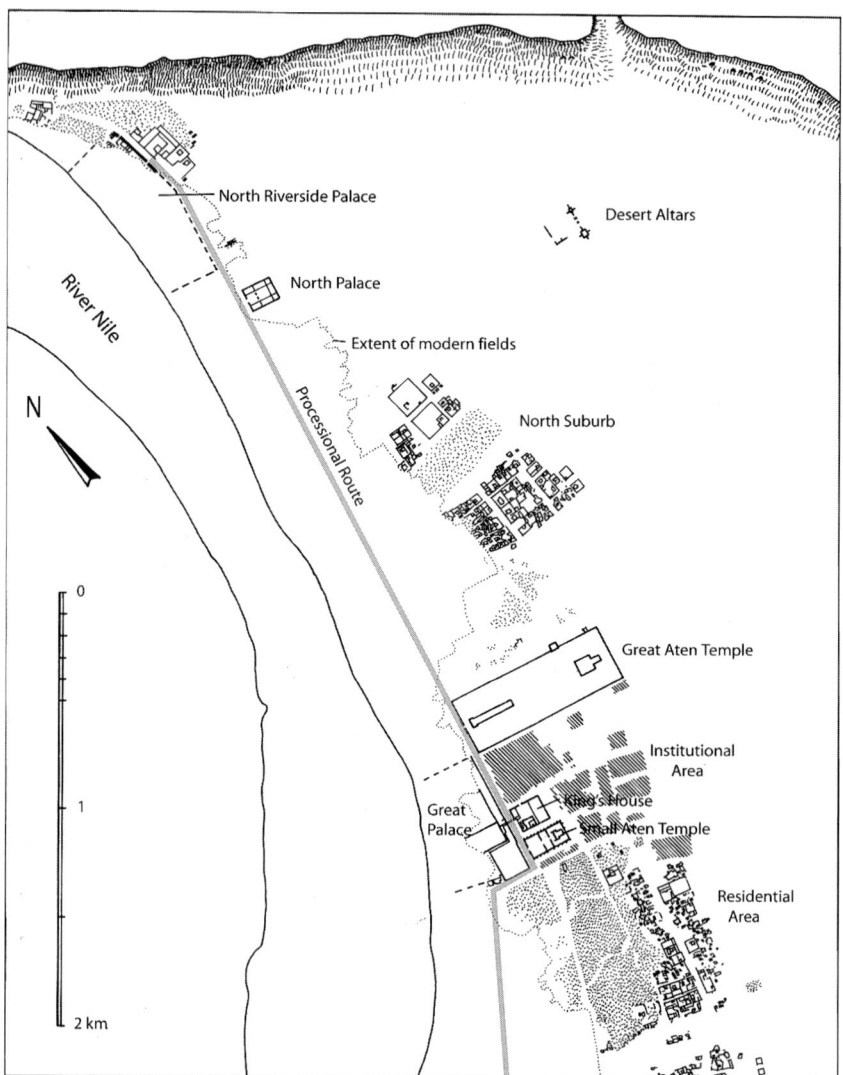

Figure 7.4 The Central City and North City at el-Amarna showing the location of the four principal palaces and the Aten Temples (adapted from Kemp 1989: figs. 89 and 91).

preserved residential palace at the far north of the site (the North Riverside Palace), while in the 'Central City' the enormous ceremonial Great Palace is linked by a bridge to the smaller King's House. Alongside the palaces, the two major state temples to the Aten dominate the Central City, whilst administrative buildings and institutional headquarters cluster around the King's House, clearly marking the palace as the institutional and governmental hub of the city (Kemp 1976). Residential suburbs were constructed to the north and south of the Central City. Akhenaten was probably the only king of the New Kingdom to construct his tomb outside Thebes: he began work on a new royal necropolis in a prominent valley to the east of his city. A series of diverse ceremonial settings were constructed around the outskirts of the natural bay in which the city was sited (Kemp 1995). He thus reintegrated state cult and the royal necropolis with the governmental and ceremonial aspects of kingship within a single residence city.

The area within the palace walls was the setting for most aspects of court life, and the very different architectural settings in existence in the distinct palaces at Amarna or Thebes suggest varied activities, although ascribing function to whole palaces or rooms within palaces remains problematical given the nature of our evidence.[36] In some palaces, the presence of members of the court is apparent and is structured architecturally through the provision of housing. The small palace of Amenhotep III at Kom el-'Abd was constructed on a raised brick platform which was approached by a broad ramp (Fig. 7.5).[37] Within the same enclosure wall, but built at ground level and divided from the palace itself by walls and courtyards, were the remains of seven houses within a single courtyard. One house is larger than the rest, although its whole plan is still smaller than the major room of the palace. Four smaller houses of identical plan and size are grouped together, while at the back of the court are two further houses, similar in scale to those found in the group of four but with a slightly different arrangement of rooms which suggests that they were of lesser importance. The complex perhaps provides accommodation for seven courtiers and their own families and staff, carefully differentiated from the king's residence and also distinguished from each other to reflect three ranking groups. To be chosen to accompany the king in such a restricted entourage must have been a sign of great favour, and the specific allocation of houses within would presumably have been carefully noted by contemporaries.

Residences for officials and court staff have also been found at Malkata (Lacovara 1997: 56–7, fig. 20). Close to the main palace complex was a group of three large houses and eleven smaller dwellings, clearly planned as a unit and built as an integral part of the complex. Further small houses were constructed behind the North Palace at the site, while the nearby unexcavated 'north village' shows signs of organic growth suggesting that it was not built as a part of the complex. The provision of housing for essential members

---

[36] O'Connor (1989) divides the palaces into governmental, ceremonial and residential palaces. There is likely to have been significant overlap in these functions between palaces.

[37] Such raised construction appears to have been common in New Kingdom palace architecture and is found in palaces at Ezbet Helmi and Deir el-Ballas (Lacovara 1997: fig. 43).

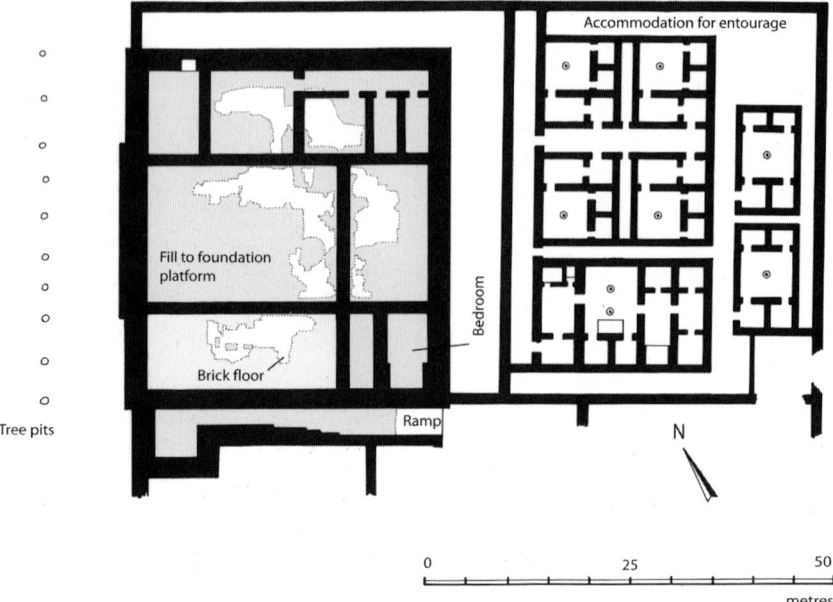

Figure 7.5 The remains of the palace of Amenhotep III at Kom el-'Abd. The palace itself has eroded down to below the level of the brick floor in many places and only the raised foundations remain. Accommodation for the entourage is to the east (adapted from Kemp 1977: fig. 2).

of the court or royal household thus appears to be a feature even of this larger palace, but the accommodation is still very limited indeed. Malkata served as the setting for important jubilee celebrations and presumably the majority of courtiers gathered there for the occasion were expected to find their own accommodation, camp or travel back to their houses in the main city on the east bank of the Nile.

At Amarna, very little in the way of accommodation for courtiers is found within palaces. Both the King's House (Fig. 7.6) and the North Palace (Fig. 7.7) contain a fairly large house within the grounds in addition to the palatial accommodation. It seems likely that this was for the use of a palace overseer as, in the case of the North Palace, it is situated within the service quarters. Other than that, only very small lodgings are found within the palace, presumably for more humble attendants and servants, although even then the provision of such accommodation seems very limited.[38] Houses also

[38] It should also be noted that dwellings can be very difficult to distinguish from places of work or 'offices' as in some cases the architecture is very similar. The role of smaller units within the palaces is therefore difficult to establish with certainty.

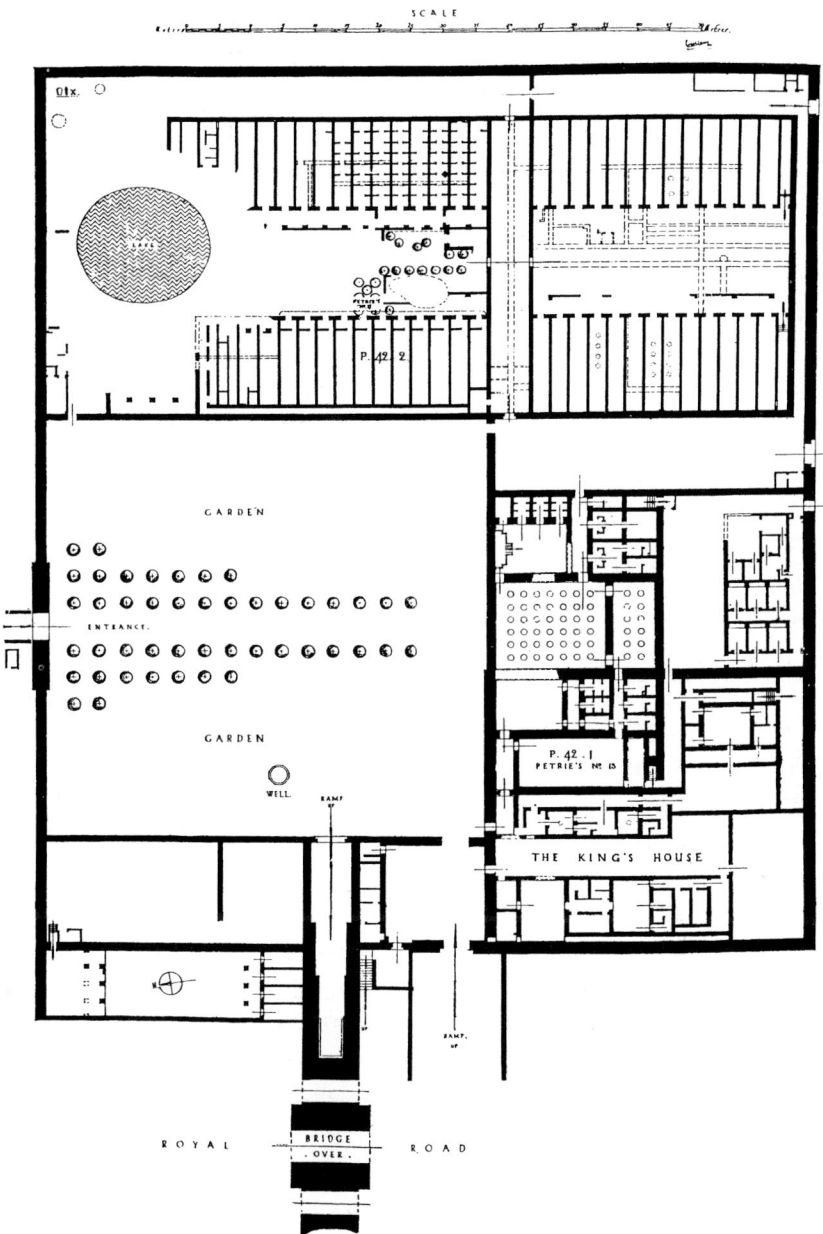

Figure 7.6 The King's House at el-Amarna. A bridge linked this palace with the Great Palace on the opposite side of the royal road (Pendlebury 1951: pl. XVI).

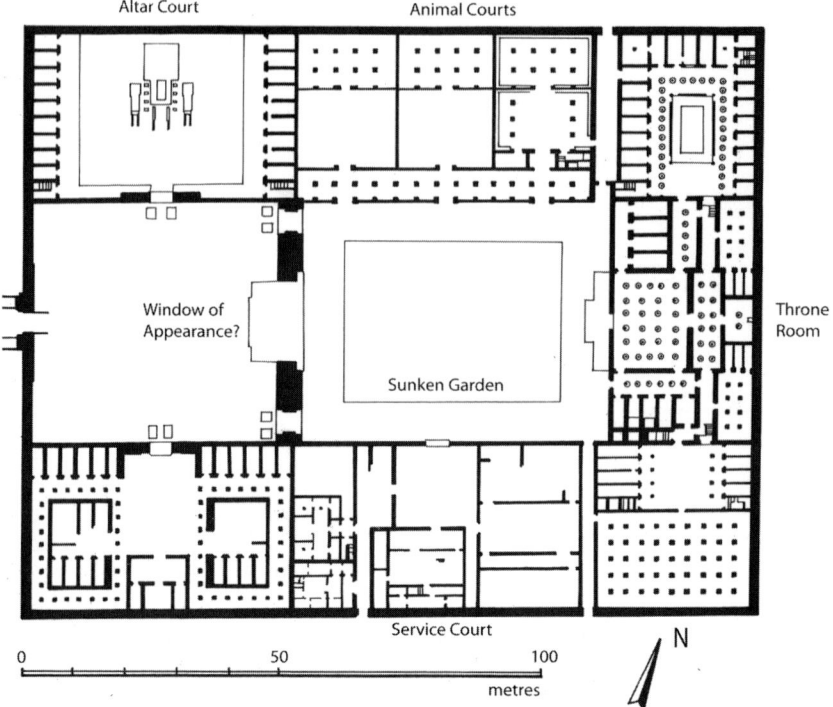

Figure 7.7 The North Palace at el-Amarna (adapted from Stevenson Smith 1981: fig. 304).

seem to have been provided for chief priests in proximity to their temples and for the overseers of institutions within those compounds. The majority of courtiers at Amarna seem to have been expected to construct their own houses, which they did in large numbers, creating residential suburbs to the north and south of the royal and administrative heart of the city. These houses in turn were surrounded by the smaller dwellings of dependants (Kemp 1989: fig. 97). Kemp (1989: 314) estimates that about half the houses at the site have been excavated and that, on the basis of size, we should estimate that between 120 and 240 of these belonged to 'officials'. These would have included those employed in the governmental and military institutions and the priesthood; among the largest of these are presumably found those who served as courtiers. The vast majority of these people probably also had dwellings in Thebes and/or Memphis, and many must also have had holdings in their home towns.

The architecture of palaces serves to differentiate the king from his people and to structure the relationships between the king and his courtiers. All palaces are walled and internally subdivided with varying degrees of complexity. To the majority of the population the interior of the palace would have been a mystery; to be allowed access to even the outer parts of a palace would have differentiated an individual from the majority of Egyptians and marked him or her out as privileged. Access within the palace was further controlled by door-keepers and courtiers, such as the overseers of the various parts of the inner palace (Murnane 1998: 216). How far a courtier was allowed to progress towards the inner parts of the palace would have been clearly readable to all others as a mark of status. Horemheb's Edict from Karnak makes it clear that it was a question not only of access but also of the manner of entry: 'They enter through the portals of . . . quickly, by horse, to the holy area, with a dog at their feet and an attendant at the rear' (Murnane 1995: 240). Presumably only the very privileged were permitted to ride into the palace and enter quickly with servants and dogs. Again, such specific details of behaviour, for which evidence very rarely survives in Egypt, would have been immediately readable both to eye-witnesses (i.e. other courtiers and servants) and, by report, to those excluded from the palace.

The status achieved through access to inner parts of the palace and other royal structures perhaps also goes some way towards explaining a couple of the more unusual aspects of Amarna period elite art. Private tombs at Amarna often depict plans of palaces and temples. These can be difficult to relate to the archaeological remains found on the ground; the confusion stemming partly from Egyptian drawing conventions but also unquestionably from a degree of inaccuracy, which was clearly not considered a problem by the artists and tomb owners. These depictions provide a temporal setting for the royal activities depicted in scenes, but the architectural representations also give the impression that the tomb owner has knowledge of the layout of the interior of royal buildings (however mistaken this actually is) and that he therefore has unfettered access to all parts of palaces and temples. The representations could then be interpreted as an indication of status. Secondly, stelae depicting intimate scenes of the royal family relaxing beneath the rays of the Aten (e.g. Arnold 1996: fig. 88) have been found as objects of devotion in prominent locations in a few private houses at the site. Although the emphasis in interpreting these objects and their contexts has been on the royal family as the major focus of private devotion (Ikram 1989) it is perhaps also significant that these individuals are depicting private activities of the royal family within their homes, again displaying prominently their privileged access.

Differentiation between the king and those around him is also established architecturally within the palace building. The focus of the palace is the royal throne, raised on a dais. It is usually centrally positioned within the throne room, and the approach to the dais is carefully structured architecturally and often reflected in decoration (Kemp 1989: fig. 77; Weatherhead 1992). Palaces usually also contain a private suite including a niched bedroom for the king. Elsewhere I have divided the architectural ordering of Egyptian palaces into axial, semi-axial and non-axial structures based on the relationship between the entry and the approach to the throne room. This distinction most probably reflects the nature of ceremonial activity that took place within them, although it should be emphasised that there is likely to be considerable overlap (Spence 1998: 209–14; forthcoming). The bilateral symmetry found in axial palaces throws emphasis on the enthroned king and focuses attention on the distance between a person arriving at the gate and the king, an impression further heightened by the many liminal spaces which must be crossed in order to enter his presence. The North Palace (Fig. 7.7) and the Great Palace at Amarna are examples of axial palaces.[39]

Non-axial palaces feature a large columned hall approached through a smaller columned hall. Beside or near the large columned hall is a smaller room containing a throne dais. There is no grand or formal entrance to the interior of the palace and no axial entrance into the throne room. This is a more private setting for the king, perhaps even the 'audience hall' in which he conducted day-to-day business and consulted with his most important officials and courtiers. The King's House at Amarna (Fig. 7.6) and the North Palace at Malkata are of this type. Semi-axial palaces have non-axial entrance sequences but internal structures which relate the throne room of the king to a number of subordinate chambers; examples include the so-called Harim Palace at Malkata and parts of the eastern wing of the Amarna Great Palace.

The remote location of Amenhotep III's palace at Kom el-'Abd (a non-axial palace) suggests that it served as a retreat from the centres of court life (Kemp 1977), and the palace within it thus seems likely to represent the bare minimum of an architectural setting within which the king could function and court life could take place. The majority of smaller royal palaces in the New Kingdom are actually of a very similar size, as are the more private suites of rooms within much larger palaces (Spence forthcoming), suggesting a common understanding of the core features making up the king's dwelling. It is interesting to note that the King's House at Amarna (Fig. 7.6), which appears from its architecture, lack of axiality and tortuous entrance sequence to be the most private of royal settings, is also the place which Kemp identifies

---

[39] Also the Palace of Merenptah at Memphis, treated in depth by O'Connor (1995).

as the likely centre of government, given the fact that it is surrounded by offices and institutional buildings (Kemp 1976; 1989: 287–8). Although this combination seems counter-intuitive to modern architectural readings, the role of the domestic setting as the site of royal decision-making is well attested in court studies (Duindam 2003: 223, 234–48) and goes some way towards explaining the prominent role and influence that might be accorded to the royal family, favourites and members of the household.

Within the many royal palaces, the king, and sometimes also his family, interacted with courtiers and members of his household. In addition to his architectural setting and throne, he was distinguished from those around him by his dress, crowns and other royal regalia, perhaps by his authoritative speech and also by his posture, gestures and behaviour. Amarna tomb scenes suggest that few stood upright in the presence of the king and there are clear degrees of bowing, grovelling and scraping the ground adopted by foreign dignitaries, courtiers and servants in the presence of the king (Figs. 7.2, 7.3, 7.8–7.10). It seems likely that this is a fair representation of interaction in the palace. The Amarna tomb scenes and other objects from the site also show the royal family embracing, kissing, relaxing and eating in a manner entirely alien to the strict decorum usually governing Egyptian art (e.g. Arnold 1996: figs. 88, 93–8, 108). Yet courtiers are not depicted acting in the same relaxed manner and it seems that such familiar behaviour may also have served to differentiate the king's interaction with his family from his formal engagement with inferiors.[40]

Court ceremonial

Ceremonial at court covers a range of activities, from occasional festivals of kingship such as coronations, *sed*-festivals (jubilees) and funerals,[41] through specific court ceremonies, such as the appointment and rewarding of officials, to ritualised everyday activities of the king including his regular

---

[40] The only other representations of such behaviour are found in ceramic statuettes of monkeys, which are sometimes shown driving chariots or embracing each other with a similar lack of reserve. However, while these have been interpreted as satirical, potentially indicating resistance to such practices and disapproval of the regime (Frankfort and Pendlebury 1933: 99), it is worth noting that the majority of the statuettes derive from the houses of the courtiers who profited most from the king (Freed et al. 1999: 156), and also that the king himself included a silver statuette of a monkey and her child in gifts sent to one of his counterparts in the Near East: '1 (female) monkey, with its daughter on its lap, of silver' (Moran 1992: 30).

[41] In Tutankhamun's tomb a group of courtiers headed by the vizier is shown dragging the king's mummy in its bier (Reeves 1990: 72).

interaction with courtiers; I will discuss briefly examples of major festivities involving the court, the 'Window of Appearance' reward scenes and the everyday activities of the court.

Major festivals

Akhenaten celebrated a *sed*-festival at Karnak in the early years of his reign before the residence was moved to Amarna (Gohary 1992). The timing of his jubilee celebration was unusual: this ancient ceremony associated with the renewal of divine kingship was usually celebrated after thirty years on the throne and perhaps more frequently thereafter; Amenhotep III had celebrated jubilees in years 30, 34 and 37 (Kemp 1989: 213–17). Much of the evidence for Akhenaten's *sed*-festival derives from a building he constructed at East Karnak, consisting of a massive colonnaded court decorated with statues of the king and relief scenes depicting episodes in the jubilee festivities; relief scenes deriving from other structures built by Akhenaten at Karnak are also known. The king obviously features very prominently in the decoration but courtiers, priests, guards and members of the household are also shown. Courtiers are repeatedly shown bowing in the presence of the king (Redford 1984: 114–15, fig. 7.13) and in one scene a courtier pours a libation (Redford 1984: 122). Servants bustle around the palaces and bearers carry the king's palanquin, while attendants and soldiers are also present. A scene reconstructed from fragments shows the king wearing his jubilee costume leaving the palace (Redford 1984: fig. 7.12). As he emerges, the chief priest of the sun cult precedes him, bowing and backing away from the king and burning incense to mark the passage of the ruler. Twelve chamberlains are shown prostrate before him. Feasting seems to have been an important part of the ceremonies.

Although the gods (or in Akhenaten's case the Aten) played an important role in the *sed*-festival, courtiers, the royal household, priests and officials would have been the major participants and witnesses, alongside the royal family. The importance of their role is clear from the surviving scenes from Karnak. Comparable but very fragmentary scenes dating to the Fifth Dynasty and the reign of Amenhotep III have been found which show that the important role played by courtiers was by no means unique to Akhenaten's reign (Redford 1984: 125). However, one very interesting difference in the representation of courtiers occurs between the reliefs carved in Amenhotep III's reign and those produced for Akhenaten. In Amenhotep III's reliefs prominent courtiers and priests are named while Akhenaten's reliefs use only titles: the courtiers are thus stripped of their personal identity in his depictions and appear in the presence of the king only as functionaries (Redford 1984: 131–2).

In year 12 of Akhenaten's reign, when king and court were well established at Amarna, Akhenaten held a 'Reception of Foreign Tribute' which is represented in some of the private tombs at the site. The reliefs in Huya's tomb (Davies 1905b: pls. XIII–XV) show the king and queen being carried to the site of the festival in a palanquin accompanied by the royal daughters and attendants, while the relief in the tomb of Meryre II (Fig. 7.8; Davies 1905a: pl. XXXVII) shows the royal family seated in a pavilion. A priest censes the empty palanquin, recently vacated by the king. Courtiers fuss near the entrance to the pavilion, and around it are lined up grandees from all over the Egyptian empire and sphere of influence, many bearing tribute or gifts and many with their arms raised in adoration of the royal family. Although these scenes do not show the detailed episodes of the Karnak *sed*-festival reliefs, the splendour of the occasion and the organisation that must have gone into it are clear from the depictions. They also illustrate the fact that Akhenaten's court did not exist in isolation: there was frequent interaction between courtiers and emissaries from other states and the Egyptian court was on display. The potential for foreign influence from royal wives, envoys (Egyptian and foreign) and gifts is very significant. An Amarna Letter chides Akhenaten for making foreign emissaries stand around in the sun for hours on end, presumably as part of one of his ceremonial reviews (Moran 1992: 39).

The 'Window of Appearance' reward scenes

The 'Window of Appearance' scene in which the king rewards and sometimes promotes a courtier is one of the most common scenes found in Amarna tombs. It is also the only common type of depiction which focuses on direct interaction between king and courtier: although courtiers appear in many Amarna period scenes of royal activity, the attention of the king is rarely focused on these individuals. The scene is always architecturally structured and highly formalised. The king, often accompanied by the queen and royal daughters, appears at a 'window' which is raised on a platform and fronted by a canopy (Fig. 7.9). The king leans out of the window and tosses golden collars to the courtier who stands in front of the window with his arms raised, while other officials tie the collars around his neck. Texts make it clear that the golden collars usually shown were accompanied by other gifts; scribes are shown making records, presumably of value given the presence of scales in some depictions (e.g. Davies 1905: pl. XVI). The ceremony singled out a

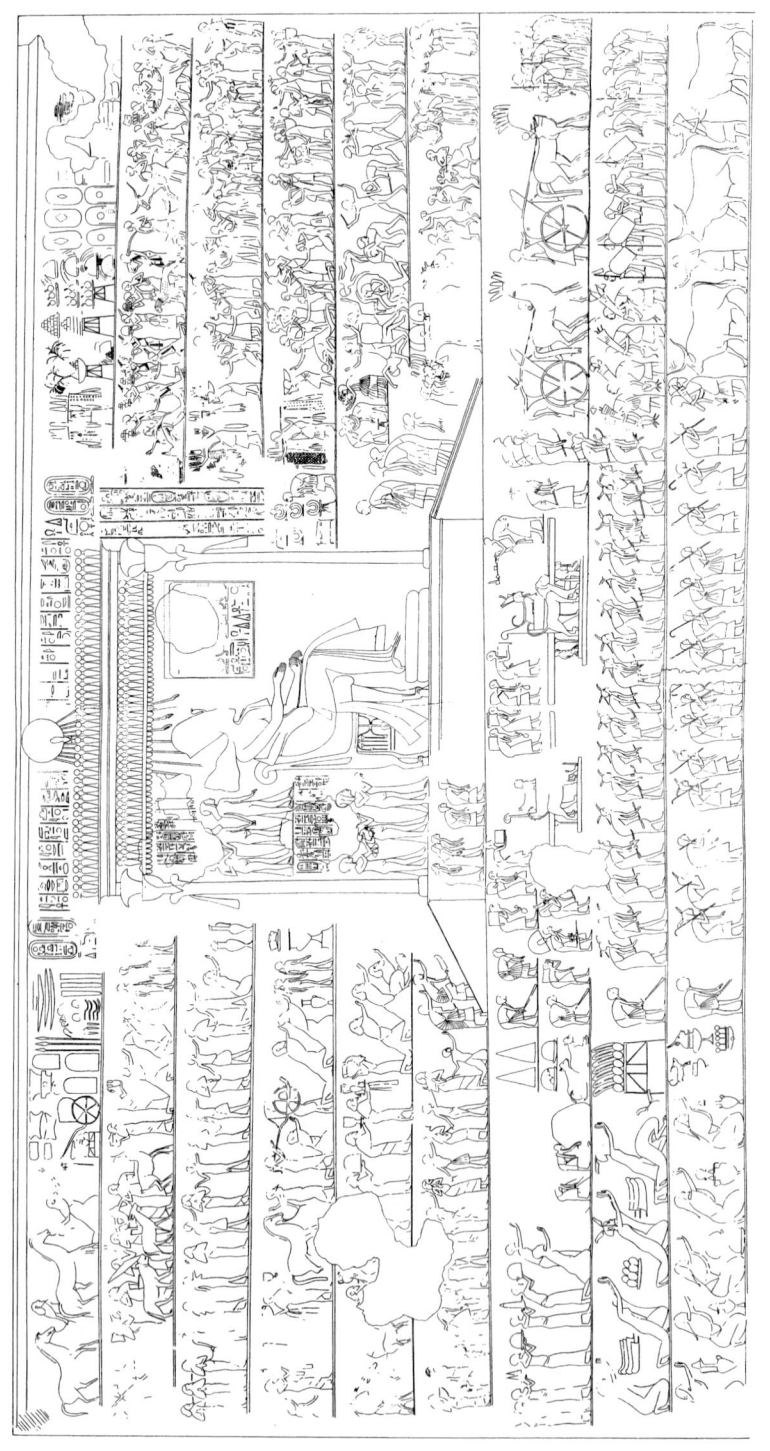

Figure 7.8 The reception of foreign tribute in year 12. From the tomb of Meryra II at el-Amarna (Davies 1905a: pl. XXXVII).

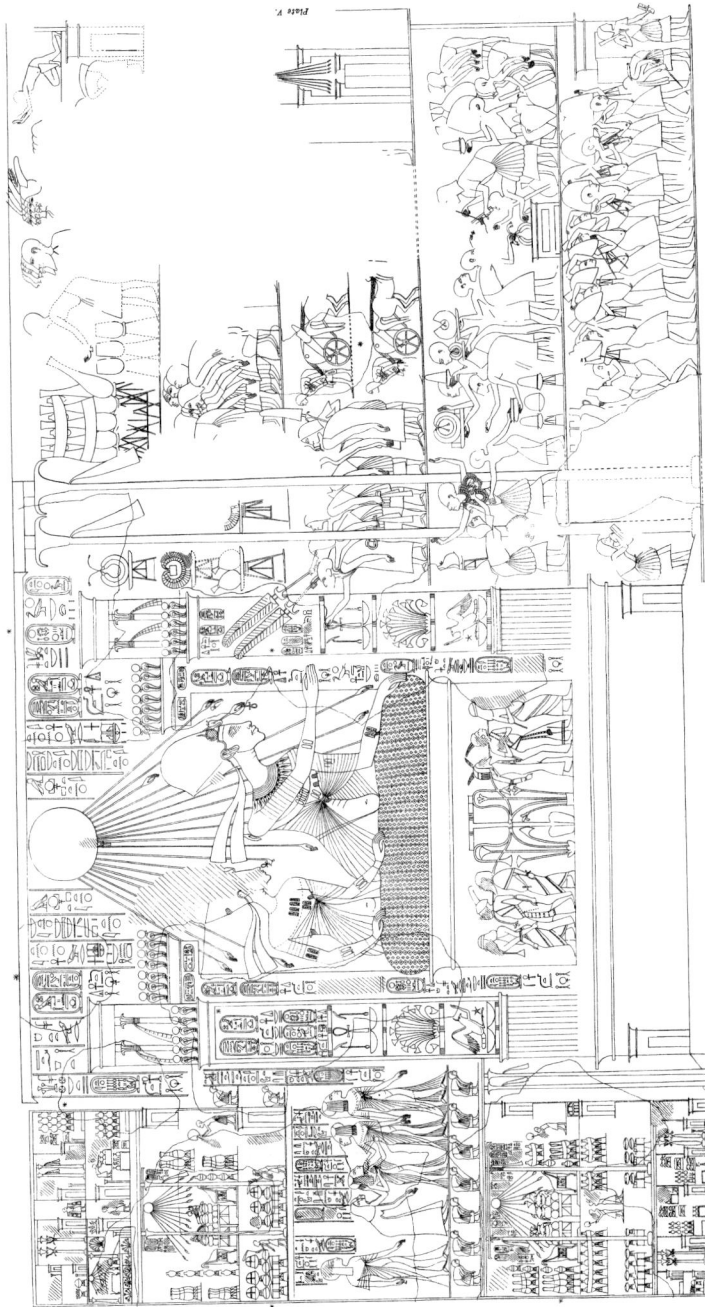

Figure 7.9 Akhenaten and Nefertiti at a Window of Appearance rewarding the official Parennefer who stands with his arms upraised (in the second register up) wearing the gold necklaces he has been thrown by the king. The palace is represented behind the window (Davies 1908b: pl. IV).

courtier, bestowing both wealth and prestige. The frequency of its depiction in the tombs at Amarna suggests that it was the highlight of an official's career.

The architectural setting of the scene is particularly interesting as it illustrates the care taken to differentiate king from courtier in representations of direct interaction. The tomb scenes situate the windows within palaces, although in one instance the depiction appears to show a window in a royal rest-house within a temple complex (Davies 1903: pls. XXV–XXVI) and a window is also shown on a royal barge (Davies 1908a: pl. V). The majority of representations appear to locate the windows between the outer court of the palace and the inner parts of the building, on the axis of the palace, where this can be established (see Fig. 7.2, top left).[42] Presence at the ceremony was thus restricted to those allowed access to the palace, temple or royal barge but participants were not allowed to enter the inner rooms. Instead the king emerged from the mysterious sanctity of the inner parts of his residence to interact formally with the courtiers. The window, lying on axis with the throne room, provides a physical barrier between king and courtier through which, crucially, neither can pass, stressing the ontological difference between humans and the divine king. Other aspects of the architecture also stress this difference: the king was raised above the level of the assembled crowd while the window was decorated with potent images of royal authority. At Amarna, where a split lintel results in the window being more of a balcony than a true window,[43] the external canopy would have thrown the façade of the window and the courtier being rewarded into shadow, whilst bright sun would have flooded down, both highlighting and rendering shadowy and indistinct the figure of the king in the window. This

[42] Egyptian drawing conventions, although highly logical, can be difficult to read. The Amarna representations of palaces are governed by schematised plans but include elements in section and elevation. The actual location of the Windows of Appearance on the ground at Amarna remains controversial. I would locate the principal windows in the North Palace (Spence 1999) and perhaps also the Great Palace. I interpret them primarily as part of axial or ceremonial palace structures. However note that Kemp (1976) locates windows in the King's House and Small Aten Temple. It is clear that they may also have formed elements of other structures from which the king made an appearance such as the royal barge.

[43] Although in the later preserved example at Medinet Habu this feature is indeed a window (Kemp 1989: 211–13, fig. 73), the Amarna examples actually seem to be balconies as they have a broken lintel and were probably unroofed. The split lintel is a common feature of religious architecture at Amarna. In traditional Egyptian architecture the lintels of doorways through which the king passed on his way through a temple were decorated with a winged sun-disk, associating his directed movement with that of the sun and all its attendant cosmological imagery. At Amarna, the lintels of doorways are instead divided so that the direct contact between the actual rays of the sun and the king remained unbroken as he moved through the building.

relationship between the sun-disk and the king is graphically depicted in the reliefs as the hands in which the sun's rays terminate reach down and touch the king.

However, many of these same courtiers were probably allowed access to the inner palace in other circumstances and presumably interacted less formally with the king during the daily routine of life in the city (for which see below). The 'Window of Appearance' scene was popular for a number of reasons. First, it formalised the relationship between king and courtier and crystallised it in a manner which allowed this relationship to be depicted; this was particularly important because each scene shows the king distinguishing one individual. Second, both the ceremony itself and the rewards distributed had important communicative value in stressing the status of the individual and his favour with the king. The rewards are likely to have had significant value (gold is prominent amongst the gifts) but luxury items are also found: among the rewards thrown to Ay is a pair of red gloves which he is shown wearing as he emerges from the ceremony to be greeted outside the palace by members of his entourage (Fig. 7.10; Davies 1908a: pls. XXIX–XXX).[44]

The Amarna tomb scenes feature only the highest officials and courtiers who had tomb chapels in which such scenes could be recorded. It is therefore difficult at Amarna to establish the frequency of such ceremonies or whether they were used to reward those other than top officials. Horemheb's edict from Karnak refers to the king's use of the Window of Appearance every ten days to watch a parade of the palace guards, during which he called to officers by name and tossed them rewards additional to their basic rations (Murnane 1995: 239–40). As part of the ceremony each man was seated (presumably in the courtyard outside the window) and served with food. This suggests that at least in the post-Amarna period the window was used regularly for formalised interactions between the king and broader sections of the royal household and other officials.

Royal favour expressed materially had significant communicative value, which was emphasised still further by the ritual nature of these reward scenes in which access to the palace, interaction with the king, individual preferment and material enrichment were combined in one representation. It seems to have been considered acceptable to beg signs of favour from the king (often in the form of burial equipment) and these were occasionally recorded. An Old Kingdom tomb inscription describes asking for a favour and receiving more than was requested: 'When I begged of the majesty of my lord that there be brought for me a sarcophagus of white stone from Tura,

---

[44] A pair of intricately woven gloves was found in the tomb of Tutankhamun (Reeves 1990: 156–7).

his majesty had a royal seal-bearer cross over with a company of sailors under his command, to bring me this sarcophagus from Tura. It came with him in a great barge of the court, together with its lid, a doorway, lintel, two doorjambs and a libation-table. Never before had the like been done for any servant' (Lichtheim 1973: 19).

Daily activity within the palace

Although we have little information on day-to-day activity within the palace there are clear indications that the king's routine was formalised and that behaviour within the palace was carefully structured. 'The Duties of the Vizier' is an important text dating to at least as early as the beginning of the Eighteenth Dynasty and outlines the principal duties of the king's chief minister (van den Boorn 1988; Lorton 1991). Every morning the vizier received reports on the 'affairs of the two lands (i.e. Egypt)' in his house. He then proceeded to the palace; his entry is described as follows:

He shall enter in the direction of the *pr-ᶜ3* (Great House) facing the treasurer, as he takes his position at the northern flagstaff, and the vizier shall then move in from the east in the doorway of the great double gate. Then the treasurer shall come to meet him and report to him, saying, 'All your affairs are sound and prosperous, and every responsible functionary has reported to me, saying, "All your affairs are sound and prosperous"'. Then the vizier shall report to the treasurer, saying, 'All your affairs are [sound] and pros[perous], and the closing of all the enclosures on time and their opening on time have been reported to me by every responsible functionary'. Then after each of the two of[ficials] has reported to the other, the vizier shall send to open every doorway of the *pr-nsw* (palace). (Lorton 1991: 296)

This shows the extent to which the meeting of the treasurer and the vizier was ritualised. Following the opening of the palace, the vizier entered and went to greet the king. The text stresses the ceremonial aspect of this activity rather than the nature of the meeting, but the fact that information on the state of affairs was passed on to the king can be inferred (Lorton 1991: 307). Old Kingdom evidence points to the importance of the royal levée with very high-status courtiers bearing titles associated with the 'House of Morning' involved with the king's toilet (Kees 1914; Blackman 1918: esp. 149–2). There is little evidence for similar activity from later periods, although the 'great chamberlain in the Great House' Amenhotep who served under Amenhotep III seems to have been involved in the ceremonial dressing of the king (Murnane 1998: 216 n. 173). Akhenaten's chamberlain, Tutu, left an account of his behaviour in the palace and morning meetings with the king, although the stress here is on the king giving orders rather than receiving information. 'My voice is not loud in the king's house. I do not swagger in the palace . . . I act only according to what he decrees as my charge . . . for every morning he rises early to instruct me.' He also reveals that he does not accept bribes and he does not think bad thoughts in the company of the favourites (Murnane 1995: 192).

Conducting temple rituals was an important aspect of royal activity and many of the tomb scenes from Amarna depict the king travelling between the palace and temple in a gilded palanquin (Davies 1905: pl. XIII) or chariot (Fig. 7.2; Davies 1903: pl. X). These become significant processions: the royal family is often accompanied by attendants, and guards line the route. Longer journeys were presumably taken in the royal barges depicted in the tomb of May (Davies 1908a: pl. V). Preparing for such journeys and accompanying the king to the temple or further afield presumably formed a major part of court life.

The process of decision-making must also have formed a prominent part of life in the palace.[45] Lorton points to texts which 'confirm the very real connection, in the eyes of the ancient Egyptians, between the physical palace and the royal throne within it, and the king's exercise of his functions of governance' (Lorton 1991: 306); he provides a particularly clear exposition of the relationship between the king and the vizier in terms of decision-making. A Middle Kingdom stela describes its owner as 'preceding the courtiers who draw nigh to the palace; knower of [the utterance (?)] of difficult (?) words (?) on the day the courtiers speak; who reports to the king in solitude; who is near of place on the day of foregathering; one to whom the king divulges his speech to act as a gateway for it' (Fischer 1960: 261). This points to the ritualised activity masking the actual exercise of decision-making: the ranking of courtiers approaching the palace, the difficulties inherent in advising the king within the setting of the council chamber, and the courtier charged with broadcasting the king's decision following a private meeting. The chamberlain Tutu's tomb inscription, quoted above, suggests a similar situation at Amarna (Murnane 1995: 192).

Königsnovelle texts refer to the king sitting in his 'audience hall' consulting with his advisors. Horemheb's Karnak Edict specifies that individuals were arranged according to role and rank within the audience hall: 'I have arranged the protocol of the inner palace, the custom of the inner quarters of the king's companions. I have set my house to . . . , they . . . the heralds

---

[45] Goelet (1986) also touches on the important governmental role of the palace although his focus is on ceremonial activity.

of the council chamber, according to their rank, while "spreading holiness" throughout the entire house, and while the members of the king's entourage are at their exact places and the Thirty are at their customary positions' (Murnane 1995: 240). The ritualised nature of activity within the palace is clear here, as is the importance attached to protocol.[46] Reports might also be made within such a context (Lorton 1991: 306) and ambassadors from important states in the Near East would presumably also have been received within the palace complex, presumably again in the audience hall.

Feasting was clearly of great importance within the palace.[47] References in the Amarna Letters suggest that foreign rulers expected invitations to dine at the palace (Moran 1992: 7) although presumably such invitations were rarely, if ever, taken up in person. Evidence for feasting or the provision of food for the court is significant (e.g. Murnane 1995: 237). Horemheb's Karnak Edict seems to suggest that the guard feasted outside in a courtyard while the king was present at the Window of Appearance (Murnane 1995: 239). Papyrus Boulaq 18 (late Middle Kingdom) lists officials feasting at the palace, although Quirke suggests that the royal family was not actually present (Quirke 1990: 42–3). It thus seems likely that the royal family actually dined separately at feasts: either in a separate room or somewhere else altogether (cf. Brosius in this volume on similar Achaemenid practices). Amarna reliefs from Karnak depict the king and queen feasting in the main room of the palace (Redford 1984: pl. 16), with food piled in front of them, waited on by servants. Reliefs from the tomb of Huya at Amarna show Akhenaten and Nefertiti dining with the king's mother, Tiye, and the royal daughters (Fig. 7.3; Davies 1905b: pls. IV–VII). Courtiers are in attendance and Huya himself directs the people waiting on the king. However, none of the courtiers is shown eating in the presence of the royal family. Troops of musicians play beneath the main scene.

External appearance was clearly considered of great importance amongst courtiers, and changing styles of dress, hair and jewellery can be traced from surviving private statues and images. Wearing clean, white linen was considered a mark of status in Egypt at all periods: presumably having clean clothes indicated that one did not engage in manual activities. However, cloth was a valuable commodity and the amount of cloth required to create a particular garment seems to have been indicative of status: thus the Amarna reliefs contrast the loin-cloths and short kilts of soldiers and servants with the three-quarter-length kilts of higher-status officials (see Fig. 7.10; for

---

[46] Compare arrangements for imperial audiences in Han China: van Ess in this volume.

[47] As it was in Egyptian society in general: scenes of feasting are prominent in Eighteenth Dynasty tombs.

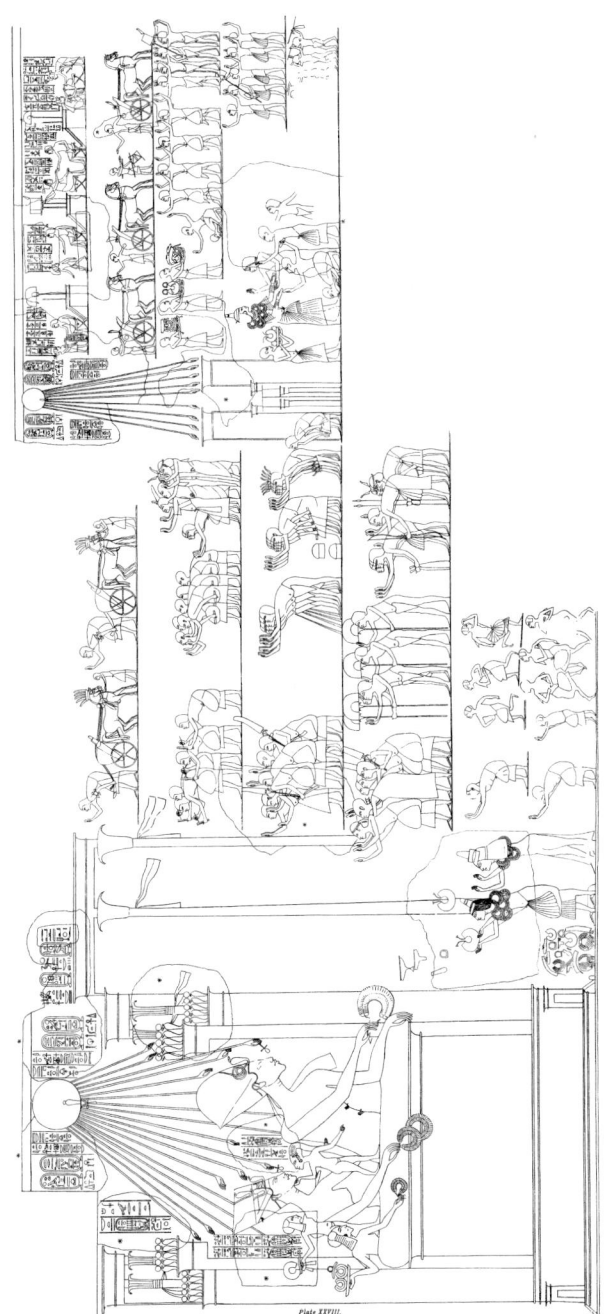

Figure 7.10 Reward scene from the tomb of Ay. Ay and his wife catch the rewards thrown from the Window of Appearance by the royal family. Outside the palace (*upper right*), Ay is greeted by his supporters (Davies 1908b: pls. XXIX–XXX).

Plate XXVIII.

clothing see Vogelsang-Eastwood 1993). The highest-ranking men wear a three-quarter-length tunic over which a kilt is tied with a billowing fold of cloth falling at the front.[48] Quality of cloth was also important and cloths were graded according to the fineness of the weave (Vogelsang-Eastwood 2000: 285). High-status clothes in the New Kingdom are also often depicted as semi-transparent, presumably an indication of the fineness and delicacy of the cloth. Coloured and embroidered clothes are known from the tomb of Tutankhamun and occasional archaeological finds (Vogelsang-Eastwood 2000: 278–81), although coloured garments are rarely depicted in tomb scenes, except on foreigners. Sandals seem frequently to have been removed as a mark of respect in the king's presence: few are shown wearing sandals in the king's presence in private tomb scenes from Amarna, while Horemheb's Karnak Edict seems specifically to refer to wearing sandals in the council chamber as a special privilege accorded to the highest officials. The Middle Kingdom story of Sinuhe refers to 'the choice perfume of the king and his favourite courtiers' (Lichtheim 1973: 233) and cosmetics and perfumes are also commonly found amongst burial goods.

The life of the Amarna courtier beyond the palace

The king and the palace thus seem to have been the major focus of elite activity both at Amarna and at other periods of Egyptian history. The extent to which officials were involved in palace life must have varied, with some based in the palace itself as court officials while others played important roles as priests or military officials and as such were presumably based at temples or in the institutional structures found in the Central City at Amarna. These men were presumably also close to the king (as is certainly suggested by many of their titles) and thus also played a role at court. The possession of a tomb was considered a mark of great status; Kemp (1989: 314–15) points out that there are too few tombs at Amarna to correspond with the number of officials, and suggests that a tomb-plot was allocated as a favour by the king. This appears to be confirmed by a statement on a small votive stela from the tomb of Any: 'We (?) have seen the good things which the good ruler has done to his Scribe of the Altar. He has ordered for him a goodly burial in Akhetaten' (Davies 1908a: 10). Other textual references from the

---

[48] Only as a result of the introduction of the vertical loom in the Eighteenth Dynasty did it become possible to weave cloths of the width to allow such differentiation in dress. Old and Middle Kingdom clothes are depicted as tighter and more restrictive.

Amarna tombs confirm that the king provides burials: 'May you grant me the good funeral which is your Ka's to give, in the tomb in which you decreed for me to rest' (Murnane 1995: 144; see also 178, 183). The Amarna tomb scenes are very focused on royal activity as the source of status, prestige and material wealth. The Window of Appearance scenes indicate time after time the importance of royal favour, and courtiers must have vied continually for positions of influence despite the paucity of evidence for such behaviour at this period.

All courtiers and officials seem to have constructed mansions at Amarna, although a few of the most important of them also had 'official' residences (found adjacent to temples and within institutional buildings and palaces). Officials were able to express their status and wealth through the size of their houses and by means of particular status symbols within them (Crocker 1985; Tietze 1985; 1986; Shaw 1992). A few houses show evidence of significant enlargement when the circumstances of the house owner improved (Spence 2004: 146–8). Hospitality also seems to have been an important part of life amongst the elite: feasting with music and dancers is frequently depicted on Theban tomb wall paintings and the scenes show both men and women gathering together. Such social activities were presumably also prominent at Amarna. The royal family was sometimes represented in these houses within shrines as objects of worship.

There are certain parallels between palace architecture and elite houses at Amarna in terms of spatial layout. This is likely to reflect parallels in the hierarchical nature of social relations structured by architecture:[49] although the individual courtier was clearly subordinate at court and existed within a strict ranking system relative to his peers, within his own home he was master. He sat to receive guests in the principal hall of his house on a chair placed on a brick dais. A separate dwelling constructed within the grounds of his house was most probably for a deputy or chief attendant: this subordinate role was in fact a privileged position which might even involve access to the palace (Murnane 1995: 240). Outside the enclosure wall of the courtier's house dependants constructed small dwellings close to the source of their own income and status (Kemp 1989: 294, fig. 98). The dual position of the

[49] Lacovara (1997: 57 60) argues that Amarna houses are not typical of Egyptian domestic architecture but are a conscious borrowing from palace design. However, clear parallels for the layout of the Amarna houses can be found in the Middle Kingdom planned town of Lahun (Arnold 1989) and in New Kingdom houses at sites such as Malkata and Amara West, suggesting that the explanation is more complex than this. The difficulty in assessing the relationship between Amarna houses and structures elsewhere has been exacerbated by difficulties in interpreting Egyptian architectural drawings (Spence 2004).

courtier within the hierarchy at court and in his own milieu is well illustrated by Ay's reward scene (Fig. 7.10; Davies 1908: pls. XXIX–XXX). In the main part of the scene Ay is rewarded by the king, the Queen and three princesses at the Window of Appearance. Ay and his wife are shown slightly bent (there are at least four distinct depths of bow visible in this one scene, apparently relating at least in part to rank) with their arms raised in adoration and to catch the rewards thrown to them. However, as soon as Ay moves beyond the palace gates he is shown standing upright. Although those waiting outside do not bow to him they raise their arms in jubilation, a few kneel before him (and the trays of rewards) and one kisses his feet. The focus of the attention of onlookers shifts from the king inside the palace to Ay himself outside it. A similar sequence of events is shown in the tomb of Tutu (Davies 1908b: pls. XIX–XX): here supporters of Tutu kiss the ground before him.

This illustrates the deeply hierarchical nature of Egyptian society and probably goes some way towards explaining the embeddedness of the social structure of the court within that society (cf. the similar observations of Brosius in this volume, on Achaemenid Persia). As discussed above, the relationship between king and courtier is expressed through service and subordination on the part of the courtier and the giving of favour in the form of rewards and titles (along with the accompanying income) on the part of the king. Manifestations of service and favour within this king–courtier relationship dominate the historical record. However, if one looks at a broader range of – admittedly rather limited – evidence, it is clear that the hierarchy stretches far beyond this. The king himself serves the gods through temple ritual and by building and fighting on behalf of the gods. Akhenaten himself is shown prostrate before the Aten, subordinating himself and his family to the gods, and even as far back as the Pyramid Texts the king makes himself useful to the gods through service in some of the texts: for example in rowing Re to the west (Faulkner 1969: 158).[50] The relationship between king and gods is usually expressed in royal texts as filial (i.e. subordinate but related). The subordination of courtiers and officials to the king has been discussed at length here, and the subordination of Ay's entourage has also been mentioned. In a fascinating study of servant figurines placed in Old Kingdom elite tombs, Ann Macy Roth has pointed out that the majority of these figures bear the names of close family members of the deceased courtier, and she interprets the relevance of these as allowing subordinates to participate in the afterlife of the courtier through provision of menial service (Roth 2002).

---

[50] In many other utterances in the Pyramid Texts, however, the gods are said to serve the king.

Conversely, the king is given favour by the gods for his service, expressed through long life, prosperity and military victories. Members of the elite would presumably reward their subordinates and dependants financially and provide them with titles and privileges. One particular favour involved depicting the dependant within the tomb chapel of the courtier or official, thus allowing him to participate in the offering cult for the tomb owner. This is particularly prominent in Middle Kingdom tombs such as those at Beni Hasan (e.g. Parkinson 1991: 78–81). However, in the small tomb of Any at Amarna were found six small votive stelae (Davies 1908a: 9–11, pls. XXI–XXIII; Murnane 1995: 124–5). Five of these show the individual dedicating the stela offering to or making recitations for Any. The sixth shows Any being driven by 'The charioteer of the Royal Scribe Any', showing that courtiers themselves must have given titles (or at least named positions) to their subordinates. All the dedicatees have titles, even if only 'servant', although it is not clear that this title was bestowed by Any himself in all cases. Each must have had the means to commission such a stela, however lowly a title such as 'servant' may appear to modern eyes.[51] These jobs presumably brought with them income and prestige within the household. As we move down the social hierarchy, evidence becomes very thin, but it is clear from differential wages paid in kind (primarily bread and beer) that some individuals would have been capable of supporting more dependants than others. This is also clear in the division of rations within a single household seen in the letters of the Middle Kingdom farmer Hekanakht (Parkinson 1991: 101–7; Allen 2002).

The symbiotic relationship between the servant and the served thus seems to stretch from the top to the bottom of Egyptian society. Service of some description ensured a position within this broad hierarchy and status was presumably reflected to some degree in the number of an individual's dependants. Those with official titles were linked into the administrative hierarchy which covered all regions of Egypt (and its empire) and all branches of the administration. The highest officials were then linked to the court and brought into the orbit of the king himself. It is the embeddedness of the court as the link between the king and the hierarchical structure of the administration and society as a whole which must have ensured its longevity despite numerous changes of kings, dynasties and court personnel.

---

[51] The six stelae vary in the quality of the carving although all appear to have been carved by professional artists. Interestingly, the stela dedicated by Any's brother May is one of the poorer examples (Davies 1908a: pl. XXIII).

Conclusions

Despite the patchy nature of the evidence, aspects of the Egyptian court can be traced from before the beginning of the historical period, through the late Eighteenth Dynasty and beyond, into the Hellenistic court of the Ptolemies, attesting to its extraordinary longevity as an institution. The existence of a king and, by extension, his court never seems to have been challenged in over 3,000 years of history, a fact that illustrates the extent to which king and court were embedded within the Egyptian world-view and social and administrative structures, but also how successfully the court managed the process of self-legitimisation, primarily through the figure of the king.

There is no doubt that the Egyptian king was clearly distinguished from both courtiers and the population as a whole by his divine status, despite the fact that he might have some decidedly human attributes. However, the evidence suggests that he was not just a divine figurehead for the country, but actively ruled it through his courtiers/administrators. There is evidence from several periods in Egyptian history of active reform of the administration – and here we might include Akhenaten's disbanding of the powerful priesthood of Amun, showing the extent to which some kings were able to shift the balance of power between themselves and their officials. While Elias (1983) suggests that kings in the early modern French court controlled their courtiers by playing them off against non-noble administrators (but see the Introduction; also Paterson in this volume), the Egyptian king's courtiers also doubled up as administrators. Thus important officials were kept focused on life and competition at court rather than their institutional power, and the king could keep his courtiers occupied and accountable.

It is easy, however, to fall into the snare set by the Egyptian historical documents which encourage us to view the king as all-powerful and acting in isolation. Courtiers clearly did have power, as the troubled accession of Hatshepsut as co-regent with Tuthmosis III suggests. Although there was technically no hereditary nobility and those from humble backgrounds did occasionally rise to positions of power, there can be no doubt that much of the time positions of power close to the king were monopolised by a small number of powerful families, sometimes also linked to the royal family by marriage. It was at times of succession of a new king that courtiers were at their most powerful, as is shown by the few conspiracies that we know of, but also by the royal practice of appointing co-regents to ensure that control was established before the death of the reigning king. There are a significant number of instances in which a prominent courtier managed to take over the throne at the death of the king: the processes of legitimisation rapidly established him as a divine ruler and the court continued with its business. We see only the extremes, and search for the 'power behind the throne' in the case of child-kings or female rulers, but how many of the other kings who form the subject of our histories were strong individuals and how many were manipulated by their advisors? We are unlikely ever to know, but it is worth occasionally re-examining our assumptions. Ultimately, the dynasties who monopolised the office of kingship changed many times, and it is the court and not kingship itself that underpins the stability of the Egyptian social system.

Any study of the Egyptian court rests on generations of excellent work by Egyptologists in many branches of the discipline: literature, history and social history, prosopography, and art, architectural history and archaeology. Focusing on the court, however problematical it may prove as a topic, allows reflection on the nature and context of our evidence and the interrelationships between interpretations derived from the various sources. Instruction texts, for example, take on added significance in the light of the world of faction, competition and intrigue highlighted by studies of court society (e.g. Elias 1983), despite the virtual absence of information on this aspect of Egyptian court society from the primary sources (Coulon 2002). The same might be said of domestic architecture. Comparative studies of courts prove invaluable in reminding us just how much evidence we are missing in Egypt and in suggesting how we might go about reassembling the surviving pieces of the jigsaw.

Although the Amarna period and its aftermath tend to be treated with great caution by historians as a result of the upheavals surrounding Akhenaten's religious changes, the wide range of sources it yields provide rich material for examining the court. Courts tend to be configured and conceived spatially, and the scope for examining architectural settings is widely acknowledged in court studies (e.g. Baillie 1967; Elias 1983; Duindam 2003). Amarna provides an excellent opportunity for exploring such configurations and settings through the archaeological record, while there is enough comparative evidence in the form of palace architecture and art that we can rest assured that conclusions drawn from this period are not irrelevant to broader trends within the Egyptian court. The Window of Appearance, for example, which was developed as an essential component of court life in the Amarna period, remained an important element of palace architecture at least for the remainder of the New Kingdom. There remains considerable scope for study in this area.

The Egyptian evidence also offers a fascinating opportunity to examine the origins of the court as it emerged alongside kingship as part of a complex process of social stratification that can be observed in the archaeological record. Duindam (2003: 318) writes that 'it makes no sense to use "court" as a bland equivalent for group dynamics around leaders'. This may be true, but the origins of the court in such behaviour are clear, as are the various culturally determined strategies for legitimising existing political power through processes of differentiation – whether that power was gained rapidly through conquest or built up gradually over centuries. This perhaps explains both the frequency with which courts are encountered around the world across the centuries, and the fact that they prove so difficult to model. It is the processes that can be modelled, while the courts themselves remain diverse although with frequent parallels. In a long-term view, the Egyptian evidence also illustrates the extent to which court society was continually evolving in unexpected directions as the actors sought to cope with the fluid nature of power relations between king and courtier and to find new ways of expressing the differentiation between king and courtier and courtier and subject, so essential to maintaining the status quo.

Bibliography

Abka'i-Khavari, M. 2000. *Das Bild des Königs in der Sasanidenzeit*. Munich

Adamson, J. 1999a. The making of the ancien-régime court 1500–1700. In Adamson 1999b: 7–41

   (ed.) 1999b. *The Princely Courts of Europe: Ritual, Politics and Culture under the Ancien Régime 1500–1700*. London

Aldred, C. 1988. *Akhenaten: King of Egypt*. London

Alföldi, A. 1952. *A Conflict of Ideas in the Late Roman Empire*. Oxford

   1962. A coin portrait of Julian Apostata. *AJA* 66: 403–5

   1970. *Die monarchische Repräsentation im römischen Kaiserreiche*, Darmstadt (reprint of: (i) Die Ausgestaltung des monarchischen Zeremoniells im römischen Kaiserhofe. *MDAI(R)* 49 (1934): 3–188; (ii) Insignien und Tracht der römischen Kaiser. *MDAI(R)* 50 (1935): 3–158)

Allen, J. P. 2002. *The Hekanakht papyri*. New York

Altheim, F. 1962. *Geschichte der Hunnen*, Bd V. Berlin

Altheim, F. and Stiehl, R. 1954. *Ein asiatischer Staat: Feudalismus unter den Sasaniden und ihren Nachbarn*. Wiesbaden

   1957. *Finanzgeschichte der Spätantike*. Frankfurt

Andronicos, M. 1984. *Vergina*. Athens

Anson, E. M. 1985. Macedonia's alleged constitutionalism. *Classical Journal* 80: 303–16

Antoine, M. 1989. *Louis XV*. Paris

Apostolidès, J.-M. 1981. *Le roi-machine: spectacle et politique au temps de Louis XIV*. Paris

Archibald, Z. 1999. Macedonian administration. *CR* n.s. 49: 163–5

Arnold, D. 1996. *The Royal Women of Amarna: Images of Beauty from Ancient Egypt*. New York

Arnold, F. 1989. A study of Egyptian domestic buildings. *Varia Aegyptiaca* 5: 75–93

Asch, R. G. 2003. *Nobilities in Transition 1550–1700: Courtiers and Rebels in Britain and Europe*. London

Asch R. G. and Birke, A. M. (eds.) 1991. *Princes, Patronage and the Nobility: The Court at the Beginning of the Modern Age*. Oxford

Atkinson, J. E. 1994. *A Commentary on Q. Curtius Rufus'* Historiae Alexandri Magni Books 5 to 7,2. Amsterdam

Aujolat, N. 1983. Eusébie, Hélène et Julien I–II. *Byzantion* 53: 78–109 and 421–52

Avery, W. 1940. The *adoratio purpurae* and the importance of the imperial purple in the 4th century. *MAAR* 17: 66–79

Badian, E. 1958. Alexander the Great and the unity of mankind. *Historia* 7: 425–44

　1981. The deification of Alexander the Great. In H. J. Dell (ed.), *Ancient Macedonian Studies in Honor of C. F. Edson*, 28–71. Thessaloniki

　1985. Alexander in Iran. In I. Gershevitch (ed.), *The Cambridge History of Iran*, vol. II: *The Median and Achaemenian Periods*, 420–501. Cambridge

　1996. Alexander the Great between two thrones and heaven: variations on an old theme. In A. Small (ed.), *Subject and Ruler: The Cult of the Ruling Power in Antiquity*, *JRA* Suppl. 17: 11–26

　2000. Conspiracies. In Bosworth and Baynham 2000: 50–95

Baer, K. 1960. *Rank and Title in the Old Kingdom: The Structure of the Egyptian Administration in the Fifth and Sixth Dynasties*. Chicago

Baillie, H. M. 1967. Etiquette and the planning of state apartments in baroque palaces. *Archaeologia* 101: 167–99

Baines, J. 1990. Restricted Knowledge, Hierarchy, and Decorum: Modern Perceptions and Ancient Institutions. *Journal of the American Research Centre in Egypt* 27: 1–23

　1995. Origins of Egyptian kingship. In D. O'Connor and D. Silverman (eds.), *Ancient Egyptian Kingship*, 95–156. Leiden

　1998. The dawn of the Amarna age. In D. O'Connor and E. H. Cline (eds.), *Amenhotep III: Perspectives on His Reign*, 271–312. Ann Arbor, MI

Balsdon, J. P. V. D. 1962. *Roman Women*. London

　1969. *Life and Leisure in Ancient Rome*. London

Bang, M. 1921. Die Freunde und Begleiter der Kaiser. In Friendländer 1921: 56–76

Bard, K. 1994. *From Farmers to Pharaohs: Mortuary Evidence for the Rise of Complex Society in Egypt*. Sheffield

Bardill, J. 1997. The Palace of Lausus. *AJA* 101: 67–95

　1999. The Great Palace of the Byzantine emperors. *JRA* 12: 217–28

Barnes, T. 1981. *Constantine and Eusebius*. London

　1982. *The New Empire of Diocletian and Constantine*. Cambridge, MA and London

　1989. Emperors on the move. *JRA* 2: 247–61

Bartsch, S. 1994. *Actors in the Audience: Theatricality and Doublespeak from Nero to Hadrian*. Cambridge, MA

Baynes, N. 1955. *Byzantine Studies*. London

Beik, W. 1985. *Absolutism and Society in Seventeenth Century France*. Cambridge

Bek, L. 1983. *Quaestiones Convivales*: the idea of the *Triclinium* and the staging of convivial ceremony from Rome to Byzantium. *Analecta Romana* 12: 81–107

Berger, P. 1981. *The Insignia of the* Notitia Dignitatum. New York

Berve, H. 1926. *Das Alexanderreich auf prosopographischer Grundlage*, 2 vols. Munich

Bickerman, E. 1963. A propos d'un passage de Chares de Mytilene. *PdP* 18: 241–55

Bielenstein, H. 1954. The restoration of the Han Dynasty, part I. *Bulletin of the Museum of Far Eastern Antiquities* 26: 1–209

1976. Lo-yang in Later Han times. *Bulletin of the Museum of Far Eastern Antiquities* 48: 1–144

1979. The restoration of the Han Dynasty, part IV. *Bulletin of the Museum of Far Eastern Antiquities* 51: 1–300

1980. *The Bureaucracy of Han Times.* Cambridge

1986a. The institutions of Later Han. In Twitchett and Loewe 1986: 491–519

1986b. The Later Han Dynasty. In Twitchett and Loewe 1986: 279–87

Bird, H. (trans. and comm.) 1993. *Eutropius:* Breviarium. Liverpool

(trans. and comm.) 1994. *Sextus Aurelius Victor:* De Caesaribus. Liverpool

Blackman, A. M. 1918. The House of the Morning. *Journal of Egyptian Archaeology* 5: 148–65

Blockley, R. 1983. *Fragmentary Classicizing Historians of the Later Roman Empire.* Liverpool

Boardman, J. 2000. *Persia and the West.* London

Borchardt, L. 1913. *Das Grabdenkmal des Königs S'a³ Hu-Re'. Band* II: *Die Wand-bilder.* Leipzig

Borza, E. 1983. The symposium at Alexander's court. *Ancient Macedonia* 3: 45–55. Thessaloniki

1999. *Before Alexander: Constructing Early Macedonia.* Publications of the Association of Ancient Historians 6. Claremont, CA

Bosworth, A. B. 1980. Alexander and the Iranians. *Journal of Hellenic Studies* 100: 1–21

1988. *Alexander the Great: Conquest and Empire.* Cambridge

1995. *A Historical Commentary on Arrian's History of Alexander,* vol. II: *Commentary on Books IV–V.* Oxford

1996. *Alexander and the East: The Tragedy of Triumph.* Oxford

2000. A tale of two empires: Hernán Cortés and Alexander the Great. In Bosworth and Baynham 2000: 23–49

Bosworth, A. B. and Baynham, E. J. (eds.) 2000. *Alexander the Great in Fact and Fiction.* Oxford

Boucharlat, R. 1997. Susa under Achaemenid rule. In J. Curtis (ed.), *Mesopotamia and Iran in the Persian Period: Conquest and Imperialism 539–331 BC,* 54–67. London

2001a. Pasargades 2001. Rapport sur les travaux de la mission conjointe soumis à l'Organisation du Patrimoine culturel de l'Iran, Direction de la recherche, www.achemenet.com/recherche/sites/pasargades/pasargades.htm

2001b. The palace and the royal Achaemenid city. Two case studies – Pasargadae and Susa. In I. Nielsen (ed.), *The Royal Palace Institutions in the First Millennium BC,* 113–24. Aarhus

Bourriau, J. 2000. The Second Intermediate Period (c. 1650–1550 BC). In Shaw 2000: 185–217

Bowersock, G. 1996. The vanishing paradigm of the Fall of Rome. *Bulletin of the American Academy of Arts and Sciences* 49: 29–43

2000. *Selected Papers on Late Antiquity*. Bari

Bowersock, G., Brown, P. and Grabar, O. 1999. *Late Antiquity: A Guide to the Post-classical World*. London

Bremmer, J. 1978. An imperial palace guard in heaven: date of the Vision of Dorotheus. *ZPE* 75: 82–8

Brent, A. 1999. *The Imperial Cult and the Development of Church Order*. Supplement to VC Texts and Studies 45. Leiden, Boston and Cologne

Briant, P. 1985. Les Iraniens d'Asie mineure après la chute de l'Empire achéménide. A propos de l'inscription d'Amyzon. *DHA* 11: 167–95

1989a. Histoire et idéologie: les Grecs et la 'décadence' perse. In M.-M. Mactoux and E. Geny (eds.), *Mélanges Pierre Lévêque*, vol. II, 33–47. Besançon

1989b. Table du roi, tribut et redistribution chez les Achéménides. In P. Briant and C. Herrenschmidt (eds.), *Le tribut dans l'empire perse*, 35–44. Paris and Louvain

2001. *Bulletin d'histoire achéménide*, vol. II. Paris

2002 (French original 1996). *From Cyrus to Alexander: A History of the Persian Empire*. Winona Lake, MN

2003. *Darius dans l'ombre d'Alexandre*. Paris

Brilliant, R. 1963. *Gesture and Rank in Roman Art*. New Haven (= MCAAS 14)

Brooker, G. 1977. *The Civic World of Early Renaissance Florence*. Princeton

Brosius, M. 2000. *The Persian Empire from Cyrus II to Artaxerxes I*. London

2002. *Women in Ancient Persia 559–331 BC*. Oxford

2003. Alexander and the Persians. In J. Roisman (ed.), *Alexander the Great*, 169–93. Leiden

2006. Investiture I. Achaemenid times. *EncIr* XIII: 181–7

Brown, P. 1971. *The World of Late Antiquity*. London

1992. *Power and Persuasion in Late Antiquity*. Madison, WI

1995. Review of T. F. Mathews, *The Clash of Gods* (1993). *Art Bulletin* 77: 449–502

1997. The world of late antiquity revisited: a report. *SO* 72: 5–32

1998. Christianization and religious conflict. In A. Cameron and P. Garnsey (eds.), *The Cambridge Ancient History*, vol. XIII, 632–64. Cambridge

Brunt, P. A. 1976–83. *Arrian* History of Alexander *and* Indica, 2 vols. Loeb Classical Library. Cambridge, MA

1988. The emperor's choice of *amici*. In P. Kneissl and V. Losemann (eds.), *Alte Geschichte und Wissenschaftsgeschichte: Festschrift für Karl Christ zum 65 Geburtstag*, 39–56. Darmstadt

Bryan, B. 1991. *The Reign of Tuthmosis IV*. Baltimore

1998. Antecedents to Amenhotep III. In D. O'Connor & E. H. Cline (eds.), *Amenhotep III. Perspectives on His Reign*: 27–62. Ann Arbor, MI

2000. The Eighteenth Dynasty before the Amarna period (c.1550–1352 BC). In Shaw 2000: 218–71

Buck, D. 1988. The reign of Arcadius in Eunapius' Histories. *Byzantion* 68: 15–46

Burkert, W. 1985 (German original 1977). *Greek Religion.* Oxford

Butz, R. and Dannenberg, L.-A. 2004. Theoriebildungen des Hofes. In Butz et al. 2004: 1–41

Butz, R., Hirschbiegel, J. and Willoweit, D. (eds.) 2004. *Hof und Theorie: Annäherungen an ein historisches Phänomen.* Cologne, Weimar and Vienna

Cameron, A[lan]. 1968. Gratian's repudiation of the pontifical robe. *JRS* 58: 96–102

   1970. *Claudian: Poetry and Politics at the Court of Honorius.* Oxford

   1982. The empress and the poet: paganism and politics at the court of Theodosius II. *YClS* 27: 217–90

   1985. Polyonomy in the Late Roman aristocracy. *JRS* 75: 164–82

   2000. The poet, the bishop and the harlot. *GRBS* 41: 175–88

Cameron, A[veril]. (ed.) 1969/70. Agathias on the Sassanians. *DOP* 23/24: 67–183

   1976. *Corippus.* In Laudem Justini Augusti Minoris. London

   1987. The construction of court ritual: the Byzantine Book of Ceremonies. In Cannadine and Price 1987: 106–36

Cannadine, D. and Price, S. 1987. *Rituals of Royalty: Power and Ceremonial in Traditional Societies.* Cambridge

Carney, E. D. 2000a. Artifice and Alexander history. In Bosworth and Baynham 2000: 263–85

   2000b. *Women and Monarchy in Macedonia.* Norman, OK

Carrata-Thomas, F. 1995. *Il problema degli eteri nella monarchia di Alessandro Magno.* Turin

Carter, E. and Stolper, M. W. 1984. *Elam: Surveys of Political History and Archaeology.* Berkeley

Cereti, C. G. 1997. Primary sources for the history of Inner and Outer Iran in the Sasanian period. In *Archivum Eurasiae Medii Aevi* 9: 17–71

   2001. *La letteratura pahlavi.* Milano

Chavannes, E. 1895–1905. *Les mémoires historiques de Se-ma Ts'ien,* 5 vols. Paris

Cheng Ch'iao 1987. *T'ung-chih.* Peking

Chilver, G. E. F. 1979. *A Historical Commentary on Tacitus' Histories I and II.* Oxford

Ch'ü T'ung-tsu 1972. *Han Social Structure.* Seattle

Coarelli, F. 1978. Il 'grande donario' di Attalo I. In *I Galli e l'Italia* 231–55. Rome

Cohen, R. and Westbrook, R. 2000. *Amarna Diplomacy: The Beginnings of International Relations.* Baltimore

Costa, E. 1972. The office of *castrensis sacri palatii* in the 4th century. *Byzantion* 42: 358–87

Cotton, H. 1984. The concept of *indulgentia* under Trajan. *Chiron* 14: 245–66

Coulon, L. 2002. Cour, courtisans et modèles éducatifs au moyen empire. *Egypte Afrique & Orient* 26: 9–20

Couvreur, S. 1899. *Li Ki ou Mémoires sur les bienséances et les cérémonies,* 2 vols. Ho Kien Fou

Crocker, P. 1985. Status symbols in the architecture of el-Amarna. *Journal of Egyptian Archaeology* 71: 52–62

Crook, J. A. 1955. *Consilium Principis: Imperial Councils and Counsellors from Augustus to Diocletian.* Cambridge

  1996. Augustus: power, authority, achievement. In A. K. Bowman et al. (eds.), *The Cambridge Ancient History*, 2nd edn, vol. X, 113–46. Cambridge

Da Vinha, M. 2004. *Les valets de chambre de Louis XIV.* Paris

Dagron, G. 1974. *Naissance d'une capitale: Constantinople et ses institutions.* Paris

  1996. *Empereur et prêtre: étude sur le 'césaro-papisme'.* Paris

Dalby, A. 1996. *Siren Feasts: A History of Food and Gastronomy in Greece.* London and New York

Dandamayev, M. A. 2002. Courts and courtiers. In *EncIr* 6: 356–9

D'Arms, J. 1990. The Roman *convivium* and the idea of equality. In O. Murray (ed.), *Sympotica*, 308–20. Oxford

Daryaee, T. 1995. National history or Keyanid history? The nature of Sasanid Zoroastrian historiography. *Iranian Studies* 28: 129–141

  2001/02. Memory and history. The reconstruction of the past in late antique Persia. *Nâme-ye Irân-e Bâstân* 1/2: 1–14

  2002. Mind, body, and the cosmos: chess and backgammon in ancient Persia. *Iranian Studies* 35: 281–312

Daskalopoulos, M. 1993. Divinités et cultes en Macédoine dans l'antiquité. Unpublished PhD thesis, University of Tours

Davidson, J. 1997. *Courtesans and Fishcakes.* London

Davies, N. de G. 1903. *The Rock Tombs of El Amarna*, Part I: *The Tomb of Meryra.* EEF Memoir 13. London

  1905a. *The Rock Tombs of El Amarna*, Part II: *The Tombs of Panehesy and Meryra II.* EEF Memoir 14. London

  1905b. *The Rock Tombs of El Amarna*, Part III: *The Tombs of Huya and Ahmes.* EEF Memoir 15. London

  1906. *The Rock Tombs of El Amarna*, Part IV: *Tombs of Penthu, Mahu, and others.* EEF Memoir 16. London

  1908a. *The Rock Tombs of El Amarna*, Part V: *Smaller Tombs and Boundary Stelae.* EEF Memoir 17. London

  1908b. *The Rock Tombs of El Amarna*, Part VI: *Tombs of Parennefer, Tutu, and Aÿ.* EEF Memoir 18. London

de Blois, F. 1990. *Burzōy's Voyage to India and the Origin of the Book of Kalilah wa Dimna.* London

de Buck, A. 1937. The Judicial Papyrus of Turin. *Journal of Egyptian Archaeology* 23: 152–64

de Crespigny, R. 1975. The harem of Emperor Huan: a study of court politics in Later Han. *Papers on Far Eastern History* 12: 1–42

Deichmann, F. 1989. *Ravenna: Haupstadt des spätantiken Abendlandes* 2.3, Stuttgart

Delmaire, R. 1995. *Les institutions du Bas-Empire romain de Constantin à Justinien.* I. *Les institutions civiles palatine.* Paris

  1997. Les usurpateurs du Bas-Empire et le recrutement des fonctionnaires. In Paschoud and Szidat 1997: 111–27

Demandt, A. 1989. Der Hof. In Demandt, *Die Spätantike*, vol. II.1.b, 231–44. Munich

Dickmann, J. A. 1999. *Domus frequentata: Anspruchsvolle Wohnen in pompeianischen Stadthaus*. Munich

Dodson, A. 1990. Crown Prince Dhutmose and the royal sons of the Eighteenth Dynasty. *Journal of Egyptian Archaeology* 76: 87–96

Dorman, P. 1988. *The Monuments of Senenmut*. London

Drake, H. A. 2000. *Constantine and the Bishops*, Baltimore

Dubs, H. 1938, 1944, 1955. *The History of the Former Han Dynasty*, 3 vols. Baltimore

Duindam, J. 1995. *Myths of Power: Norbert Elias and the Early Modern European Court*. Amsterdam

   2003. *Vienna and Versailles: The Courts of Europe's Dynastic Rivals, 1559–1780*. Cambridge

   2004. Norbert Elias and the history of the court: old questions, new perspectives. In Butz et al. 2004: 91–104

Dumser, E. A. (ed.) 2002. *Mapping Augustan Rome. Journal of Roman Archaeology* Supplementary Series 50, Portsmouth, RI

Dunbabin, K. M. 1991. Triclinium and stibadium. In W. J. Slater (ed.), *Dining in a Classical Context*, 121–48. Ann Arbor, MI

Duval, N. 1997. Les résidences impériales. In Paschoud and Szidat 1997: 127–55

Dvornik, F. 1955. The emperor Julian's 'reactionary' views on kingship. In F. Weitzmann (ed.), *Late Classical and Medieval Studies in Honour of A. M. Friend*, 71–81. Princeton

Eck, W. 2000. The emperor and his advisers. In A. K. Bowman, P. Garnsey and D. Rathbone (eds.), *The Cambridge Ancient History* 2nd edn, vol. XI, 195–213. Cambridge

   2002. Imperial administration and epigraphy: in defence of prosopography. In A. K. Bowman, H. M. Cotton, M. Goodman and S. Price (eds.), *Representations of Empire: Rome and the Mediterranean World*. Proceedings of the British Academy 114, 131–52. London

Eck, W., Caballos, A. and Fernàndez, F. 1996. *Das senatus consultum de Cn. Pisone patre*. Vestigia 48. Munich

Edwards, C. 2003. Incorporating the alien: the art of conquest. In C. Edwards and G. Woolf (eds.), *Rome the Cosmopolis*, 44–70. Cambridge

Eichert, O. 1967 (1893). *Vollständiges Wörterbuch zu dem Geschichtswerke des Quintus Curtius Rufus*. Hildesheim

Elias, N. 1983. *The Court Society*. Oxford

Elliott, J. H. and Brokliss, B. (eds.) 1999. *The World of the Favourite*. New Haven and London

Elster, J. 1993. *Political Psychology*. Cambridge

Enderlein, V. and Sundermann, W. (eds.) 1988. *Schāhnāme Das persische Königsbuch. Miniaturen und Texte der Berliner Handschrift von 1605*. Leipzig and Weimar

Engler, F. K. 1980. *Der Goldherr besteigt den weißen Tiger*. Zurich

Erman, A. and Grapow, H. 1930. *Wörterbuch der Ägyptischen Sprache*, vol. IV. Leipzig

Errington, M. 1996. Assembly, Macedonian. In *OCD*[3] 192–3

Faulkner, R. O. 1962. *A Concise Dictionary of Middle Egyptian*. Oxford
  1969. *The Ancient Egyptian Pyramid Texts*. Oxford

Favro, D. G. 1996. *The Urban Image of Augustan Rome*. Cambridge

Finsen, H. 1969. *La résidence de Domitien sur le Palatin*. Copenhagen

Fischer, H. G. 1960. The Inscription of *'In-it.f*, Born of *Tfi*. *Journal of Near Eastern Studies* XIX: 258–68

Fowden, E. 1999. *The Barbarian Plain: Saint Sergius between Rome and Iran*. The Transformation of the Classical Heritage 28. Berkeley

Fraisse, J. C. 1974. *Philia: la notion d'amitié dans la philosophie antique*. Paris

Frank, R. I. 1969. Scholae Palatinae: *The Palace Guards of the Late Roman Empire*. Rome

Franke, D. 1991. The career of Khnumhotep III of Beni Hasan and the so-called "decline of the nomarchs". In S. Quirke (ed.), *Middle Kingdom Studies*, 51–67. New Malden

Frankfort, H. and Pendlebury, J. D. S. 1933. *The City of Akhenaten*, Part II: *The North Suburb and the Desert Altars*. EEF Memoir 40. London

Fredricksmeyer, E. 2000. Alexander and the kingship of Asia. In Bosworth and Baynham 2000: 136–66

Freed, R. E., Markowitz, Y. J. and D'Auria, S. H. 1999. *Pharaohs of the Sun: Akhenaten, Nefertiti, Tutankhamun*. Boston

Friedländer, L. 1921. *Darstellung aus der Sittengeschichte Roms in der Zeit von Augustus bis zum Ausgang der Antonine*, 9th–10th revision, vol. IV, ed. George Wissowa with contributions by M. Bang, F. Drexel, U. Kahrstedt and O. Weinreich. Leipzig (English translation: Friedländer, 1908. *Roman Life and Manners under the Early Empire*, trans. of 7th edn by J. H. Freese, A. B. Gough and L. A. Magnus, London)

Friedrich, C. and Brzezinski, Z. 1965. *Totalitarian Dictatorship and Autocracy*. Cambridge, MA

Fu Lo-ch'eng 1977. Hsi Han de chi ko cheng-chih chi-t'uan. In *Han T'ang shih lun chi*. Taipei

Gagé, J. 1971. *Les classes sociales dans l'empire romain*, 2nd edn. Paris

Garnsey, P. and Humfress, C. 2001. *The Evolution of the Late Antique World*. Cambridge

Garnsey, P. and Saller, R. 1987. *The Roman Empire: Economy, Society, and Culture*. London

Garrison, M. B. and Root, M. C. Forthcoming. *Seals of the Persepolis Fortification Tablets*, II. *Images of Human Activity*. Chicago

Gascou, J. 1981. Un énigme épigraphique: Sévère Alexandre et la titulature de Giufi. *AntAfr* 17: 231–40

Geertz, C. 1983. *Local Knowledge*. New York

Gelzer, M. 1968. *Caesar, Politician and Statesman*, trans. P. Needham. Oxford

Geyssen, J. 1998. Presentations of Victory on the Theodosian obelisk base. *Byzantion* 68: 47–55

Gibson, S., Delaine, J. and Claridge, A. 1994. The triclinium of the Domus Flavia: a new reconstruction. *Papers of the British School at Rome* 62: 67–100

Giele, E. 2006. *Imperial Decision-Making and Communication in Early China: A Study of Cai Yong's* Duduan. Opera Sinologica 20. Wiesbaden

Gignoux, P. (ed.) 1991. *Les quatre inscriptions du mage Kirdir: textes et concordances.* Cahiers de Studia Iranica 9. Paris

　　2006. Prolégomènes pour une histoire des idées de l'Iran sassanide: convergences et divergences. In Wiesehöfer and Huyse 2006: 71–81

Giles, F. J. 1997. *The Amarna Age: Western Asia.* Warminster

Gnirs, A. M. 1996. *Militär und Gesellschaft: ein Beitrag zur Sozialgeschichte des Neuen Reiches.* Studien zur Archäologie und Geschichte Altägyptens; Bd. 17. Heidelberg

Gnoli, G. 1989. *The Idea of Iran: An Essay of Its Origin.* SOR 62. Rome

　　1993. *Iran als religiöser Begriff im Mazdaismus.* Rheinisch-Westfälische Akademie der Wissenschaften, Vorträge G 320. Opladen

　　1999. Farr(ah). In *Encyclopaedia Iranica* IX: 312–19

Goelet, O. 1985. *Two Aspects of the Royal Palace in the Egyptian Old Kingdom.* Ann Arbor, MI

　　1986. The term *stp-s3* in the Old Kingdom. *Journal of the American Research Center in Egypt* 23: 85–97

Goffman, E. 1967. The nature of deference and demeanor. In Goffman (ed.), *Interaction Ritual: Essays on Face-to-Face Behavior*, 47–95. Garden City, NY

Gohary, J. 1992. *Akhenaten's Sed-festival at Karnak.* London

Goukowsky, P. 1978. *Essai sur les origines du mythe d'Alexandre (336–270 av. J.-C.)*, vol. I. *Les origines politiques.* Nancy

Grabar, A. 1936. *L'empereur dans l'art byzantin.* Paris

　　1967. *Christian Iconography: A Study of Its Origins.* Princeton

Greatrex, G. and Bardill, J. 1996. Antiochus the *praepositus*: a Persian eunuch at the court of Theodosius II. *DOP* 50: 171–98

Gregor, W. 1997. Interaktion, Repräsentation und Herrschaft. Der Königshof im Hellenismus. In Winterling 1997b: 27–71

Grenet, F. 2001. *La geste d'Ardashir fils de Pâbag: Kārnāmag i Ardaxšēr ī Pābagān.* Paris

Griffin, M. 2003. *De Beneficiis* and Roman society. *JRS* 93: 92–113

Grzybek, E. 1999. Le meutre et son châtiment dans la Macédoine antique. In *Ancient Macedonia. Sixth International Symposium* (Ancient Macedonia 6), vol. I, 463–9. Thessaloniki

Güterbock, K. 1906. *Byzanz und Persien in ihren diplomatisch-völkerrechtlichen Beziehungen im Zeitalter Justinians.* Berlin

Guidi, M. and Morony, M. 1991. Mazdak. In *The Encyclopaedia of Islam.* New edn, vol. VI: 949–52

Guilland, R. 1955. Les titres auliques reservé aux eunuques. *REB* 13: 65

    1969. *Etudes de topographie de Constantinople byzantine.* Amsterdam

Gundlach, R. 1998. *Der Pharao und sein Staat: die Grundlegung der Ägyptischen Königsideologie im 4. und 3. Jahrtausend.* Darmstadt

    2004. Zu Strukturen und Aspekten Pharaonischer Residenzen. In Butz et al. 2004: 225–47

Gutsfeld, A. 2004. Der Prätorianerpräfekt und der kaiserliche Hof. In Winterling 1998: 75–102

Gyselen, R. (ed.) 1999. *La science des cieux: sages, mages, astrologues.* Res Orientales 12. Bures-sur-Yvette

    (ed.) 2002. *Charmes et sortilèges: magie et magicians.* Res Orientales 14. Bures-sur-Yvette

Hall, E. 1989. *Inventing the Barbarian.* Oxford

Hallock, R. T. 1969. *Persepolis Fortification Tablets.* Chicago

    1978. Selected Fortification texts. *CahDAFI* 8: 109–36

Hammond, M. 1959. *The Antonine Monarchy.* Rome

Hammond, N. G. L. 1983. *Three Historians of Alexander the Great.* Cambridge

    1989. *The Macedonian State: Origins, Institutions and History.* Oxford

    1990. Royal pages, personal pages, and boys trained in the Macedonian manner during the period of the Temenid monarchy. *Historia* 39: 261–90

    1991. The various guards of Philip II and Alexander III. *Historia* 40: 396–418

Han-shu 1962. Ed. Peking: Chung-hua shu-chü

Hardy, G. 2000. *Worlds of Bronze and Bamboo,* New York

Harries, J. 1988. The Roman imperial quaestor from Constantine to Theodosius II. *JRS* 78: 148–72

Hartmann, U. 2002. Geist im Exil. Römische Philosophen am Hof der Sasaniden. In M. Schuol, U. Hartmann and A. Luther (eds.), *Grenzüberschreitungen: Formen des Kontakts zwischen Orient und Okzident im Altertum.* OrOcc 3. Stuttgart: 123–60

Hatzopoulos, M. 1988. *Un donation du roi Lysimaque.* Meletemata 5. Athens and Paris

    1994. *Cultes et rites de passage en Macédoine.* Athens

    1996. *Macedonian Institutions under the Kings,* vol. I: *A Historical and Epigraphic Study* and vol. II: *Epigraphic Appendix.* Meletemata 22. Athens and Paris

Heather, P. 1998a. Senators and senates. In A. Cameron and P. Garnsey (eds.), *The Cambridge Ancient History,* vol. XIII, 184–210. Cambridge

    1998b. Themistius: a political philosopher. In Whitby 1998: 125–49

Heisserer, A. J. 1980. *Alexander the Great and the Greeks.* Norman, OK

Helck, W. 1954. *Untersuchungen zu den Beamtentiteln des ägyptische Alten Reiches.* Glückstadt

    1958. *Zur Verwaltung des Mittleren und Neuen Reiches.* Probleme der Ägyptologie 3. Leiden

    1986. *Politische Gegensätze im alten Ägypten.* Hildesheimer Ägyptologische Beitrage 23. Hildesheim

Heltzer, M. 1994. Neh.11,24 and the provincial representative at the Persian court. *Transeuphratène* 8: 109–19

Herman, G. 1987. *Ritualised Friendship and the Greek City*. Cambridge

    1997. The court society of the Hellenistic Age. In P. Cartledge, P. Garnsey and E. Gruen (eds.), *Hellenistic Constructs: Essays in Culture, History, and Historiography*. Berkeley, CA: 199–211

Hermann, A. 1938. *Die ägyptische Königsnovelle*. Leipziger Ägyptologische Studien 10. Glückstadt

Herrmann, G. and Curtis, J. 1998. Reflections on the four-winged genie: a pottery jar and an ivory panel from Nimrud. *IrAnt* 33: 107–33

Hirsch, S. W. 1985. *The Friendship of the Barbarians: Xenophon and the Persian Empire*. Hanover, NH

Hoffmeier, J. K. 1985. *Sacred in the Vocabulary of Ancient Egypt: The Term DSR, with Special Reference to Dynasties I–XX*. Orbis Biblicus et Orientalis 59. Göttingen

Holum, K. 1977. Pulcheria's Crusade AD 421–2 and the ideology of imperial victory. *GRBS* 18: 153–72

    1982. *Theodosian Empresses*. Berkeley, CA

Hopkins, K. 1961. Social mobility in the later Roman empire: the evidence of Ausonius', *CQ* 11: 239–49

    1963 [1978]. Eunuchs in politics in the late Roman empire, *PCPS* 1963 (= Hopkins, *Conquerors and Slaves*, Cambridge 1978: 172–96 (= ch. IV, with revisions))

    1978a. *Conquerors and Slaves*. Cambridge

    1978b. The political power of eunuchs. In Hopkins 1978a: 172–96

    1980. Taxes and trade in the Roman Empire, 200 BC–AD 400. *JRS* 70: 101–25

    1995/6. Rome, taxes, rents and trade. *Kodai: Journal of Ancient History* 6–7: 41–75 (reprinted in W. Schiedel and S. von Reden (eds.) 2002. *The Ancient Economy*. Edinburgh)

Hou Han shu 1965. Ed. Chung-hua shu-chü. Peking

Hours, B. 2002. *Louis XV et sa cour: le roi, l'étiquette et le courtesan*. Paris

Howard-Johnston, J. D. 1995. The two great powers in late antiquity: a comparison. In A. Cameron (ed.). *The Byzantine and Early Islamic Near East*, III: *States, Resources and Armies*. Studies in Late Antiquity and Early Islam 1. Princeton: 157–226

Humbach, H. and Skjærvø, P. O. 1978–83. *The Sassanian Inscription of Paikuli*, 3 pts. Wiesbaden

Hunt, T. D. 1998. The Church as a public institution. In A. Cameron and P. Garnsey (eds.), *The Cambridge Ancient History*, vol. XIII, 238–76. Cambridge

Huyse, P. 1999. *Die dreisprachige Inschrift Šābuhrs I. an der Ka'ba-i Zardušt (ŠKZ)* (CII, pt. III, vol. 1, texts I), 2 vols. 1–2. London

    2002. La revendication de territoires achéménides par les Sassanides: une réalité historique? In Huyse (ed.). *Iran: questions et connaissances. Actes du IVe Congrès européen des études iraniennes organisé par la Societas Iranologica Europaea*, I: *La période ancienne*. Studia Iranica, cahier 25. Paris: 297–311

    (in press). *Histoire orale et écrite en Iran ancien entre mémoire et oubli*

Ikram, S. 1989. Domestic shrines and the cult of the royal family at el-'Amarna. *Journal of Egyptian Archaeology* 75: 89–101

Inwood, B. 1995. Politics and paradox in Seneca's *De Beneficiis*. In A. Laks and M. Schofield (eds.), *Justice and Generosity*, 241–65. Cambridge

Jacobs, B. 1994. *Die Satrapienverwaltung im Perserreich zur Zeit Darius' III.* Wiesbaden

Joannès, F. 2004. *The Age of Empires: Mesopotamia in the First Millennium BC*, trans. Antonia Nevill. Edinburgh

Johnson, D. 1977. *The Medieval Chinese Oligarchy.* Boulder, CO

Jones, A. H. M. 1964. *The Later Roman Empire 284–602: A Social, Economic and Administrative Survey.* Oxford

1966. *The Decline of the Ancient World.* London

Jones, B. W. 1992. *The Emperor Domitian.* London

Jones, C. 2002. *The Great Nation: France from Louis XV to Napoleon.* Harmondsworth

Jugel, U. 1976. *Politische Funktion und soziale Stellung der Eunuchen zur späteren Hanzeit (25–220 n.Chr.).* Wiesbaden

Kanawati, N. 1977. *The Egyptian Administration in the Old Kingdom: Evidence on Its Economic Decline.* Warminster

1980. *Governmental Reforms in Old Kingdom Egypt.* Warminster

2003. *Conspiracies in the Egyptian Palace: Unis to Pepy I.* London

Kantorowicz, E. 1963. Oriens Augusti: lever du roi. *DOP* 17: 119–77

Kaptan, D. 1996. The Great King's audience. In F. Blakolmer et al. (eds.), *Fremde Zeiten*, 2 vols., 259–71. Vienna

Kay, N. M. 1985. *Martial Book XI, A Commentary.* London

Kees, H. 1914. *Pr-dw3t* and *Db3t. Recueil de Travaux* 36: 1–15

Kelly, C. 1994. Later Roman bureaucracy: going through the files. In A. Bowman and G. Woolf (eds.), *Literacy and Power in the Ancient World*, 161–76. Cambridge

1998. Emperors, government and bureaucracy. In A. Cameron and P. Garnsey (eds.), *The Cambridge Ancient History*, vol. XIII, 138–83. Cambridge

1999. Empire building. In Bowersock, Brown and Grabar 1999: 170–95

Kemp, B. J. 1976. The Window of Appearance at El-Amarna and the structure of this city. *Journal of Egyptian Archaeology* 62: 81–99

1977. A building of Amenophis III at Kôm El-'Abd. *Journal of Egyptian Archaeology* 63: 77–8

1978. The Harîm-Palace at Medinet el-Ghurab, *Zeitschrift für Ägyptische Sprache und Altertumskunde* 105: 122–33

1989. *Ancient Egypt: Anatomy of a Civilization.* London

1995. Outlying temples at el-Amarna. In Kemp (ed.), *Amarna Reports VI.* EES Occasional Publications 10. London: 411–62

Kettenhofen, E. 2002. Die Einforderung der achaimenidischen Territorien durch die Sāsāniden – eine Bilanz. In S. Kurz (ed.). *Festschrift I. Khalifeh-Soltani zum 65. Geburtstag.* Aachen: 49–75

Kettering, S. 1986. *Patrons, Brokers, and Clients in Seventeenth Century France.* Oxford

Kienast, D. 1973. *Philip II von Makedonien und das Reich der Achaimeniden.* Munich

Kiilerich, B. 1993. *Late Fourth Century Classicism in the Plastic Arts.* Odense

Kirkpatrick, J. 1982. *Dictatorship and Double Standards: Rationalism and Realism in Politics.* New York

Kitchen, K. A. 1982. *Pharaoh Triumphant: The Life and Times of Ramesses II.* Cairo

Klodt, C. 2001. *Bescheidene Grösse. Die Herrschergestalt, der Kaiserpalast und die Stadt Rom: Literarische Reflexionen monarchischer Selbstdarstellung.* Göttingen

Kloft, H. 1970. *Liberalitas Principis.* Boehlau

Kokkinos, N. 1992. *Antonia Augusta: Portrait of a Great Roman Lady.* London

Kolb, F. 2001. *Herrscheridiologie in der Spätantike.* Berlin

Konstan, D. 1997a. Friendship and monarchy: Dio of Prusa's 3rd Oration on Kingship. *SO* 72: 124–43

1997b. *Friendship in the Classical World.* Cambridge

1983. *Three Imperial Capitals: Topography and Politics.* London

Krautheimer, R. 1986. *Early Christian and Byzantine Architecture*, 4th edn. Harmondsworth

Krentz, P. and Wheeler, E. L. 1994. *Polyaenus: Stratagems of War*, vol. I. Chicago

Kroll, W. 1931. Kuss. *RE* Suppl. 5: 512–20

Kühn, W. 1987. Der Kuss des Kaisers: Plinius paneg.24.2. *Würzburger Jahrbücher fur die Altertumswissenschaft* 13: 263–87

Kuhrt, A. 1995. *The Ancient Near East 3000–300 BC*, 2 vols. London

2001. The palace(s) of Babylon. In I. Nielsen (ed.), *The Royal Palace Institutions in the First Millennium BC*, 77–93. Aarhus

Kuran, T. 1995. *Private Truths, Public Lies: The Social Consequences of Preference Falsification.* Cambridge, MA

LÄ: W. Helck, E. Otto and W. Westendorf (eds.) 1975–92. *Lexikon der Ägyptologie*, vols. I–VII. Wiesbaden

Lacovara, P. 1997. *The New Kingdom Royal City.* London

Lane Fox, R. J. 1997. The Itinerary of Alexander: Constantius to Julian. *CQ* 47: 239–52

Lanfranchi, G. B., Roaf, M. and Rollinger, R. (eds.) 2003. *Continuity of Empire? Assyria, Media, Persia.* Padua

Larsen, M. T. (ed.) (in press). *Palace, King and Empire.* Copenhagen

Laurence, R. and Paterson, J. J. 1999. Power and laughter: imperial dicta. *Papers of the British School at Rome* 67: 183–97

Lavagne, H. 1988. *Operosa antra: recherches sur la grotte à Rome de Sylla à Hadrien.* BEFAR 212. Rome

Lee, A. D. 1993. *Information & Frontiers: Roman Foreign Relations in Late Antiquity.* Cambridge

Legge, J. 1861–72. *The Chinese Classics*, 5 vols. Hong Kong and London

1885. Li-chi, *Sacred Books of the East*, vols. XXVII and XXVIII. Oxford

Lendon, J. E. 1997. *Empire of Honour: The Art of Government in the Roman World.* Oxford

Leprohon, R. J. 1995. Royal ideology and state administration in Pharaonic Egypt. In J. M. Sasson (ed.), *Civilizations of the Ancient Near East*, vol. I, 273–87. New York

Lévy, E. 2001. Review of Hatzopoulos 1996. *Gnomon* 73: 267–70

Lewis, D. M. 1977. *Sparta and Persia.* Cincinnati

  1987. The king's dinner (Polyaenus IV, 3, 32). *AchHist* 2: 79–87

Lichtheim, M. 1973. *Ancient Egyptian Literature*, vol. I: *The Old and Middle Kingdoms.* Berkeley

  1976. *Ancient Egyptian Literature*, vol. II: *The New Kingdom.* Berkeley

  1996. Didactic literature. In A. Loprieno (ed.), *Ancient Egyptian Literature: History and Forms*, 243–62. Leiden

Liebeschuetz, J. H. W. 1972. *Antioch: City and Imperial Administration in the Late Roman Empire.* Oxford

  2001. The uses and abuses of the concept of 'decline'. In L. Lavan (ed.), *Recent Research in Late-Antique Urbanism. JRA* Suppl. Ser. 42, 233–8. Portsmouth, RI

Liverani, M. 1990. *Prestige and Interest: International Relations in the Near East ca. 1600–1100 BC.* Padua

Loewe, M. 1974. *Crisis and Conflict in Han China.* London

  1986a. The concept of sovereignty. In Twitchett and Loewe 1986: 726–46

  1986b. The structure and practice of government. In Twitchett and Loewe 1986: 463–90

  1992. The imperial tombs of the Former Han dynasty and their shrines. *T'oung Pao* 78: 302–40

Loprieno, A. 1996. The 'King's Novel'. In Loprieno (ed.), *Ancient Egyptian Literature: History and Forms*, 277–95. Leiden

Lorton, D. 1991. What was the *pr-nsw* and who managed it? Aspects of royal administration in 'The Duties of the Vizier'. *Studien zur Ägyptischen Kultur* 18: 291–316

MacCormack, S. 1981. *Art and Ceremony in Late Antiquity.* Berkeley, CA

McCormick, R. 1985. Analysing imperial ceremonies. *Jahrbuch der Österreichischen Byzantinistik* 35: 1–19

  2000. Emperor and court. In A. Cameron, B. Ward-Perkins and M. Whitby (eds.) *The Cambridge Ancient History*, vol. XIV, 135–61. Cambridge

MacDonald, W. L. 1982. *The Architecture of the Roman Empire*, vol. I, rev. edn. New Haven

McManners, J. 1998. *Church and Society in Eighteenth Century France*, 2 vols. Oxford

MacMullen, R. 1962. Roman bureaucratese. *Traditio* 18: 364–78 (= MacMullen 1990: ch. 8)

  1964a. Some pictures in Ammianus Marcellinus. *Art Bulletin* 46: 435–56 (= MacMullen 1990: ch. 9)

  1964b. Social mobility and the Theodosian Code. *JRS* 54: 49–53

1988. *Corruption and the Decline of Rome.* New Haven

1990. *Changes in the Roman Empire: Essays in the Ordinary.* Princeton

Macuch, M. 1992. Charitable foundations, I. In the Sasanian period. In *Encyclopaedia Iranica* V: 380–2

1994. Die sasanidische Stiftung 'für die Seele' – Vorbild für den islamischen *waqf?* In P. Vavroušek (ed.), *Iranian and Indo-European Studies: Memorial Volume of Otakar Klima*, Prague: 163–80

Maguire, H. 1999. The good life. In Bowersock, Brown and Grabar 1999: 238–57

Mango, C. 1981. Daily life in Byzantium. *JÖB* 31: 337–53

Manley, B. 1996. *The Penguin Historical Atlas of Ancient Egypt.* Harmondsworth

Mansel, P. 2006. The globalisation of court history. *The Court Historian* 11, 1: 77–101

Marmon, S. 1990. *Eunuchs and Sacred Boundaries in Islamic Society.* Oxford

Mathew, G. 1963. *Byzantine Aesthetics.* London

Matthews, J. F. 1975. *Western Aristocracies and Imperial Court AD 364–425.* Oxford

1989. *The Roman Empire of Ammianus.* London

Mathews, T. F. 1993. *The Clash of Gods.* Princeton

Medrei, M. 1996. Suet. *Nero* 31.1: Elementi e proposte per la riconstruzione del progetto della Domus Aurea. In C. Panella, *Meta Sudans*, vol. I, 165–88. Rome

Mee, C. and Spawforth, A. 2001. *Greece: An Oxford Archaeological Guide.* Oxford

Meier, S. A. 2000. Diplomacy and international marriages. In Cohen and Westbrook 2000: 165–73

Millar, F. 1965. Epictetus and the imperial court. *JRS* 55: 141–8 (reprinted in H. M. Cotton and G. M. Rogers (eds.), *Rome, The Greek World, and the East*, vol. II, 105–19. Chapel Hill and London, 2004)

1967. *The Roman Empire and Its Neighbours.* London

1977. *The Emperor in the Roman World (31 BC–AD 337).* London

Millar, F. and others. 1981. *The Roman World and Its Neighbours*, 2nd edn. New York

Miller, M. C. 1997. *Athens and Persia in the Fifth Century BC: A Study in Cultural Receptivity.* Cambridge

Moles, J. L. 1985. The interpretation of the 'Second Preface' in Arrian's *Anabasis. Journal of Hellenic Studies* 105: 162–8

Mommsen, T. 1887. *Römisches Staatsrecht.* Leipzig

Montefiore, S. S. 2003. *Stalin: The Court of the Red Tsar.* London

Montserrat, D. 2000. *Akhenaten: History, Fantasy and Egyptology.* London

Mooren, L. 1975. *The Aulic Titulature in Ptolemaic Egypt: Introduction and Proso-pography.* Brussels

1977. *La hiérarchie de cour Ptolémaique: contribution à l'étude des institutions et des classes dirigeantes a l'époque hellénistique.* Studia Hellenistica 23. Louvain

Moran, W. L. 1992. *The Amarna Letters.* Baltimore

Morony, M. 1989. Bahār-e Kesrā. In *Encyclopaedia Iranica* III: 479

Morris, I. 1964. *The World of the Shining Prince: Court Life in Ancient Japan.* Oxford

Muir, E. 1997. *Ritual in Early Modern Europe.* Cambridge

Müller, C. 1979. *Untersuchungen zum Erdaltar she im China der Chou- und Han-Zeit.* Munich

Murnane, W. J. 1977. *Ancient Egyptian Coregencies.* Studies in Ancient Oriental Civilization 40. Chicago

  1995. *Texts from the Amarna Period in Egypt.* Society of Biblical Literature: Writings from the Ancient World 5. Atlanta, GA

  1998. The organization of government under Amenhotep III. In D. O'Connor and E. H. Cline (eds.), *Amenhotep III: Perspectives on His Reign*, 173–221. Ann Arbor, MI

Murnane, W. J. and van Siclen, C. C. 1993. *The Boundary Stelae of Akhenaten.* London

Murray, O. 1996. Hellenistic royal symposia. In P. Bilde et al. (eds.), *Aspects of Hellenistic Kingship*, 15–27. Aarhus

  (ed.) 1990. *Sympotica.* Oxford

Naville, E. 1898. *The Temple of Deir el Bahari. Part* III: *End of Northern Half and Southern Half of the Middle Platform.* London

Nielsen, I. 1994. *Hellenistic Palaces: Tradition and Renewal.* Studies in Hellenistic Civilization 5. Aarhus

  (ed.) 2001. *The Royal Palace Institutions in the First Millennium BC: Regional Development and Cultural Exchange between East and West*, Athens

Nienhauser, W. 1994–2002. *The Grand Scribe's Records*, vols. I, II and VII. Bloomington, IN

Nixon, C. E. V. and Rogers, B. S. 1994. *In Praise of the Later Roman Emperors: The Panegyri Latini.* Berkeley, CA

Nock, A. D. 1947. The emperor's divine comes, *JRS* 37: 102–17 (repr. in Nock 1972: 653–75)

  1972. *Essays on Religion and the Ancient World*, ed. Z. Stewart. Oxford

Noethlichs, K. 1991. Hofbeamter. *RAC* 15: 1111–58

  1998. Strukturen und Funktionen des spätantikes Kaiserhofes. In Winterling 1988: 13–50

North, D. C. 1981. *Structure and Change in Economic History.* New York

O'Connor, D. 1989. City and palace in New Kingdom Egypt. *Cahiers de Recherches de l'Institut de Papyrologie et Egyptologie de l'Université de Lille: Etudes sur l'Egypte et le Soudan anciens* 11: 73–87

  1995. Beloved of Maat, the Horizon of Re: the royal palace in New Kingdom Egypt. In D. O'Connor and D. Silverman (eds.), *Ancient Egyptian Kingship*, 263–300. Probleme der Ägyptologie 9. Leiden

Olson, M. 1993. Dictatorship, democracy and development. *American Political Science Review* 87: 567–75

Palagia, O. 2000. Hephaestion's pyre and the Royal Hunt of Alexander. In Bosworth and Baynham 2000: 167–206.

Panaino, A. 1999. *La novella degli scacchi e della tavola reale. Un' antica fonte orientale sui due giochi da tavola più diffusi nel mondo eurasiatico tra Tardoantico e Medioevo e sulla loro simbologia militare e astrologica. Testo pahlavi, traduzione e commento al Wizārišn ī čatrang ud nihišn ī nēw-ardaxšīr 'La spiegazione degli scacchi e la disposizione della tavola reale'.* Milan

2001. Greci e Iranici: confronto e conflitti. In Settis, S. (ed.), *I Greci,* vol. III: *I Greci oltre la Grecia.* Turin: 79–136

2003. The baγān of the Fratarakas: gods or 'divine' kings? In C. G. Cereti, M. Maggi. and E. Provasi (eds.), *Religious Themes and Texts of Pre-Islamic Iran and Central Asia: Studies in Honour of Prof. Gherardo Gnoli on the Occasion of His 65th Birthday on 6th December 2002.* Beiträge zur Iranistik 24. Wiesbaden: 265–88

Pandermalis, D. 1997. *Dion.* Athens

1999. *Dion. Hê Anaskaphê.* Athens

Pani, M. 2003. *La corte dei Cesari: fra Augusto e Nerone.* Rome

Parkinson, R. B. 1991. *Voices from Ancient Egypt: An Anthology of Middle Kingdom Writings.* London

Paschoud, F. and Szidat, J. (eds.) 1997. *Usurpationen in der Spätantike.* Historia Einzelschriften 111. Stuttgart

Paterson, J. 2004. Autocracy and political economy. *Mediterraneo Antico* 7.2: 571–89

Patlagean, E. 1992. De la chasse et du souverain, *DOP* 46: 257–63

Pearson, L. 1960. *The Lost Historians of Alexander the Great.* American Philological Monographs 20. New York

Peck, E. H. 1992. Clothing, IV. In *Encyclopaedia Iranica* V: 739–52

Peet, T. E and Woolley, C. L. 1923. *The City of Akhenaten,* Part I: *Excavations of 1921 and 1922 at el-'Amarneh.* EES Memoir 38. London

Pendlebury, J. D. S. 1951. *The City of Akhenaten,* Part III: *The Central City and the Official Quarters.* EES Memoir 44. London

Perron, Y. 1990. D'Alexandre à Néron: le motif de la tente d'apparat. La salle 29 de la Domus Aurea. In J. M. Croisille (ed.), *Neronia IV: Alejandro Magno, modelo de los emperadores romanos,* 211–29. Collection Latomus 209. Brussels

Pharr, C. (trans.) 1952. *The Theodosian Code.* New York

Posener, G. 1960. *De la divinité du Pharaon.* Cahiers de la Société Asiatique 15. Paris

Postgate, N., Wang, T. and Wilkinson, T. 1995. The evidence for early writing: utilitarian or ceremonial? *Antiquity* 69: 459–80

Potter, D. S. 2004. *The Roman Empire at Bay AD 180–395.* London

Potts, D. T. 1999. *The Archaeology of Elam.* Cambridge

Price, M. J. 1991. *The Coinage in the Name of Alexander the Great and Philip Arrhidaeus,* 2 vols. Zurich and London

Price, S. 1984. *Rituals and Power: The Roman Imperial Cult in Asia Minor.* Cambridge

Quirke, S. 1990. *The Administration of Egypt in the Late Middle Kingdom: The Hieratic Documents.* New Malden

1999. Visible and invisible: the King in the administrative papyri of the late Middle Kingdom. In R. Gundlach and W. Seipel (eds.), *Das frühe ägyptische Königtum: Akten des 2. Symposiums zur ägyptischen Königsideologie in Wien,* 63–71. Wiesbaden

Raedler, C. 2004. Die Wesire Ramses' II.– Netzwerke der Macht. In R. Gundlach and A. Klug (eds.), *Das ägyptische Königtum im Spannungsfeld zwischen Innen- und Außenpolitik im 2. Jahrtausend v. Chr.* Wiesbaden

Forthcoming. Rank and favour at the early Ramesside court. In R. Gundlach and J. Taylor (eds.), *Egyptian Royal Residences: Structure and Function*

Rance, P. 2000. Simulacra pugnae: the literary and historical tradition of mock battles in the Roman and early Byzantine army, *GRBS* 41: 223–75

Rawski, E. S. 1998. *The Last Emperors: A Social History of Qing Imperial Institutions.* Berkeley, CA

Rawson, E. 1975. Caesar's heritage: Hellenistic kings and their Roman equals. *JRS* 65: 148–59

1985. *Intellectual Life in the Late Roman Republic.* London

Redford, D. 1984. *Akhenaten: The Heretic King.* Princeton

1986. *Pharaonic King-Lists, Annals and Day-Books: A Contribution to the Egyptian Sense of History.* Mississauga

1995. The concept of kingship during the Eighteenth Dynasty. In D. O'Connor and D. Silverman (eds.), *Ancient Egyptian Kingship*, 157–84. Probleme der Ägyptologie 9. Leiden

Reeves, N. 1990. *The Complete Tutankhamun.* London

Richter-Bernburg, L. 1998. On the diffusion of medical knowledge in Persian court culture during the fourth and fifth centuries A.H. In Z. Vezel et al. (eds.), *La science dans le monde iranien à l'époque islamique.* Tehran: 219–33

1999. Iran's contribution to medicine and veterinary science in Islam AH 100–900/AD 700–1500. In J. A. C. Greppin et al. (eds.), *The Diffusion of Greco-Roman Medicine into the Middle East and the Caucasus.* Delmar: 139–67

2000. Medicine, pharmacology and veterinary science in Islamic eastern Iran and Central Asia. In C. E. Bosworth and M. S. Asimov (eds.), *History of Civilizations of Central Asia*, vol. IV: *The Age of Achievement: AD 750 to the End of the Fifteenth Century*, pt 2, *The Achievements.* Paris

Ringrose, K. 2003. *The Perfect Servant: Eunuchs and the Social Construction of Gender in Byzantium.* Chicago

Rist, J. 1967. *Plotinus: The Road to Reality.* Cambridge

Roddaz, J.-M. 1984. *Marcus Agrippa.* Rome

Rogers, R. S. 1947. Roman emperors as heirs and legatees. *Transactions of the American Philological Association* 78: 140–58

Roller, M. B. 2001. *Constructing Autocracy: Aristocrats and Emperors in Julio-Claudian Rome.* Princeton

Rollinger, R. 2003. The western expansion of the 'Median' empire: a re-examination. In Lanfranchi, Roaf and Rollinger 2003: 289–319

Root, M. C. 1979. *The King and Kingship in Achaemenid Art.* Acta Iranica 3. Leiden

Roth, A. M. 1991. *Egyptian Phyles in the Old Kingdom. The Evolution of a System of Social Organization.* Studies in Ancient Oriental Civilization, 48. Chicago

1993. Social change in the Fourth Dynasty: the spatial organisation of pyramids, tombs, and cemeteries, *Journal of the American Research Center in Egypt* 30: 33–55

1995. *A Cemetery of Palace Attendants, including G 2084–2099 G 2230 + 2231 and G 2240.* Boston

2002. The meaning of menial labour: 'servant statues' in Old Kingdom Serdabs, *Journal of the American Research Center in Egypt* 39: 103–21

Roueché, C. 1984. Acclamations in the late Roman empire: new evidence from Aphrodisias. *JRS* 74: 181–99

Royo, M. 1999. *Domus Imperatoriae: topographie, formation, et imaginaire des palais impériaux du Palatin.* Rome

Rubin, Z. 1995. The reforms of Khusro Anushirwan. In A. Cameron (ed.), *The Byzantine and Early Islamic Near East*, vol. III: *States, Resources and Armies.* Studies in Late Antiquity and Early Islam 1. Princeton: 227–97

1998. The Roman Empire in the *Res Gestae Divi Saporis* – the Mediterranean world in Sāsānian propaganda. In E. Dabrowa (ed.), *Ancient Iran and the Mediter-ranean World.* Electrum 2. Kraków: 177–85

2000. The Sasanid monarchy. In A. Cameron, B. Ward-Perkins and M. Whitby (eds.), *The Cambridge Ancient History*, 2nd edn, vol. XIV. Cambridge: 638–61

2002. *Res Gestae Divi Saporis*: Greek and Middle Iranian in a document of Sasan-ian anti-Roman propaganda. In J. N. Adams, M. Janse and S. Swain (eds.), *Bilingualism in Ancient Society: Language Contact and the Written Text.* Oxford: 267–97

Sako, L. 1986. *Le rôle de la hiérarchie syriaque orientale dans les rapports diplomatiques entre la Perse et Byzance aux Ve–VIIe siècles.* Paris

Saller, R. 1980. Anecdotes as evidence for Roman imperial history. *Greece and Rome* ser. 2, 27: 69–83

1982. *Personal Patronage under the Early Empire.* Cambridge

1989. Patronage and friendship in early Imperial Rome: drawing the distinction. In A. Wallace-Hadrill (ed.), *Patronage in Ancient Society*, 49–62. London

Salzman, M. 1990. *On Roman Time: The Codex Calendar of 354.* Berkeley

Sancisi-Weerdenburg, H. 1980. Yauna en Persai: Grieken in een ander perspectief, PhD thesis, Leiden University

1985. The death of Cyrus: Xenophon's Cyropaedia as a source for Iranian history. In *Papers in Honour of Mary Boyce*, 459–71. Acta Iranica 25. Leiden

1987. Decadence in the empire or decadence in the sources? From source to synthesis: Ctesias. *AchHist* 1: 33–45

1988. Was there ever a Median empire? *AchHist* 3: 197–212

1989. Gifts in the Persian empire. In P. Briant and C. Herrenschmidt (eds.), *Les tributs dans l'empire perse. Actes de la Table Ronde de Paris 12–13 décembre 1986*, 129–146. Paris

1993. Persian food: stereotypes and political identity. In J. Wilkins, D. Harvey and M. Dobson (eds.), *Food in Antiquity*, 286–302. Exeter

San-fu huang-t'u chiao-cheng 1980. Hsi-an

Savalli-Lestrade, I. 1998. *Les philoi royales dans l'Asie hellénistique.* Hautes Etudes du Monde Gréco-Romain 25. Geneva

Scharf, R. 1994. *Comites und comitiva primi ordinis.* Mayence and Stuttgart

Scheer, T. S. 2000. *Die Gottheit und ihr Bild.* Zetemata 105. Munich

Schlinkert, D. 1994. Der Hofeunuch in der Spätantike: ein gefahrlicher Aussenseiter?, *Hermes* 122: 342–59

   1996. Vom Haus zum Hof: Aspekte höfischer Herrschaft in der Spätantike, *Klio* 78: 454–82

   1998. Dem Kaiser folgen. Kaiser, Senatsadel und höfische Funktionselite (*comites consistoriani*) von der 'Tetrarchie' Diokletians bis zum Ende der konstantinischen Dynastie. In Winterling 1998: 133–60

   2002. Between emperor, court and senatorial order: the codification of the Codex Theodosianus, *Ancient Society* 32: 282–94

Schmidt, E. 1953. *Persepolis,* vol. I: *Structures, Reliefs, Inscriptions.* Chicago

   1957. *Persepolis,* vol. II: *Contents of the Treasury and Other Discoveries.* Chicago

   1970. *Persepolis,* vol. III: *The Royal Tombs and Other Monuments.* Chicago

Schmitt, E. 1953, 1957. *Persepolis,* vols. I–II. OIP 68.69. Chicago

Schneider, R. M. 2006. Orientalism in late antiquity: the oriental other in imperial and Christian imagery. In Wiesehöfer and Huyse 2006: 241–78

Scholten, H. 1995. *Der Eunuch in Kaisernähe: Zur politischen und sozialen Bedeutung des praepositus sacri cubiculi im 4. und 5. Jahrhundert n.Chr.* Prismata 5. Frankfurt

   1998. Der oberste Hofeunuch. Die politische Effizienz eines gesellschaftlich Diskriminierten. In Winterling 1998: 51–74

Schulman, A. R. 1978. 'Ankhsenamun, Nofretity, and the Amka affair. *Journal of the American Research Center in Egypt* 15: 43–8

   1979. Diplomatic marriage in the Egyptian New Kingdom. *Journal of Near Eastern Studies* 38: 177–93

Scott, J. 1990. *Domination and the Arts of Resistance: Hidden Transcripts.* Princeton

Seeck, O. (ed.) 1962. *Notitia Dignitatum.* Frankfurt (repr. of original 1876 edn)

Shahbazi, A. S. 2001. Early Sasanians' claim to Achaemenid heritage. *Nâme-ye Irân-e Bâstân* 1.1: 61–73

Shaw, I. 1992. Ideal homes in Ancient Egypt: the archaeology of social aspiration. *Cambridge Archaeological Journal* 2.2: 147–66

   (ed.) 2000. *The Oxford History of Ancient Egypt.* Oxford

Shepherd, M. S. 1967. Liturgical expressions of the Constantinian triumph. *DOP* 21: 57–78

Sherwin-White, S. and Kuhrt, A. 1993. *From Samarkand to Sardis: A New Approach to the Seleucid Empire.* London

Shih-chi 1959. Ed. Peking, chapter 16/759

Shih-san ching chu-shu (The Thirteen Classics). 1980. Peking

Silverman, D. 1995. The nature of Egyptian kingship. In D. O'Connor and D. Silverman (eds.), *Ancient Egyptian Kingship*, 49–92. Probleme der Ägyptologie 9. Leiden

Sivan, H. 1996. Was Theodosius I a usurper? *Klio* 78: 198–211

Smith, H. S. 1992. The making of Egypt: a review of the influence of Susa and Sumer on Upper Egypt and Lower Nubia in the 4th millennium B.C. In R. Friedman and B. Adams (eds.), *The Followers of Horus: Studies Dedicated to Michael Allen Hoffman*, 235–46. Egyptian Studies Association Publication 2. Oxbow Monographs 20. Oxford

Smith, R. B. E. 1995. *Julian's Gods: Religion and Philosophy in the Thought and Action of Julian the Apostate*. London and New York

1999. Telling tales: Ammianus' account of the Persian expedition of Julian. In J. W. Drijvers and E. D. Hunt (eds.), *The Roman World and Its Historian: Interpreting Ammianus*, 89–104. London and New York

Smith, R. R. R. 1985. Roman portraits: honours, empresses and late emperors. *JRS* 75: 209–21

1997. The public image of Licinius I: portrait sculpture and imperial ideology in the early 4th century. *JRS* 87: 170–302

2002. The statue monument of Oecumenius: a new portrait of a late antique governor from Aphrodisias. *JRS* 92: 134–56

Spalinger, A. 1982. *Aspects of the Military Documents of the Ancient Egyptians*. Yale Near Eastern Researches 9. New Haven

Spawforth, A. 2006a. *The Complete Greek Temples*. London

2006b. 'Macedonian times': Hellenistic memories in the provinces of the Roman near east. In D. Konstan and S. Said (eds.), *Greeks on Greekness: Viewing the Greek Past under the Roman Empire*. Proceedings of the Cambridge Philological Society supplementary vol. 29, 1–26. Cambridge

Spence, K. E. 1998. Orientation in Ancient Egyptian royal architecture. Unpublished PhD dissertation, University of Cambridge

1999. The North Palace at Amarna. *EA* 15: 14–17

2004. The three-dimensional form of the Amarna house, *JEA* 90: 123–52

Forthcoming. The palaces of el-Amarna: an architectural analysis. In R. Gundlach and J. Taylor (eds.), *Egyptian Royal Residences: Structure and Function*

Spencer, D. 2002. *The Roman Alexander: Reading a Cultural Myth*. Exeter

Spycket, A. 1980. Women in Persian art. In D. Schmandt-Besserat (ed.), *Ancient Persia*, 43–5 (with pls. 21–6). Malibu

St Clair, A. 1996. Imperial virtue: four late antique statuettes. *DOP* 50: 147–62

Starr, C. G. Jr. 1949. Epictetus and the Tyrant. *Classical Philology* 45: 20–9

Stausberg, M. 2002. *Die Religion Zarathushtras*, Bd I. Stuttgart

Ste Croix, G. de 1954. Suffragium: from vote to patronage, *British Journal of Sociology* 5: 33–48

Steinby, E. M. 1993–2000. *Lexicon Topographiae Urbis Romae*, vols. I–VI. Rome

Stern, H. 1954. Remarks on the adoration under Diocletian, *JWCI* 17: 184–9

Stevenson Smith, W. 1981. *The Art and Architecture of Ancient* Egypt, rev. W. K. Simpson. Harmondsworth

Straub, J. A. 1967. Constantine as Koinos Episkopos: tradition and innovation in the representation of the first Christian emperor's majesty, *DOP* 21: 57–78

Strommenger, E. 1962. *Fünf Jahrtausende Mesopotamien: Die Kunst von den Anfängen um 5000 v. Chr. bis zu Alexander dem Grossen.* Munich (Eng. trans. London 1964)

Stronach, D. 1987. Archaeology ii. Median and Achaemenid. *EncIr* 2: 288–96

  1997. Anshan and Parsa: early Achaemenid history, art and architecture on the Iranian plateau. In J. Curtis (ed.), *Mesopotamia and Iran in the Persian Period: Conquest and Imperialism 539–331 BC,* 35–53. London

Strong, R. 2002. *Feast: A History of Grand Eating.* London

Strudwick, N. 1985. *The Administration of Egypt in the Old Kingdom.* London

Summers, G. D. 2000. The Median empire reconsidered. A view from Kerkenes Dağ. *AnSt* 50: 55–73

Sundermann, W. 1977. Mazdak und die mazdakitischen Volksaufstände. *Altertum* 23: 245–9

  1981. *Mitteliranische manichäische Texte kirchengeschichtlichen Inhalts.* Schriften zur Geschichte und Kultur des Alten Orients, Berliner Turfantexte 11. Berlin

  1983. Review of Humbach/Skjærvø 1978–1983. *Kratylos* 28: 82–9

Swift, L. and Oliver, J. H. 1962. Constantius II on Flavius Philippus, *AJP* 83: 247–64

Syme, R. 1939. *The Roman Revolution.* Oxford

  1986. *The Augustan Aristocracy.* Oxford

Talbert, R. J. A. 1984. *The Senate of Imperial Rome.* Princeton

Tamm, B. 1963. *Auditorium und Palatium.* Stockholm

Tanabe, K. 1983. Iconography of the Royal-Hunt Bas-Reliefs at Taq-i Bustan. *Orient (Tokyo)* 19: 103–16

Tarn, W. 1948. *Alexander the Great,* 2 vols. Oxford

Therasse, J. 1976. *Quintus Curtius Rufus.* Index Verborum. *Relevés lexicaux et grammaticaux.* Hildesheim and New York

Thompson, D. L. 1981. The meetings of the Roman senate on the Palatine. *AJA* 85: 335–9

Tietze, C. 1985. Amarna: Analyse der Wohnhäuser und soziale Struktur der Stadtbewohner. *Zeitschrift für Ägyptische Sprache und Altertumskunde* 112: 48–84

  1986. Amarna (Teil II): Analyse der ökonomischen Beziehungen der Stadtbewohnner. *Zeitschrift für Ägyptische Sprache und Altertumskunde* 113: 55–78

Tjan Tjoe-som 1949, 1952. *Po Hu T'ung: The Comprehensive Discussions in the White Tiger Hall,* 2 vols. Leiden

Tod, M. N. 1948. *A Selection of Greek Inscriptions,* vol. II: *From 403 to 323 BC.* Oxford

Tomei, M. A. 2000. Le case di Augusto sul Palatino. *MDAI(R)* 107: 7–36

Toner, J. P. 1995. *Leisure and Ancient Rome.* Oxford

Torelli, M., 1983. Gli spettacoli conviviali di età classica: documenti archeologici su possibili fatti genetici e sviluppi. In *Spettacoli conviviali dell' antichità classica alle corte italiane del' 400: Atti del VII convegno di studio,* 51–61. Viterbo

Tougher, S. (ed.) 2002. *Eunuchs in Antiquity and Beyond.* London

Trigger, B. G. et al. 1983. *Ancient Egypt: A Social History.* Cambridge

Tuplin, C. 1987. The administration of the Achaemenid empire. In I. Carradice (ed.), *Coinage and Administration in the Athenian and Persian Empires,* 109–66. BAR International Series 34. London

Turcan, R. 1987. *Vivre à la cour des Césars.* Paris

Twitchett, D. and Loewe, M. 1986. *The Cambridge History of China,* vol. I. Cambridge

Ullmann, M. 1978. *Islamic Medicine.* Edinburgh

Unvala, J. M. 1921. *The Pahlavi Text King Husrav and His Boy. Published with Its Translation, Transcription and Copious Notes.* Paris

Vallat, F. 1998. Elam i. The history of Elam. *EncIr* 8: 301–3

Van de Mieroop, M. 1997. *The Ancient Mesopotamian City.* Oxford

    2003. *A History of the Ancient Near East ca.3000–323 BC.* Oxford

van den Boorn, G. P. F. 1988. *The Duties of the Vizier: Civil Administration in the Early New Kingdom.* London

van Dijk, J. 2000. The Amarna Period and the later New Kingdom (c.1352–1069 BC). In I. Shaw (ed.), *The Oxford History of Ancient Egypt,* 272–313. Oxford

van Ess, H. 2004. Die Aufzeichnungen des Historiographen, die erste Standardgeschichte Chinas, und das Aufkommen des bürokratisch organisierten Zentralstaates. In M. Hose (ed.), *Große Texte Alter Kulturen: Literarische Reise von Gizeh nach Rom,* 87–110. Darmstadt

Verlet, P. 1985. *Le château de Versailles,* 2nd edn. Paris

Vernus, P. 2003. *Affairs and Scandals in Ancient Egypt,* trans. D. Lorton. Ithaca, NY

Veyne, P. 1976. *Le pain et le cirque: sociologie d'une pluralisme politique.* Paris

    1981. Clientèle et corruption au service de l'état: la vénalité des offices dans le Bas-Empire. *Annales ESC* 36: 339–60

    1990. *Bread and Circuses: Historical Sociology and Political Pluralism.* Trans. Brian Pearce. London

Vogelsang-Eastwood, G. 1993. *Pharaonic Egyptian Clothing.* Leiden

    2000. Textiles. In P. Nicholson and I. Shaw (eds.), *Ancient Egyptian Materials and Technology,* 268–98. Cambridge

Völcker-Janssen, W. 1993. *Kunst und Gesellschaft an den Höfen Alexanders d. Gr. und seiner Nachfolger.* Quellen und Forschungen zur antiken Welt 15. Munich

von Gall, H. 1990. *Das Reiterkampfbild in der iranischen und iranisch beeinflußten Kunst parthischer und sasanidischer Zeit.* Teheraner Forschungen 6. Berlin

Wallace-Hadrill, A. 1982. Civilis Princeps: between citizen and king. *JRS* 72: 32–48

    1983. *Suetonius.* London

    (ed.) 1989. *Patronage in Ancient Society.* London

    1994. *Houses and Society in Pompeii and Herculaneum.* Princeton

    1996. The imperial court. In A. K. Bowman and others (eds.), *Cambridge Ancient History,* 2nd edn, vol. X, 283–308. Cambridge

Wang Zhongshu 1982. *Han Civilization,* trans. K. C. Chang and others. New Haven and London

Ward-Perkins, J. B. 1981. *Roman Imperial Architecture.* Harmondsworth

Wataghin-Cantino, C. 1966. *La Domus Augustana: personalità e problemi dell' architettura Flavia*. Turin

Watson, B. 1961. *Records of the Grand Historian of China*, 2 vols. New York
1974. *Courtier and Commoner in Han China*. New York

Weatherhead, F. 1992. Painted pavements in the Great Palace at Amarna, *Journal of Egyptian Archaeology* 78: 179–94

Weaver, P. R. C. 1972. *Familia Caesaris: A Social Study of the Emperor's Freedmen and Slaves*. Cambridge

Weber, G. 1997. Interaktion, Repräsentation und Herrschaft. Der Königshof im Hellenismus. In Winterling 1997b: 27–72

Weber, U. *Prosopographie des frühen Sasanidenreiches* (www.uni-kiel.de/klassalt/projekte/sasaniden/index.html)

Weinberg, J. 1999. The international elite of the Achaemenid empire. Reality and fiction. *ZAW* 111: 583–608

Weitzmann, K. (ed.) 1979. *The Age of Spirituality*. Princeton

Whitby, M. 1987. On the omission of a ceremony in mid-sixth century Constantinople. *Historia* 36: 462–88
(ed.) 1998. *The Propaganda of Power: The Role of Panegyric in Late Antiquity*. Mnemosyne, Bibliotheca Classica Batava. Supplementum 183. Leiden

Wiesehöfer, J. 1980. Die 'Freunde' und Wohltäter des Grosskönigs. *StIr* 9: 17–21
1994. *Die 'dunklen Jahrhunderte' der Persis*. Zetemata 90. Munich
2001. *Ancient Persia*, 2nd edn, rev. London
2005a. Rūm as enemy of Iran. In E. Gruen (ed.), *Cultural Borrowings and Ethnic Appropriations in Antiquity*. OrOcc 8. Stuttgart: 105–20
2005b. *Iraniens, Grecs et Romains*. Paris
2006. 'Randkultur' oder 'Nabel der Welt'? Das Sasanidenreich und der Westen. Anmerkungen eines Althistorikers. In Wiesehöfer and Huyse 2006: 9–28
2007a. Chusro I. und das Sasanidenreich. Der König der Könige 'mit der unsterblichen Seele'. In M. Meier (ed.), *Sie schufen Europa*. Munich: 195–215
2007b. Narseh, Diokletian, Manichäer und Christen. In A. Mustafa, J. Tubach and G. S. Vashalomidze (eds.), *Inkulturation des Christentums im Sasanidenreich*. Wiesbaden: 161–9
2007c. From Achaemenid imperial order to Sasanian diplomacy: war, peace and reconciliation in pre-Islamic Iran. In K. Raaflaub (ed.), *War and Peace in the Ancient World*. Oxford: 121–40
In press (a). *Household, Residence and Court: The Persian King and His Palace*

Wiesehöfer, J. and Huyse, P. (eds.) 2006. *Ērān ud Anērān: Beiträge zu den Beziehungen zwischen Ost und West in sasanidischer Zeit*. OrOcc 13. Stuttgart

Wilkes, J. 1986. *Diocletian's Palace, Split: Residence of a Retired Emperor*. Sheffield (repr. with corrections Oxford, 1993)

Wilkinson, T. A. H. 1999. *Early Dynastic Egypt*. London
2000. Political unification: towards a reconstruction, *Mitteilungen des Deutschen Archäologischen Instituts, Abteilung Kairo* 56: 377–95

Winter, E. 1988. Legitimität als Herrschaftsprinzip: Kaiser und 'König der Könige' im wechselseitigen Verkehr. In H.-J. Drexhage and J. Sünskes (eds.), *Migratio et Commutatio: Studien zur Alten Geschichte und deren Nachleben. Th. Pekáry zum 60. Geburtstag am 13. September 1989 dargebracht von Freunden, Kollegen und Schülern* St. Katharinen: 72–92

Winter, E. and Dignas, B. 2001. *Rom und das Perserreich: Zwei Weltmächte zwischen Konfrontation und Koexistenz.* Berlin

Winter, I. 1986. The king and the cup. Iconography of the royal presentation scene on Ur III seals. In M. Kelly-Buccellati (ed.), *Insight through Images: Studies in Honour of Edith Porada*, 253–68 and pls. 63–6. Malibu, CA

Winterling, A. 1985. *Der Hof der Kurfürsten von Köln 1688–1794. Eine Fallstudie zur Bedeutung 'absolutistischer' Hofhaltung.* Bonn

1997a. Vergleichended Perspektiven. In Winterling 1997b: 151–70

(ed.) 1997b. *Zwischen 'Haus' und 'Staat': antike Höfe im Vergleich.* Historische Zeitschrift Beiheft 23. Berlin

(ed.) 1998. *Comitatus: Beiträge zur Erforschung des spätantiken Kaiserhofes.* Berlin

1999. *Aula Caesaris: Studien zur Institutionalisierung des römischen Kaiserhofes in der Zeit von Augustus bis Commodus 31 v. Chr.–192 n. Chr.* Munich

2004. 'Hof'. Versuch einer idealtypischen Bestimmung anhand der mittelalterlichen und frühneuzeitlichen Geschichte. In Butz et al. 2004: 77–90

Wintrobe, R. 1998. *The Political Economy of Dictatorship.* Cambridge

Yarshater, E. 1983. Iranian national history. In *The Cambridge History of Iran*, vol. III/1. Cambridge: 359–477

Yü Ying-shih 1967. *Trade and Expansion in Han China.* Berkeley and Los Angeles

Zanker, P. 1988. *The Power of Images in the Age of Augustus.* Ann Arbor

2002. Domitian's Palace on the Palatine and the imperial image. In K. Bowman, H. M. Cotton, M. Goodman and S. Price (eds.), *Representations of Empire: Rome and the Mediterranean World*, 105–30. Proceedings of the British Academy 114. London

Zivie, A. 1990. *Découverte à Saqqara: le vizir oublié.* Paris

Index